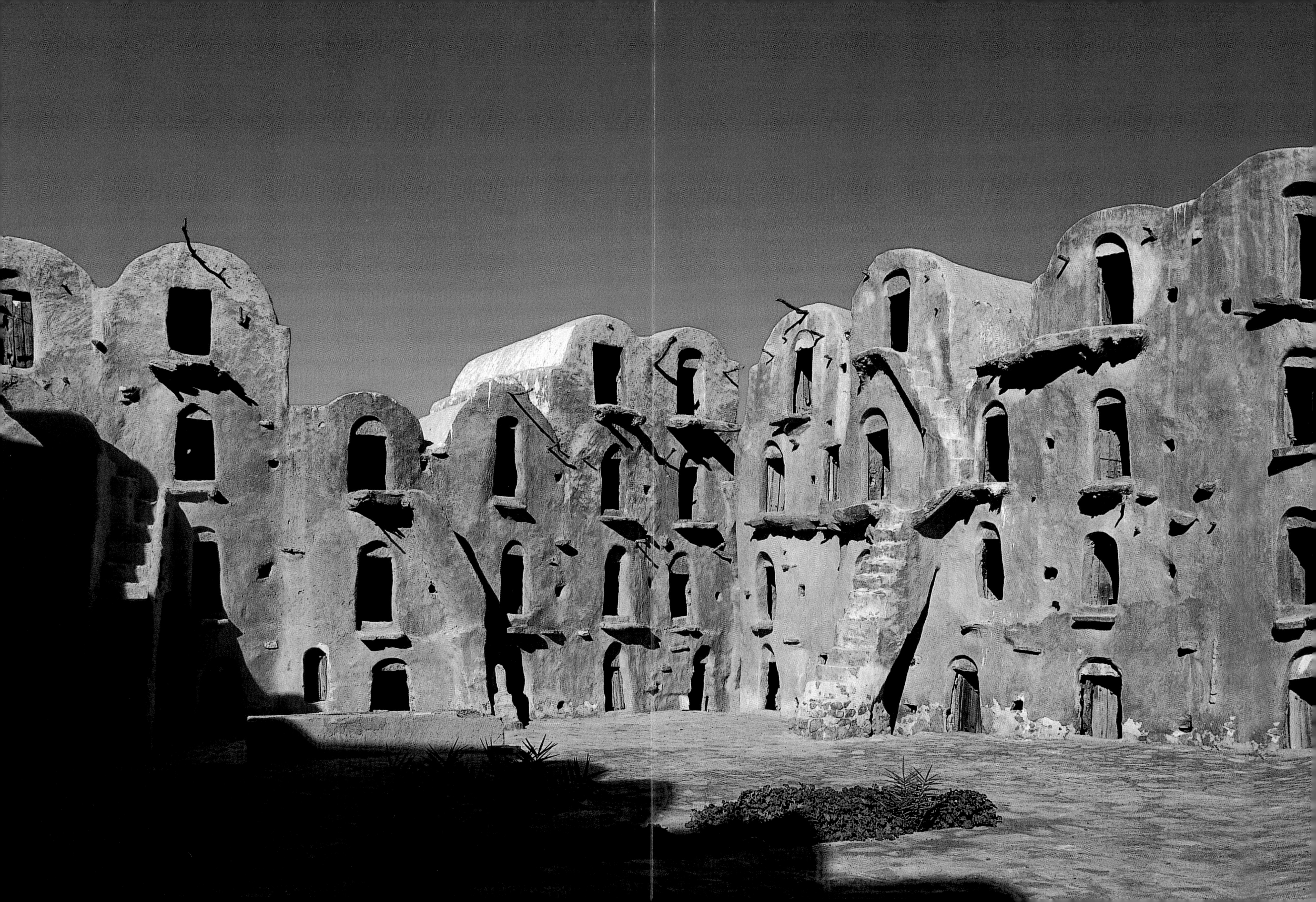

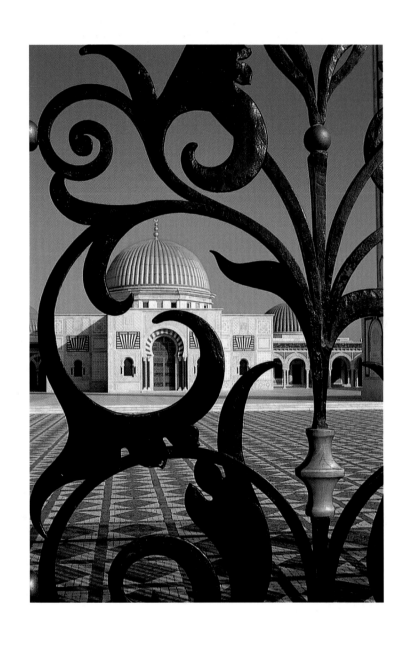

CONTENTS

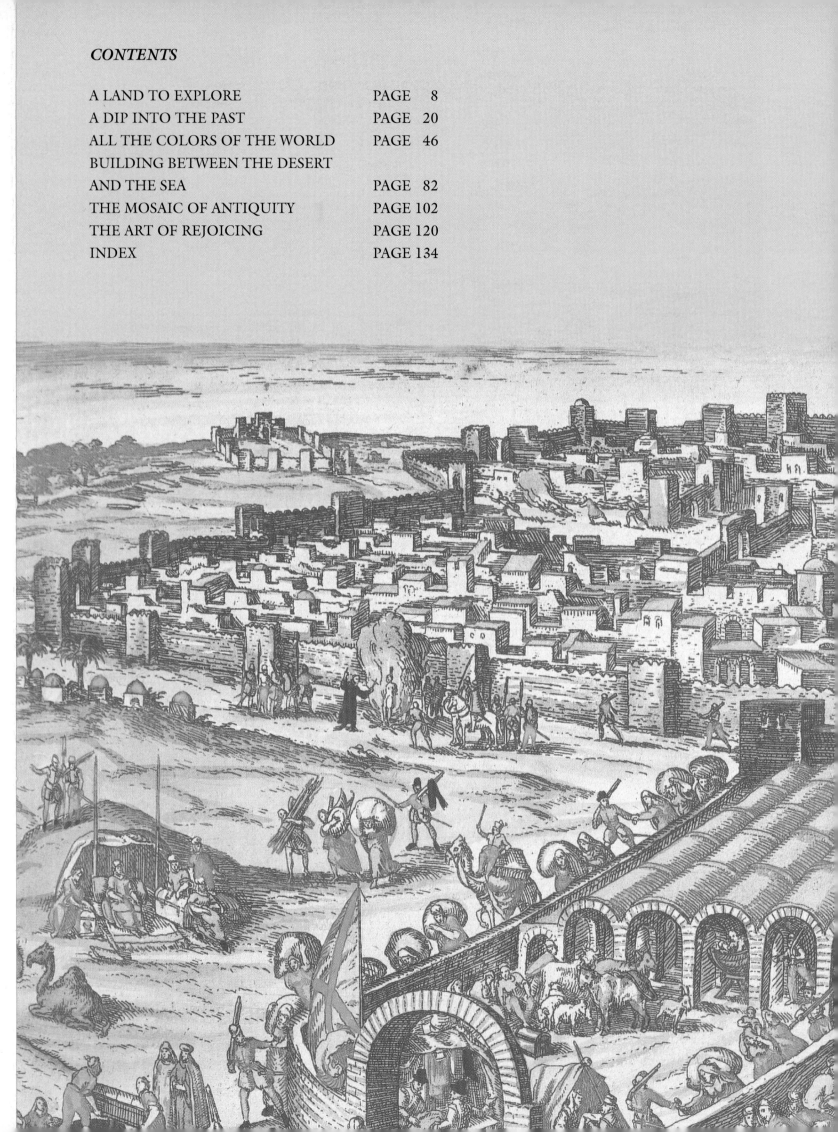

WHITE STAR
PUBLISHERS

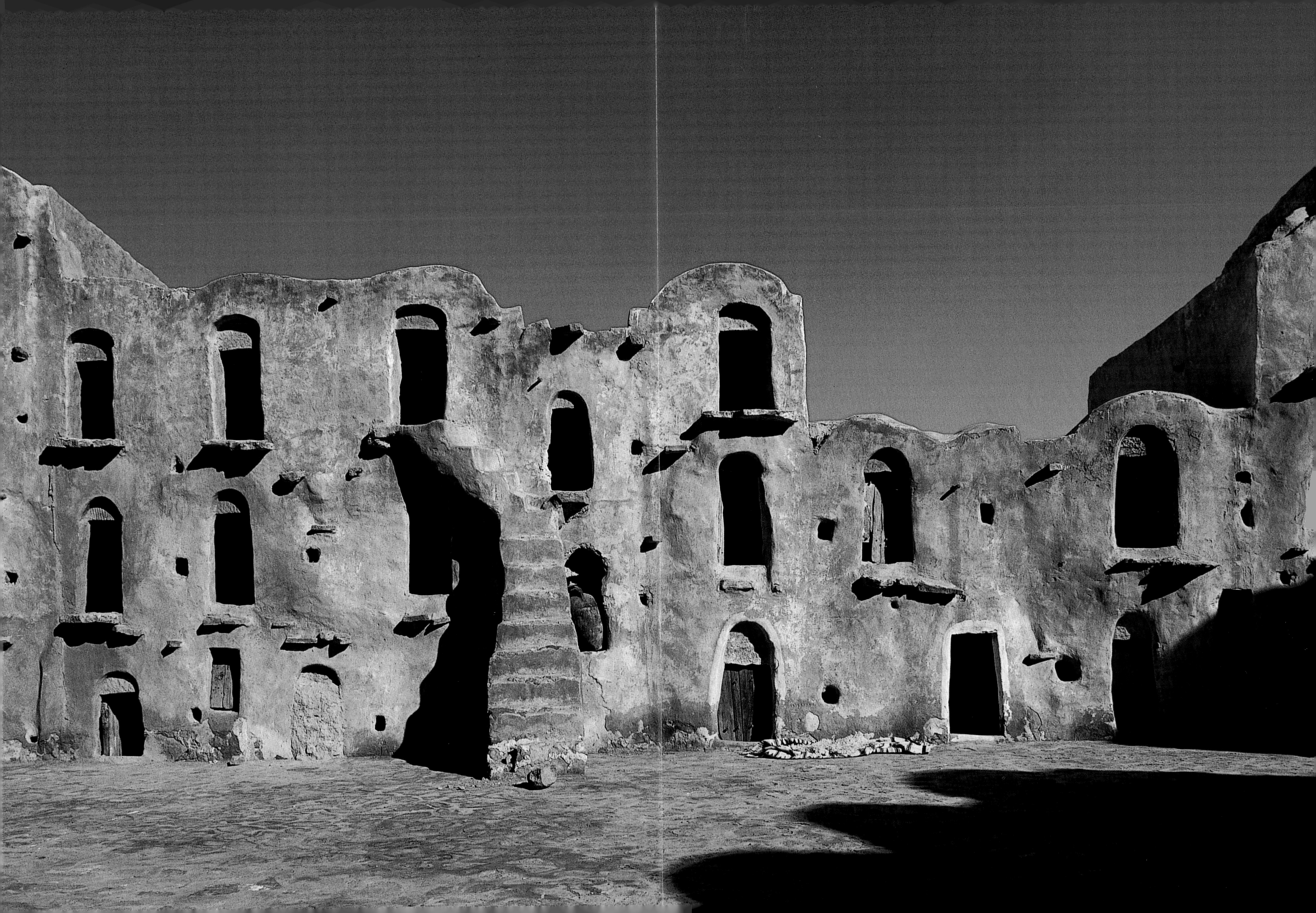

Tunisia

PLACES AND HISTORY

Text by Raffaella Piovan

1 The dome of the mausoleum of Habib Bourguiba and his family in Monastir can be glimpsed through the iron fence.

2-7 Overflowing with details, this Renaissance engraving illustrates the taking of La Goulette, the port of Tunis, by Carlos V, in 1535.

3-6 The ksar *Ouled Soltane was one of the most beautiful in southern Tunisian.* Ksour *(plural of* ksar*) are fortified collective granaries.*

Graphic design
Paola Piacco

Translation
Amy Ezrin

Via C. Sassone, 22/24
13100 Vercelli, Italy
www.whitestar.it

ISBN 88-8095-835-6
Reprints:
1 2 3 4 5 6 07 06 05 04 03

Printed in Italy by Officine Grafiche De Agostini, Novara
Color separation: Grafotitoli Bassoli srl, Sesto S. Giovanni (MI)

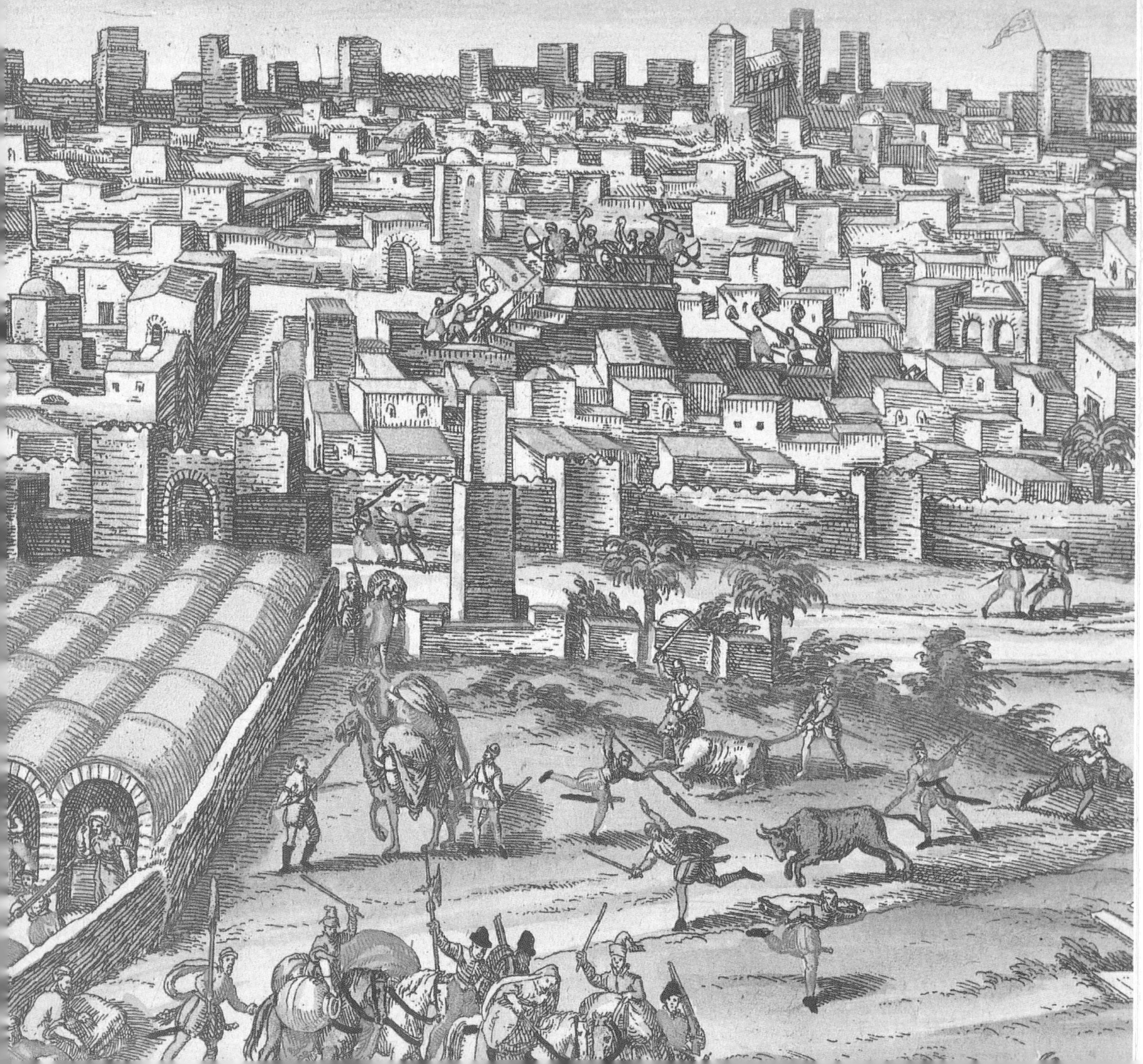

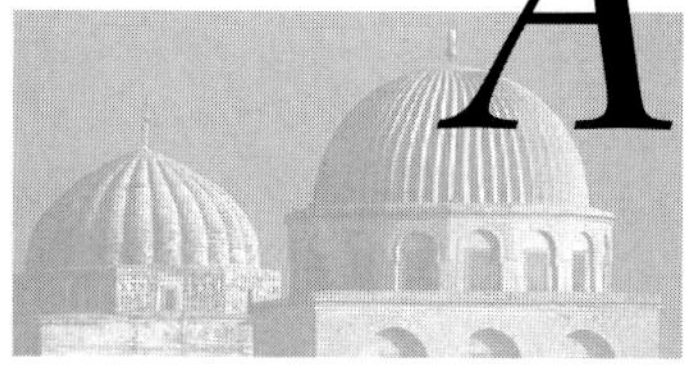

At the doors of Italy, only miles away from the island of Pantelleria, a lonely pillar of an ideal bridge between two continents, opens a universe profoundly different in respect to the familiar one on the southern shore of the Mediterranean. It is Africa of course, land of immense dimensions, full of the dramatic charm that for uncountable millennium has spread throughout the rest of the world across the ideal threshold of its borders, enclosed by sea and ocean. One of these entrances, and among the most splendid, is Tunisia, a country of transition—but not only of transit—between the north and south of the hemisphere. It is a land that offers itself to travelers as both an antechamber and a privileged destination for exploration.

A few seconds are enough for visitors to realize that they have come into a world literally 'other', made of colors and customs that smack of ancient times, of peoples and cultures that have grown from deep roots and of unfamiliar tastes and smells. In short, it is of an exotic nature that, in past epochs, has made personalities of the caliber of Paul Klee, who transfigured the wide variety of Tunisia's chromatic hues onto canvas, and Gustave Flaubert, who chose unfortunate Carthage, the ancient capital of the region today called Tunisia, as the setting for one of his most famous novels, *Salammbô*.

In terms of geographical extension the country is fairly small, covering a surface equal to about half of that of the Italian peninsula. And yet, examining it apart from the dryness of its statistical information, this microcosm is colored with variety and unexpected vastness, with peculiar rhythms and lifestyles full of calm and tranquil peace of mind; and it meets the tourist presenting immense cognitive desert spaces and infinite horizons. For whoever looks at the Black Continent for the first time through this privileged door is presented with a world in which they can lose themselves in thought while fantasizing over the view. They are presented with kaleidoscope of subdued and delicate colors and contrasts, which range from the ochre of the southern desert sands to the blue of the limitless skies, the green of the hilly forests in the north and the turquoise of the sea rich with fish and coral.

With about nine million inhabitants and more than 800 miles of coastline (370 miles of beaches) rich with gulfs and inlets, Tunisia is located in the eastern part of the Maghreb, almost at the middle of the Mediterranean coast of the continent. Looking at a map, this strip of land seems compressed and imprisoned in a virtual vise by its neighbors: Algeria to the west and Libya to the southeast. Compared to these immense geopolitical entities, Tunisia seems miniscule but, on the other hand, the proportion of desert land to inhabitable area is decisively in its favor.

Nature has given this land an environmental double personality that makes it irresistible and a region of the world to discover and admire without hesitation. It

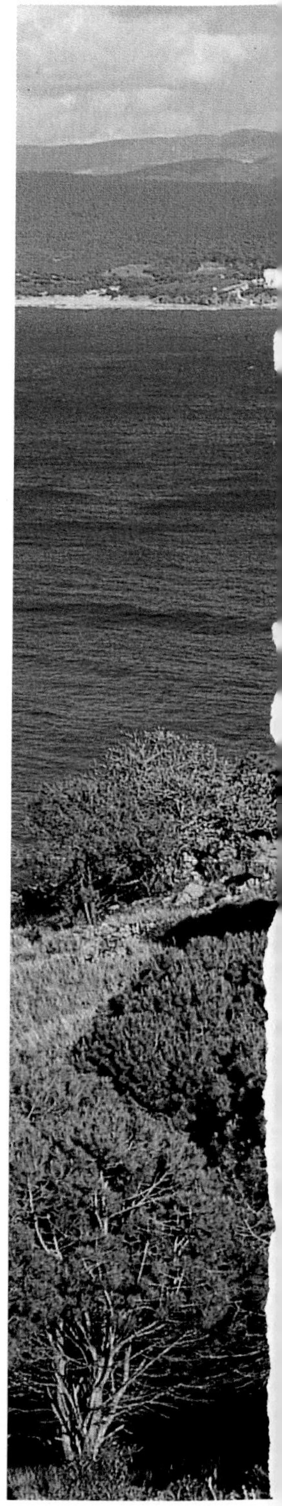

8-9 The Genoese fort at Tabarka is the building that rises highest above the city, situated on the northern coast of the country. In 1542, Emperor Carlos V gave the Genoese the little island in front of the settlement and exclusive fishing rights in the surrounding waters.

9 top left The women of Jerba often still wear the traditional costume. The dress, which even today is draped as in ancient times, usually indicates the rank and social class to which the person wearing it belongs.

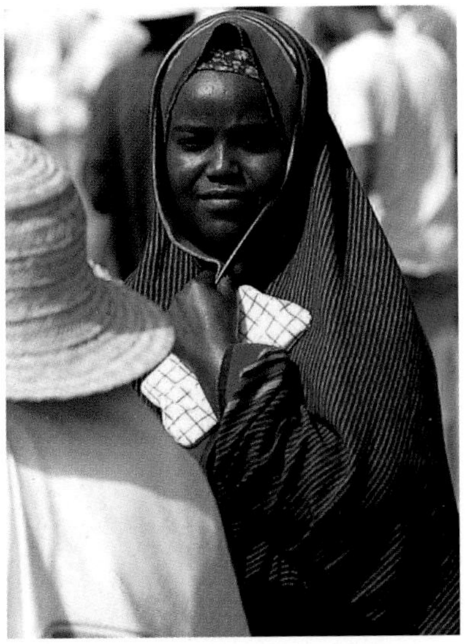

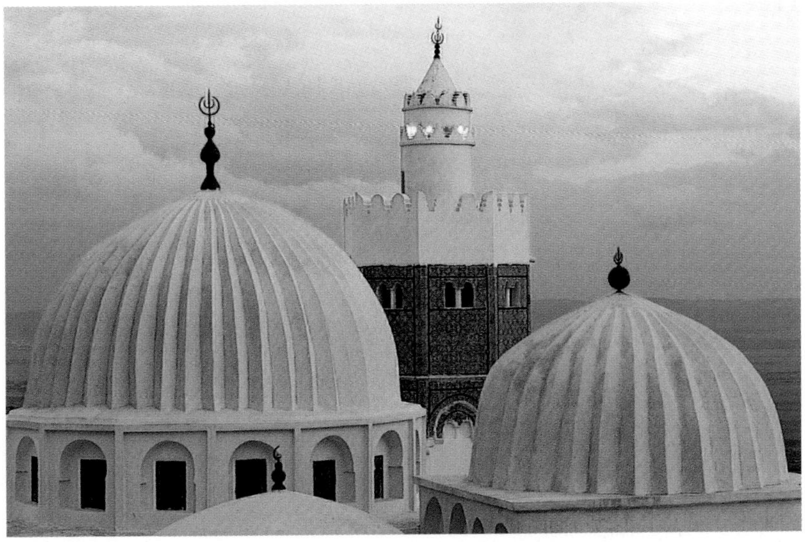

9 top right The mosque of Sidi Bou Makhlouf, in el-Kef, dates back to the seventeenth century. At sunset, its pure white dome and octagonal minaret add a touch of charm to the old city. The mosque is today the headquarters of the Brotherhood of the Aissaoua, founded at the beginning of the 1500s.

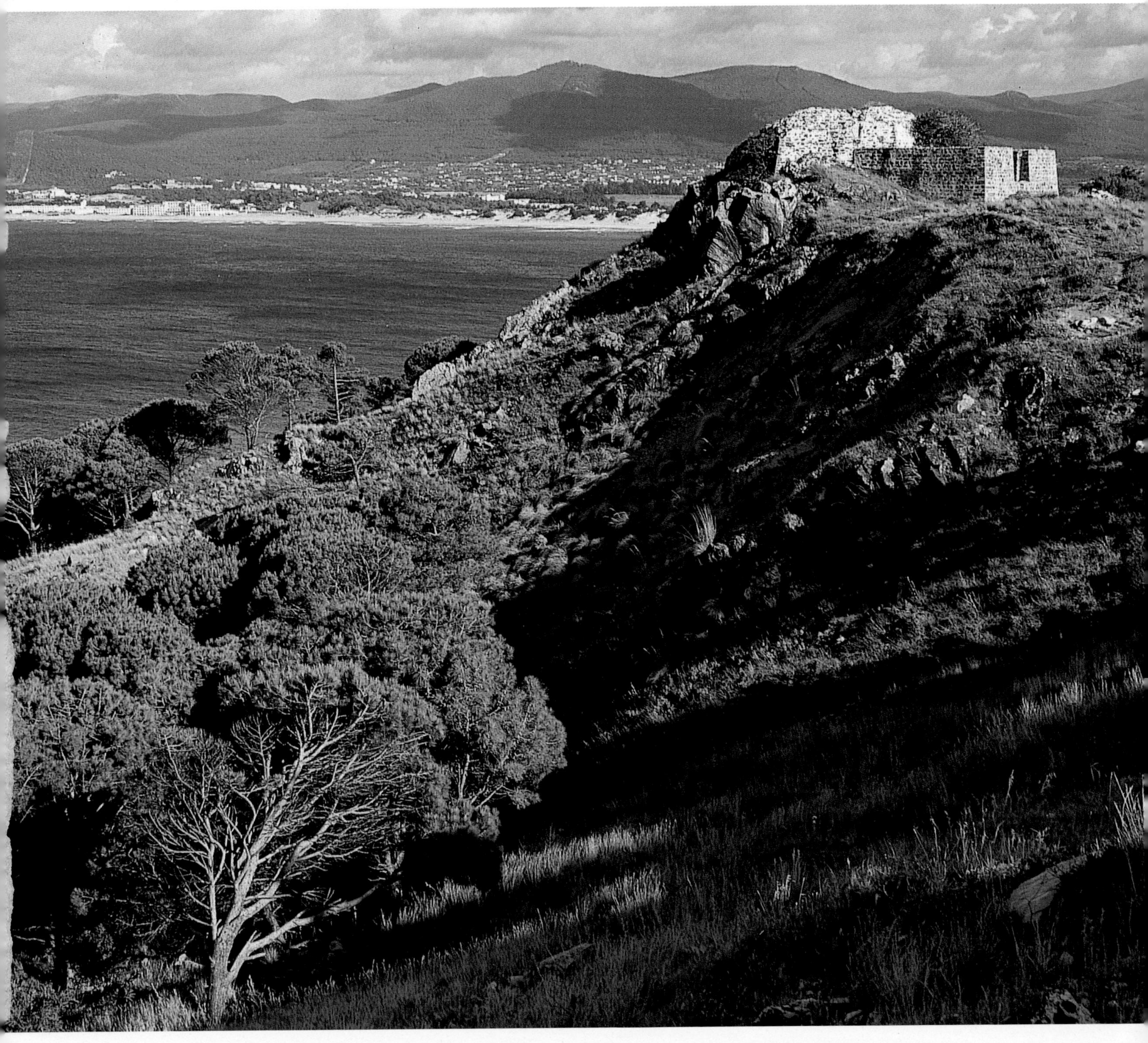

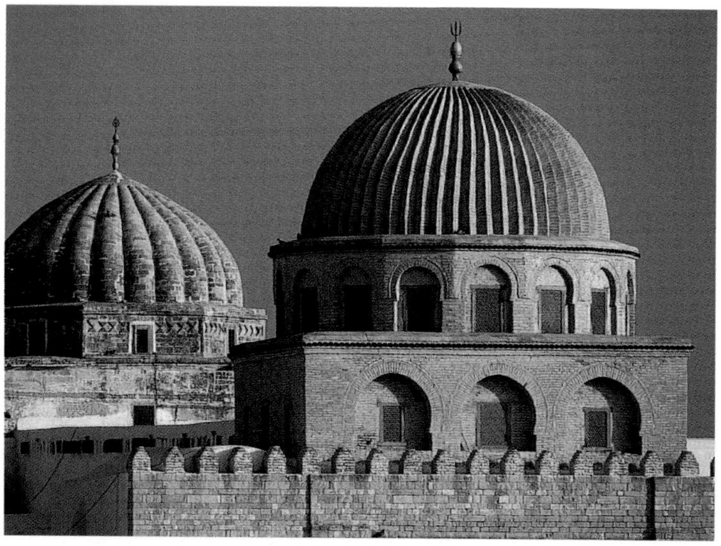

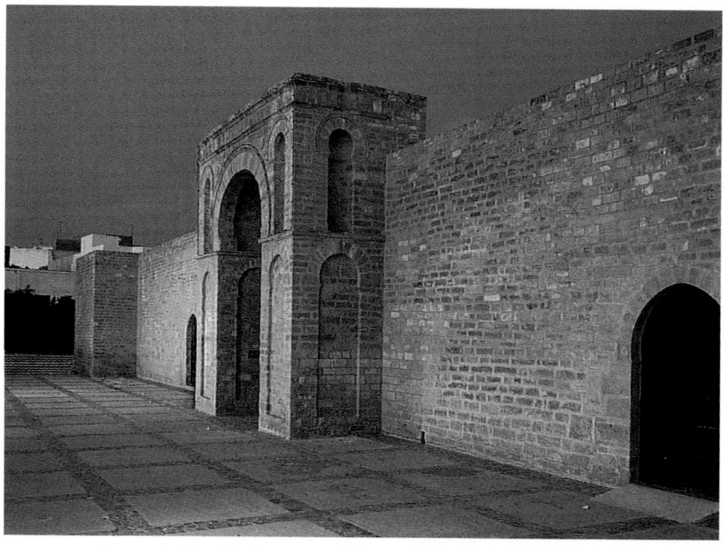

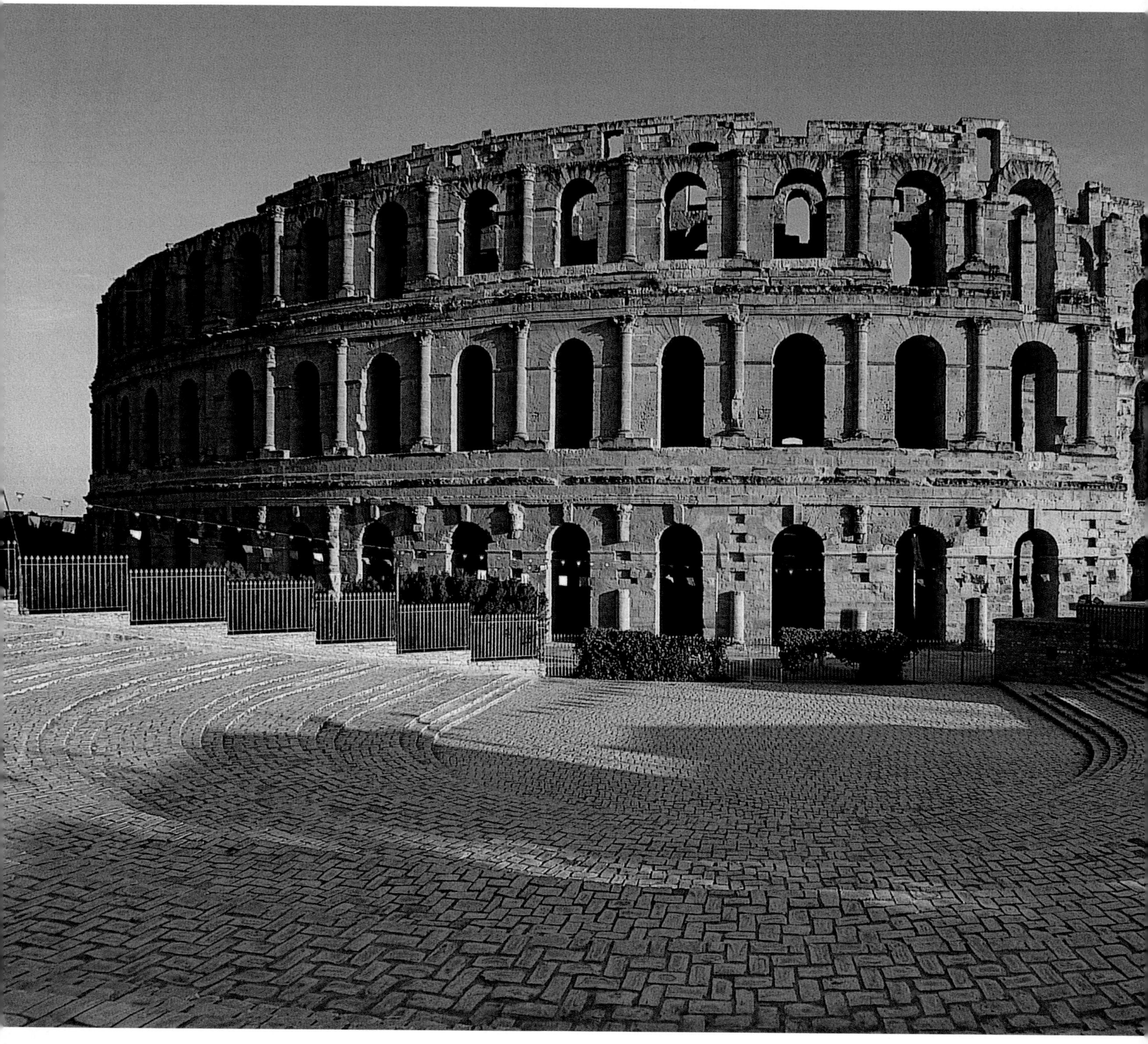

10 top left The Great
Mosque of Kairouan,
dating back to AD
670, is considered the
oldest place of worship
in the western Islamic
world.

10 top right Situated
in a strategic position
on Cape Africa,
Mahdia was
founded in AD 916
by Caliph Obeid
Allah, known as
'Mahdi', founding
father of the dynasty
of Fatimid caliphs.

is endowed with extremely diversified landscapes and natural scenes with places that, for as much as they can be opposites, provide visitors with an overall view packed with harmony and a serene equilibrium.

The country is substantially divided into two morphological areas. Half of the territory is quite varied: the horizons that are encountered traveling the long and seductive northern routes of Tunisia range from the limitless cultivated stretches that characterize the plains to the coasts rich with fish and tourism to the enormous salt lakes of Chott el-Fejaj, el-Jerid and el-Gharsa to the forests and valleys of the Great Ridge (the most important and massive local mountain chain, an orographic system that, at its highest point, Jebel Chambi, reaches its maximum height of 5,066 feet). This last area is where the economic activities of the country are more developed. Great spaces, cultivated mainly with cereals, grape vines, olives and citrus fruits, sustain about 40 percent of the active population. The intense green prairies allow for raising livestock in great quantities but the sea and the richness it offers of course represent one of the country's main resources. The crystal waters of the sea provide markets and restaurants on the coast with fresh fish every day, in particular anchovies, tuna, sardines and lobsters—true delicacies.

Artisans produce excellent quality carpets, and the entire zone is the headquarters for important industrial sectors from the textile industry to the chemical, min-

ing and oil industries. Continuing on towards the south, beyond the area of the salt lakes, one penetrates a totally new geographical dimension. Having passed the Great Ridge, one enters the interior of an immense geological depression that gives way to the desolation of the steppes, the actual transition zone towards the Sahara, located in the strip further to the southeast of the country. The desert, with the infinite silence broken only by the blowing of the wind and the dunes that disappear into the infinity of the horizon, always ready to let their shape be altered by the action of the sandstorms, is the African universe *par excellence* for all those who are not African.

Here, the dreams and fantasies of tourists are coordinated in thrilling synthesis. Under a pitiless and burning sun, which often causes the mercury to rise well over 104°F, an undulating, unending sea of golden sand is crossed to reach

10-11
The amphitheater of
el-Jem takes third
place for size following
those of Rome and
Capua. Dated to
between the second and
third centuries AD, it
may never have been
completed.

11 top The ksar er-
Ribat in Sousse is one
of the most important
Islamic buildings in
the Maghreb. Datable
to the beginning of the
ninth century AD, this
sort-of coastal fortress
was inserted in a
defensive line meant to
resist Christian
incursions.

11 bottom Dedicated
to Jupiter, Juno and
Minerva, the three
gods of the Capitoline
triad, the Capitol of
Dougga was erected in
the second half of the
second century AD.

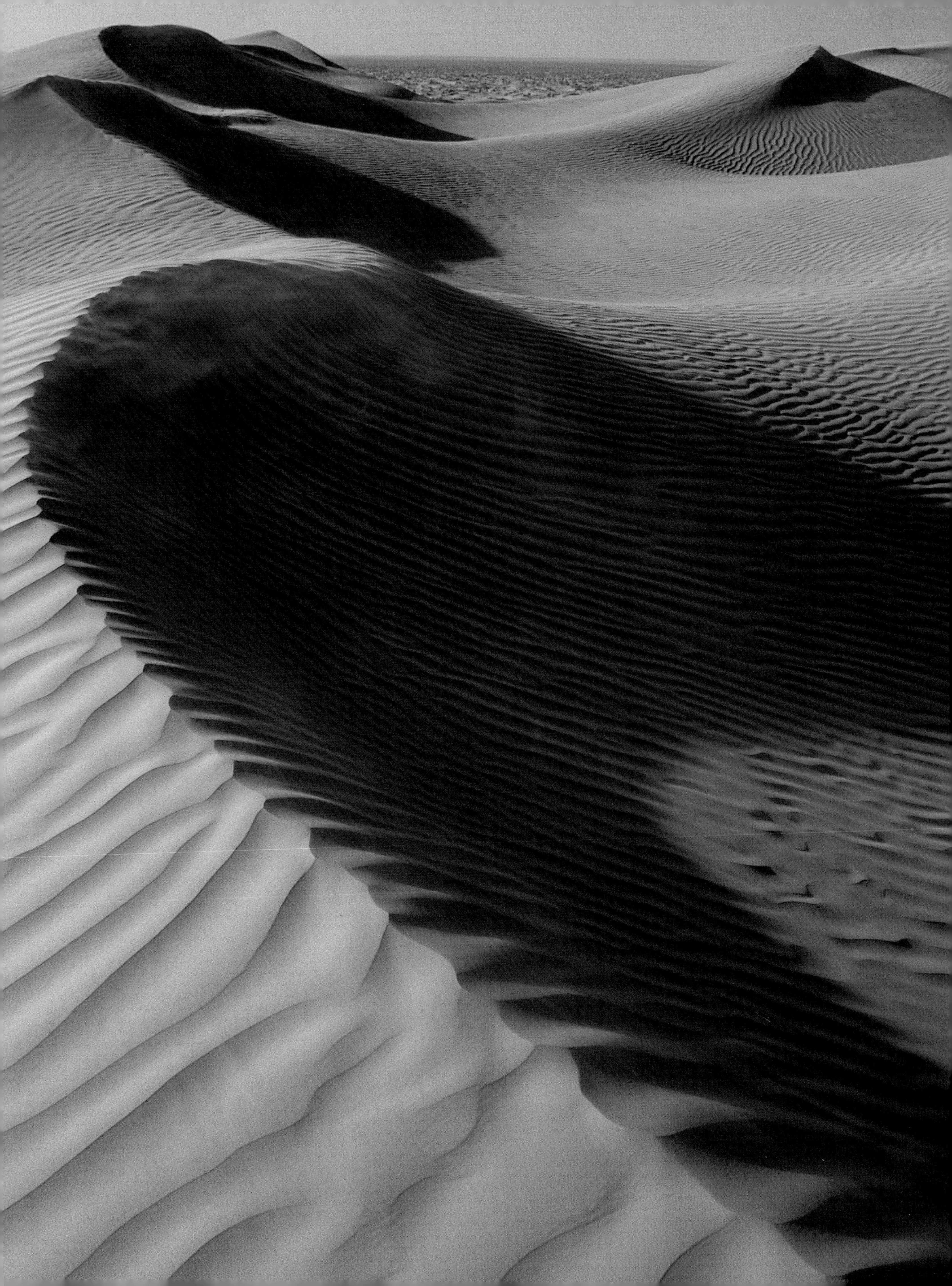

its constant state as a conquered land—or perhaps actually thanks to it—Tunisia has learned over the centuries to cultivate its own cosmopolitan soul, absorbing into its heart a dense multiplicity of cultures and traditions and becoming, among the countries within the Islamic culture, one of the most open, moderate and tolerant in the world.

From the oases to the modern cities of the north, from desert dunes to Roman ruins, from nomadic shepherds to Mediterranean fisherman, Tunisia introduces itself to foreigners through the characteristic hospitality of its people with their peaceful disposition along with the splendor of its intense, star-filled nights and the indescribable quiet of its enchanting landscapes and itineraries. In order to fully appreciate these qualities it is sufficient to abandon oneself totally to the gentle sensations of harmonic peace of mind that are magically triggered, liberating the imagination while letting oneself be sweetly rocked by the serene atmosphere admirably transmitted by the enormous open spaces.

13 bottom left Dominated by shades of ochre, la region of the ksour, to the south of Gafsa, receives about four inches of water a year.

13 top right A flock silhouetted against the whiteness of the Tunisian steppe is one of the most common sights for travelers. Despite the aridity, important local resources are the cultivation of dates in the oases and transhumant livestock rearing.

13 bottom right Matmata is famous for troglodyte dwellings, still in use today. This evocative village is one of the most touristic destinations in the country, but the way of life of the population has been kept relatively intact.

the peaceful rhythms of legendary oases, an all-time classic feature of the cinema that really exists with all the intense romantic zest. In this arid area, cultivation possibilities are scarce but man has always managed to grow various types of dates, famous throughout the world, and patiently raise sheep, goats and dromedaries. The environmental differences that exemplify Tunisia radically influence its economy, directly tied to the diverse characteristics of the climate variable from zone to zone: more humid and temperate in the north and drier and more arid in the center and the southeast region.

Tunisia bears a similarly stratified history: a past that goes back by now more than three millennia imposes itself on the shoulders of the modern nation. Thousands of years of human events are testified to everywhere by traces and monuments left by peoples and civilizations that from time to time have invaded and molded this ancient patch of Africa. Even in this a peculiarity is manifested: despite

12 A veritable sea of sand extends around Douz: this is the antechamber to the Grand Erg, a fragile ecosystem of dunes in perennial movement, an environment as fascinating as it is hostile and absolutely uncontaminated.

13 top left Chott el-Jerid, together with chotts el-Fejaj and el-Gharsa, is one of the enormous, pure salt lakes that are found in the middle of Tunisia, a prelude to the big stretches of desert. Here, vegetation is totally absent and not even a trace of man is seen, except for a few vehicles that plough along the long track that borders the lake. In compensation, mirages are numerous.

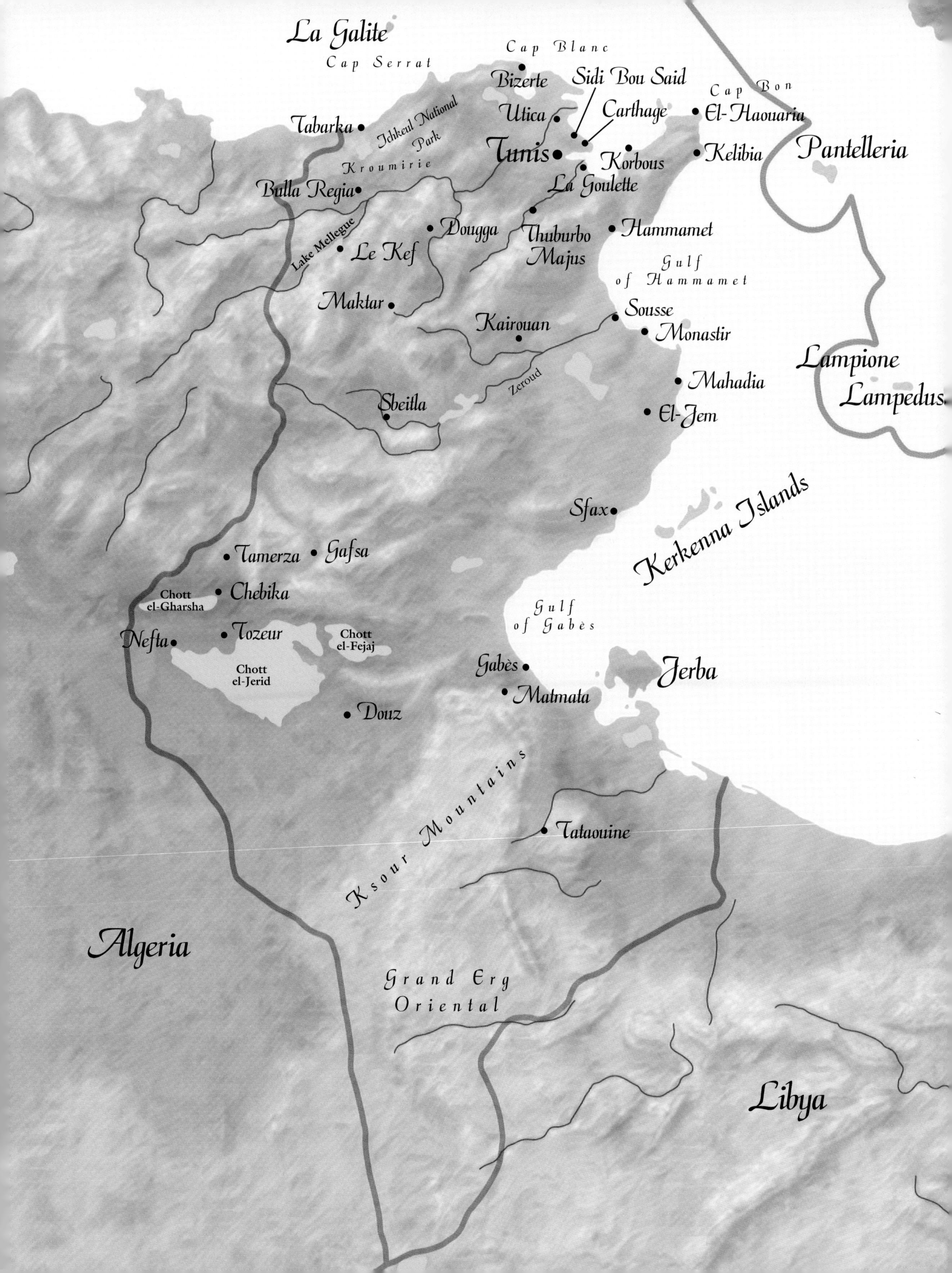
La Galite
Cap Serrat
Cap Blanc
Bizerte
Sidi Bou Said
Cap Bon
Utica
Carthage
El-Haouaria
Tabarka
Ichkeul National Park
Tunis
Korbous
Kelibia
Pantelleria
Kroumirie
Bulla Regia
La Goulette
Dougga
Thuburbo Majus
Hammamet
Lake Mellegue
Le Kef
Gulf of Hammamet
Maktar
Sousse
Kairouan
Monastir
Lampione
Zeroud
Mahadia
Lampedus
Sbeitla
El-Jem
Sfax
Kerkenna Islands
Tamerza
Gafsa
Chott el-Gharsha
Chebika
Gulf of Gabès
Nefta
Tozeur
Chott el-Fejaj
Chott el-Jerid
Gabès
Jerba
Matmata
Douz
Ksour Mountains
Tataouine
Algeria
Grand Erg Oriental
Libya

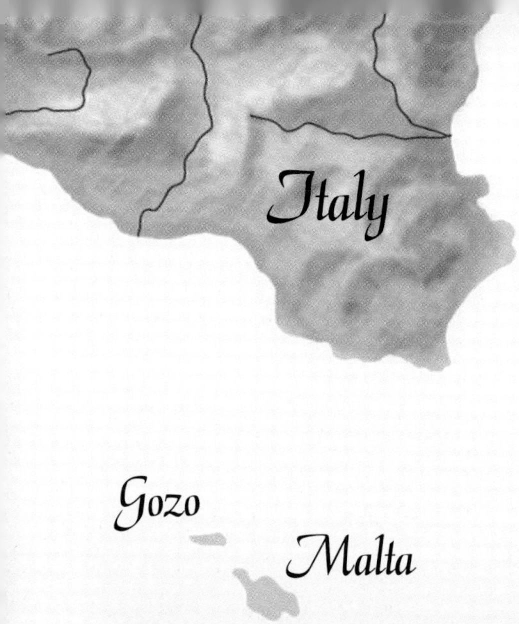
Italy
Gozo
Malta

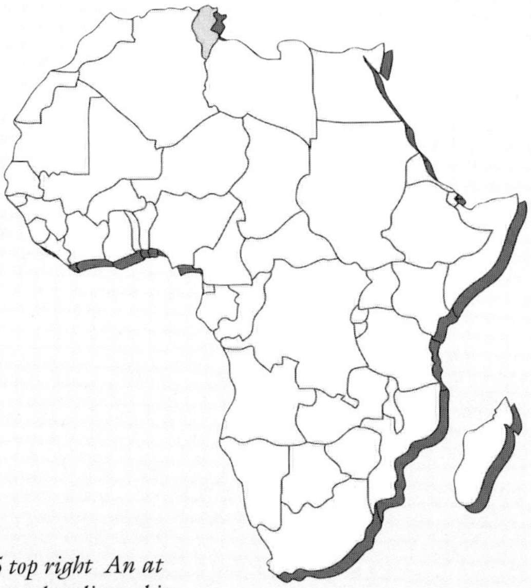

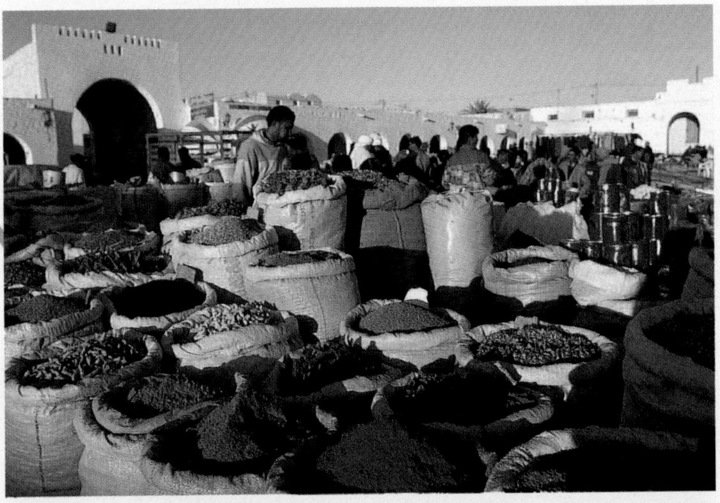

15 top left Every Thursday, the market in Douz welcomes nomads coming from the surrounding oases, who gather here to sell their wares.

15 bottom left Besides beaches, Tabarka offers a good level of cultural tourism, thanks to the Punic, Roman and Genoese ruins.

15 top right An at times dazzling white dominates Tunisian architecture.

15 bottom right The dunes of Douz offer classic excursions for thrill-seeking tourists.

16-17 Raised in 1963 in Monastir, the design of the mosque dedicated to the country's most beloved president, Habib Bourguiba, was inspired by the mosque of Hammouda Pacha in the capital.

18-19 Hunting with greyhounds, camel battles, parades and folkloristic shows animate the festival of Douz held at the end of December.

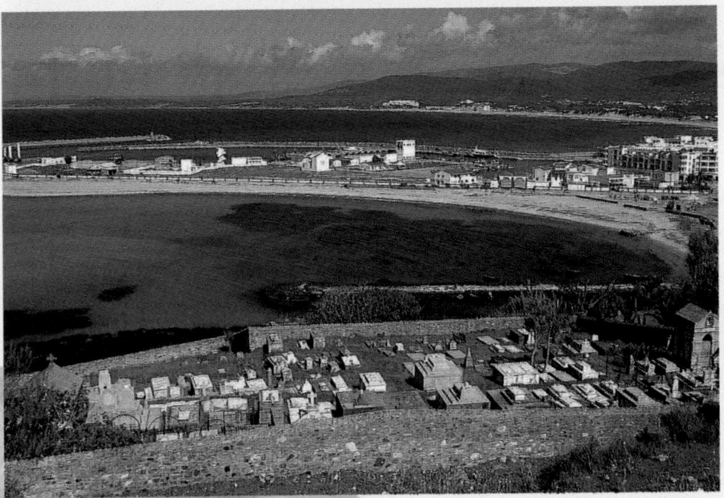

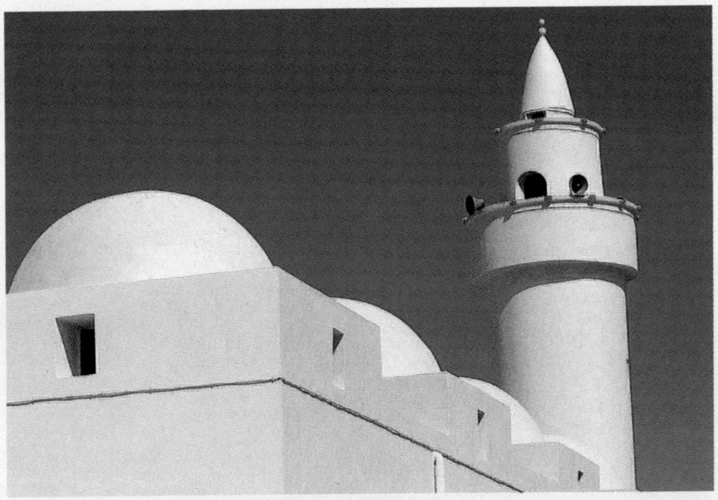

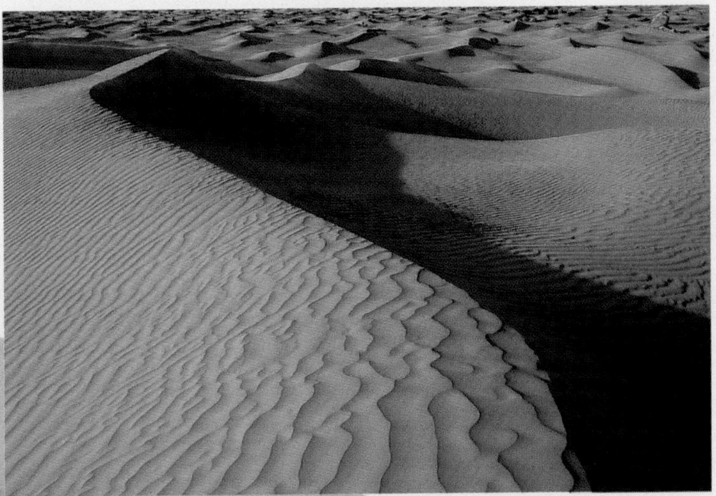

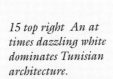

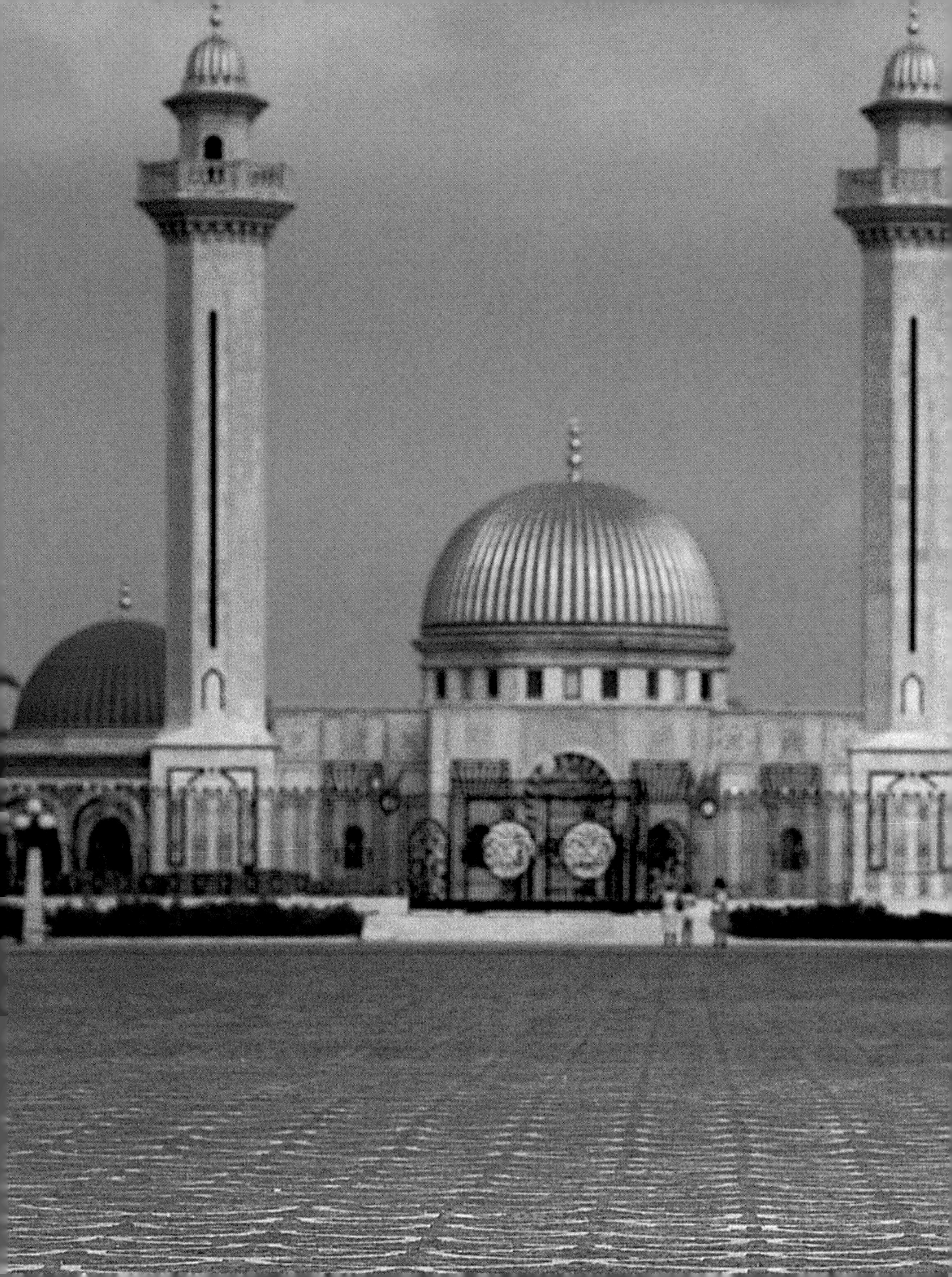

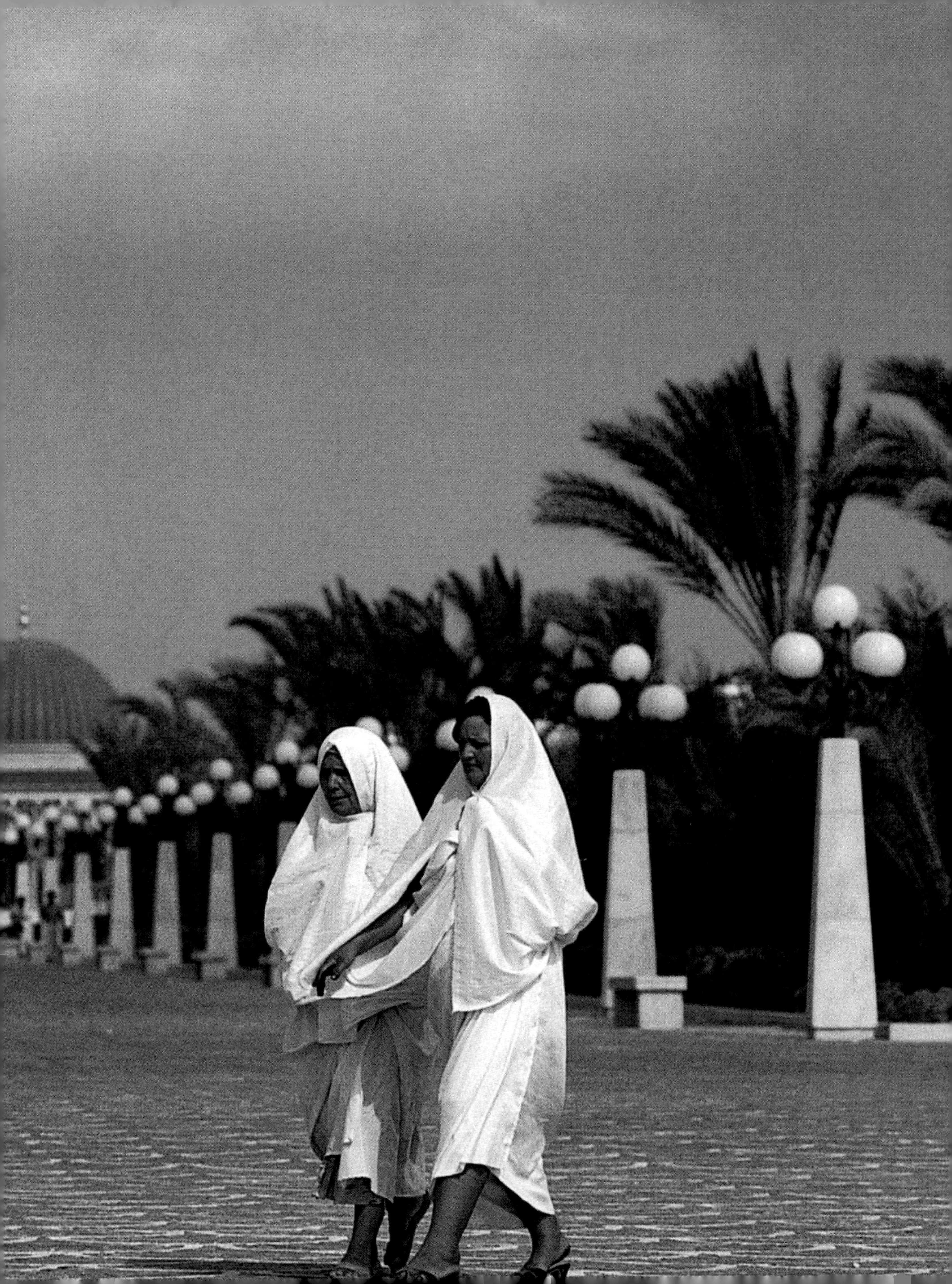

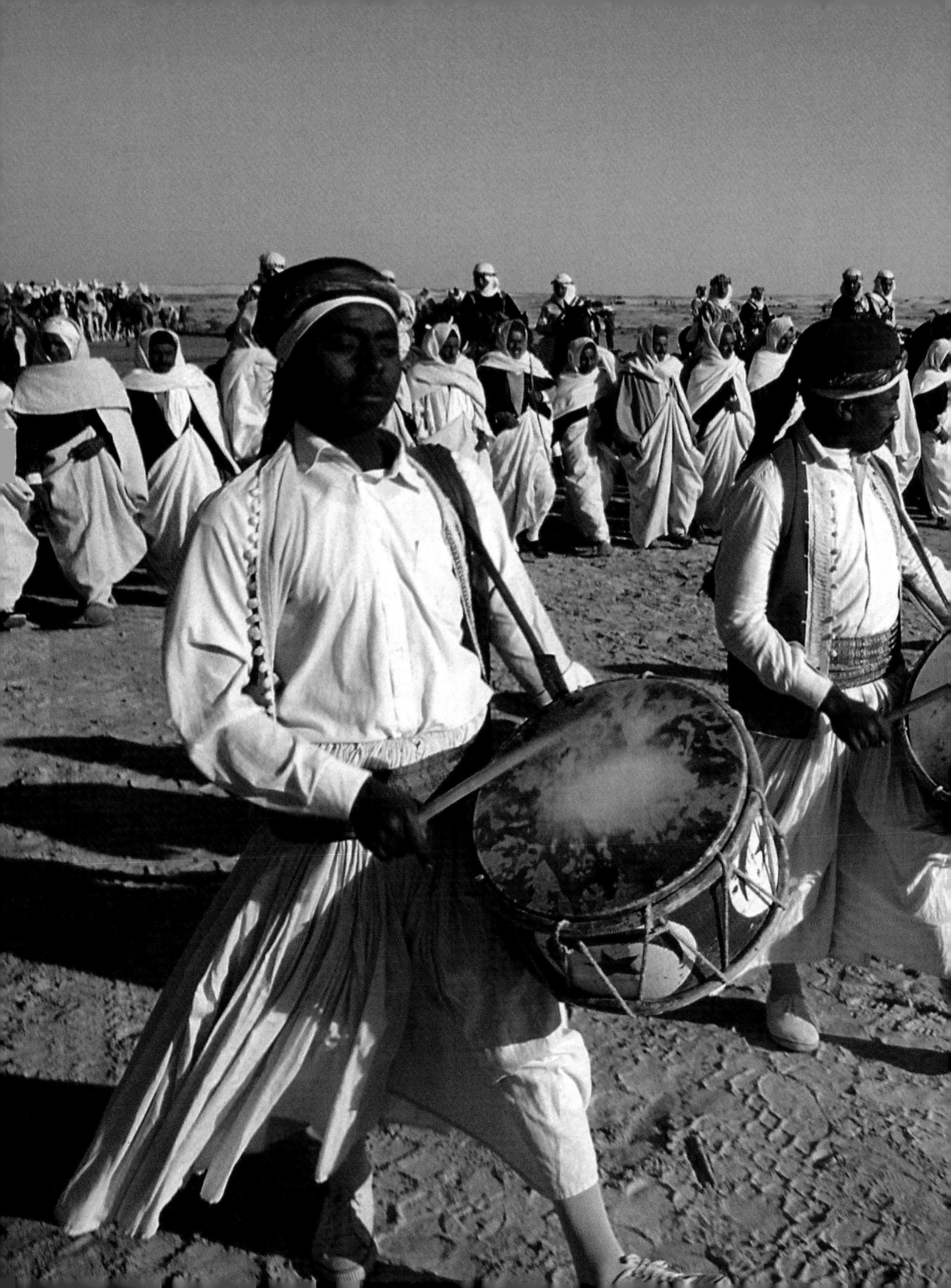

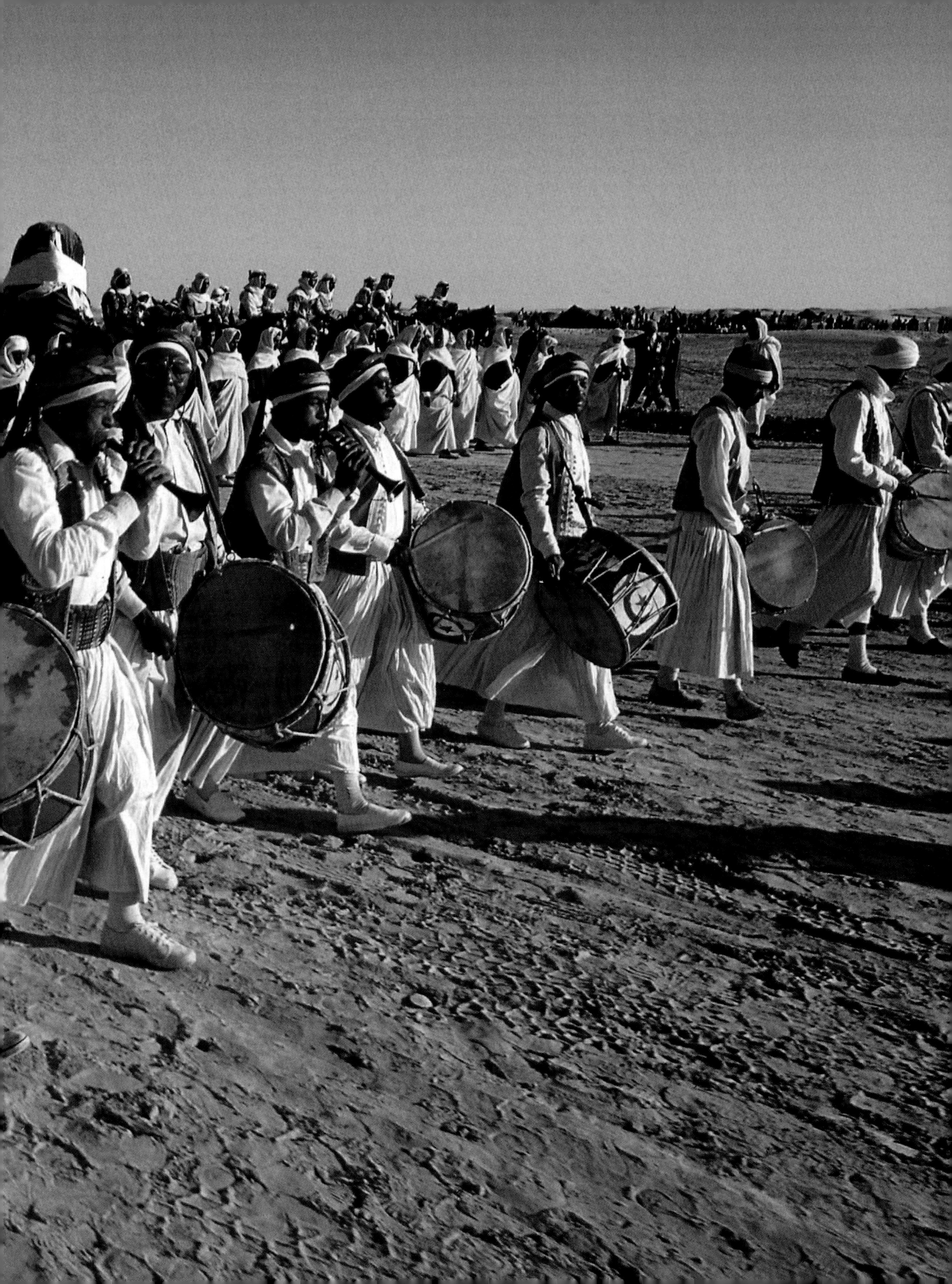

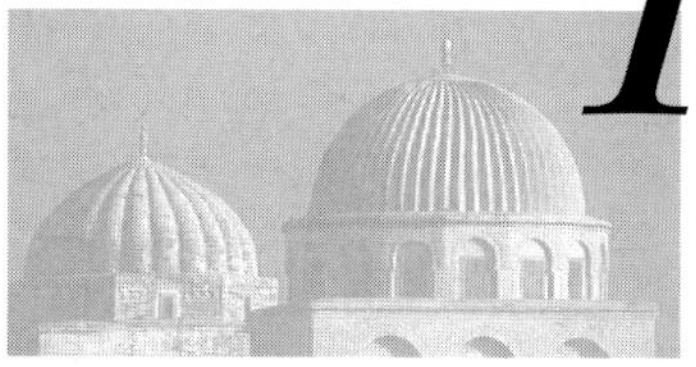

20 top *On this stone stela dating back to the second to first centuries BC and of Carthaginian origin is engraved a dedication to Baal, the most powerful masculine divinity worshiped by the Phoenicians. Today conserved in the British Museum in London, the find was dedicated to the god by Caius Julius Arish.*

20 bottom *Carthage is also the place of origin of this stela, dating back to the first century AD. The sculptured figure is Tanit, the main Phoenician goddess, often represented by peculiar symbols: a disc, a half moon and occasionally, as in this case, sacrificial victims.*

It began in the remote prehistory of the Tunisian epic because here in North Africa *Homo sapiens* took their first steps around the ninth millennium BC. Founded upon hunting and stone-wielding, the earliest civilization documented in Tunisia was the Capsian, which developed in the area of the Gafsa Oasis in the heart of the modern-day country between the Paleolithic and the Neolithic eras. From this branch evolved the Proto-Libyan Civilization, later called Berber (from the *Latin barbarus*), through a combination of the native peoples and populations arriving from the Egyptian east and the North African coasts that penetrated the interior owing to climatic changes affecting and drying the Sahara region around the third millennium.

The lifestyle long remained primitive. The foundation of Utica in 1101 BC, the work of the Phoenicians who needed a port along the route to Gibraltar, did not alter the situation but did culturally enrich the Berber population and generate the historical event crucial to the successive development of the Mediterranean area. The foundation of Carthage in 814 BC supplanted Utica in strategic importance, and as a result the Punic civilization (the name by which the Romans called the Phoenicians) was born.

21 *In the Bardo Museum in Tunis this earthenware protome is exhibited, datable to between the sixth and fourth centuries BC and featuring the head of the goddess Tanit. In the local religion, Tanit was the goddess of fertility that, together with Baal-Hammon, formed the divine protective couple of Carthage.*

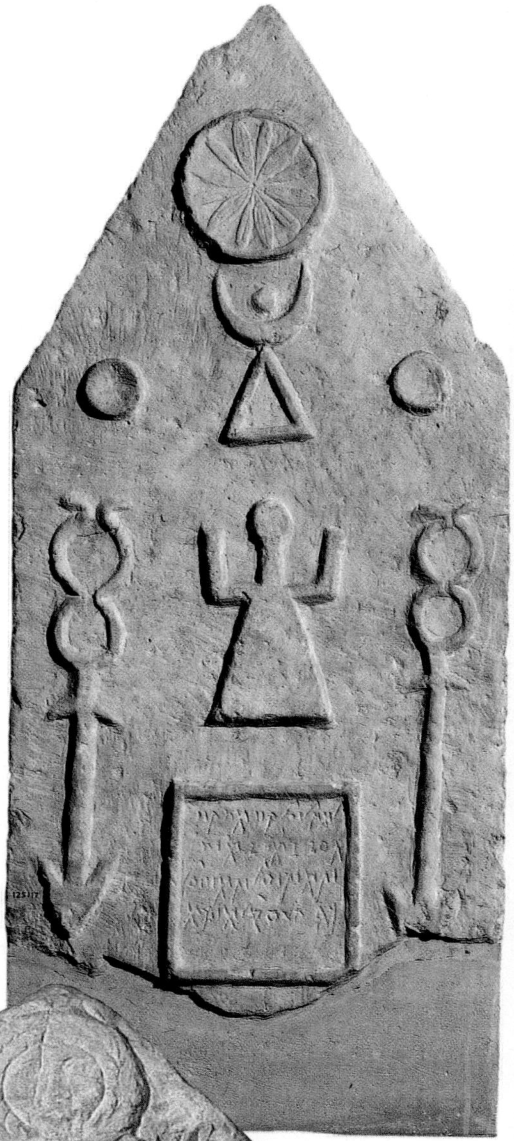

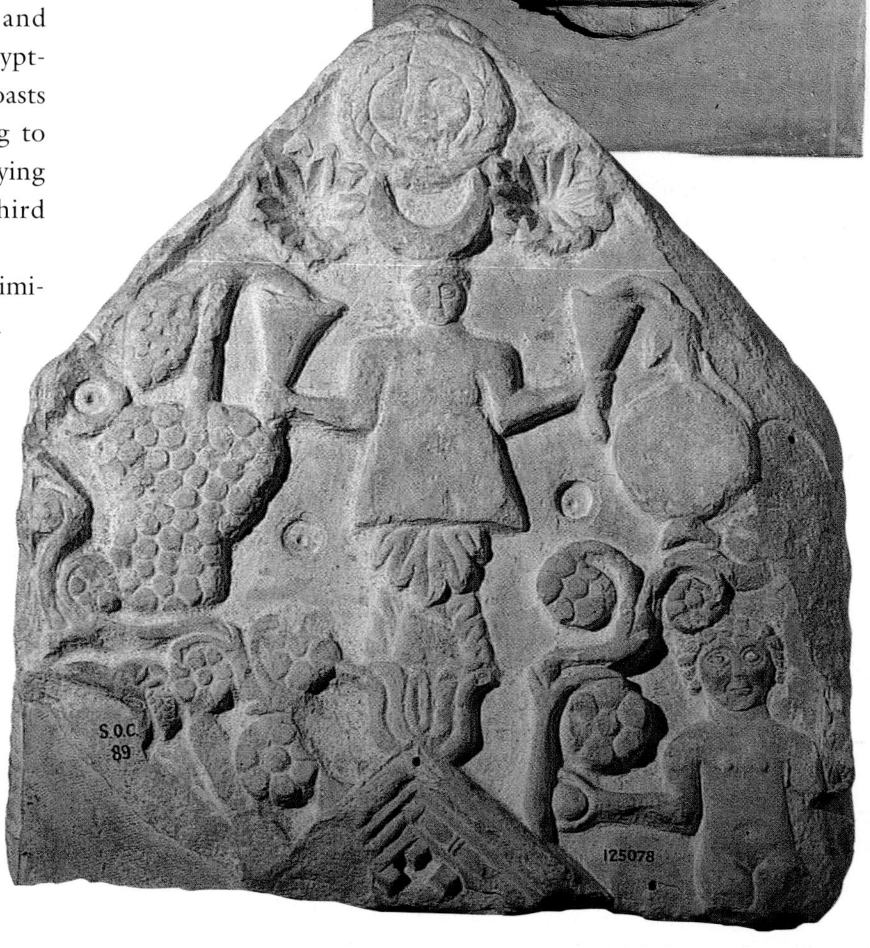
S.O.C.
89
125078

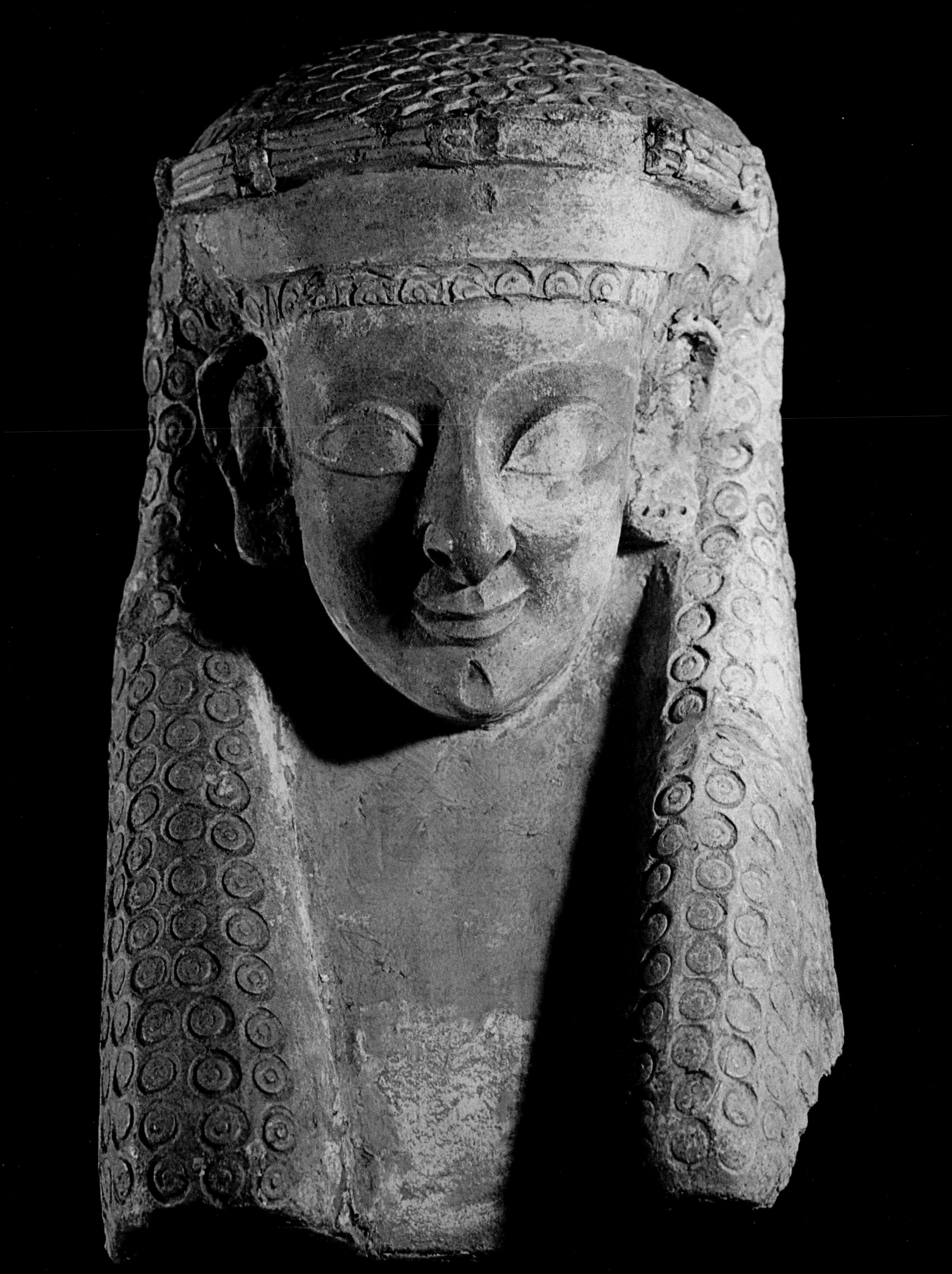

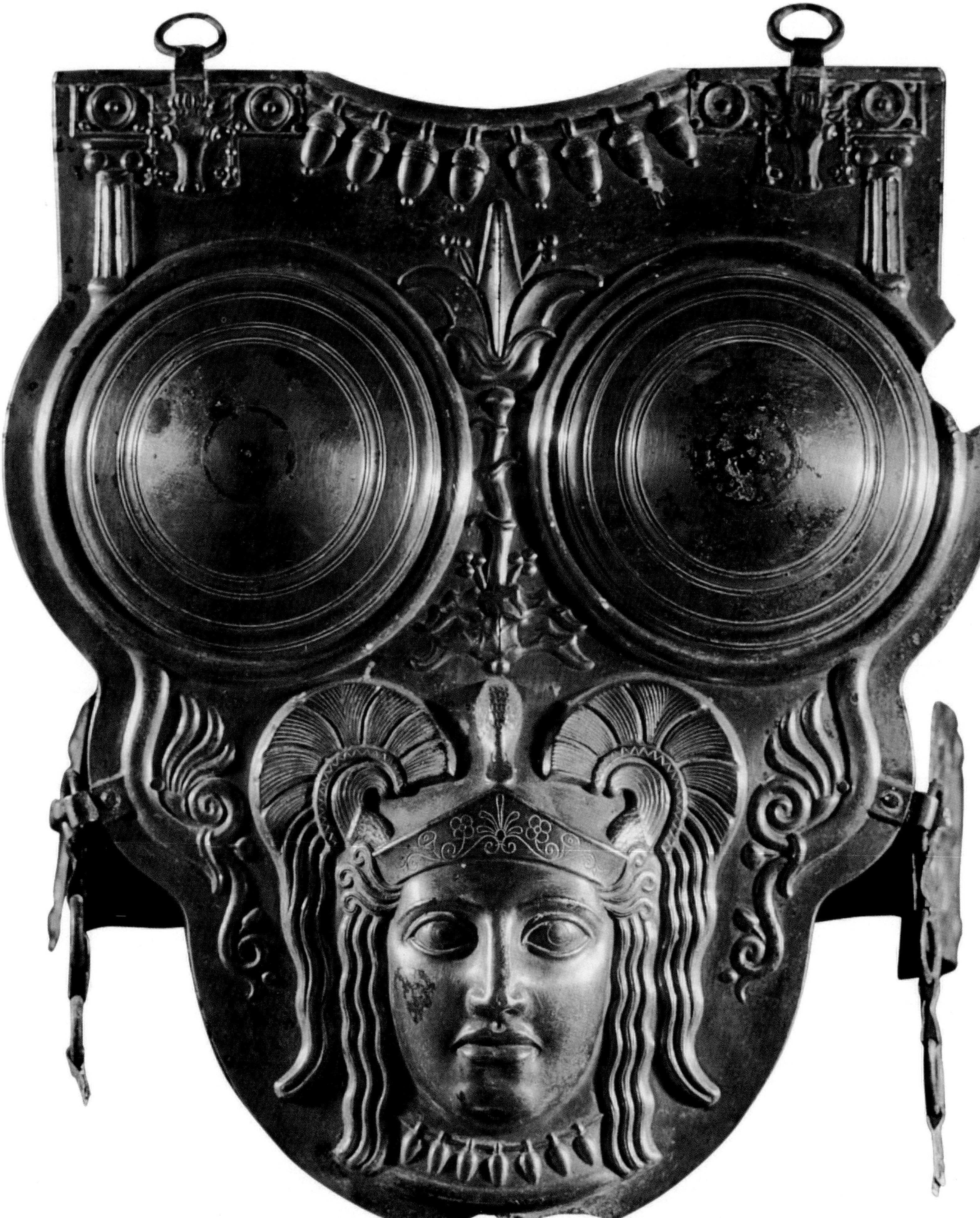

22 The splendid bronze breastplate shown here is Punic made and probably dates back to the third to second centuries BC. In the lower section of the object stands out a woman's head adorned with an elaborate crown and surrounded by floral motifs.

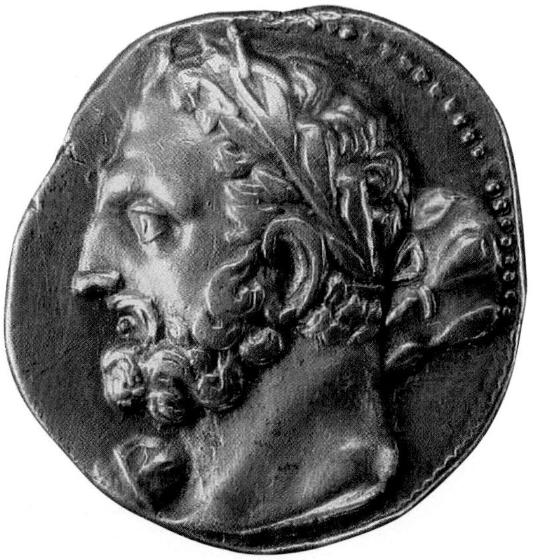

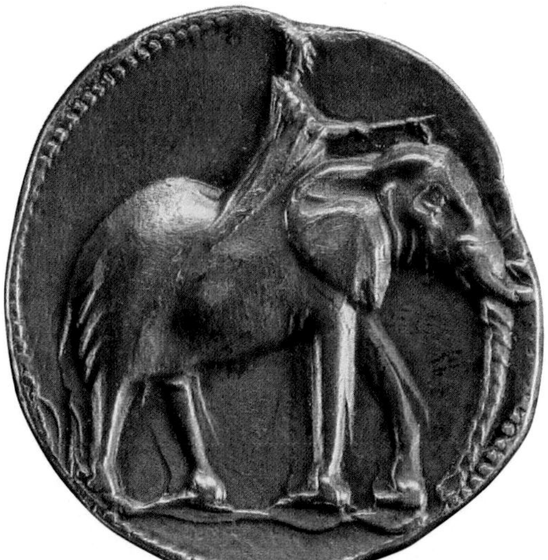

23 top On this shekel, a silver coin of Carthage, an elephant with his driver and a man's face are portrayed. They are references to Hannibal and his conquests. Dated to 230 BC, the coin was found in Spain, in the area of Valencia.

Before the fifth century BC little is known about Carthage. However, it is known that it became the center of an empire that was in continuous expansion. The Phoenicians peppered the Tunisian coast with layover ports that were part of a system built to monitor commercial activities in the Mediterranean and, at the same time, manage the inland regions, thanks to which an enormous agricultural potential was put at their disposal. This created closer relationships and more frequent cultural exchanges with the Berber population. The first nucleuses of Tunis, Bizerte, Sousse, Gabès and other important cities were formed. Carthage, grown big and powerful, freed itself from subordination to the local people, having been forced until then to pay rent to occupy the land, and committed itself to a vigorous campaign to colonize the surrounding lands, hence conquering Sardinia and dominating commercial traffic destined for Spain, France and even Ireland. However, their expansionist aims were met with an immediate defeat in Sicily, the eternal aspiration of the Phoenicians, to the Greeks who were still militarily strong. However, foreign relations produced significant treaties, symptom of the soon-to-come recognition of Carthage's important role in the Mediterranean area. With the Etruscans, Carthage stipulated alliance pacts that showed themselves to be efficient in limiting the Greek forces in Tyrrhene, while treaties with Rome were shaped as early as 509 BC.

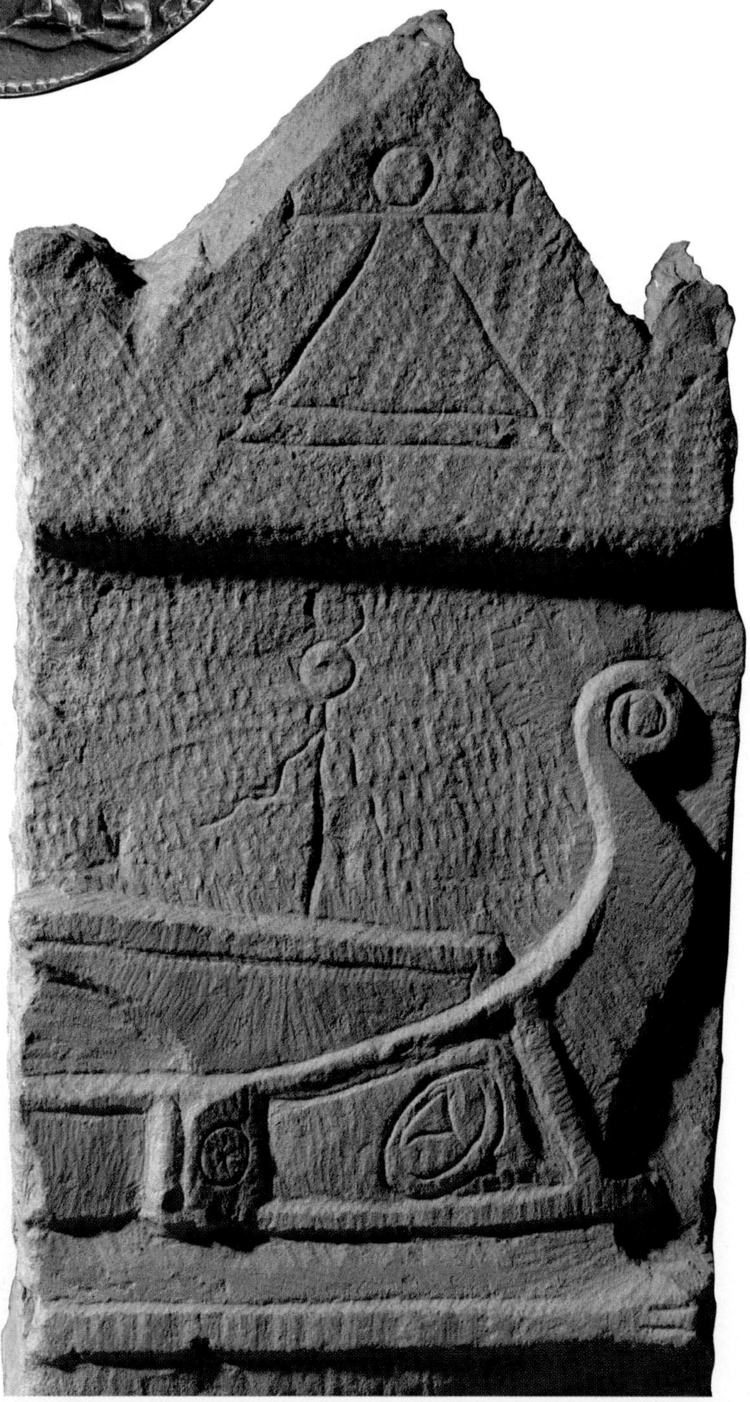

23 bottom From the Tophet of Carthage, this votive stela is 181/2 inches high and dates back to the third century BC. In the top part, one of the symbols of the goddess Tanit is reproduced: a stylized praying figure with open arms. In the lower part is the bow of a ship.

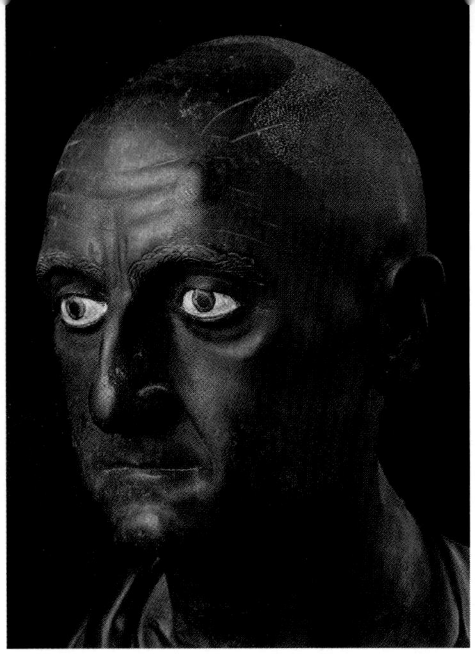

24 top Publius Cornelius Scipio, known as 'Africanus', owes his nickname to the victorious mission conducted on Carthaginian terrain in 202 BC. The battle of Zama, which brought an end to the Second Punic War, constituted a first step towards Roman hegemony in the Mediterranean.

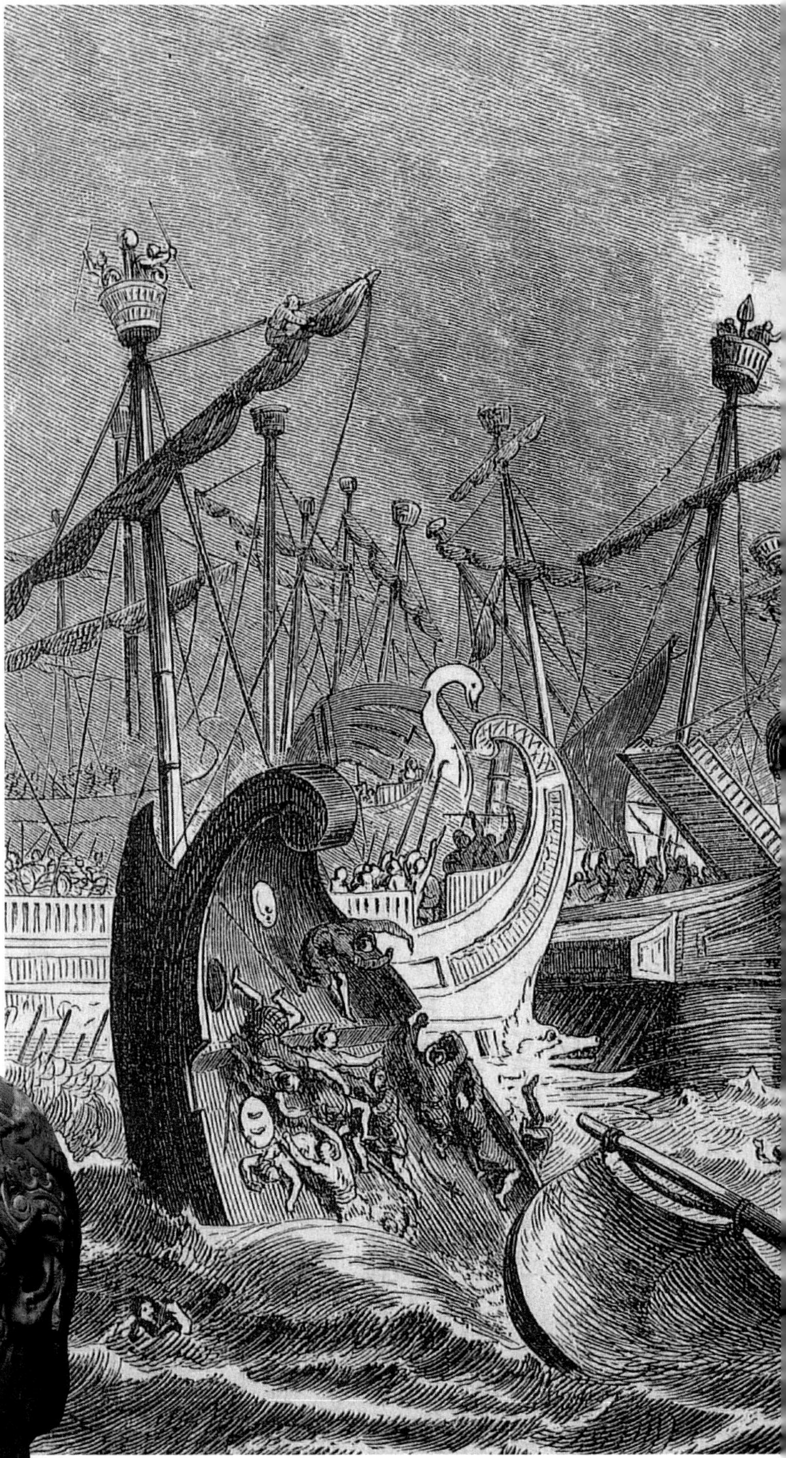

24 bottom The African general Hannibal, here portrayed in a marble bust datable to between the third and second centuries BC and conserved in the National Museum in Naples, was one of the most extraordinary characters in the conflict between Rome and Carthage, the two powers that contested for hegemony in the Mediterranean for decades.

However, the clash with the great power of Rome would explode soon thereafter: the attempted conquest of Sicily (270 BC) cost the Punic city a century of conflicts, marked by the three unfortunately famous wars (the first from 264 to 241 BC; the second from 218 to 201 and the third from 149 to 146). With the taking of Messina, the Carthaginians found themselves in direct contact with the sphere of influence of a Rome in full expansion, which was also seeking to get its hands on the Sicilian city. Following two major defeats, a Roman assault lasting three years led the city to its total destruction. *'Delenda est Carthago'*, meaning 'Carthage must be destroyed', thundered Cato, and despite the valiant resistance of Hamilcar followed by that of his celebrated commander Hannibal—who managed to inflict a crushing defeat on his enemy at Zama—Carthage was later razed to the ground by Scipio the Africanus in 146 BC.

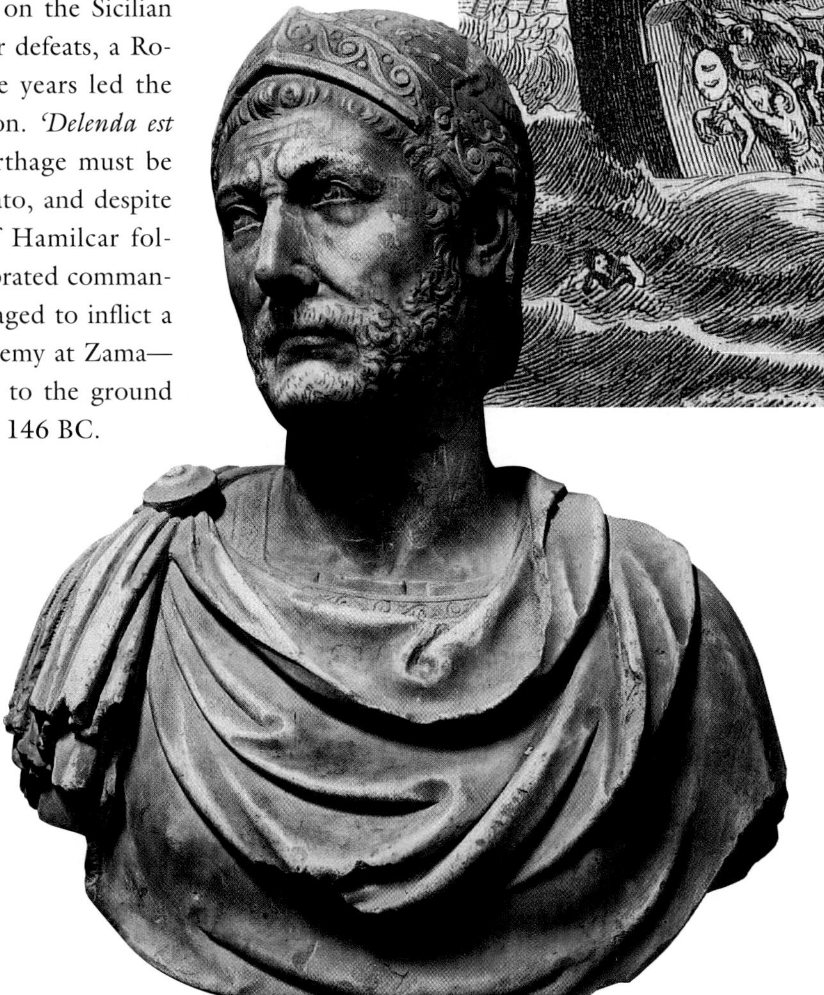

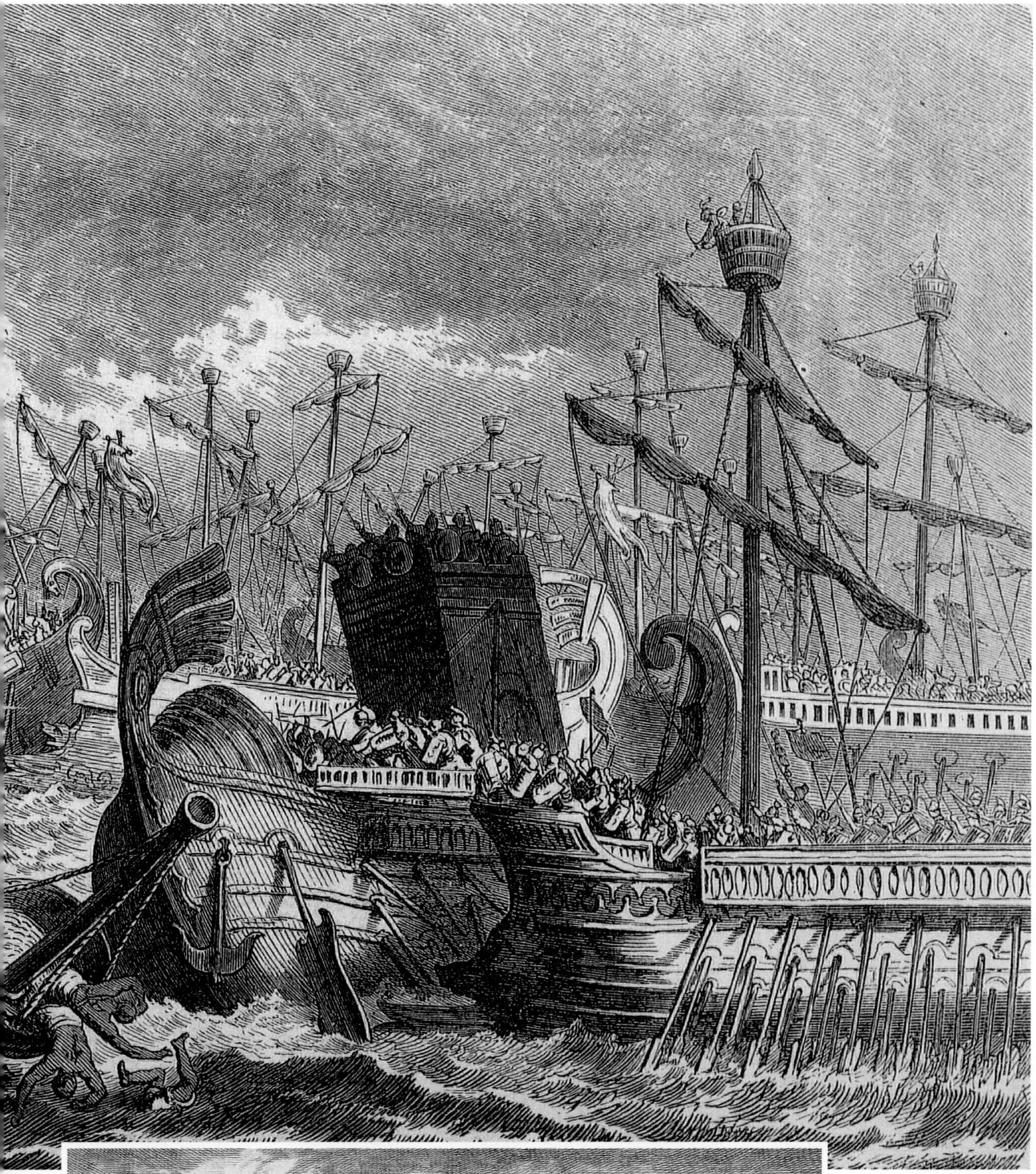

24-25 During the course of the naval battle of Aegusa, fought in the area of Favignana Island on 10 March 241 BC at the end of the First Punic War, the Roman Caius Lutatius Catulus captured 70 enemy ships and sunk 50.

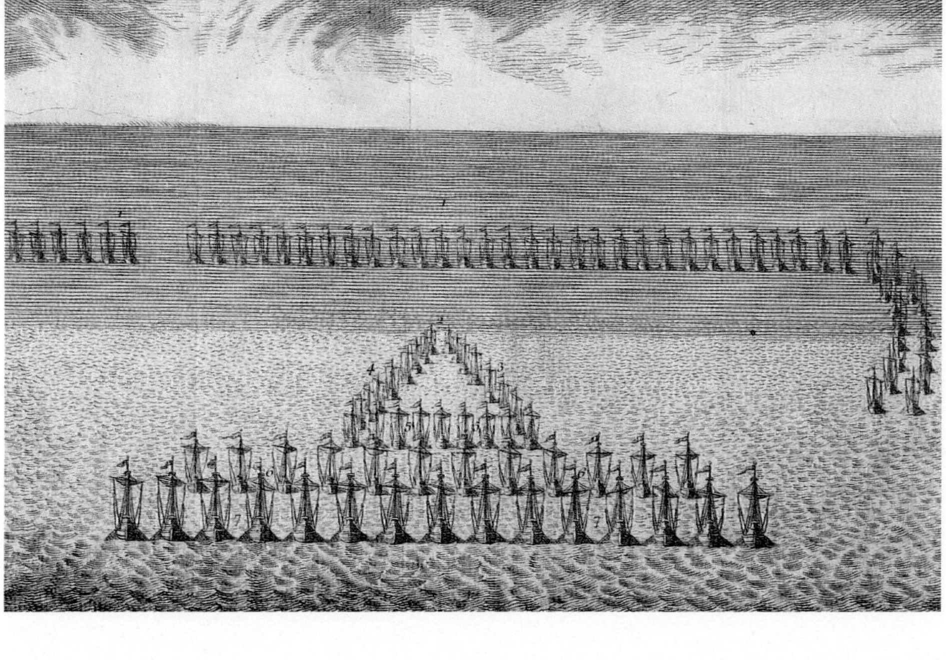

25 bottom In the naval battle of Ecnomus, which unfolded in 256 BC during the course of the First Punic War (264-241 BC), the Roman fleet, after a violent fight, was able to defeat the impressive Carthaginian armada.

26-27 Conserved by the Bardo Museum in Tunis, this precious Carthaginian mosaic from the second century BC portrays circus attractions.

27 top left A goddess rides a lion on the face of this gold coin of Carcalla. The inscription reads, 'Indugentia Aug. in Carth'.

27 top right The production of mosaics had a prominent role in Punic art, finding opportunities for expression both in public as well as private sectors. This photo shows a Carthaginian funereal mosaic dating back to the earliest Christian times.

27 bottom Born in 354 in Tagaste, today in Algeria, Saint Augustine studied in Carthage, where he formed his theological convictions.

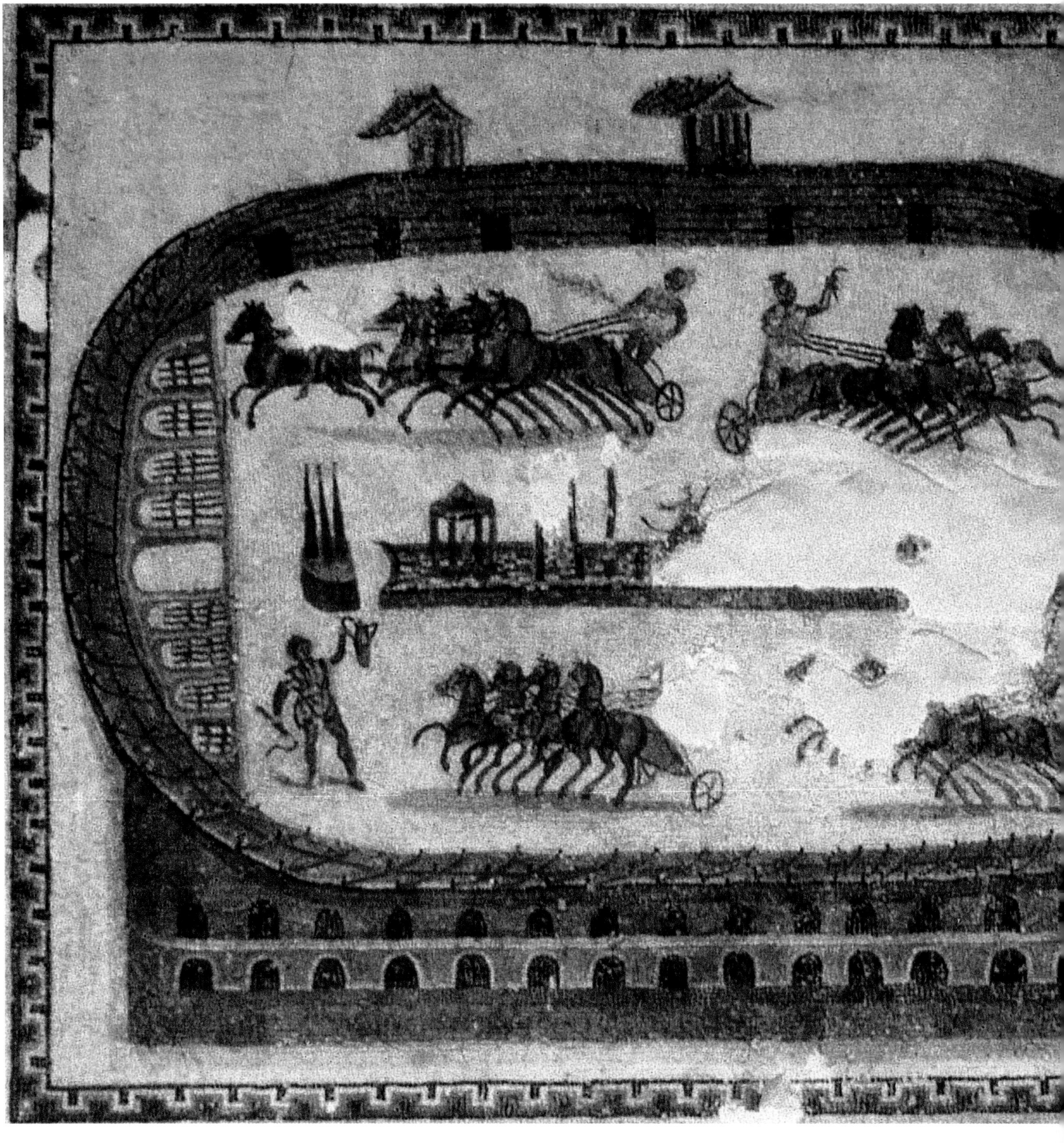

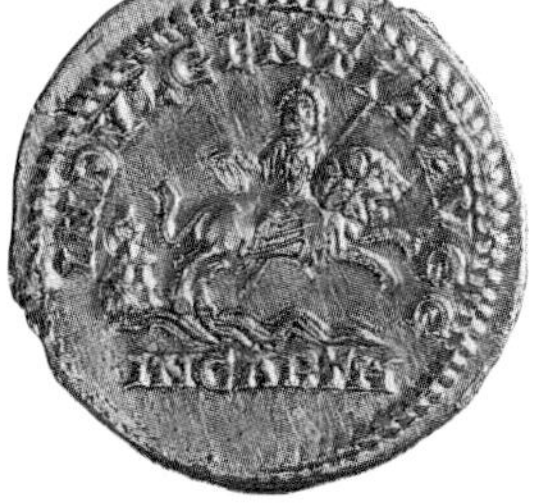

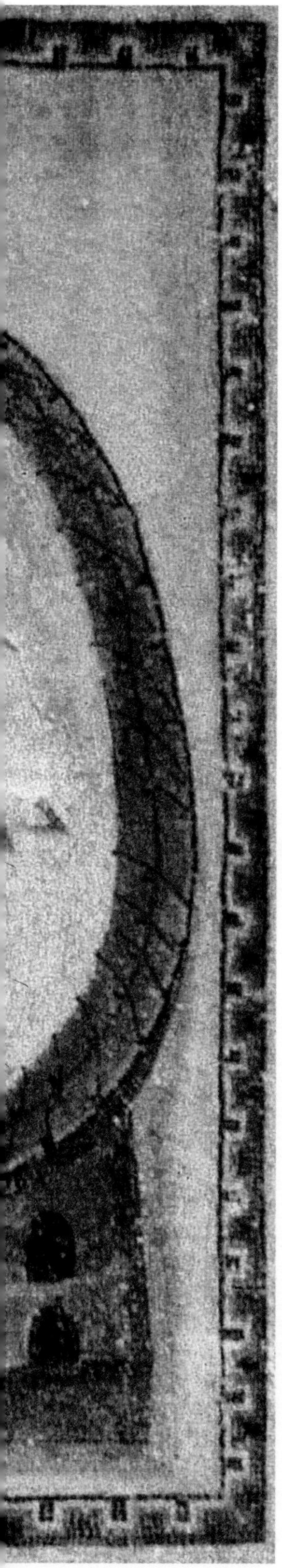

Rome's victory did not break up the cultural order of the Punic civilization. The language, arts and religious cults survived, integrating themselves into the Hellenistic culture to the point that the Romans conceded the *suffeti* (the Punic magistrates) command of many cities. Carthage was later founded again by Octavian Augustus, thus becoming capital of the province of Africa and, for a brief period, the second-most important urban center of all the Empire. New ports and cities were constructed in Tunisia and progressively, from the second century on, they passed on the models of the imperial governmental and municipal institutions to the entire area. Meanwhile, art, architecture and Roman urbanization permeated the country, with traces of their presence still visible today. Despite persecution, Christianity spread widely, mixing with the pagan practices of the region, thanks to the active preaching of prestigious figures such as Saint Augustine (who lived and studied in Carthage), Tertullian and Saint Ciprian. However, the climate of peace was destined to explode, compromising the Roman dominion in the area. Following the fourth century AD, certain social tensions within the economic and religious matrix, deriving from increasing agricultural crises and cults ever more in contrast with the Christian presence, embittered the population to the point of initiating a revolt that affected a large portion of North Africa. The difficulty with which the Romans reinforced their presence brought to light their weakness and prepared the land for their eventual overthrow.

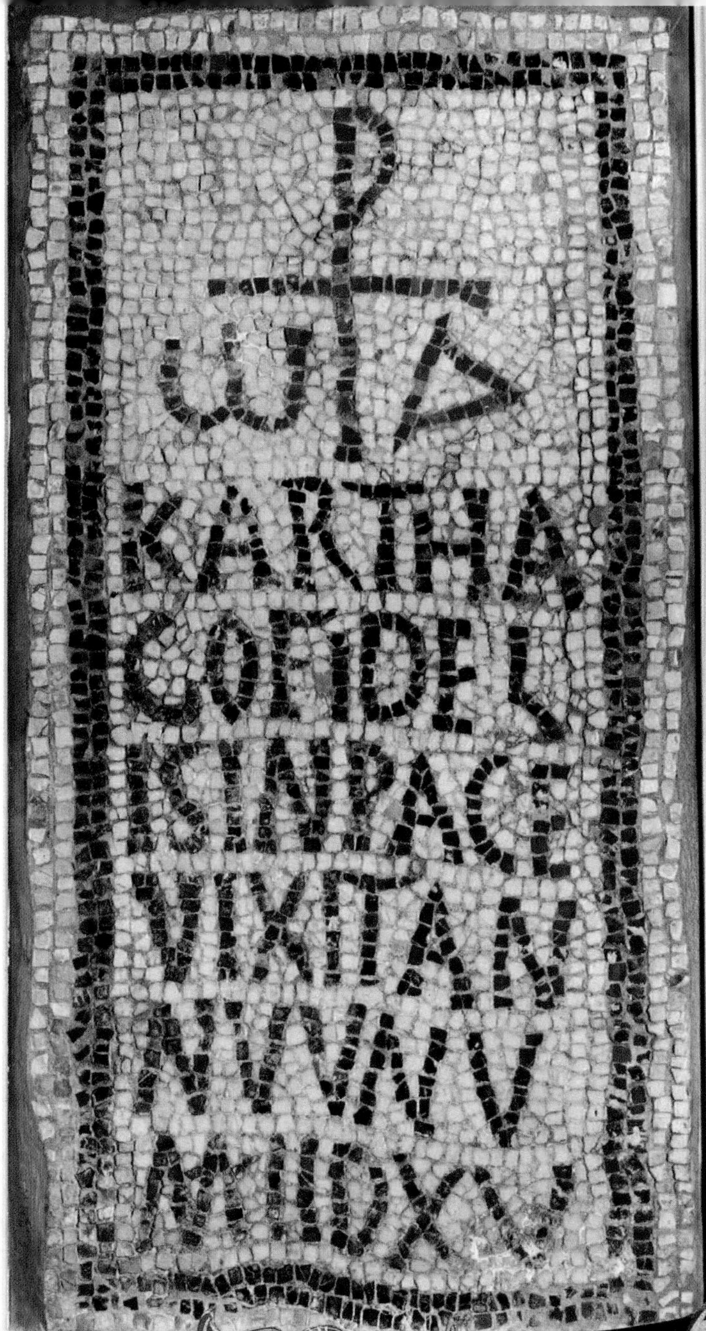
KARTHA

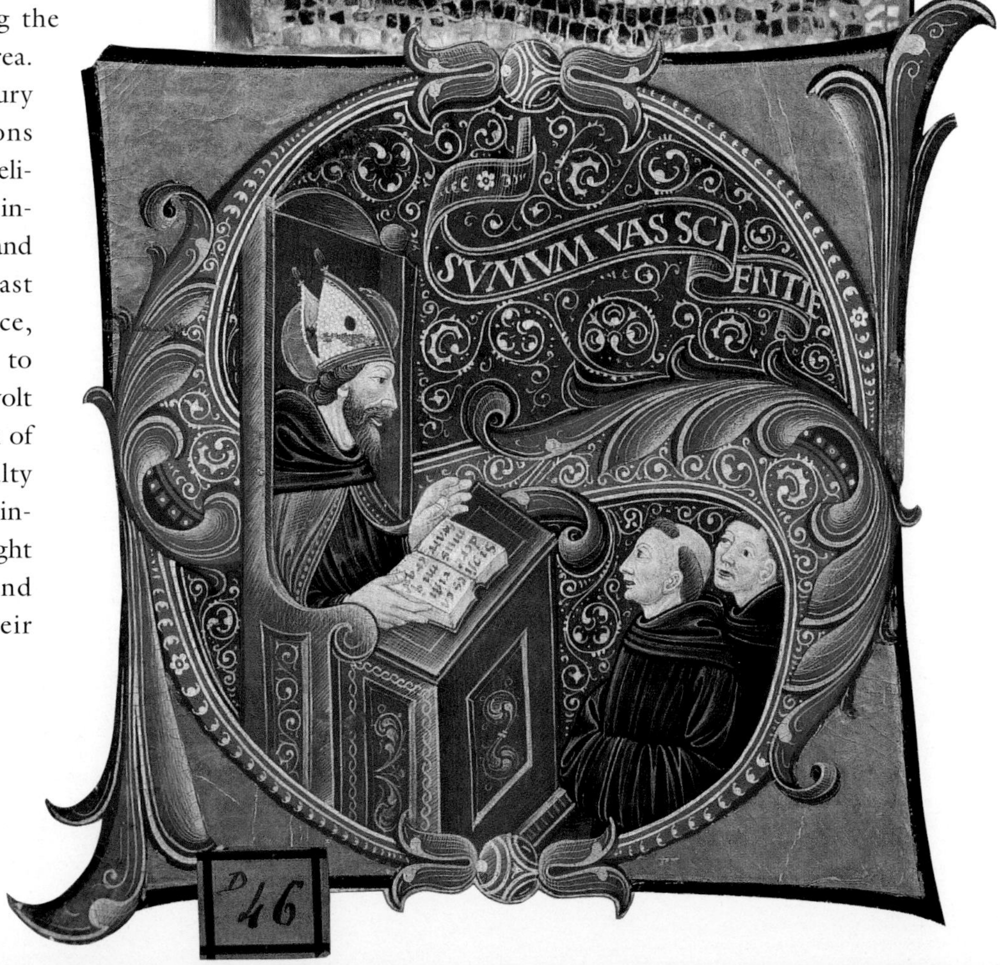
SVMVM VAS SCI
ENTIE
46

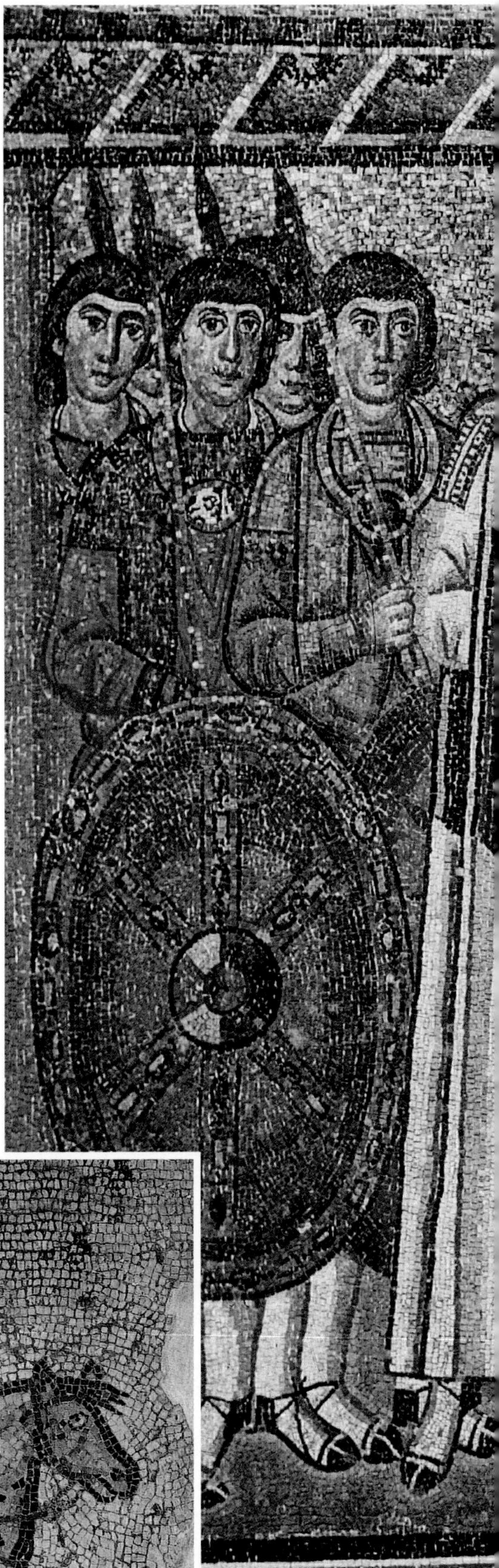

This event was finally accomplished in 429 with the arrival of the Vandals of Genseric who stormed into the region and conquered Carthage in 439. However, their fragile dominion never achieved systematic control of the inland territory but remained limited to the cities and the coast allowing the Berber population, which never disappeared, to reinforce their autonomy.

In 533, the Byzantine Empire, which wanted to annex the African regions to Constantinople, expelled the Vandals and installed itself in the area of Tunisia. The fiscal and agrarian reforms adopted were unfortunately not sufficient: the new occupants had to learn quickly to defend themselves from the rehabilitated Berber forces that, in the second half of the seventh century, greatly contributed to the fall of the Empire in the territory, which came about in 698 with the Arab conquest of Carthage. These events exposed Tunisia to the Islamic incursions into the African region, which had been increasing drastically for decades and left the foundations for a conflict between the Arabs and Berbers that did not end before 702 with the assassination of the heroic Berber queen Kahina, who had led the courageous insurrection against the Muslims.

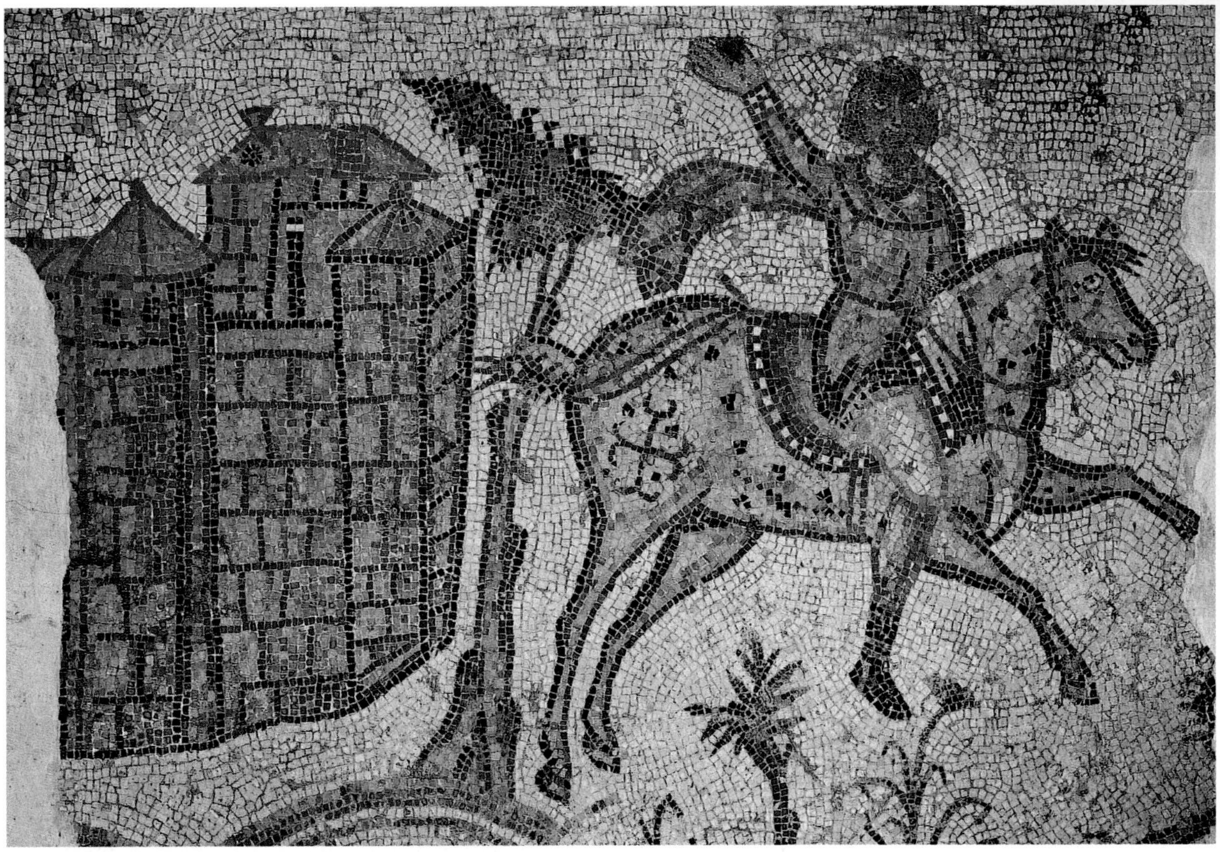

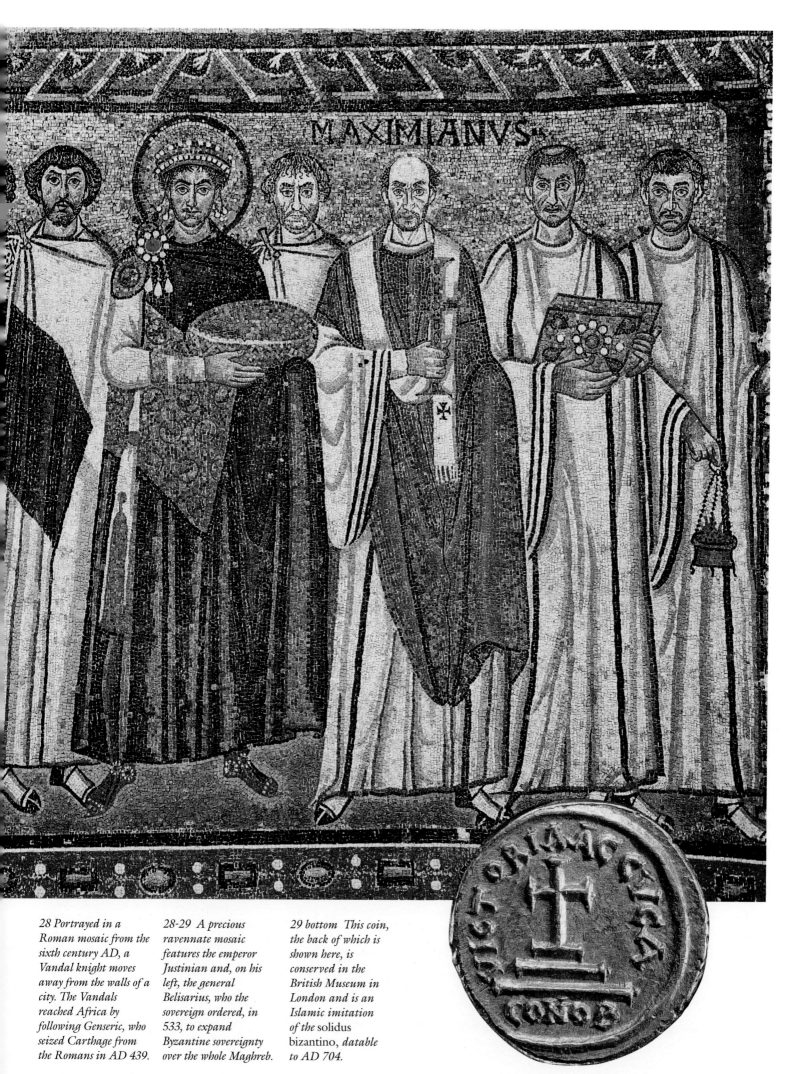

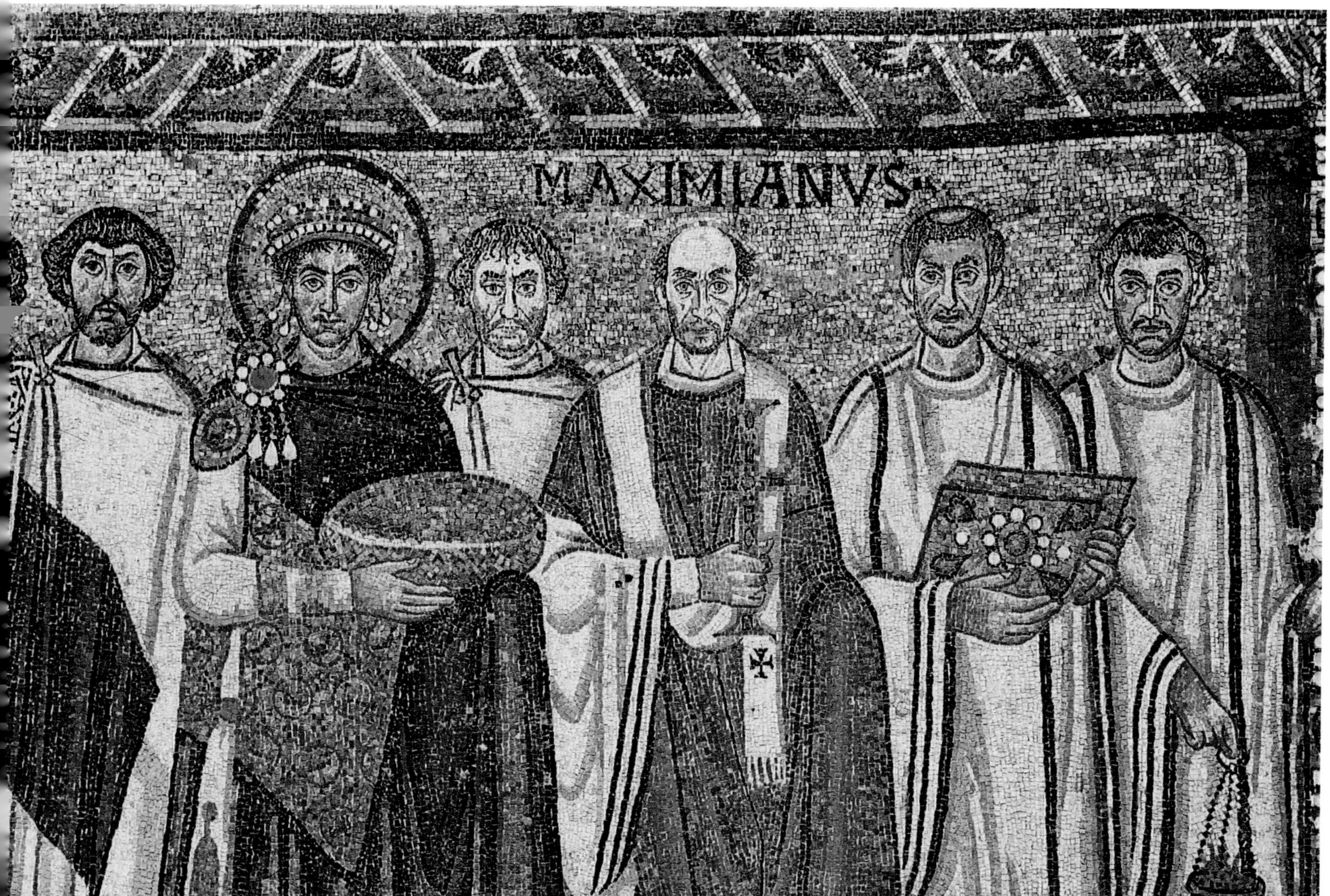
MAXIMIANVS

28 Portrayed in a Roman mosaic from the sixth century AD, a Vandal knight moves away from the walls of a city. The Vandals reached Africa by following Genseric, who seized Carthage from the Romans in AD 439.

28-29 A precious ravennate mosaic features the emperor Justinian and, on his left, the general Belisarius, who the sovereign ordered, in 533, to expand Byzantine sovereignty over the whole Maghreb.

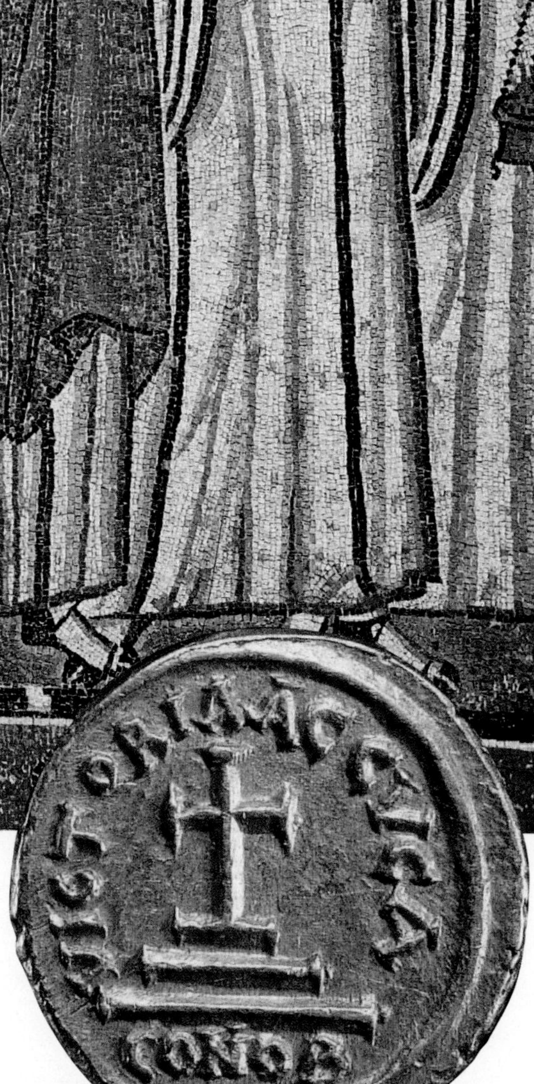
CONOB

29 bottom This coin, the back of which is shown here, is conserved in the British Museum in London and is an Islamic imitation of the solidus bizantino, *datable to AD 704.*

Under the new Arab domination, Tunisia began its own process of Islamization as it was absorbed into the Arab-Muslim Empire, first under order of the Umayyad Caliphate of Damascus and later under that of the Abbasids in Baghdad. The Abbasid reign had a short life however, provoking the break-up of the Muslim world. The birth of a new emirate followed, that of the Aghlabids, founded by Ibrahim ibn el-Aghlab, which brought an extraordinary period of social-economic progress over the next 110 years. Agriculture was intensified thus building numerous infrastructures while palaces and mosques were erected in Tunis, Sousse and Kairouan—just to name a few—and the sciences, arts and theology were developed. However, a new conflict with the Berbers would soon explode: the dynasty was routed in 909 by Obeid Allah who, with the support of the Kutama Berbers and claiming direct descent from Fatima, daughter of the prophet Mohammed, proclaimed himself caliph and founded the famous Shiite Fatimid Dynasty, which would reign in Tunisia for over 250 years.

Conquest did not wait long: with the acquisition of Egypt, the Fatimids took a central role in the conflict that in the tenth century put the caliphates of Cordoba and Cairo in competition for control of the northern commercial routes crossing the Sahara. The clash involved the Berber tribes of the entire Maghreb, who allied themselves with one or the other of the contending caliphates. In Ifriqiyya—the name given to north-central Africa by the Arabs, which included Tunisia, Tripolitania

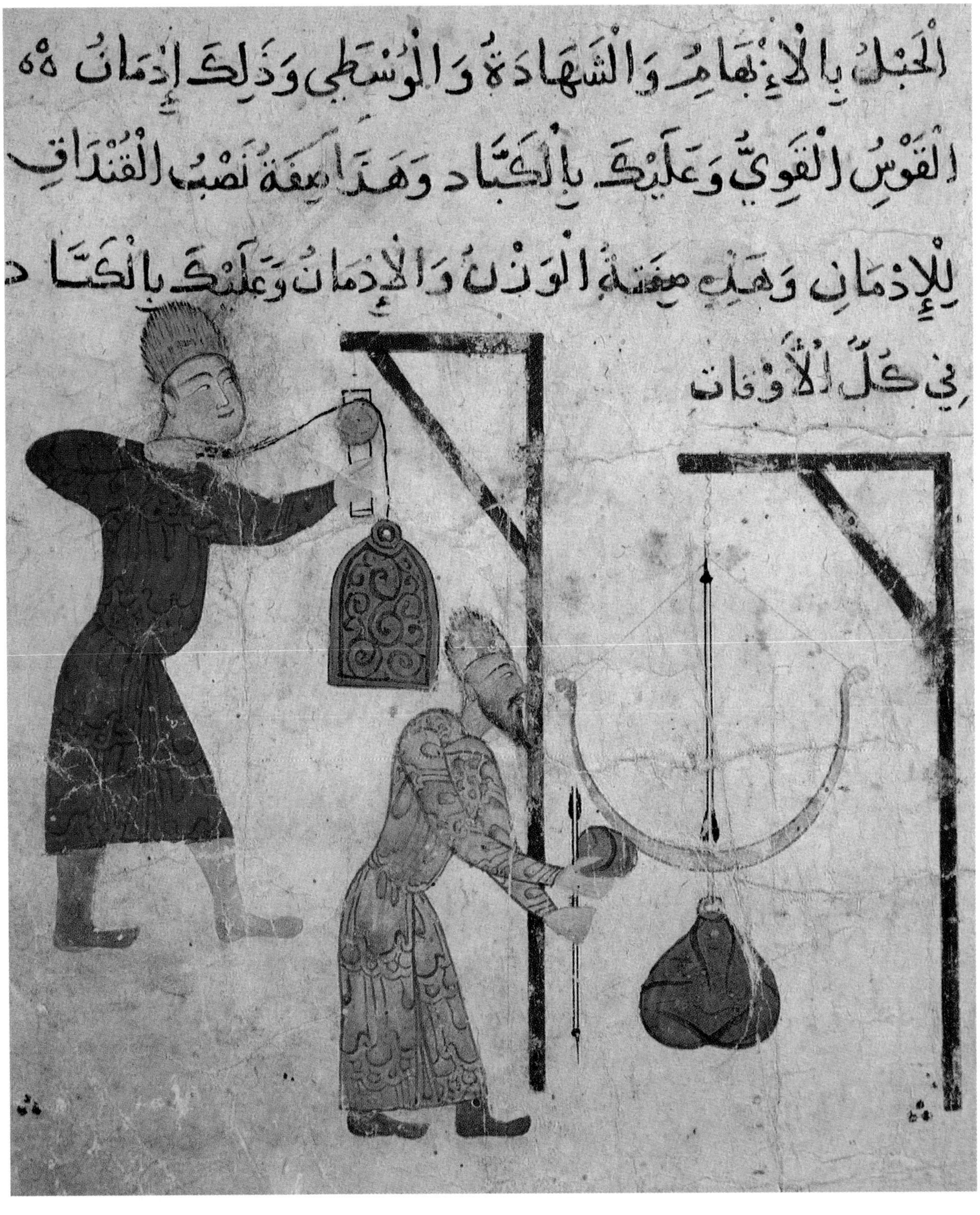
الحبل بالابهام والشهادة والوسطى وذلك إدمان
القوس القوي وعليك بالكباد وهذا صفة نصب القنداق
للإدمان وهذه صفة الوزن والإدمان وعليك بالكباد
في كل الأوقات

30 The 'weighing of good deeds', the subject of this remarkable Fatimid miniature (tenth to twelfth century), is rather unusual in Islamic iconography, even if in the Koran it is written that on Judgment Day everything that one has done in their life, even an atom of bad or good, will be weighed.

31 top Also dating back to the Fatimid era, this illustration portrays a contest between knights. The Shiite dynasty of the Fatimids claimed that their origin could be traced back to Fatima, beloved daughter of Mohammed and one of the few feminine cult figures in Islam.

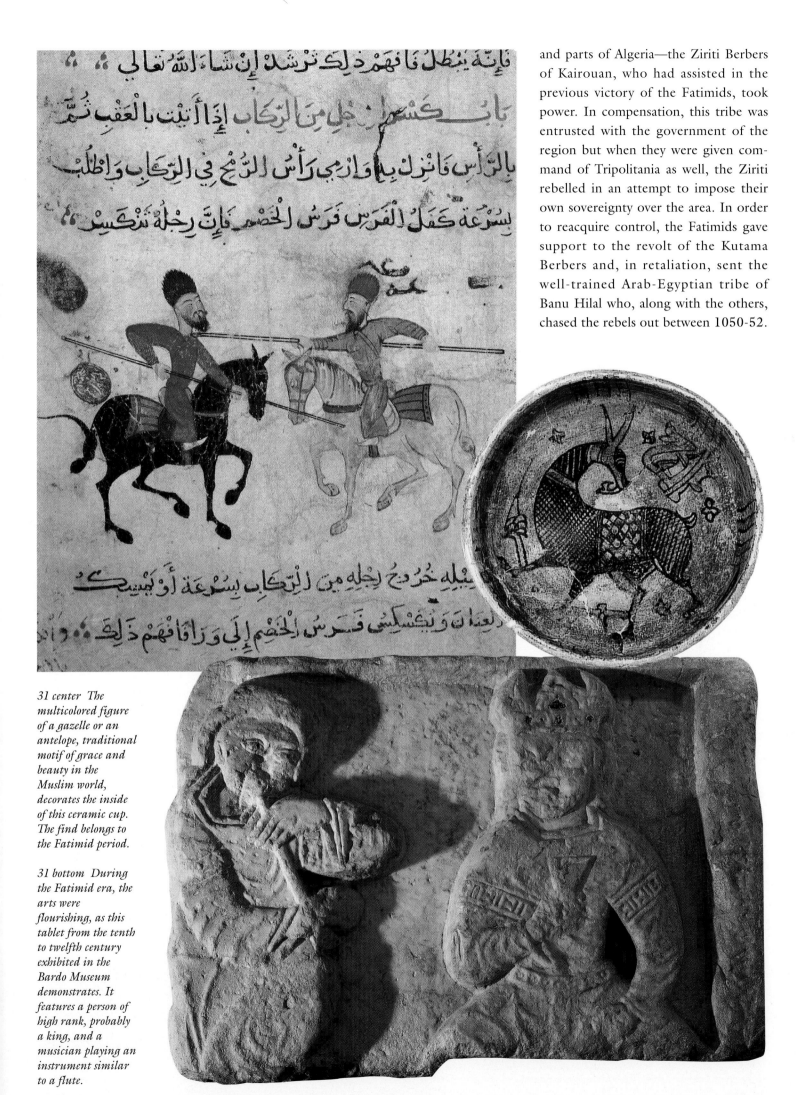

and parts of Algeria—the Ziriti Berbers of Kairouan, who had assisted in the previous victory of the Fatimids, took power. In compensation, this tribe was entrusted with the government of the region but when they were given command of Tripolitania as well, the Ziriti rebelled in an attempt to impose their own sovereignty over the area. In order to reacquire control, the Fatimids gave support to the revolt of the Kutama Berbers and, in retaliation, sent the well-trained Arab-Egyptian tribe of Banu Hilal who, along with the others, chased the rebels out between 1050-52.

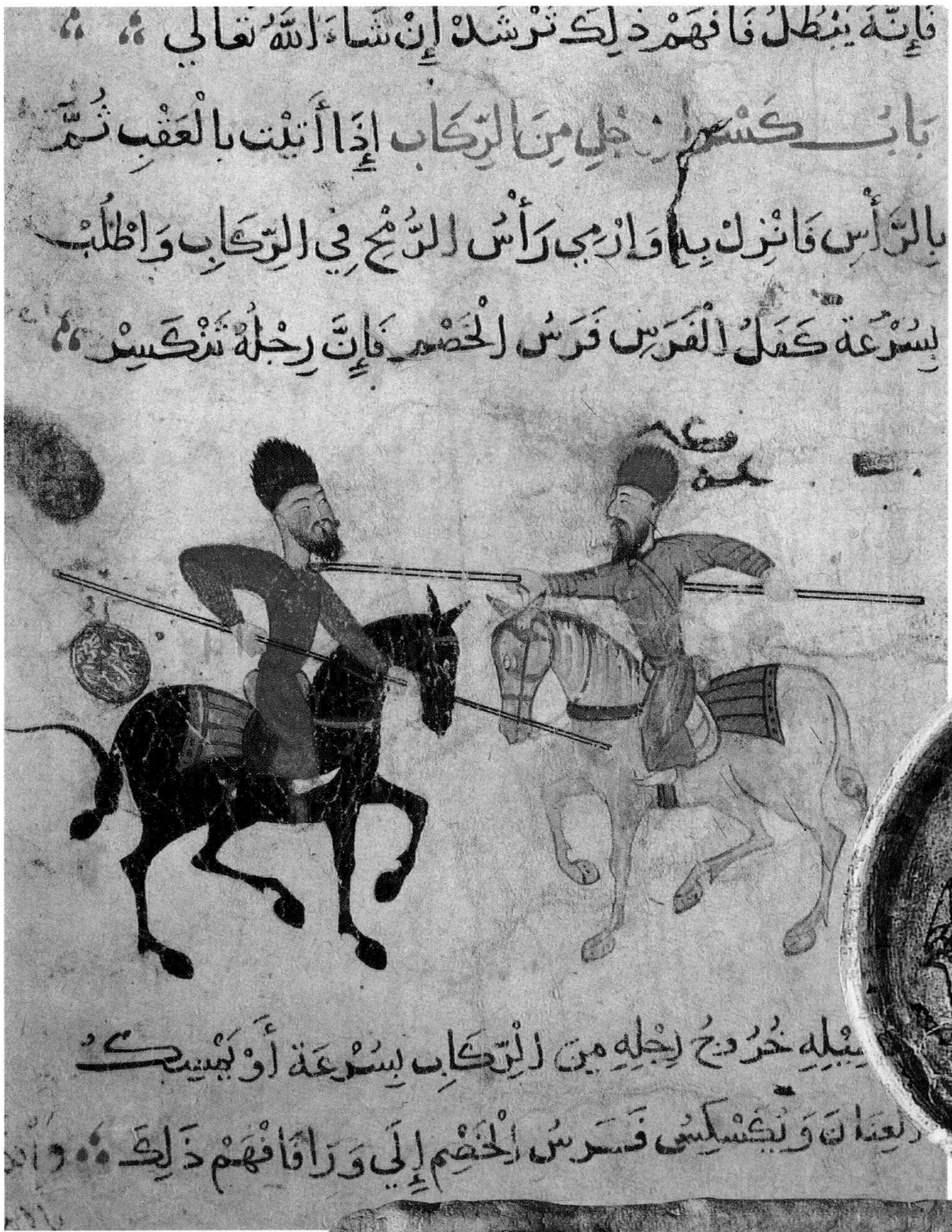

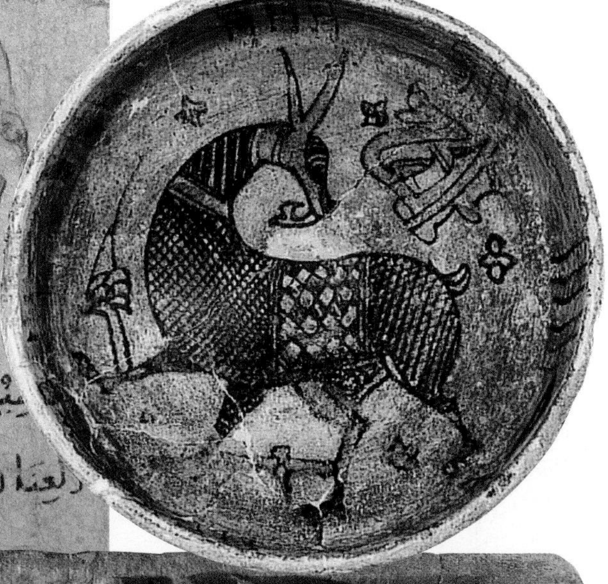

31 center The multicolored figure of a gazelle or an antelope, traditional motif of grace and beauty in the Muslim world, decorates the inside of this ceramic cup. The find belongs to the Fatimid period.

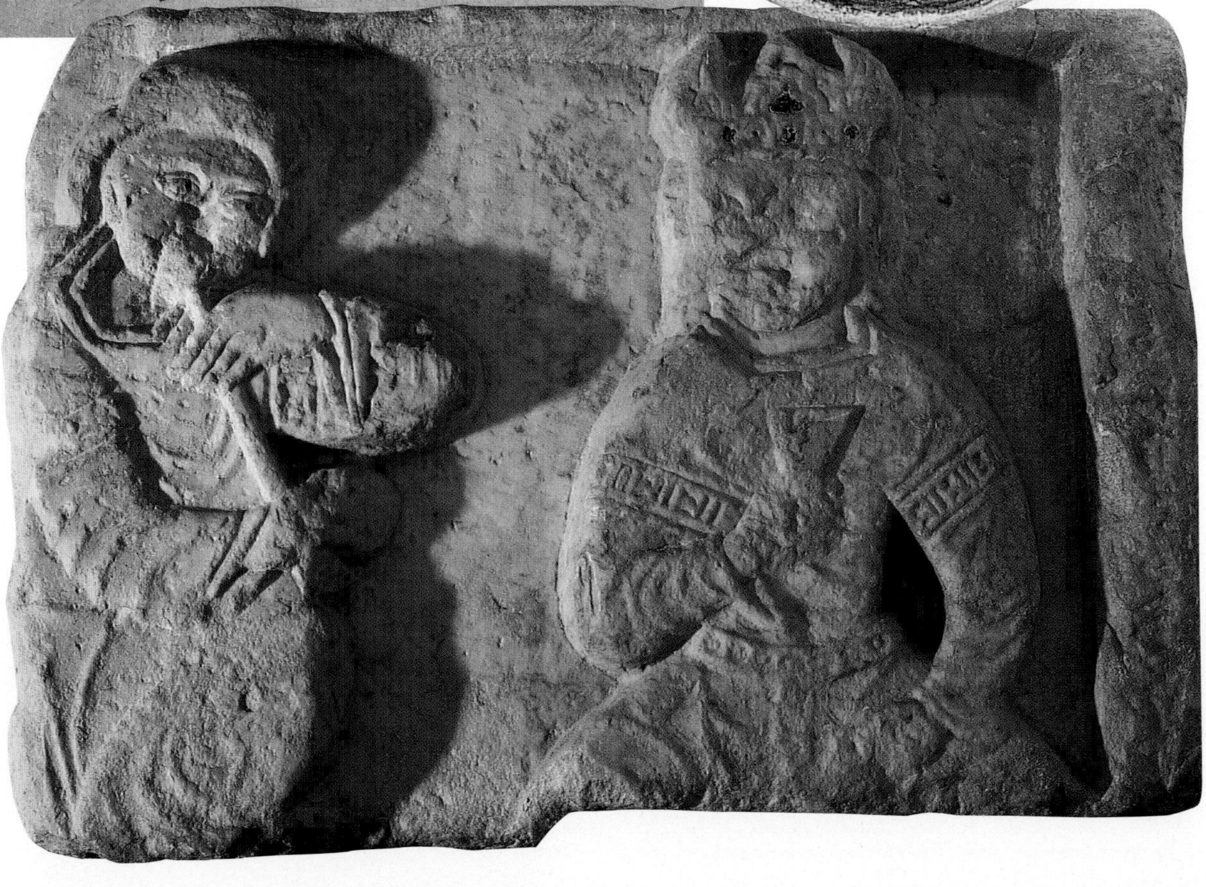

31 bottom During the Fatimid era, the arts were flourishing, as this tablet from the tenth to twelfth century exhibited in the Bardo Museum demonstrates. It features a person of high rank, probably a king, and a musician playing an instrument similar to a flute.

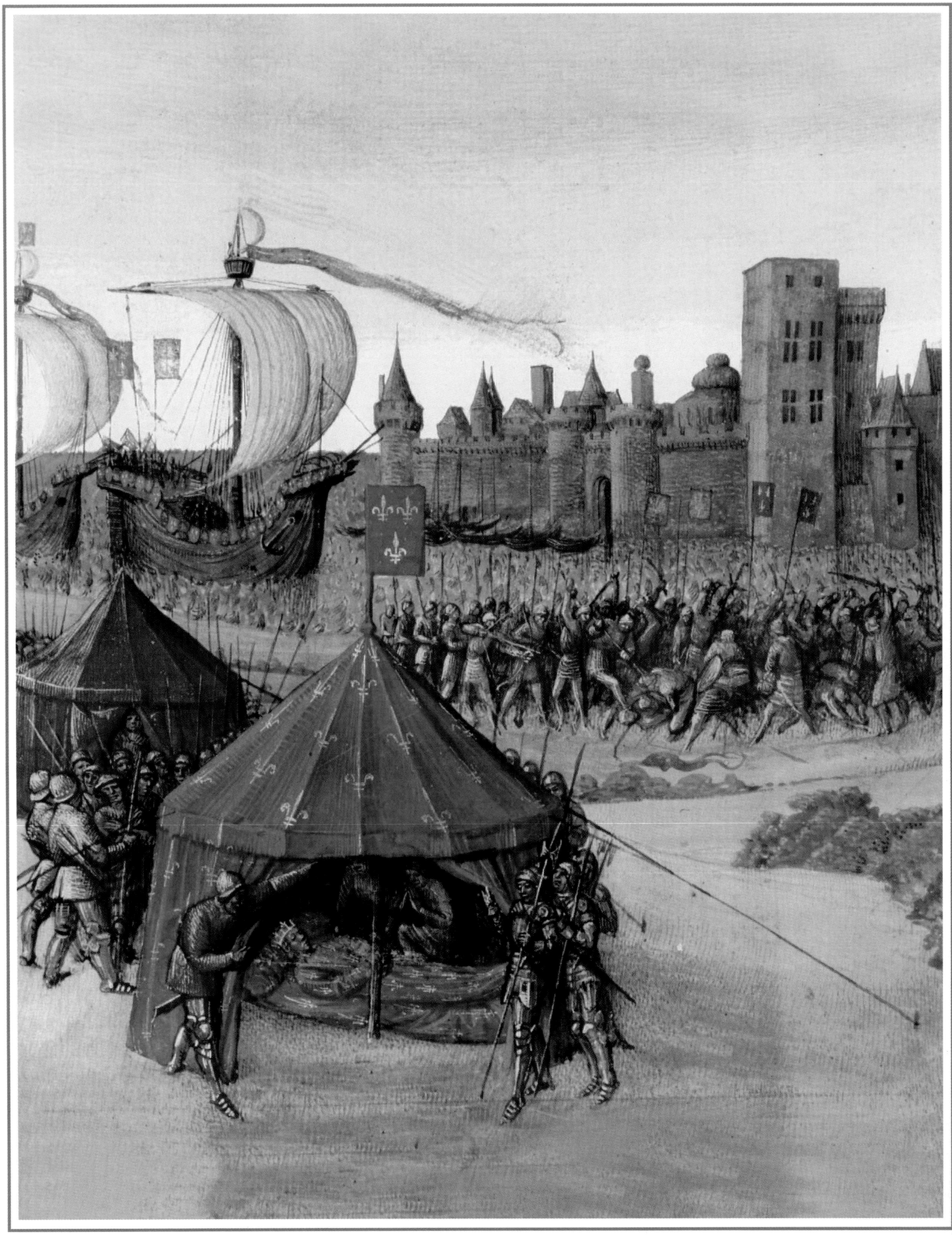

33 center From the Grand Chroniques de France, *a sixteenth-century manuscript conserved in the Bibliothéque Nationale de France, this illustration features the disembarking of the Crusaders before the siege of Tunis.*

33 bottom Moulay Hasan, sovereign of the Hafsid Dynasty, is here portrayed in an oil painting on wood of the Italian school that dates back to the last quarter of the sixteenth century. Hasan, who took the throne of Tunis in 1526, was deposed in 1542 and died in exile in Italy.

32 Tunis is put under siege by the Crusader forces in an illustration from the thirteenth century. Louis IX, canonized in 1297, lost his life during the siege of the city in 1270. The king of France had involved the major European states in the Eighth Crusade.

33 top Crusaders attack an Islamic citadel in an illuminated first letter. Besides religious motives, the crusade promoted by Louis IX was also dictated by tactical and economic reasons, owing to the fact that Tunis was a big, prosperous city and strategically well-connected.

The confusion created thus allowed the Normans, lodged in Sicily, to occupy the eastern Tunisian coast and Jerba Island, while the whole economic system began to collapse. Agriculture was abandoned and Tunisia entered a backward phase, both culturally and economically, that made it spiral towards desperate levels of poverty.

Its comeback began with the Berber kingdom of the Almohads who, between 1152-60, defeated the Normans and reunified the Maghreb. A governor was installed in Tunis and the position was handed down from father to son. The Almohad Dynasty was followed by the Hafsid Dynasty, founded in 1230 by Abou Zakkariya Yahya, governor of the city, who proclaimed himself emir. He made Tunis his capital and established an autonomous regime by taking advantage of the political weakness of the Almohads. This situation lasted until al-Mustansir, his son, proclaimed himself Prince of the Believers and tried to make the nearby countries recognize him as such. He had not taken into account, however, the indomitable spirit of King Louis IX 'the Saint' of France, who announced a crusade in 1270, mobilizing the forces of Europe against the Muslims.

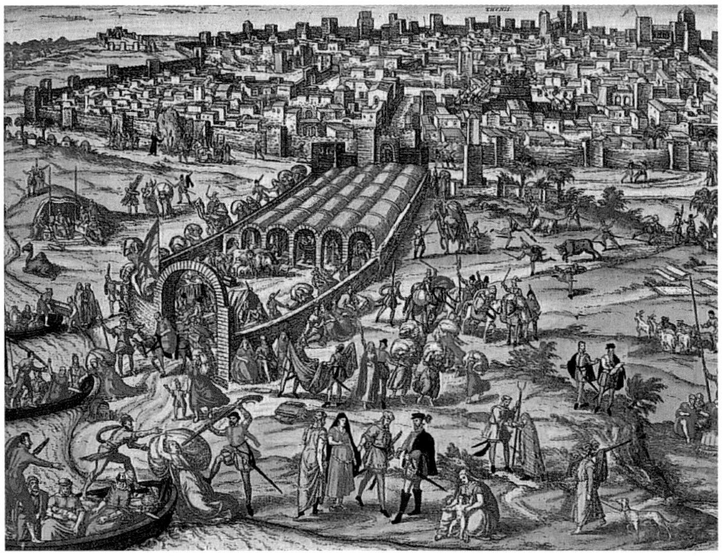

All the marine powers of the time aspired to conquer the Tunisian city, having since become big and prosperous with a population of around 100,000 inhabitants. The new power base brought about a period of restored prosperity that revived the country, by now nearly completely Arab, opening itself to Europe. But despite artistic and economic growth, the fourteenth century was a difficult period, also because of war, famine and the terrible Black Plague epidemic in 1348. Soon enough, Tunisia found itself caught between the Catholic kings of unified Spain and the Ottoman caliphs of Istanbul, by now both at the heights of their powers. The result was the conquest of the city by Carlos V in 1535.

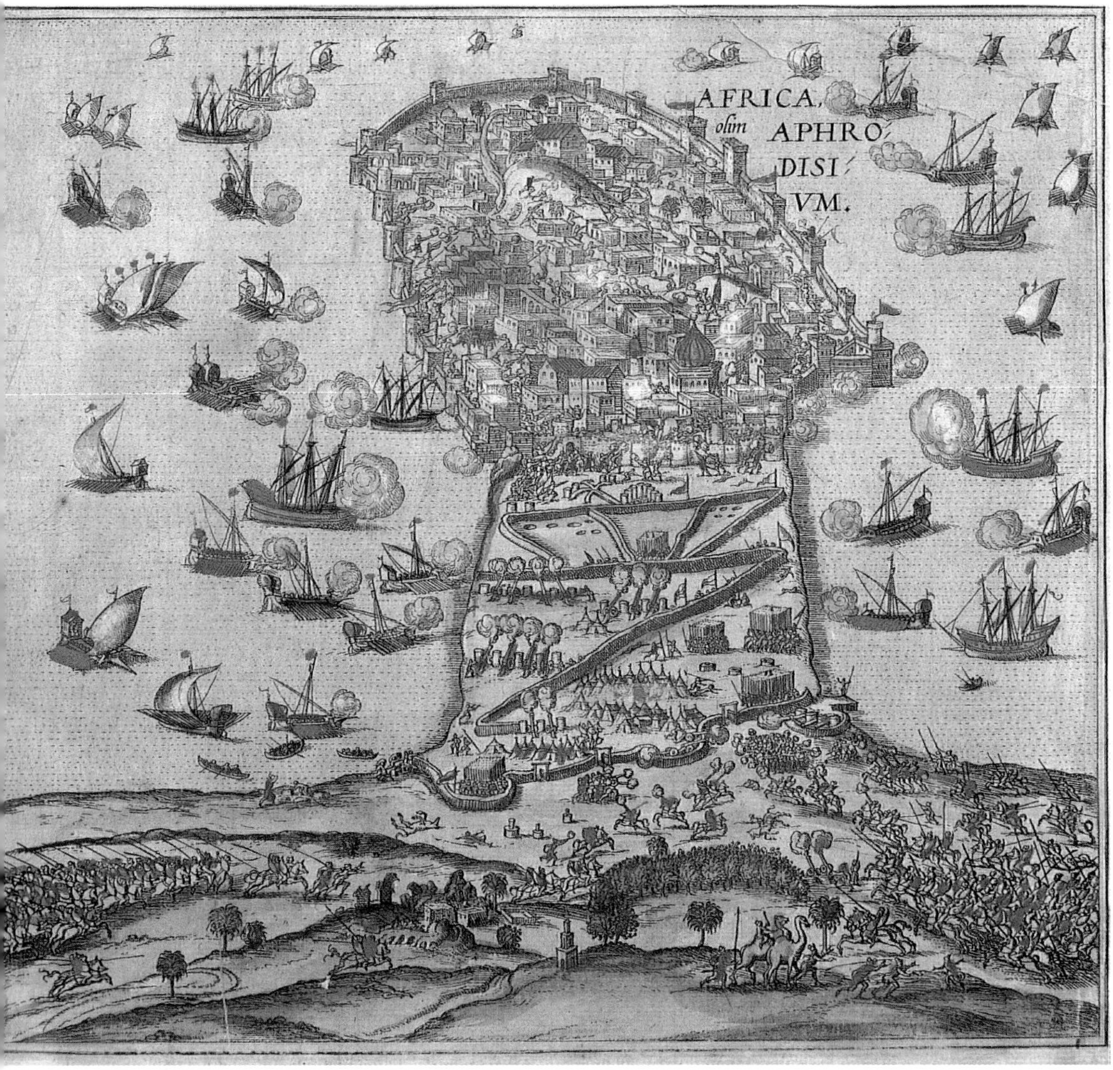
AFRICA, olim APHRODISIVM.

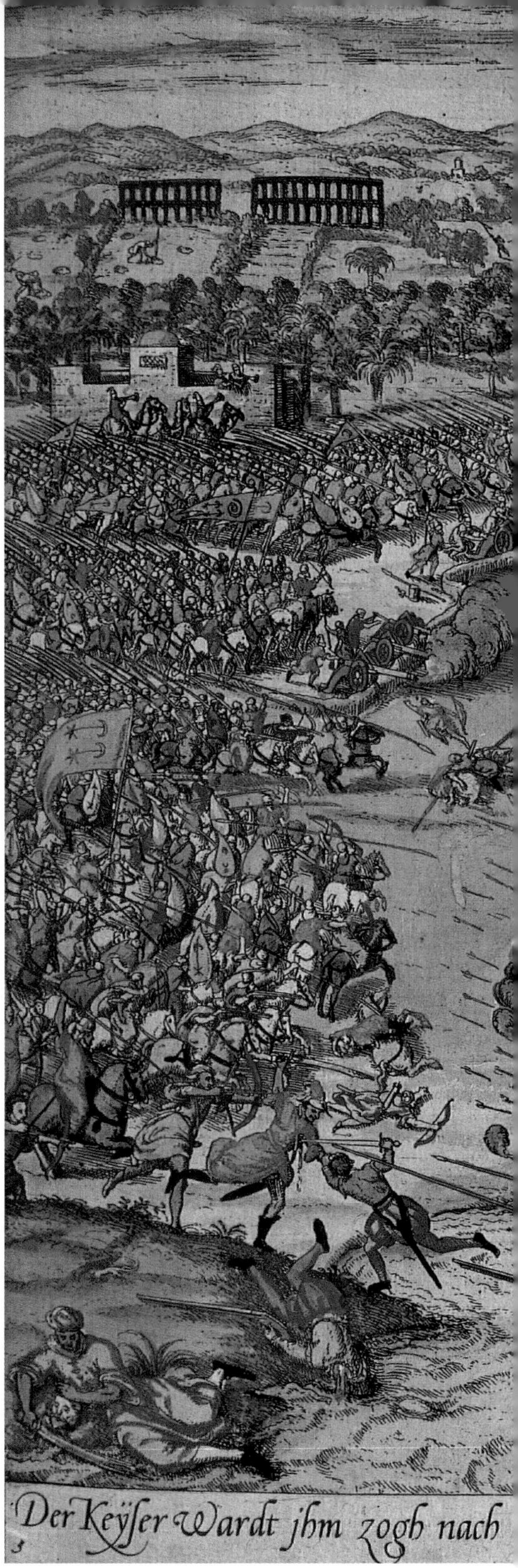
Der Keÿſer Wardt jhm zogh nach

34 top The old port of Tunis, La Goulette, was besieged by the armada of the Spanish emperor Carlos V in 1535. This remarkable renaissance work is conserved in the University Library of Geneva.

34 bottom The Spanish fleet attacks the walls of Tunis in a coeval aerial view of particular effect. The episode must undoubtedly be placed among the most dramatic in the Tunisian capital's history.

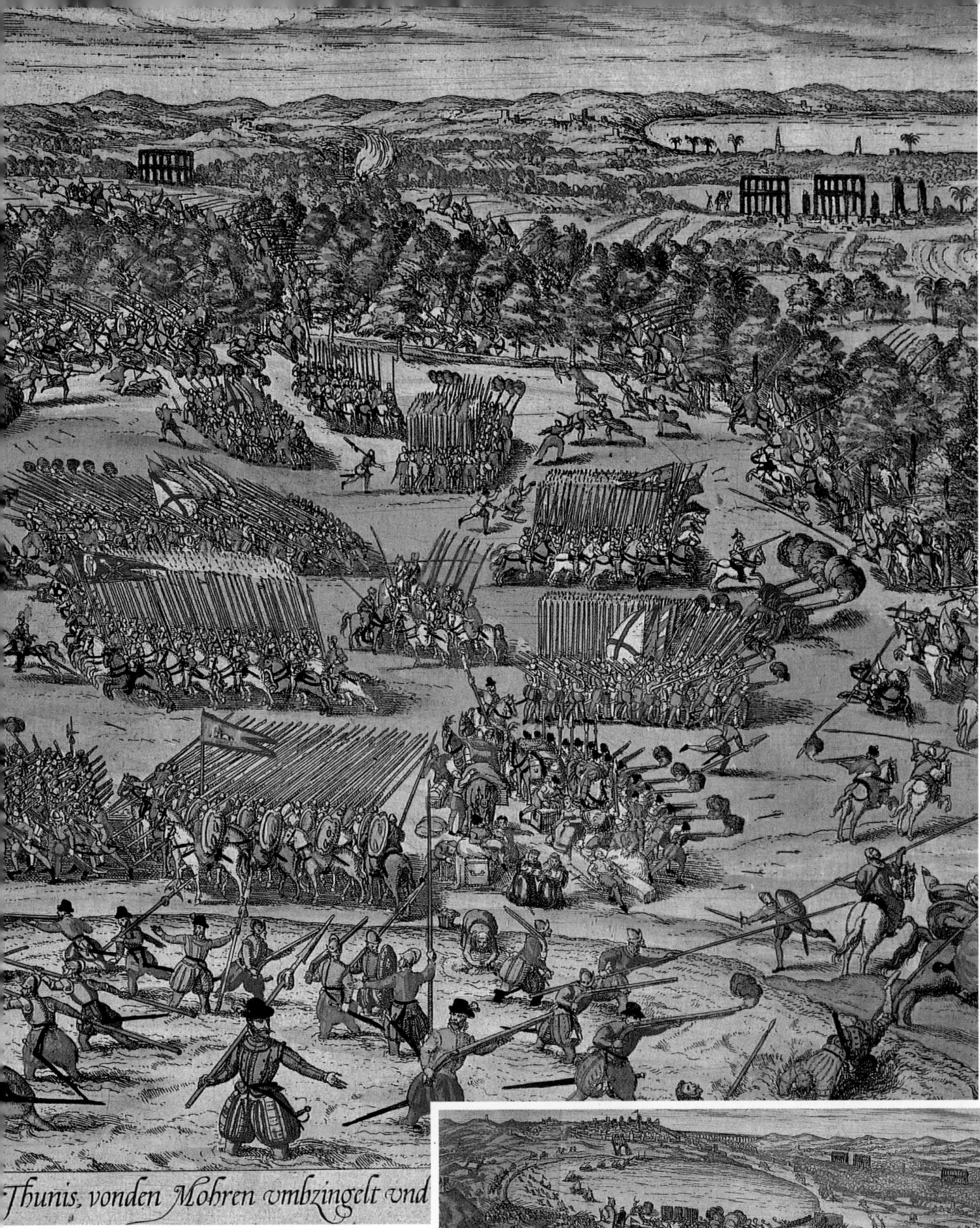
Thunis, vonden Mohren vmbzingelt vnd

34-35 The fall of Tunis brought about by Carlos V took place after three weeks of siege, during which thousands of helpless people were massacred. With this enterprise, which closely resembled a crusade, the emperor believed to have also liberated the Mediterranean of pirates. This conviction, nonetheless, did not last long because after only three years the Ottoman fleet destroyed the European one.

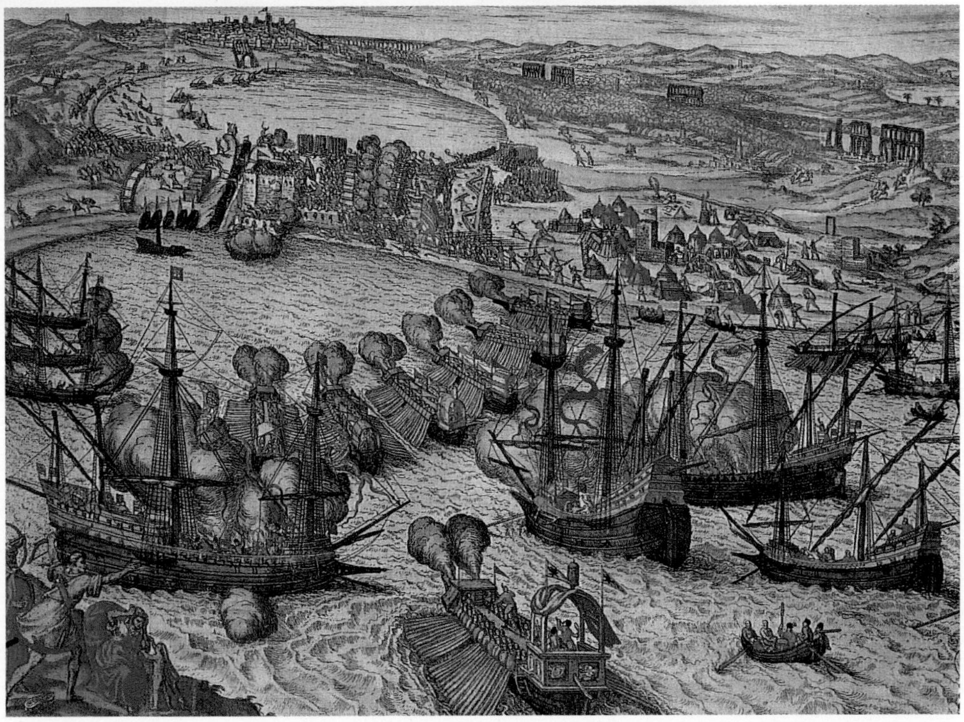

35 bottom As this illustrated engraving recalls, Tunis was relentlessly cannonaded by the Spanish fleet. Carlos V counted on an armada of 64 galleys, 300 transport vessels and 30,000 men, among them the Knights of Malta.

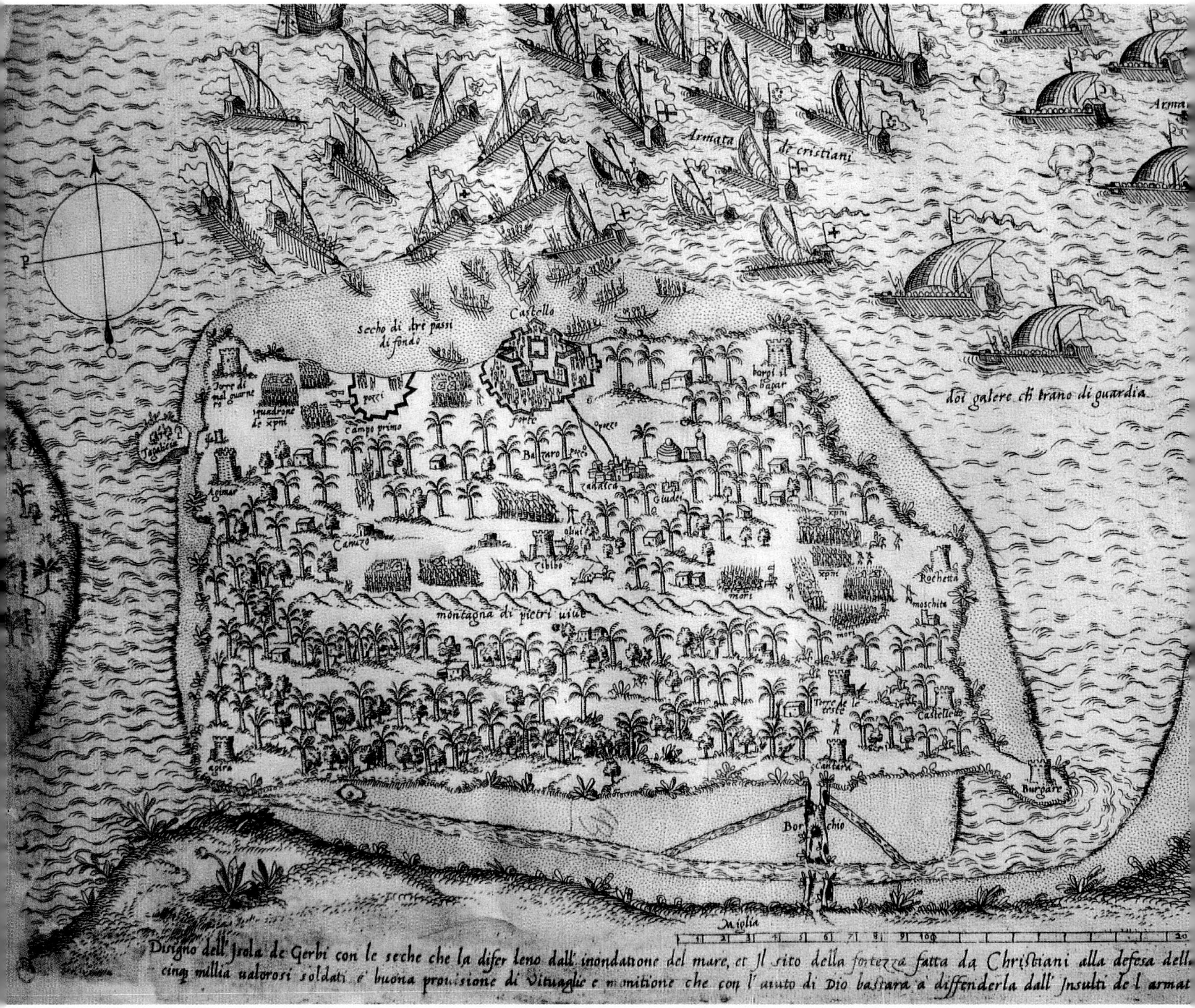
Armata de cristiani
secho di tre passi di fondo
Castello
borgi il bagar
doi galere ch'erano di guardia
squadrone de xpni
campo primo
forte
zadaica
Giudei
Camizo
montagna di pietri uiue
xpni
mori
Rochetta
moschite
Castelletto
Cantara
Burgare
Miglia
Disegno dell' Isola de Gerbi con le seche che la difer leno dall' inondatione del mare, et Il sito della fortezza fatta da Christiani alla defesa dell
cinq millia ualorosi soldati é buona prouisione di Vituaglie e monitione che con l'aiuto di Dio bastara a diffenderla dall' Insulti de l armat

36-37 In 1560, the sieges and massacres followed one another thanks to Dragut, one of the most famous pirates of the Mediterranean. At a certain point, the French, Spanish and Papal troops joined forces with the Knights of Malta to destroy once and for all the pirate hideout, which was located on Jerba Island. Only 5,000 to 6,000 Christians survived the first encounter, which took place in May of that year, and escaped to Borj el-Kebir.

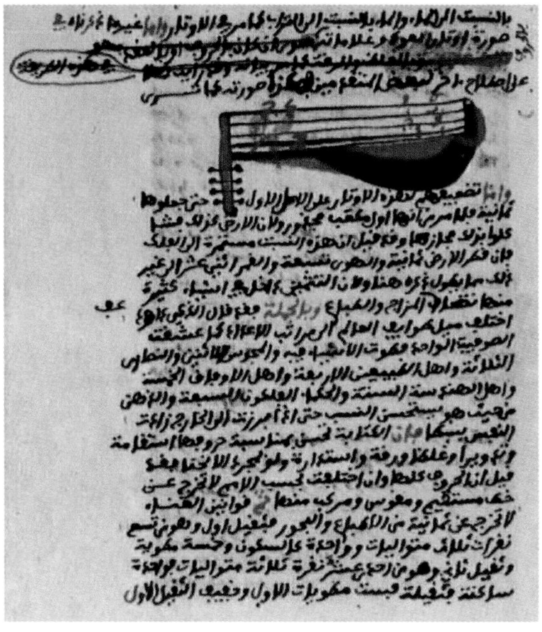

36 bottom This manuscript, work of Mahmoud b. Mohammed al-Siyala al-Safakusi, is a treatise on musicology. The pages of the volume are illustrated with miniatures that exemplify various musical instruments (on this page a lute is depicted).

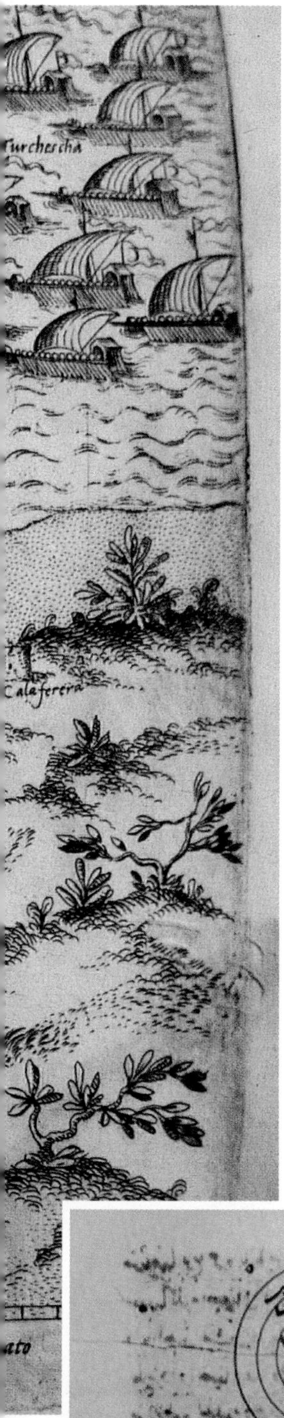

37 left Tunisian academics produced numerous works on all kinds of subjects, from military arts to sporting practices, from nutrition to medicine, as is shown on the page illustrated here, taken from Hallu al-Mudjaz, a medical treatise composed in 1377.

37 right On 16 August 1534, the fleet of Admiral Khair ad-Din, better known as a pirate and by the nickname 'Barbarossa', portrayed here, opened fire against the forts that protected Tunis. King Mumlay Hasan had no choice but to flee.

In 1574, Tunisia, because of the decadence of the Hafsid regime and by now objective of the two strongest powers in the Mediterranean, Spain and Turkey, saw the victory of the Turks and the annexation of its territory to the Ottoman kingdom. Their rule, initially labored with military uprisings, would last 131 years and produce the fusion of the local and Turkish cultures. In 1628, the Turkish dynasty Muradid reestablished peace and order, leading the country to a genuine period of renaissance that lasted until 1705. An internal revolt brought about the foundation of a new local dynasty, that of the Husainids, which gained independence from the Turks by garnering support from the European powers, with which they began to stipulate economic treaties and agreements with growing frequency.

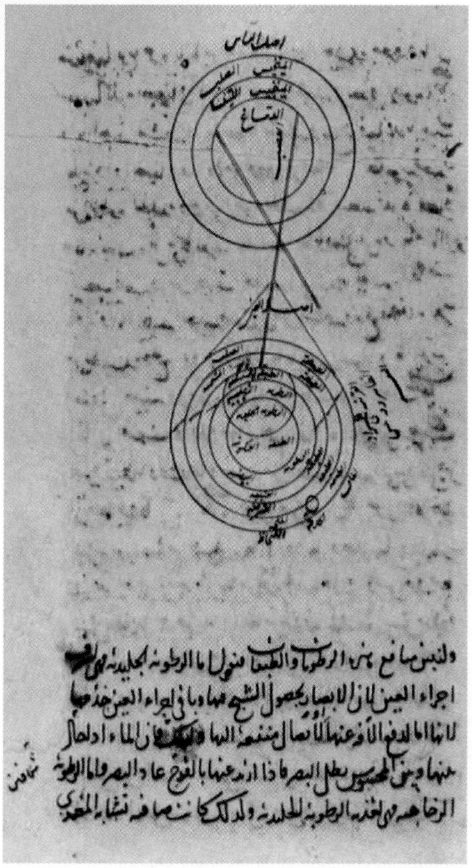

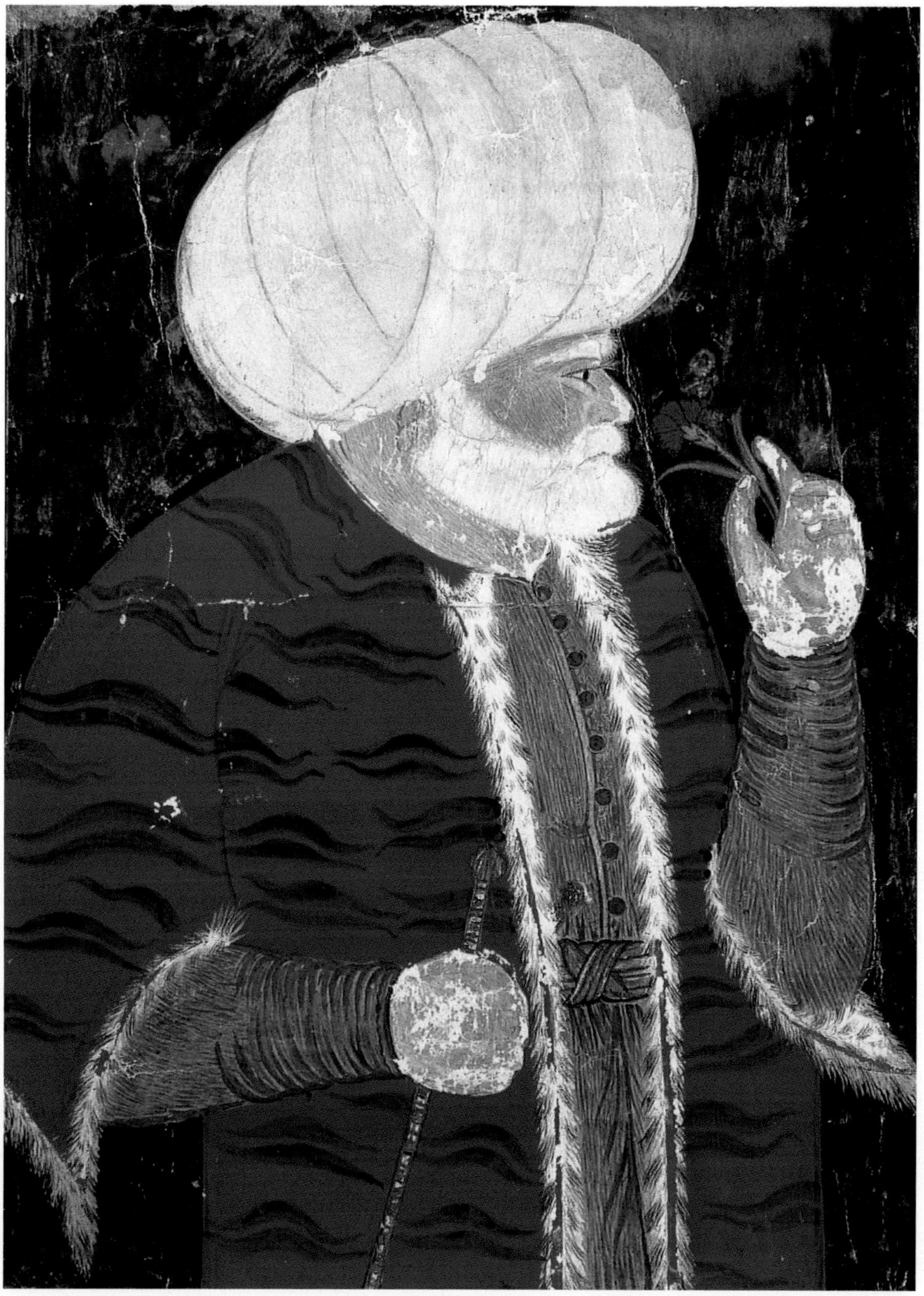

38 top At the Congress
of Berlin, between 13
June and 13 July
1878, the French were
given permission to
invade Tunisia,
putting a stop to the
designs that Italy and
Great Britain had on
the North African
country.

38 bottom The
functionaries of
Muhammed as-Sadiq,
Bey of Tunis, pose for a
group photograph on the
occasion of the
stipulation of the Treaty
of Bardo of 1881, by
which the French
imposed its protectorate
on Tunisia.

The relationship that would unite Tunisia and France was already taking shape. In 1830, the French occupied Algeria, creating the foundation for that which would be their historic presence in Africa. At the Congress of Berlin in 1878, and with the Bardo Treaty in 1881, France was given consent to invade Tunisia, thus blocking the claims made on the country by both Italy and Great Britain. Under the pretext of violations of the Algerian border by a Tunisian tribe, the French entered Tunisia and imposed their own Protectorate in 1883. This brought a decent level of progress to the area and the construction of roads and railroads but it favored above all the French society, which exploited the territory in every way.

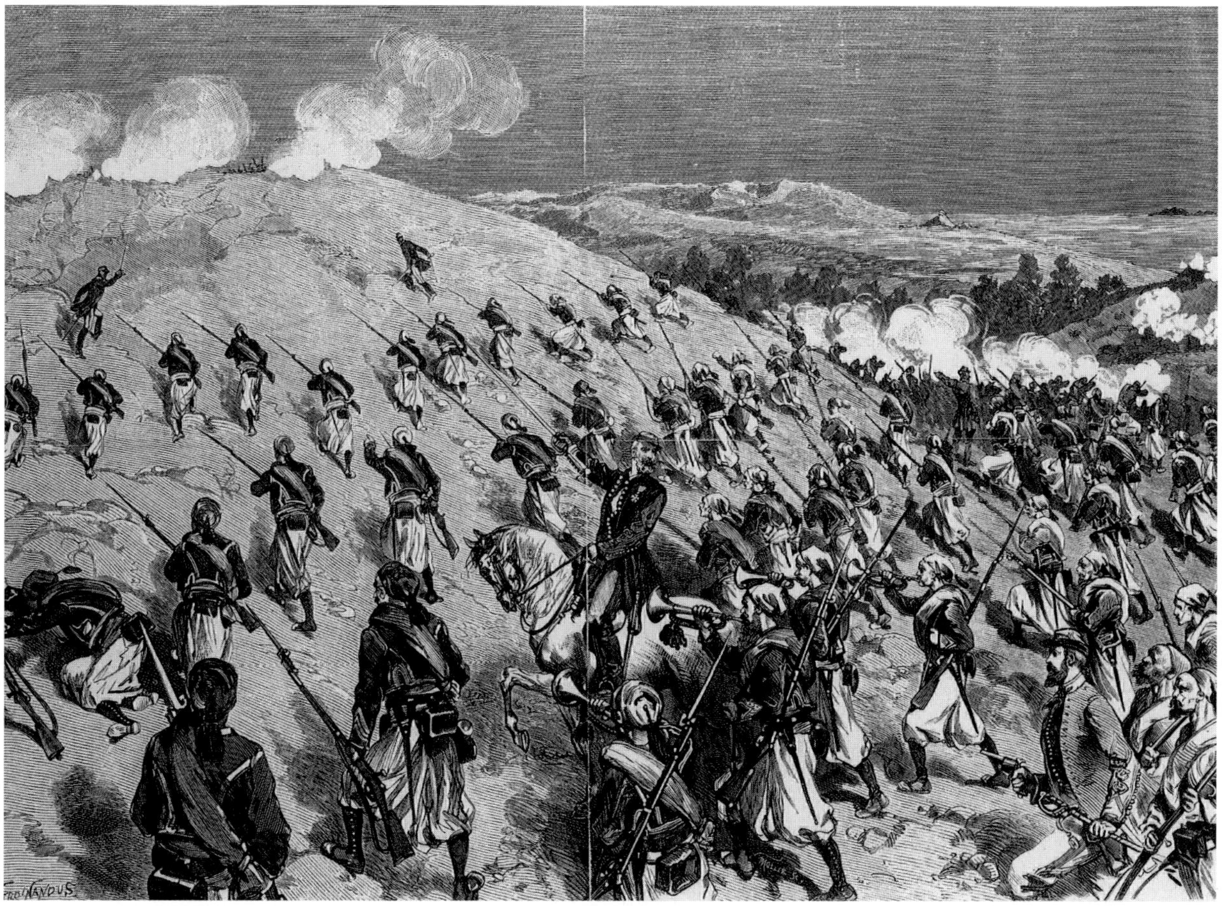

39 top This bustling drawing by Alexandre Ferdinandus recalls a battle of French soldiers on Tunisia in 1881. With the Treaty of Bardo, signed in the same year, the legitimacy of the European nation's invasion that, in 1883, imposed its protectorate was definitively sanctified.

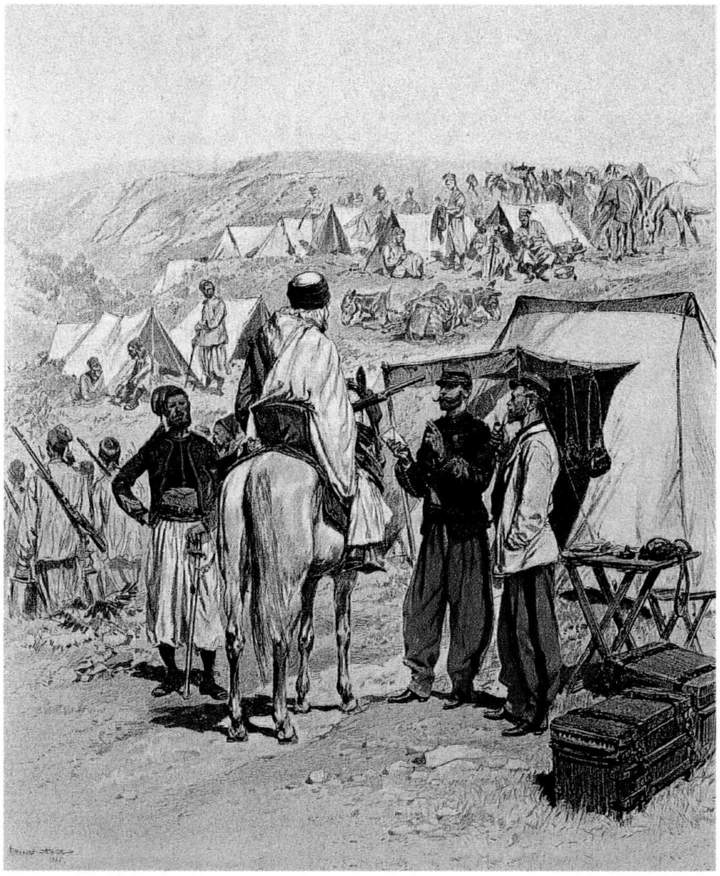

39 bottom left French officials argue with a dispatch rider in a military camp. In 1883, France occupied Tunisia on the basis of a pretext.

39 bottom right The Bey of Tunis was crowned in 1902. For the Turks, the title of bey *was attributed to vassals of the sultan or to high-ranking officials.*

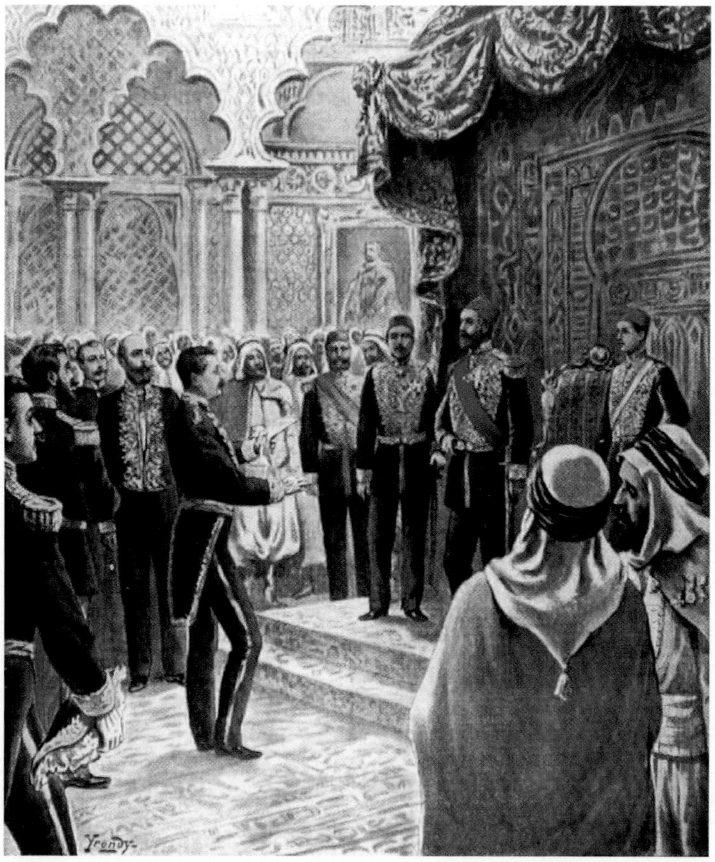

40 top left The French premier Edouard Daladier visits Sousse, south of the capital, during the course of an inspection of the colonies. In this photograph, taken in 1939, the politician is accompanied by General Erik Labonne, resident in the country.

40 top right Risen in 1920, the Tunisian Constitutionalist Party, Destour, split into two factions. In this photograph are gathered the members of the New Destour, democratic, as opposed to the Old Destour, devoted to the recuperation of Islamic traditions.

40 bottom A delegation of Destour waits to address their complaints to Bey Naceur. The name of the Tunisian Liberal Constitutionalist Party derives from the Arab word dastour, which means 'constitution'.

40-41 At the outbreak of the First World War, a group of Tunisians gathers in the enclosure of a mosque as they wait for the call to arms. There were 63,000 soldiers to fight alongside the French.

41 top In September 1939, cavalry troops paraded through the streets of Tunis in honor of the French premier Daladier's visit to the city.

Education and cultural development fostered a fervent elite that would become essential to the nationalistic current opposing the Protectorate that took shape in 1907. Popular support for this interest group, the Movement of Young Tunisians, grew to the point of pushing the French to prohibit free press and to impose martial law in1912, which remained active until 1921.

Even Tunisia was later involved in the Great War, World War I, which claimed around 10,000 victims in the country. Arab participation in the conflict alongside the French rendered hopes for compensation in the form of much-longed-for independence ever more popular. Consequently, as Tunisians saw their hopes inexorably frustrated, they established numerous political movements run not only by intellectuals but also by bank and industry employees or functionaries and advocates of the new social classes. For this reason tensions rose quickly, and the ever-growing desire for freedom saw the birth, on 4 June 1920, of Destour, the Liberal Constitutionalist Party. It was followed in 1924 with the writing of the constitution of the General Confederation of Tunisian Workers—whose leader, Mohammed Ali, was accused of communist activities and exiled—and by Neo-Destour, which, in 1934, split off from its predecessor thanks to a young secular lawyer, Habib Bourguiba, who, over the course of a brilliant political career, would work to gain independence without trauma through gradual steps.

This moderate strategy was maintained for about 20 years, despite the fact that even Bourguiba was arrested in 1938 and sent into exile.

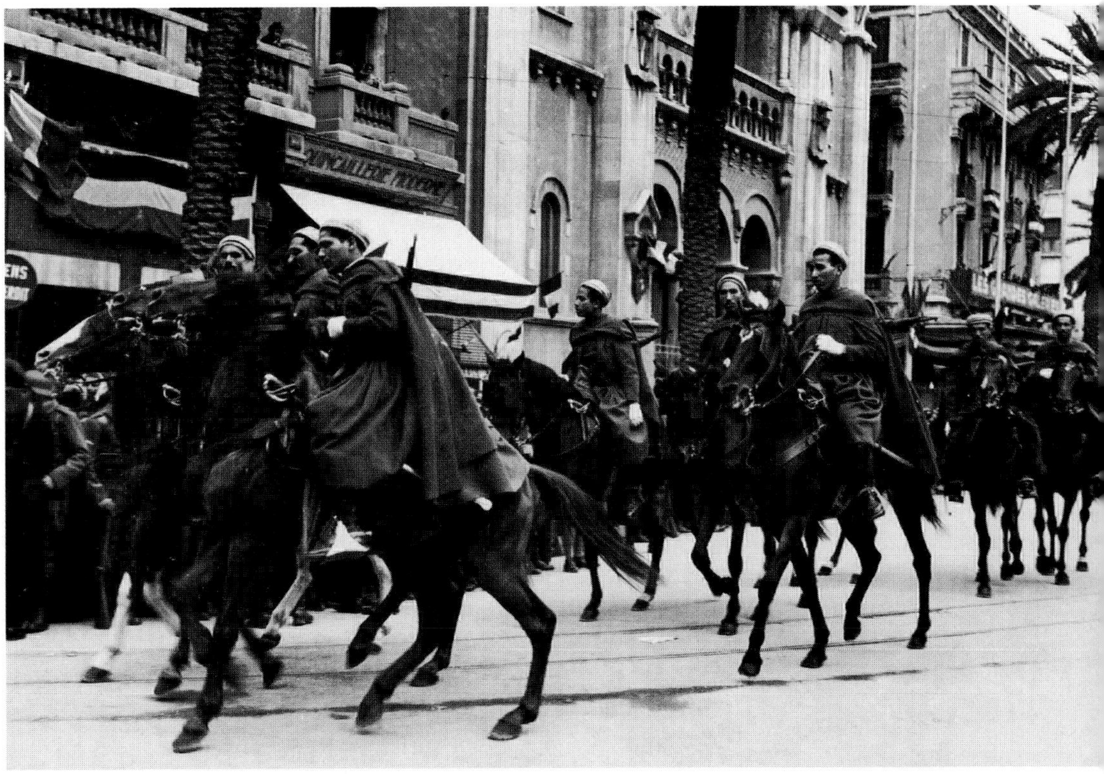

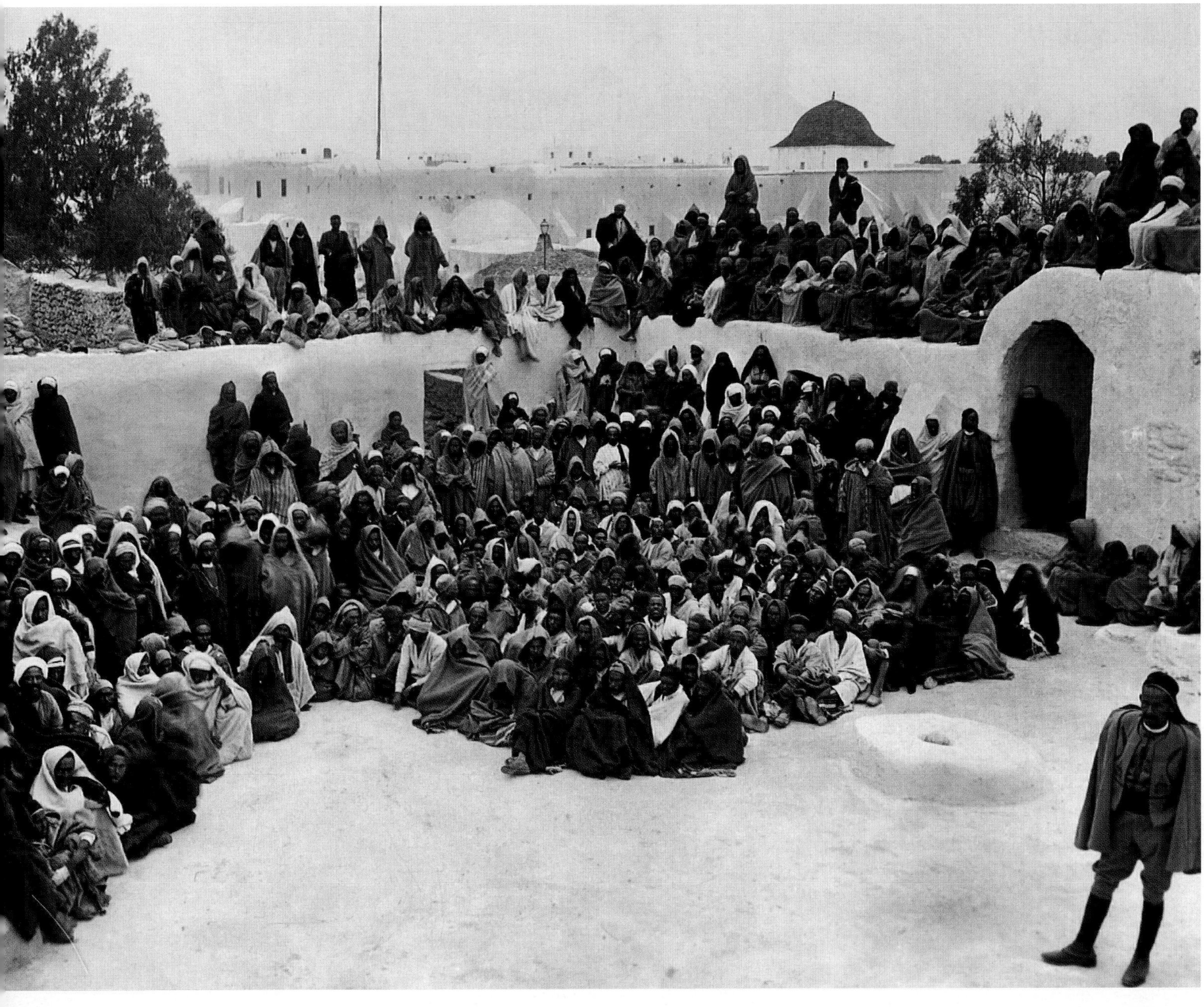

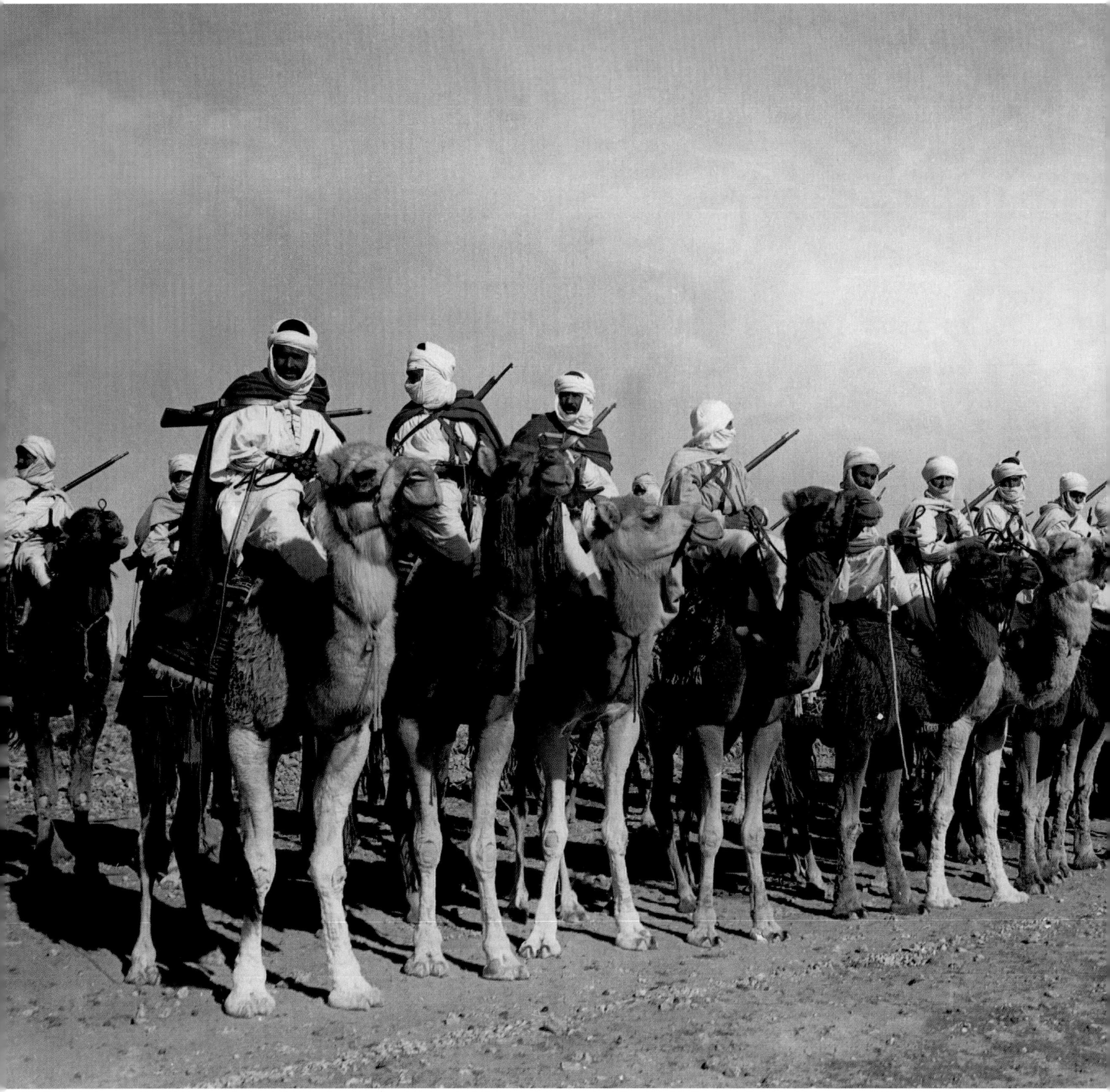

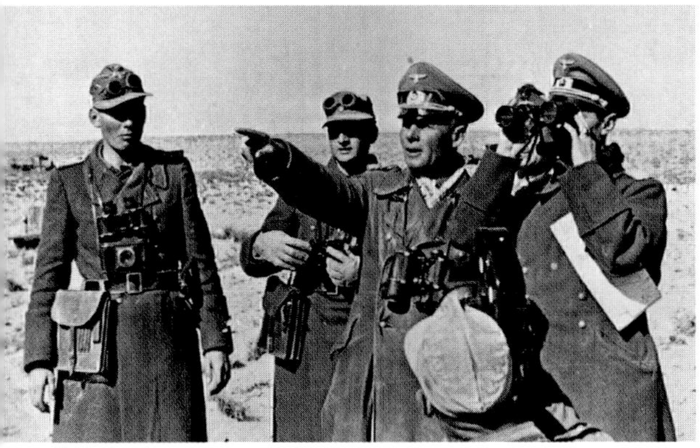

Two years later Tunisia entered into the bellicose vortex of the Second World War: in 1940 it was attacked from the south by the Italians who found themselves obligated to ask for help from the Rommel's Afrika Korps troops.

The country was then broken at the end of 1942 by the German intervention, becoming the last Nazi stronghold in North Africa. However, it was liberated six months later (May 1943) by the Allies, led by General Patton and Field Marshal Montgomery, who launched a series of bloody battles.

The most important fighting took place in central Tunisia, around Kasserine, and in the northern part of the country in Cap Bon and Tunis, from where the English-American forces

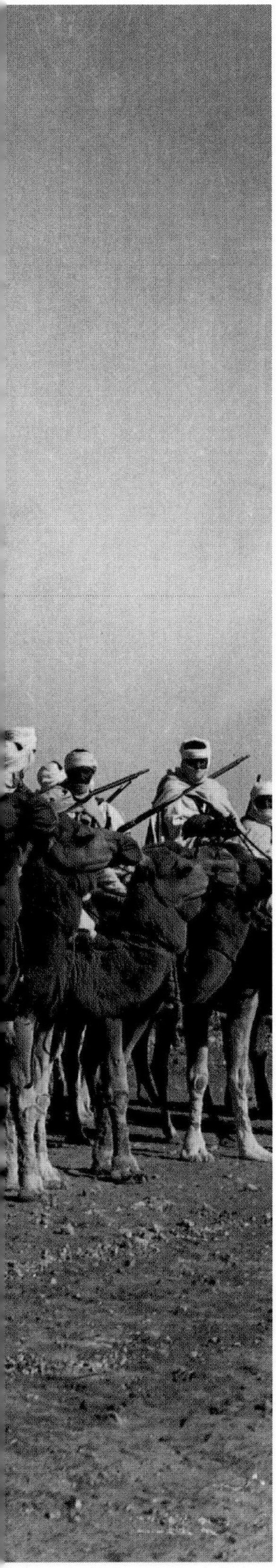

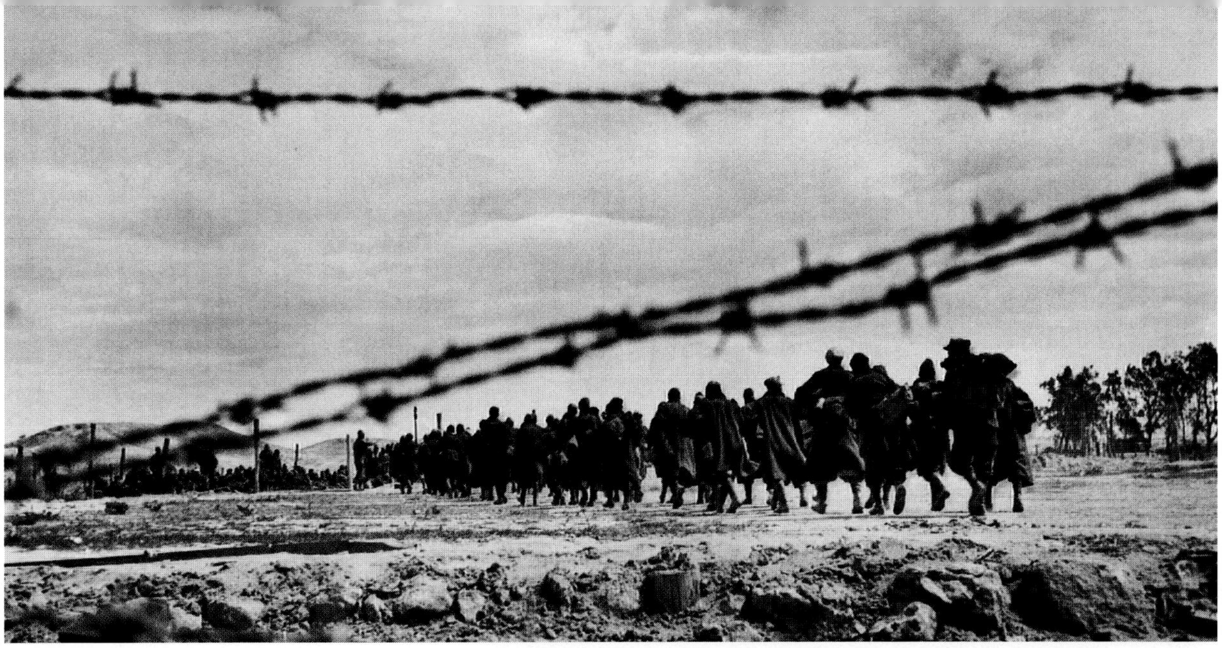

reached Pantelleria and Lampedusa, finally disembarking in Sicily.

As for Bourguiba, the Italians also made an attempt to use this political figure in anti-French activities, but the leader did not allow himself to be seduced by the Fascist promises. He reentered Tunisia in 1949 and was arrested in 1952 along with 150 party members, at which point an armed movement came to life that, stationed in the mountains, began fighting the French forces.

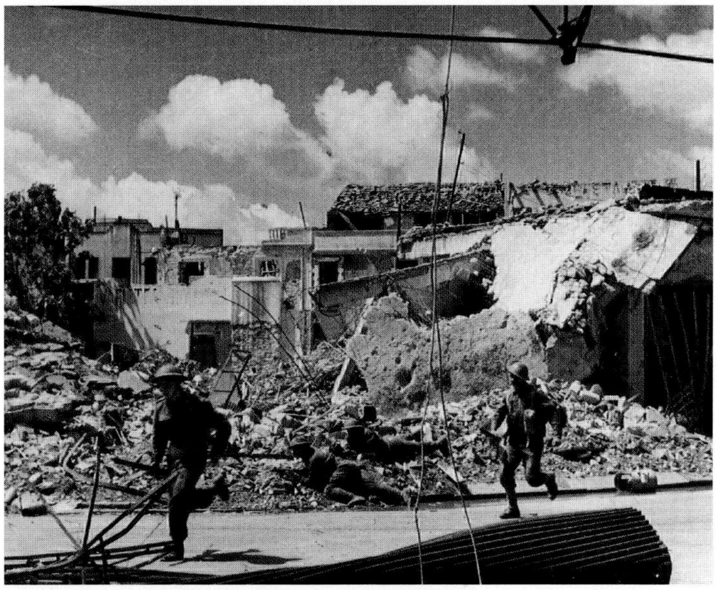

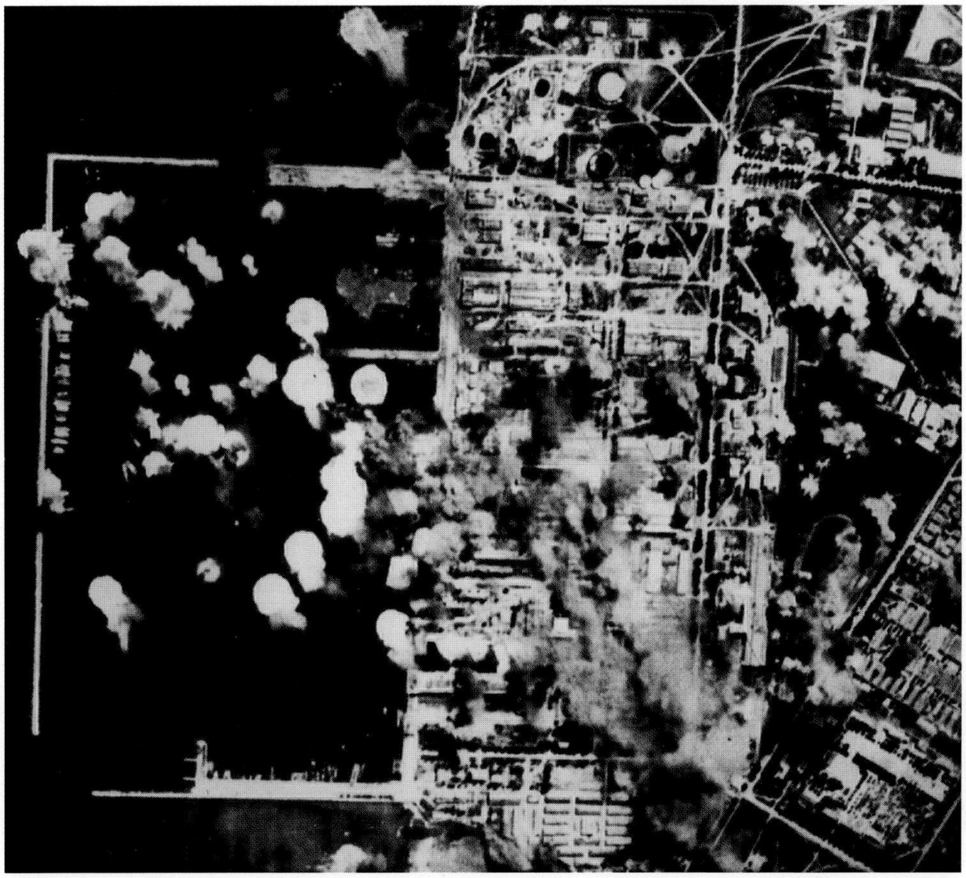

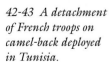

42-43 A detachment of French troops on camel-back deployed in Tunisia.

42 bottom Erwin Rommel gives orders in the field in March 1943. In that year, Tunisia had become the last Nazi bulwark in North Africa.

43 top An unending line of Italian prisoners, escorted by American soldiers, is led toward a prisoner-of-war camp. This photograph was taken in April 1943, three years after Tunisia entered the war.

43 center On 6 May 1943, the patrols of the French-British corps entered Bizerte.

43 bottom The American 'flying fortresses' heavily bomb the city of Bizerte on 6 May 1943. Once the German forces in Tunisia were annihilated, the Allies moved north to land in Sicily.

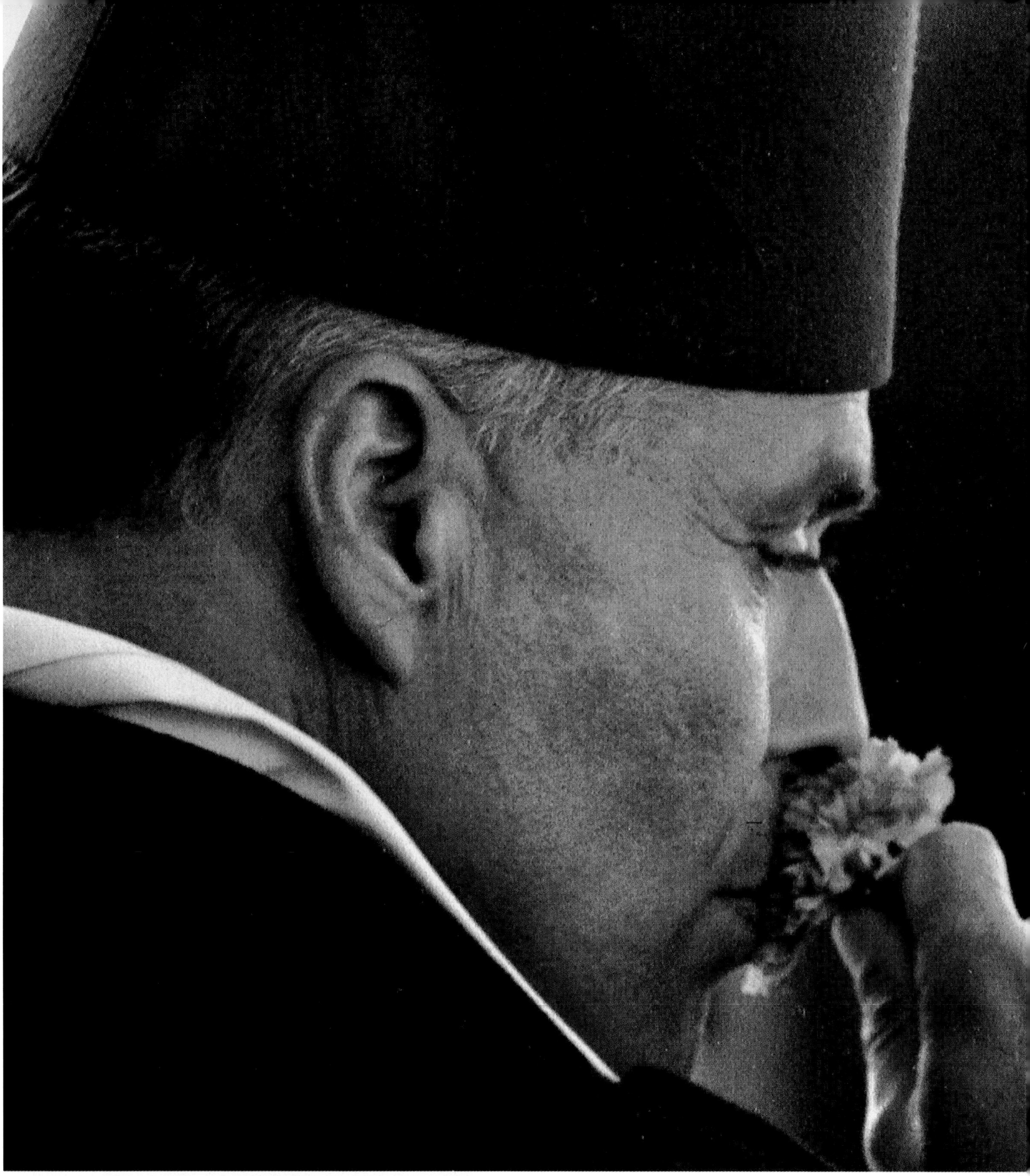

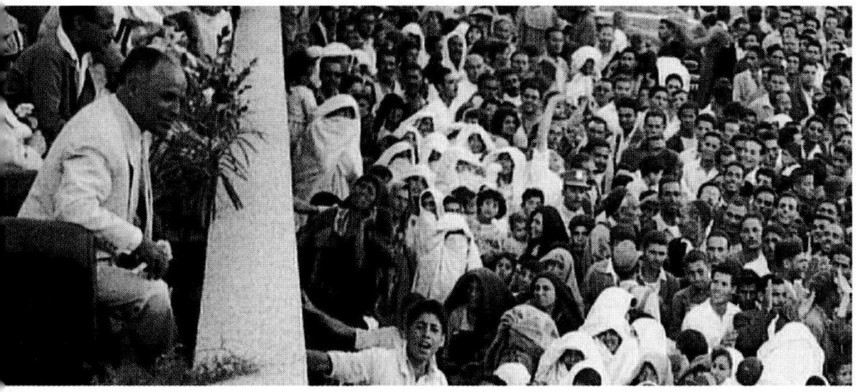

44-45 Habib Bourguiba worked to achieve the country's independence without suffering, through gradual steps. This moderate strategy was maintained for about 20 years, despite the arrest, in 1938, and the successive exile of the leader.

44 bottom Tunisia's independence was declared on 20 March 1956, following a massive wave of strikes that paralyzed life in the country. Proclaimed a republic on 25 July 1957, Habib Bourguiba became president.

45 top Habib Bourguiba triumphed on 23 March 1956, at the end of his exile in France. As soon as he was elected president, Bourguiba enacted modifications to the most archaic customs of the country, among them abolition of the obligation for women to wear a veil.

45 bottom Zine el-Abdine Ben Ali, Tunisian president, formally salutes the body of Habib Bourguiba. The ex-president, who had governed the country from 1956 to 1987, died on 6 April 2000, at the age of 97. He was buried in Monastir, his birthplace.

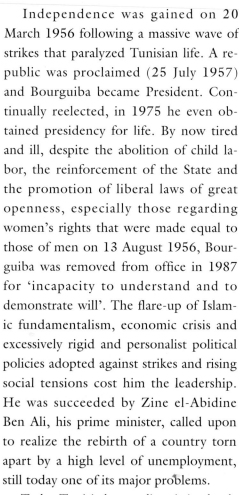

Independence was gained on 20 March 1956 following a massive wave of strikes that paralyzed Tunisian life. A republic was proclaimed (25 July 1957) and Bourguiba became President. Continually reelected, in 1975 he even obtained presidency for life. By now tired and ill, despite the abolition of child labor, the reinforcement of the State and the promotion of liberal laws of great openness, especially those regarding women's rights that were made equal to those of men on 13 August 1956, Bourguiba was removed from office in 1987 for 'incapacity to understand and to demonstrate will'. The flare-up of Islamic fundamentalism, economic crisis and excessively rigid and personalist political policies adopted against strikes and rising social tensions cost him the leadership. He was succeeded by Zine el-Abidine Ben Ali, his prime minister, called upon to realize the rebirth of a country torn apart by a high level of unemployment, still today one of its major problems.

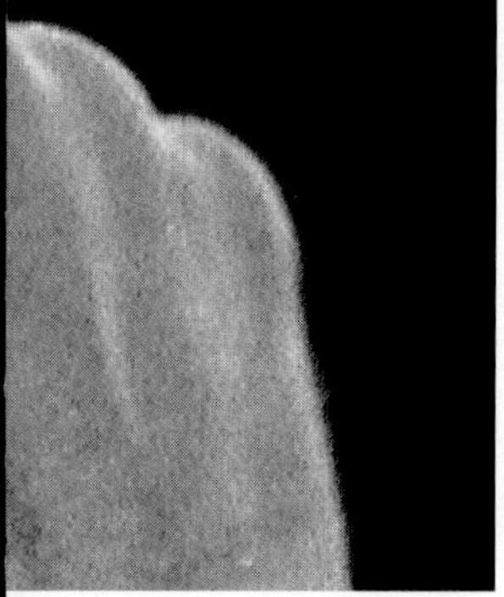

Today Tunisia hosts a linguistic plurality that summarizes its historic identity: languages widely spoken are classical Arabic, the official language, dialectal Arabic and French. Alongside these exist linguistic traces of Berber, especially in the villages of the interior. Defined 'the cradle of tolerant Islam', Tunisia shines for its moderation in the field of religious law and the status of women is an emblematic example. In fact, Tunisian women are among the most emancipated in the Arab world and enjoy high esteem, bringing the country closer to Western standards. The laws of 1956, the abolition of polygamy and the concession of the right to ask for a divorce and to choose one's husband, not to mention the right to a complete education, are only the most incisive of the reforms that gave a vast human aspect to this splendid land.

On 2 April 1989, General Zine el-Abidine Ben Ali was elected President of the Republic. After taking over the leadership of the country for the second time on 20 March 1994, he received his third mandate in 1999. Still in power today, his presidency has been characterized, by giving life to a new era of economic reconstruction, adopting democratic reforms and promoting laws concerning the respect.

ALL THE COLORS OF THE WORLD

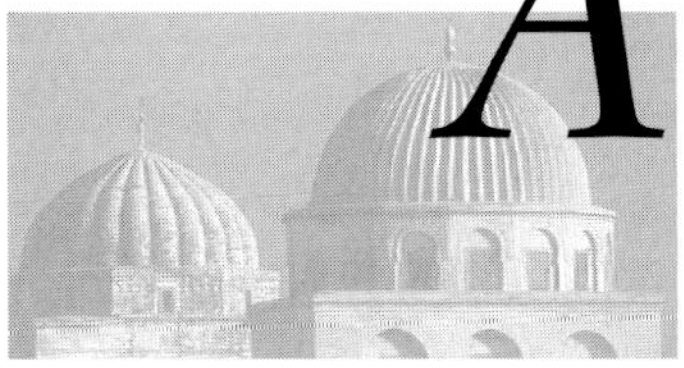

As they say in these parts, Eden was not open to everyone. Tunisia's northernmost stretch of coastline is in fact a Mediterranean delight, as yet uncontaminated because it is not easy to reach. Considering Tabarka as the country's western border and proceeding eastward, the coast is a succession of white sandy shores and blue waves against the background of the intense green of the internal vegetation, reachable only by off-road vehicle or boat. It has always been a magnificent place, assuming it was precisely in these sweet and sunny lands that, during the Neolithic era, the practice of farming was unusual and that the first herds were domesticated, great-great grandparents of those that today trot along the hills and among the brush of Mediterranean scrub. From these crystalline waters rise the Aiguilles ('the needles') of Tabarka—imposing, evocative stacks that tickle the sky with their sharp peaks. From here starts a picturesque road, excavated from the side of the mountain and shadowed by cork trees, that runs as far as Algeria. The sea here is the favorite of coral fisherman, who manage to find specimens of great beauty to be transformed into jewels, scuba divers, who can swim with a thousand types of fish, and sailors, who appreciate the shape of the coast with about 60 miles of bays and coves that offer quiet and shelter from the strong wind.

Rounding Cap Negro, the remains of Cap Serrat (the construction requested in the sixteenth century by grain-trading colonists, the French citizens of the Royal Africa Company), embellished by poplars and willows, and Sidi Mechrig, with its incredibly white sandy shores, can both be seen. The waters here are very clean and host a colony of endangered monk seals in the archipelago of La Galite. Evidently the seals live a cloistered life because they are rarely seen.

Even further east, Cap Blanc appears like a kind of sugar loaf; it represents the northernmost point of all of Africa. As if from the bow of the Titanic, from here one looks onto a simply spectacular panorama that touches the earth, sea and sky in a palette of tones as fleeting as the changing light.

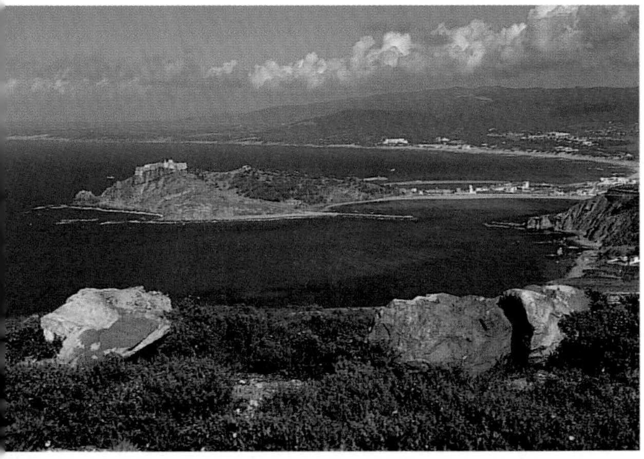

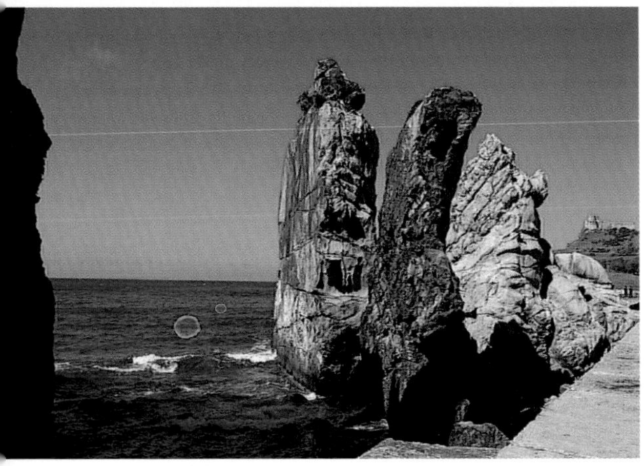

46 top left A bay that looks Corsican or Ligurian dominated by a Genoese fort overlooked by an intensely green landscape: it would seem to be a place located much farther north, but this is Tabarka, on the north coast of the country.

46 bottom left The Aiguilles ('the needles'), imposing, evocative calcareous stacks, are reflected in the limpid waters of Tabarka.

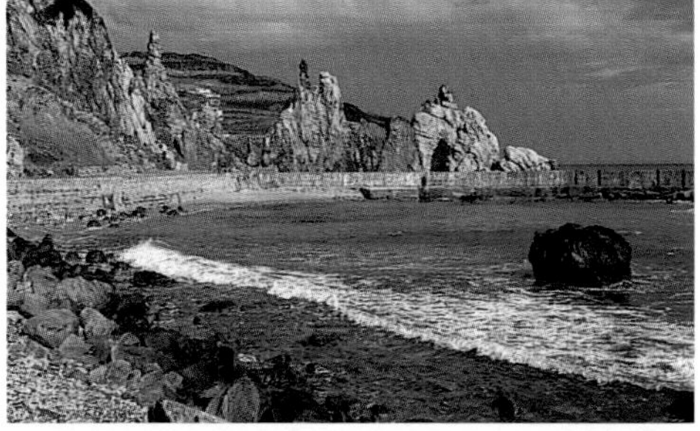

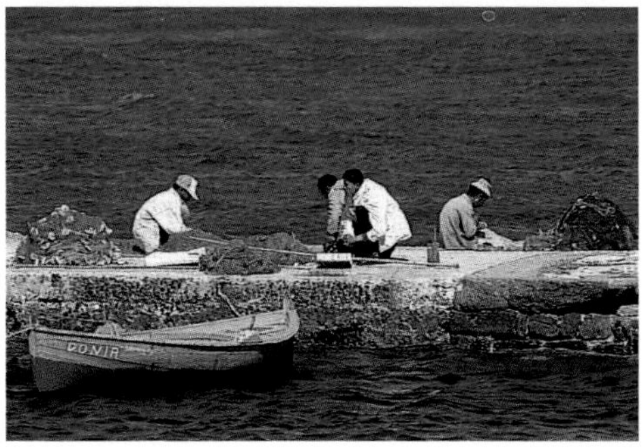

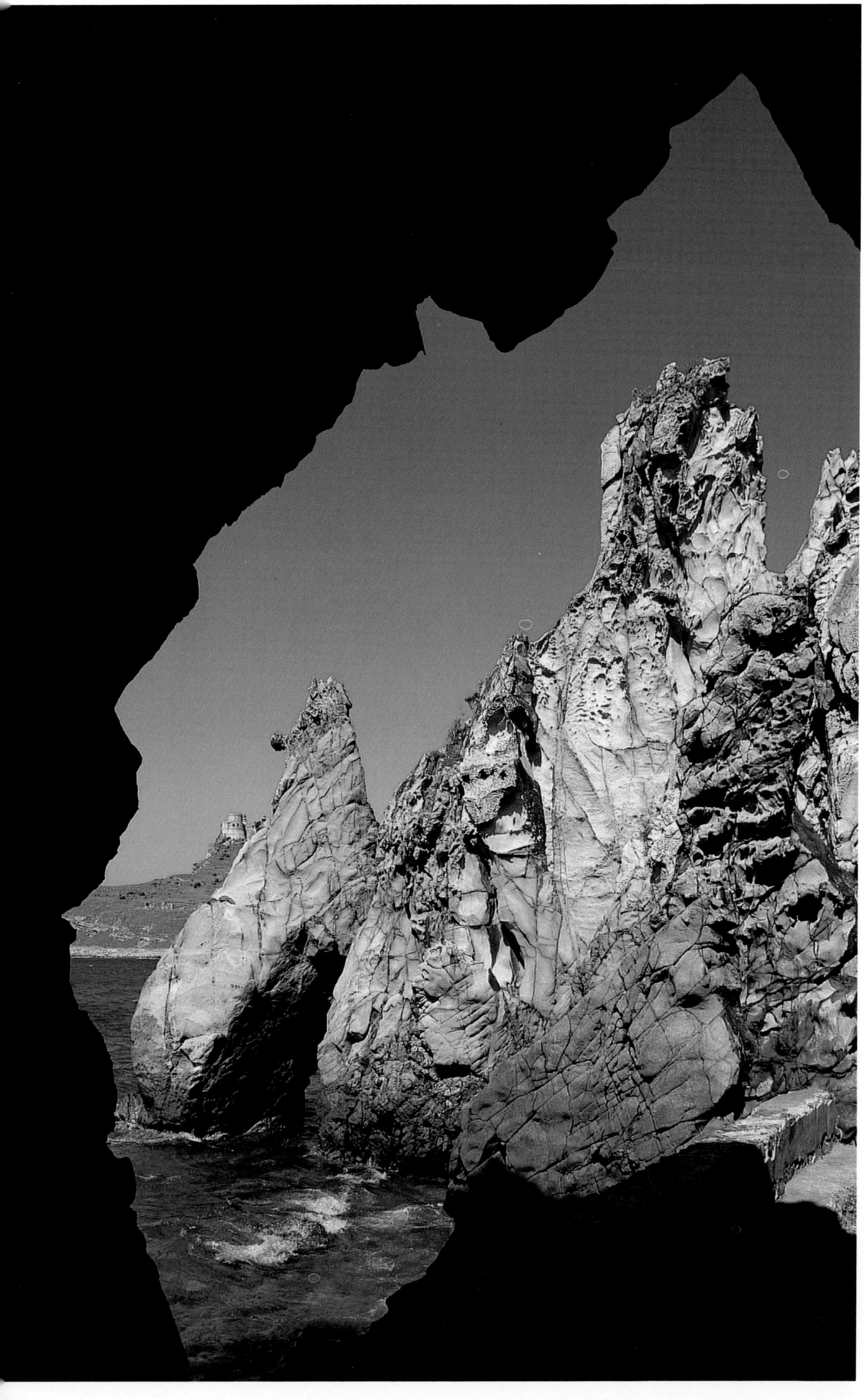

46 top right From the stacks of Tabarka, an undeniably picturesque road, entirely excavated from the side of the mountain and shaded by cork trees, unravels towards the west until it reaches the first lands of Algeria.

46 bottom right In Tabarka, the fishermen dedicate themselves, besides to their idiosyncratic profession, to harvesting red coral, which in this area is still found in substantial amounts and maintains a high quality.

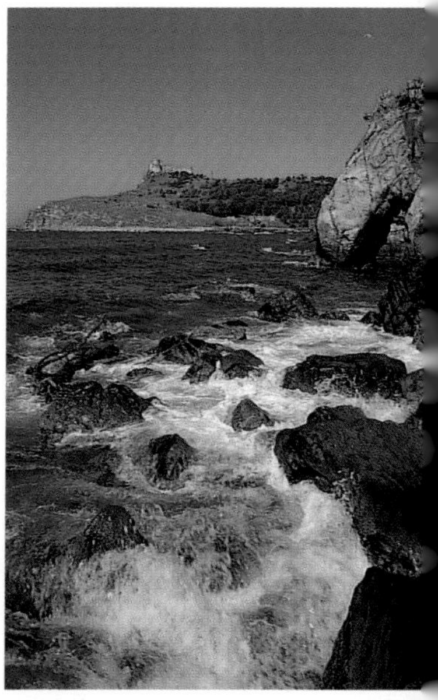

47 left The coast of Tabarka is highly appreciated by tourists: stretching for over 50 miles, it is indented by uncountable, splendid bays and small coves.

47 right Tabarka is a gathering places for scuba divers from around the Mediterranean: its sea is populated by a great amount of fish of several species and, it is said, by a colony of monk seals.

48-49 Lake Ichkeul, the largest in the Maghreb, has a special characteristic: in summer it is shallow and salty because of the penetration of seawater and the powerful evaporation; in winter, thanks to the rains and the contribution of four tributaries, it is fresh.

49 top left In the Ichkeul Reserve, 180 species of migratory birds, for an estimated total of around 200,000 exemplars, make their nests from October to March. Just to name a few, ruddy ducks, coots and whistle ducks can be admired here.

49 top right The Kroumirie is an extremely green region. Here, the palms give way to cork trees and, until the end of the nineteenth century, it was still possible to encounter lions and panthers. Today, only the wild boar remain, which can be hunted in the reserve provided for this purpose.

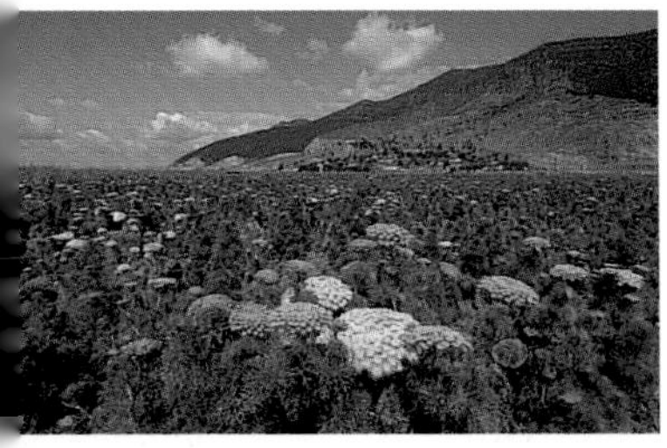

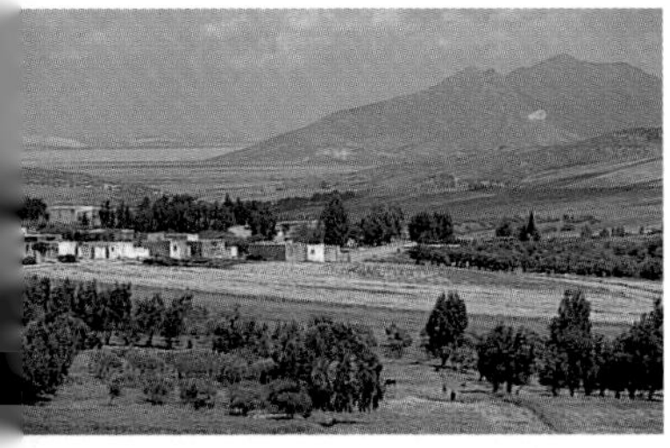

48 top The Ichkeul Nature Reserve, in the hinterlands of Bizerte, takes its name from the lake that is located at the fulcrum. This zone, once surrounded by swamps but now drained, has been protected by law since 1980.

48 bottom The territory surrounding Lake Ichkeul is ideal for bird-watching fans. Here, it is possible to also come across Asian buffaloes, jackals, foxes, wild boar and otters, which hide among the vegetation consisting of tamarisks, ditch reed, cyclamens and wild orchids.

Once arrived in the area surrounding Bizerte, one enters the Ichkeul Nature Reserve, which takes its name from the lake situated as if it were the reserve's belly button. About nine miles wide from one shore to the other, the lake along with a 1,677-foot-high mountain with spiky rocks that shoot out into the fresh water are the outstanding features of this area protected since 1980 and once surrounded by swamps that have since been drained. It is a place of big numbers: there are 180 species of migrant birds that make their nests here, from October to March, making a total of 200,000 flourishing specimens, among which stand out 40,000 ruddy ducks, 30,000 coots and other whistle ducks, plus 8,000 wild ducks and a few exemplars of the rare white-headed duck, just to name a few. At this crossroads of wings, a back-and-forth of both feathered and non-feathered guests alternates in an environment similar to that of the Camargues of the Old Continent.

The land seems made just for bird-watchers. Not lacking are Asian buffaloes, jackals, foxes, wild boar and otters that peep out curiously from the thickets of greenery comprised of tamarisks, ditch reed, cyclamens and wild orchids. The lake, the biggest in the Maghreb with its 22,239 acres, presents a unique phenomenon in the world: in the summer it is low, extremely salty because of the seawater that penetrates it and quickly evaporates, and therefore rightly snubbed by that which is considered the largest bird community in all of the Mediterranean basin, while in winter, as the rains increase and its four tributaries fill, it becomes fresh and hospitable again. For this reason, the lake is part of at least two international conventions besides that of UNESCO, and between November and December it is populated by humans from around the world that roam the woods armed with binoculars.

Behind the coastal zone, still in the northwestern region of the country nearly at the Algerian border, stretches another notably evocative landscape: the Kroumirie. It takes its name from the Khrumir, the Berber tribe that dabbled in piracy and violated the Algerian border in 1881, giving the French the excuse to invade Tunisia. Since then, the word *'khrumir'* has assumed a negative connotation.

Shimmering with dew in the early morning, the intense green of this area covered by cork-tree forests extends into the low undulating mountains, which obtain a maximum height of 2,625 feet, dense with forests, waterfalls and springs fed by the intense winter rains generated by cyclonic weather depressions coming from the Atlantic Ocean. Under the leafy branches myrtle, strawberry, heather and viburnum proliferate. The pastures nurture the 'Atlas brown', a local free-range cow with a dark coat. When the herd must be gathered, an honest-to-goodness western-type battle is unleashed.

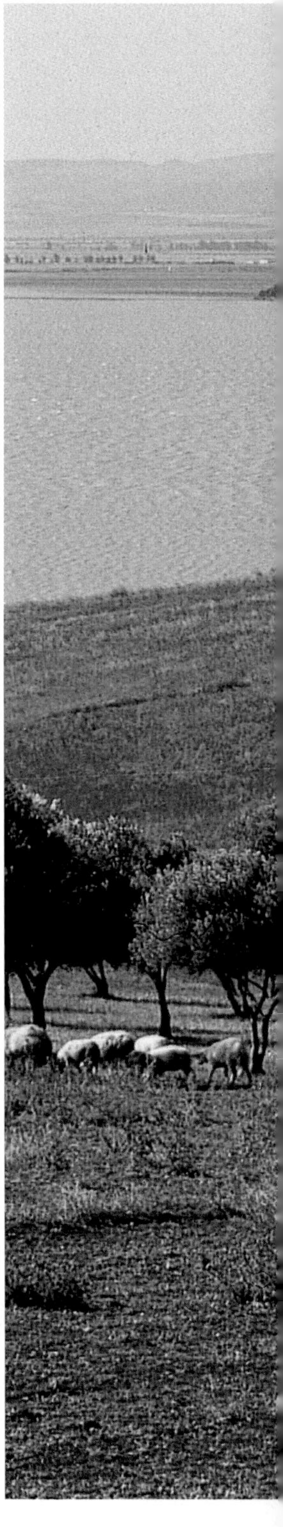

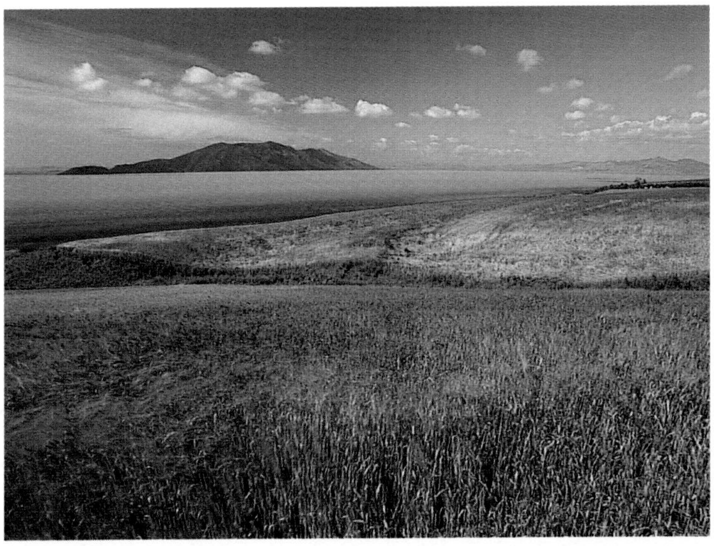
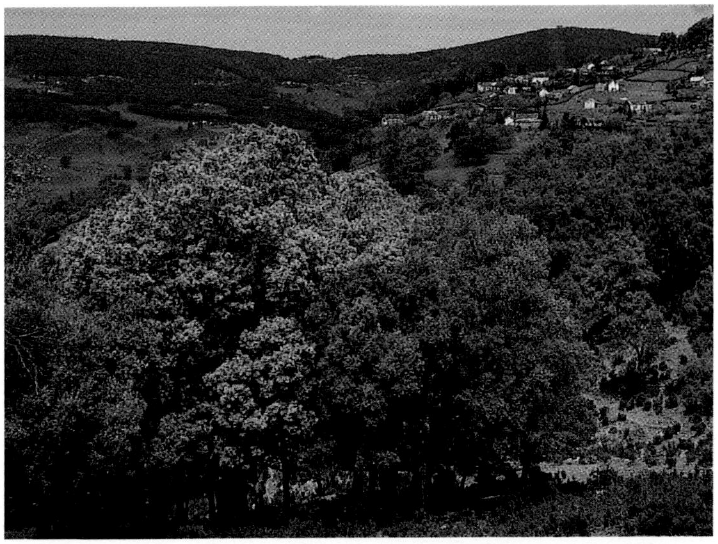
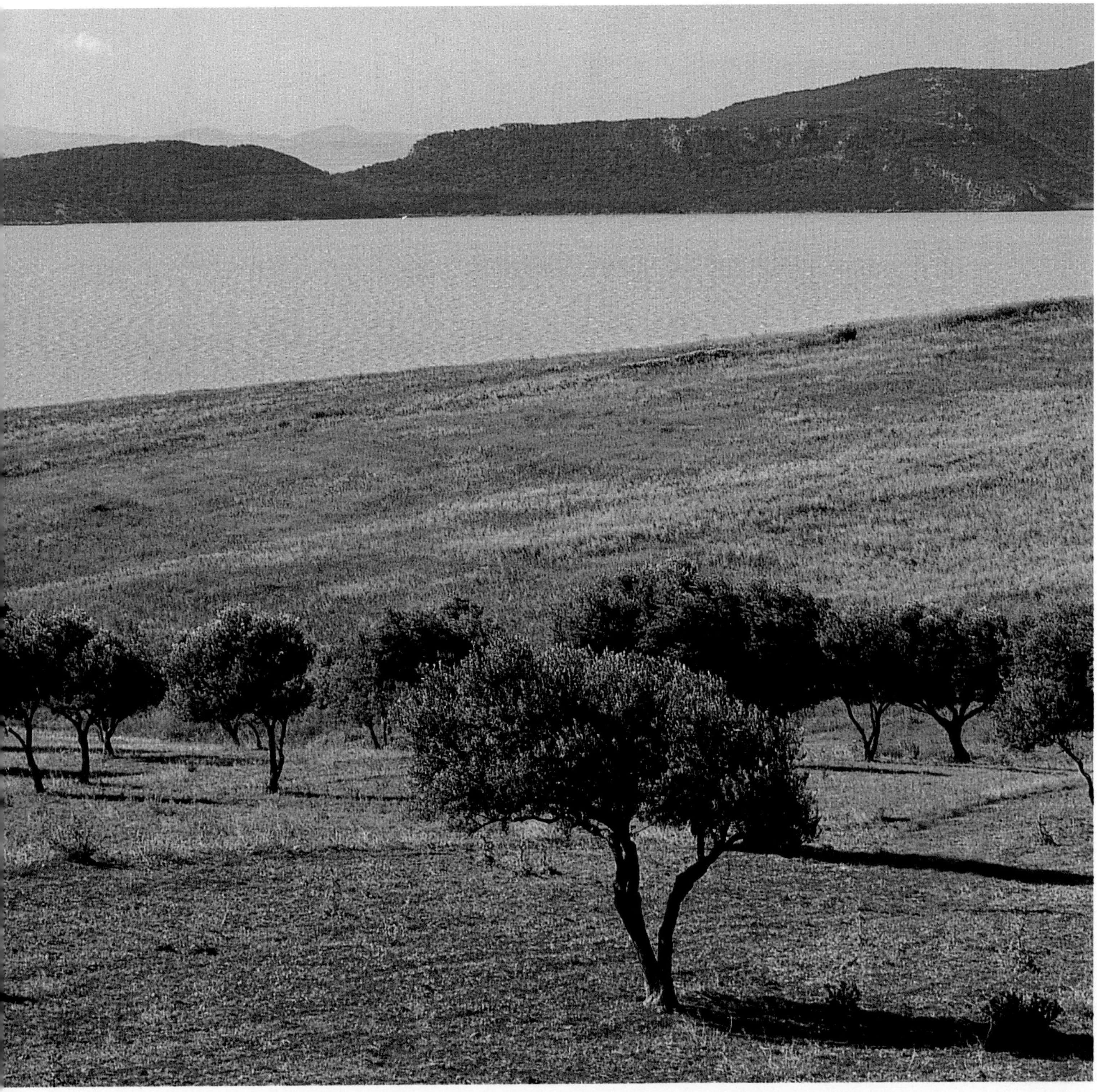

50 top The white domes and the octagonal minaret of the mosque of Sidi Bou Makhlouf dominate the village of Le Kef, 'the rock', at an altitude of 2,625 feet.

50 center The zaouia, or the seat of the religious brotherhood of Sidi Ali ban-Aissa, in Le Kef, today contains an interesting museum of arts and local traditions.

50 bottom The shepherds of Le Kef often push towards areas near the Algerian border, where the Numidian settlement of Naraggara stood. Some historians have placed here the historic battle between Scipio and Hannibal that, in 202 BC, brought the Second Punic War to an end. Traditionally, it is called Zama.

50-51 Le Kef occupies the site of ancient Sicca Veneria, a Roman colony that stood on a spot sacred to the Punic goddess Astarte.

All together, this forest territory accounts for 40 percent of the national woodland property. Besides cork trees, whose industrial-scale exploitation employs a large portion of the population, zen oaks, elms and willows appear towards the mountain peaks, while the perfume of the cypress wafts through the air. Here, in the past both remote and not so remote, animals such as the wild boar found themselves right at home. At one point in time, wild animals provided entertainment to the spectators of the games that took place in the amphitheaters of the Roman empire, and today, amusement for hunters that in 1891 killed the last lion and in 1932 the last panther in the area.

Further into the interior, still in the northwest, retreating into the heart of the country, a stop must be made at Le Kef, a town chiseled into the side of a mountain at around 2,625 feet high and whose name means, by the way, 'the rock'. It boasts whitewashed alleys, a Roman bath complex, two mosques—one with truly elaborate decorations on majolica tiles that gleam in the sun—and a museum of art and folk traditions. Substantially dominating a boundless plain, the city is the remnant of the ancient Sicca Veneria, which owed its name to a temple dedicated to the phoenix-goddess Astarte (analogous to the Greek Aphrodite and the Roman Venus). A starting-point for the main excursions in the archeological areas of the north, in the Second World War it was the headquarters of the Tunisia Free from the Italian-German Forces group.

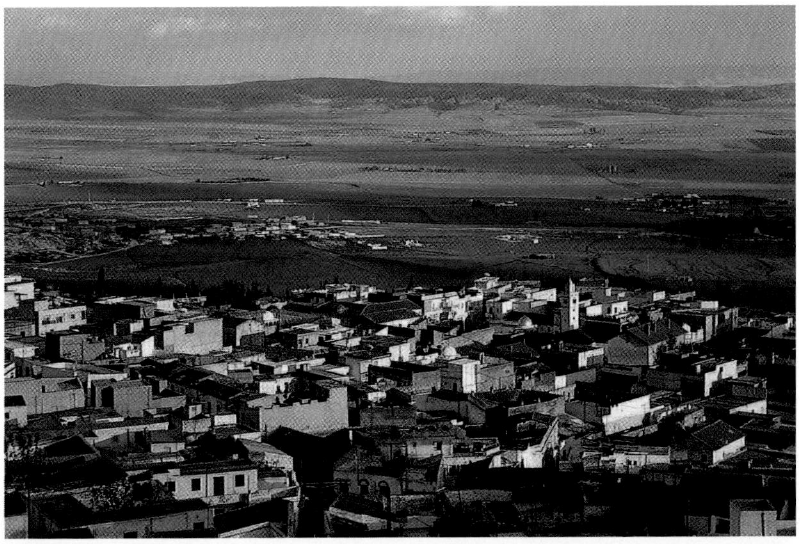

51 top Le Kef overlooks a landscape of endless plains, low-lying hills and woods of pine and cork trees. Far from the main tourist routes, it has stayed a place full of fascination.

52-53 The city of Korbous is situated on a very famous section of the Tunisian coast: Cap Bon, the 'beautiful promontory', as the Greeks called it, which extends out into the sea east of Tunis.

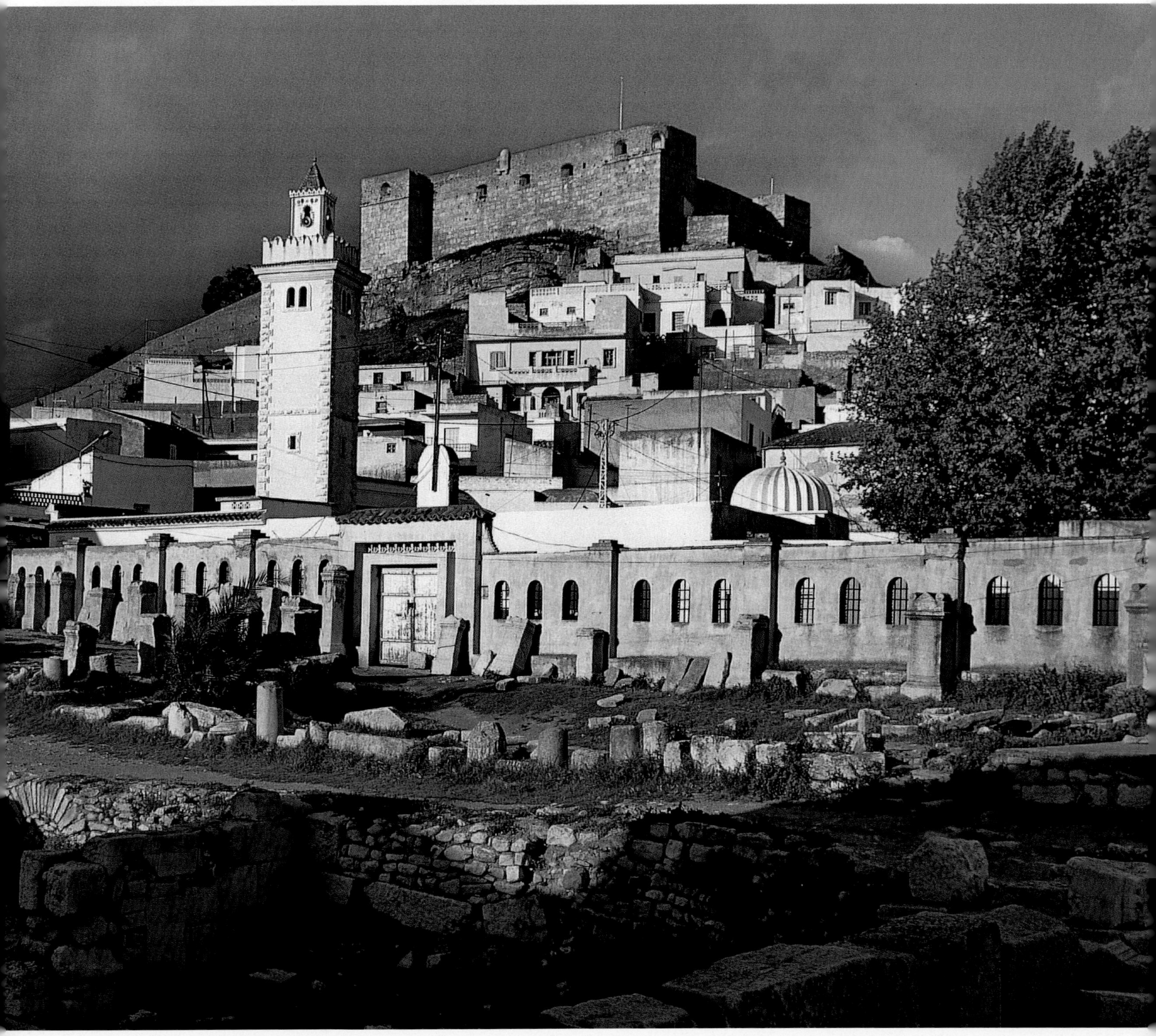

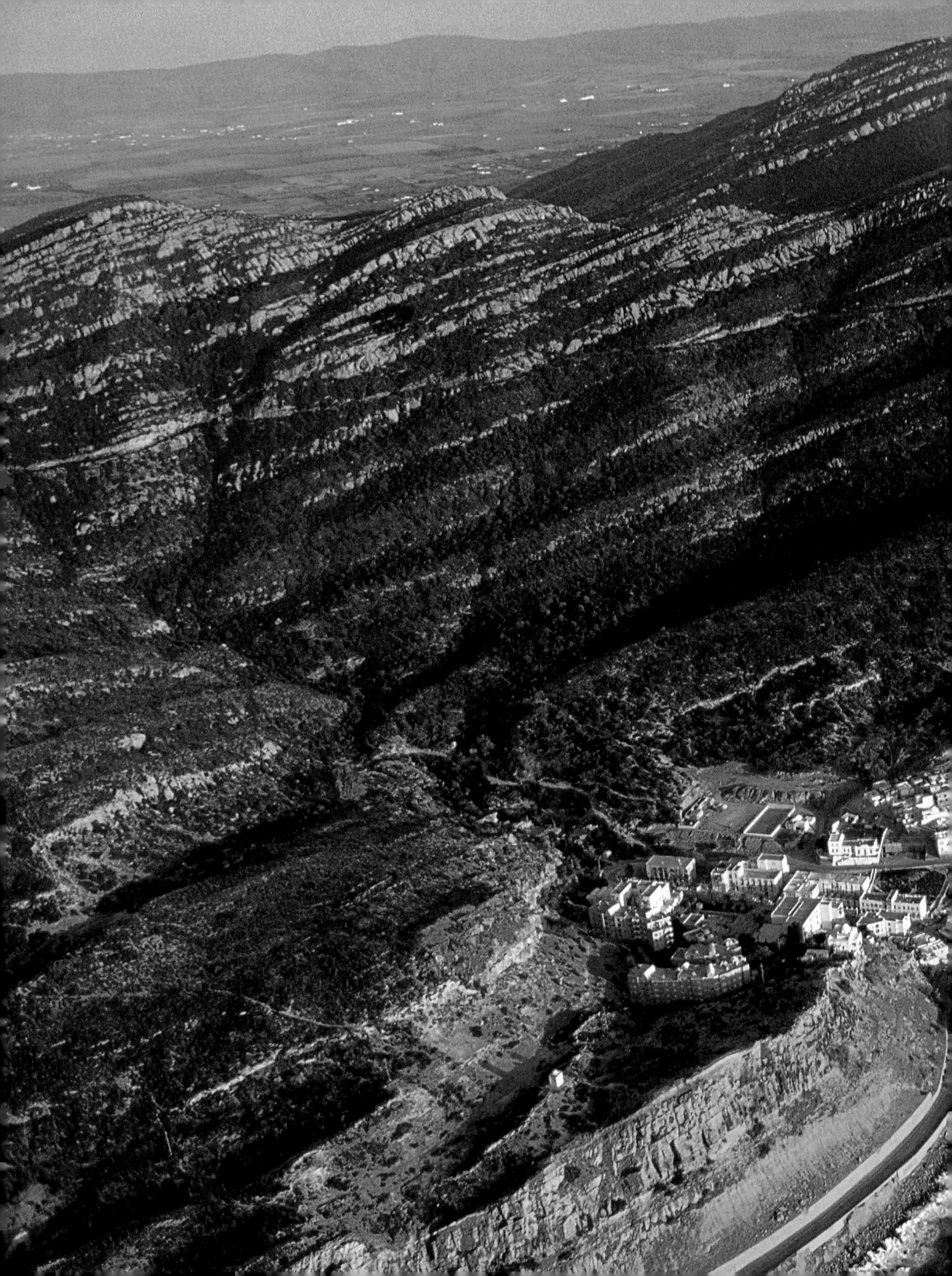

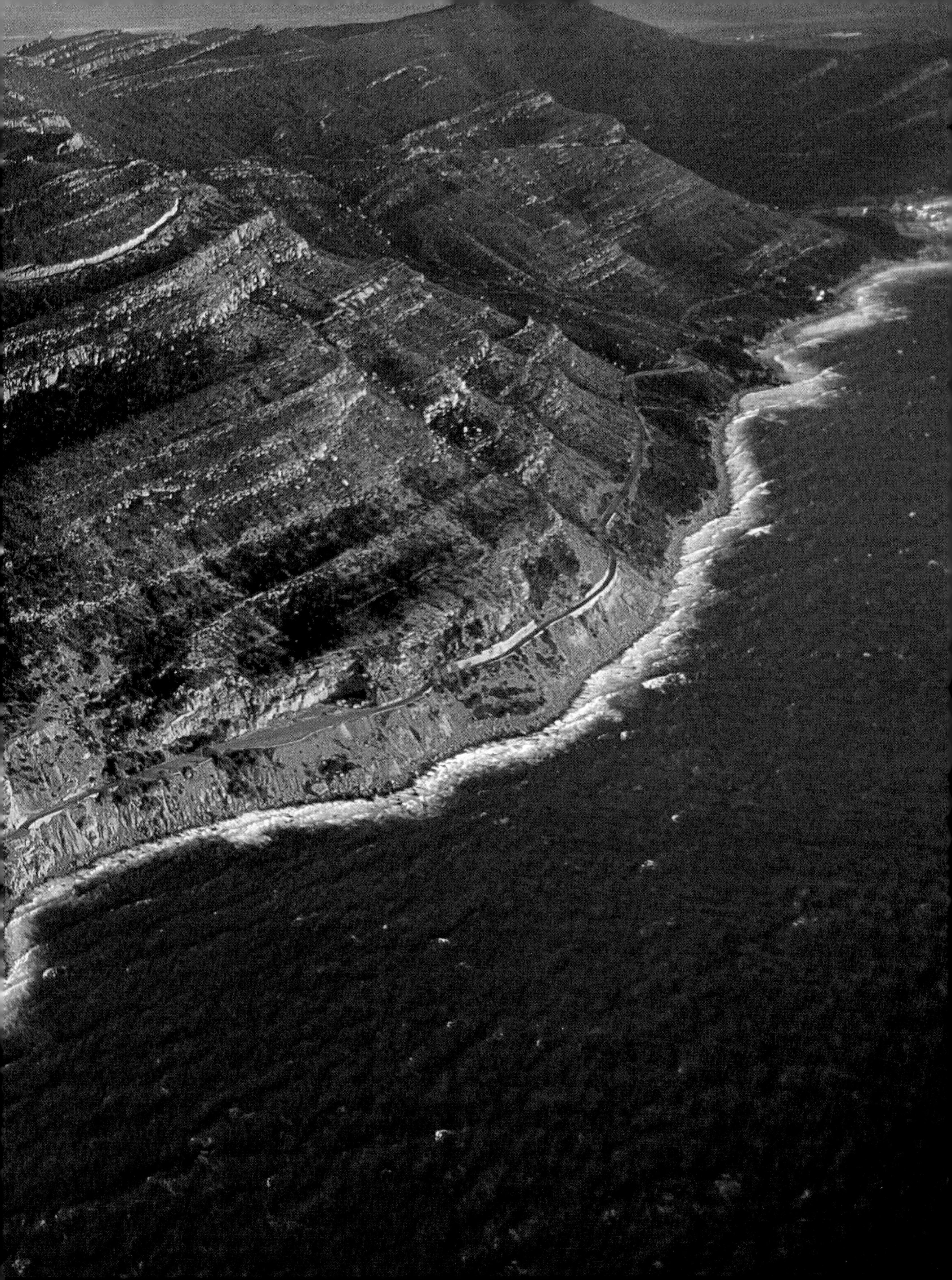

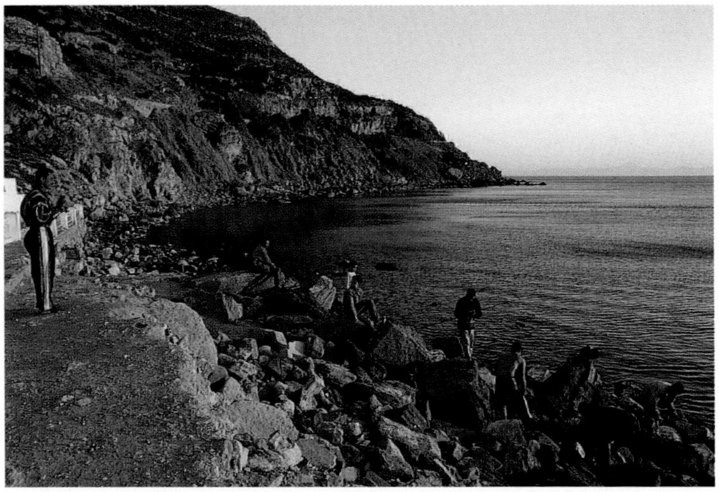

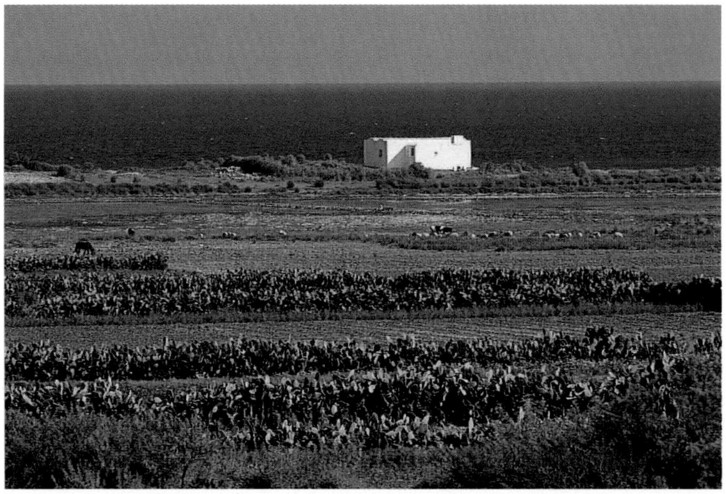

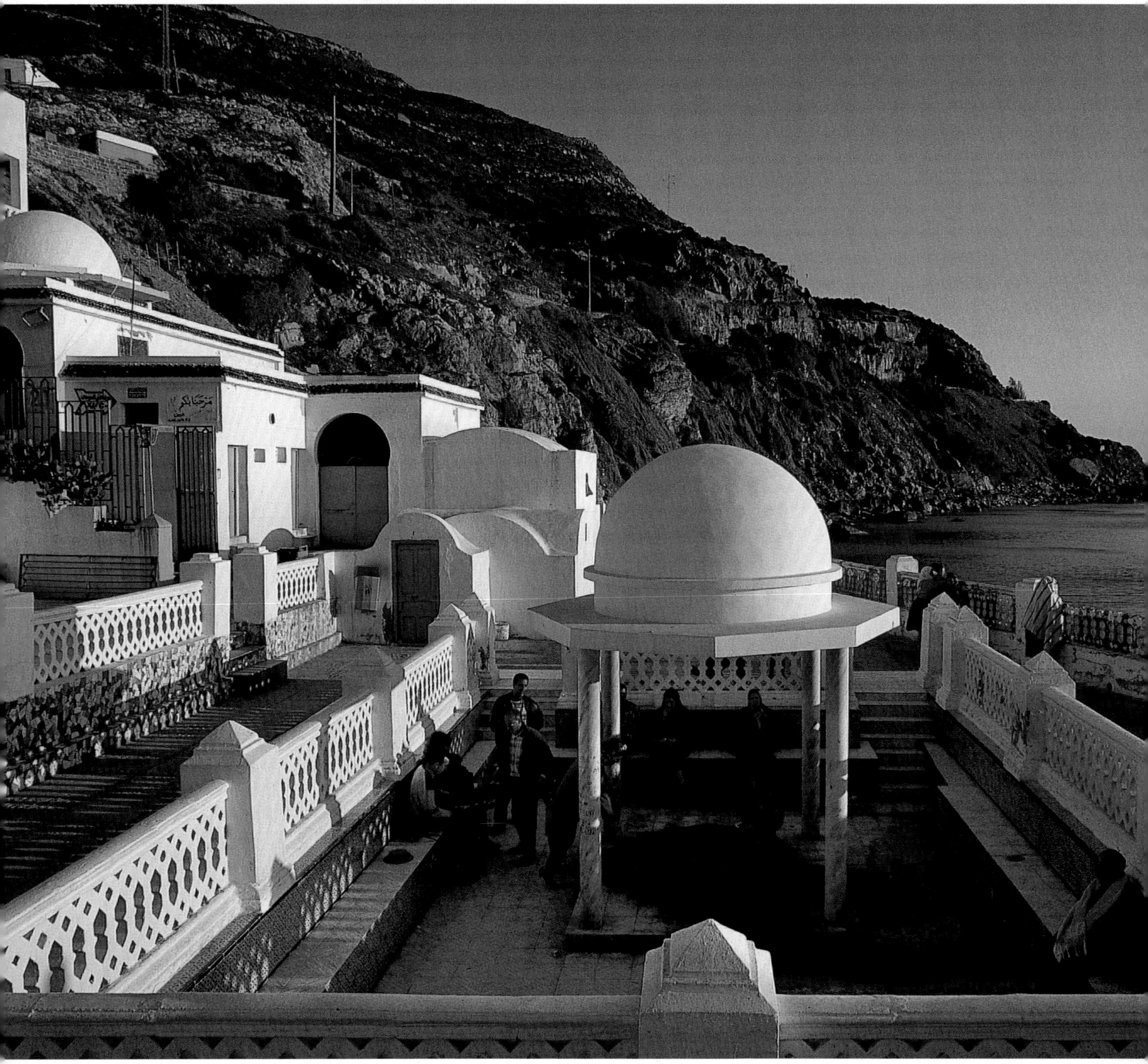
مرحبا بكم

54 top left The section of coast between Cap Bon and Korbous is today a beautiful area equipped for tourism. In the past, the Carthaginian aristocrats stayed here, also to take care of their farming properties.

54 top right In the generous zone of Cap Bon, numerous agricultural holdings follow one after the other—orchards, vegetable gardens and citrus groves, almost creating a garden on the sea—characterize this stretch of land with customs much like those of Sicily.

54-55 In the thermal establishments of Korbous, the water gushes out at an average temperature of 122-140°F. These hot springs, among the most important in the country, possess highly acclaimed purgative and digestive properties, as well as beneficial effects for eczema sufferers.

If one wants to return to the coastal landscapes, the other seashore that truly deserves attention is that of Cap Bon, east of Tunis—called *kalós akroteriós* or the 'beautiful promontory' by the Greeks.

It is still beautiful, full of orchards, vegetable gardens and citrus plantations, like a garden by the sea where an Italian echo is felt. Leaning in towards its interior, the place is packed with hard-working people and customs—such as the killing of tuna—similar to the Italians.

The circumnavigation of the cape is also pleasant, as one may encounter serene villages like Korbous, the pristine *Aquae Calidae Carpitanae* of the Romans nestled into a small, rocky bay, where puffs of vapor exit from underground promising thermal springs renowned for their effectiveness. Or, there is El-Haouaria, where falconers live.

In spring, they throw out their nets and catch the fierce raptors, which are then trained to hunt. A bit further on appears the site of Kerkouane, the very ancient city that produced the scarlet-red dye so dear to the empire. Here can be seen the sacred 'sign of Tanit', the Punic fertility goddess: a stylized human symbol traced in white on the dark rock. Finally, along the last part of the southern coast, until and beyond Hammamet—the largest Tunisian tourist site—there is a continuous line of hotels and residences where life passes pleasantly between shopping and taking a dip in the rightly-dubbed emerald sea.

55 top Looking onto the Gulf of Tunis, Korbous was already famous in ancient times for its salubrity. After a period of oblivion, it became popular again in the ninth century and since then has never ceased to welcome local and foreign tourists.

55 bottom Korbous, the Roman Aquae Calidae Carpitanae, is settled comfortably in a small, rocky bay, where puffs of vapor often come out of the ground. The thermal hot springs are also numerous in the surrounding area.

56 top In the area of el-Haouaria, the quarries of Ghar el-Kebir are found, vast caverns exploited for the extraction of stone. The locally produced blocks served to build Punic Carthage, and the caverns themselves were used as barracks by the Byzantines.

56 center and bottom The coast of el-Haouaria offers views of great beauty, often in a secluded atmosphere. The caves are numerous in the region, both on the coast and inland: one of these is famous for the bat colonies that live there.

56-57 The village of el-Haouaria, lying at the base of modest slopes, is famous throughout the country for hunting with falcons, which is practiced in spring. With the raptors, quails, partridges and migratory birds are hunted.

57 top left The sea around el-Haouaria is particularly full of fish (in this area ritual tuna fishing is practiced) and rich with flora. For this reason, the nearby island of Zembra is included within a marine reserve.

57 top right El-Haouaria is the outmost point of Cap Bon, reaching out towards Pantelleria. Every year, during the migration season, the passage of tens of thousands of birds can be admired from the promontory.

Moving further down the coast, one enters the territory that goes from Sousse to Sfax: the Sahel. 'The coast' is the meaning of this Arabic name, which indicates, effectively, the coastal zone and its hinterlands contained between the two famous cities. Here, the hills are modest, of a low altitude, subject to heavy erosion and sometimes tricky to navigate since they conceal the *sebka*, depressions that contain brackish swamps. The actual coast is almost one big sandy tongue of land that over time has advanced, stealing ever more ground from the sea to the point that it has managed to incorporate the primitive islands of Monastir and Mahdia.

This is a particular region, where tourism has deeply taken root. The first signs of the 'African dream' made of oases and palm trees, Bedouin tents and thousands of olive trees in tidy rows under the hot sun start to be seen. For centuries and centuries this land has produced fruit and vegetables—which arrive on European tables months ahead of time—oils and cereals because both the Romans and the Carthaginians replenished their resources at this commercial crossroads that reunited the tribes of the zone. The olive groves, those planted in the 1930s by French colonists and local farmers, are concentrated in the area between Sousse and Ksour Essaf where they are cultivated in big valleys among the hills, giving the gift of beautiful views to attentive travelers. It is like a watershed between the Mediterranean and the desert.

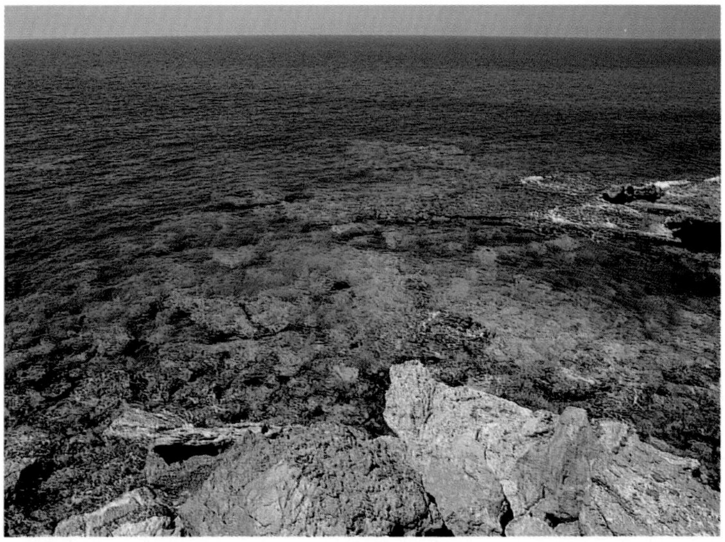

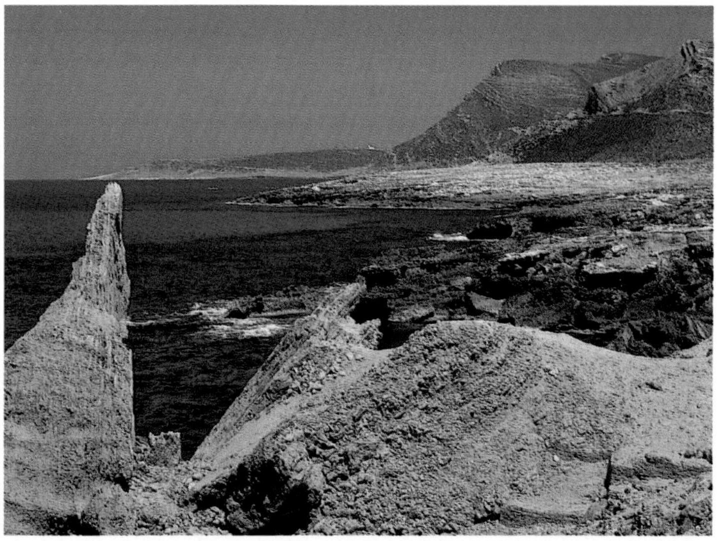

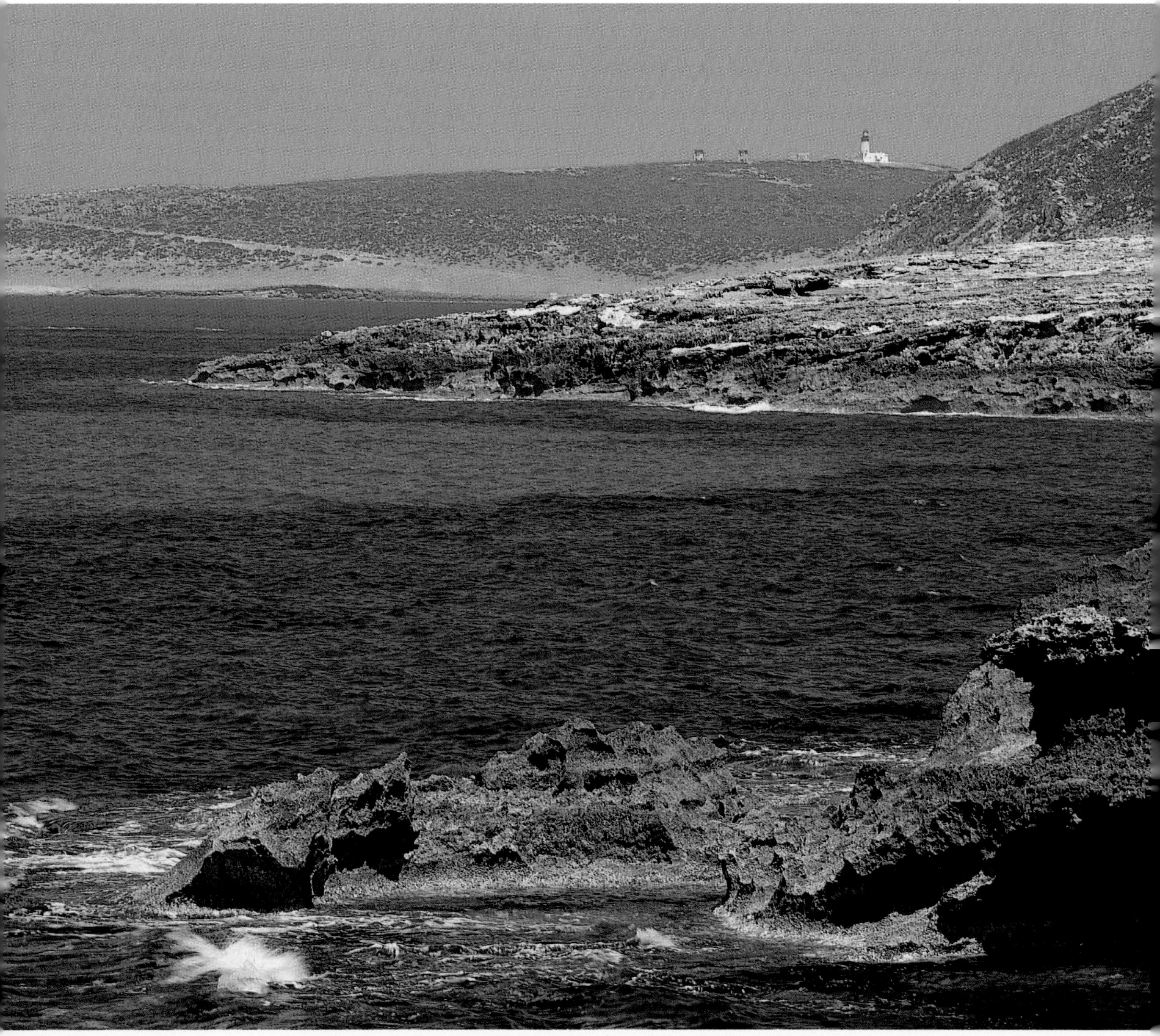

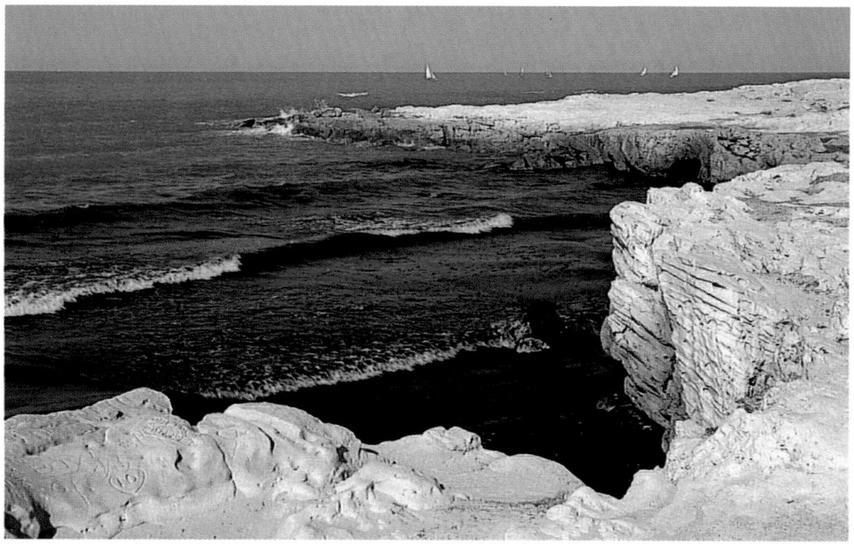

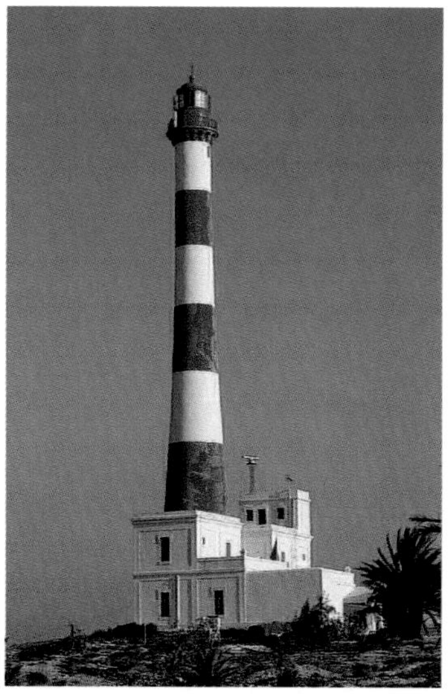

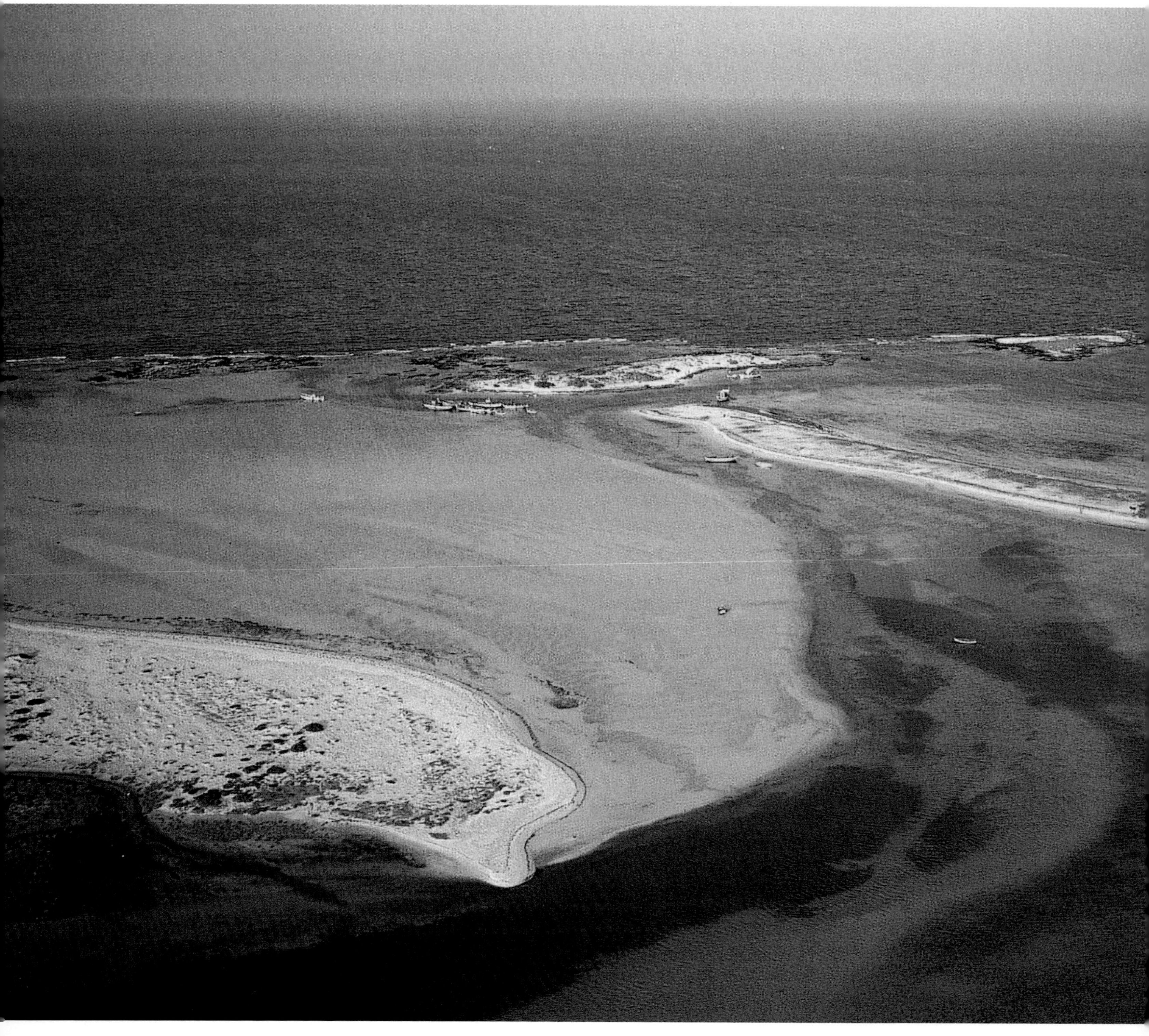

58 top left The southern coast of Jerba is less frequented by tourists looking to relax, which have a preference for the white, long beaches typical of the eastern part of the island.

58 top right There are two lighthouses on the island of Jerba: shown here, at the north-westernmost point, is Borj Jillij; the other is in the mid-east region, around the village of Taguermess.

58-59 Jerba is an ideal destination for a relaxing vacation. The sea that laps the eastern coast, shallow and gently sloping, makes it possible to take long walks in the surf.

In the descent towards the south, the landscape changes again as it nears the Gulf of Gabès. Here passed slave merchants and caravans coming from the north, stopping in the shade of the hundreds of thousands of palm trees—an obligatory stop for all. The climate, being milder than that inland, made possible an explosion of long and winding palm trunks, with rustling, intensely green leaves that stand out against the yellow of the surroundings like a single emerald set in an empty jewelry box. The trees border on—a unique situation in all of the Maghreb—the powder-fine sand of the beach, a white ribbon framed by the waves of the sea.

The attraction of the Gabès Oasis palm tree groves, through which to-day it is possible to ride in a cart, leaves its mark in the heart and mind as it did in that of Pliny the Elder, who wrote, 'Under a very tall palm tree grows an olive tree, under the olive tree, a fig tree, under the fig tree, a pomegranate tree and under the latter, a grape vine; under the grape vine, wheat is planted and then vegetables and fodder, and all this happens within one year, and every plant grows in the shadow of the next.'

All of this is made possible thanks to the dense network of irrigation canals, which take advantage of the fresh water that runs above and under ground.

59 top In Jerba, some places are still found where the palms, which once covered literally the whole island, arrive at the waterline, creating an evocative situation.

59 bottom From the sky the morphology of the eastern coast of Jerba can be fully appreciated, moderately 'colonized' by hotels and all-inclusive resorts.

60 top left In the area of Matmata, the white dome of a marabout, *a tomb of a cleric warrior or a saintly man devoted to Islam, stands out against the golden ochre of the surrounding hills.*

60 bottom left In the troglodytic houses of Matmata, time seems to stand still. The handmade furnishings are objects of everyday use for the women of the place but they seem reminiscent of the past.

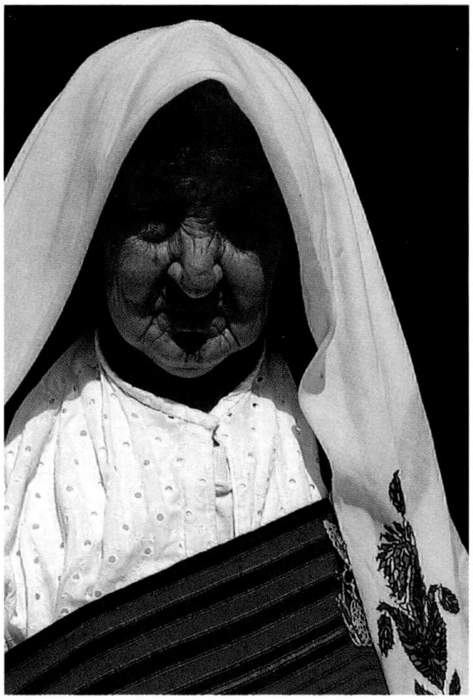

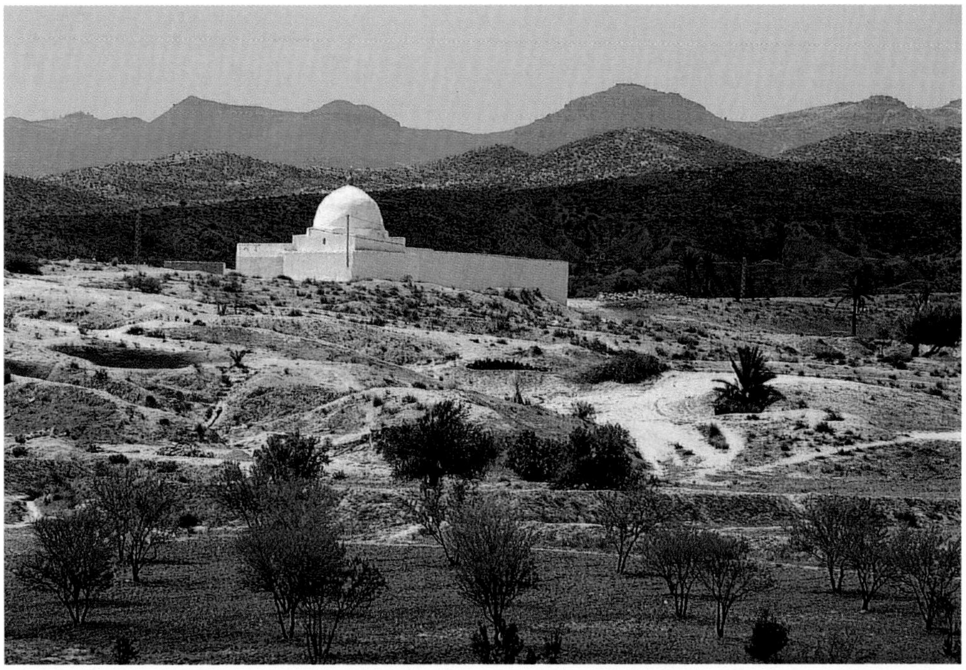

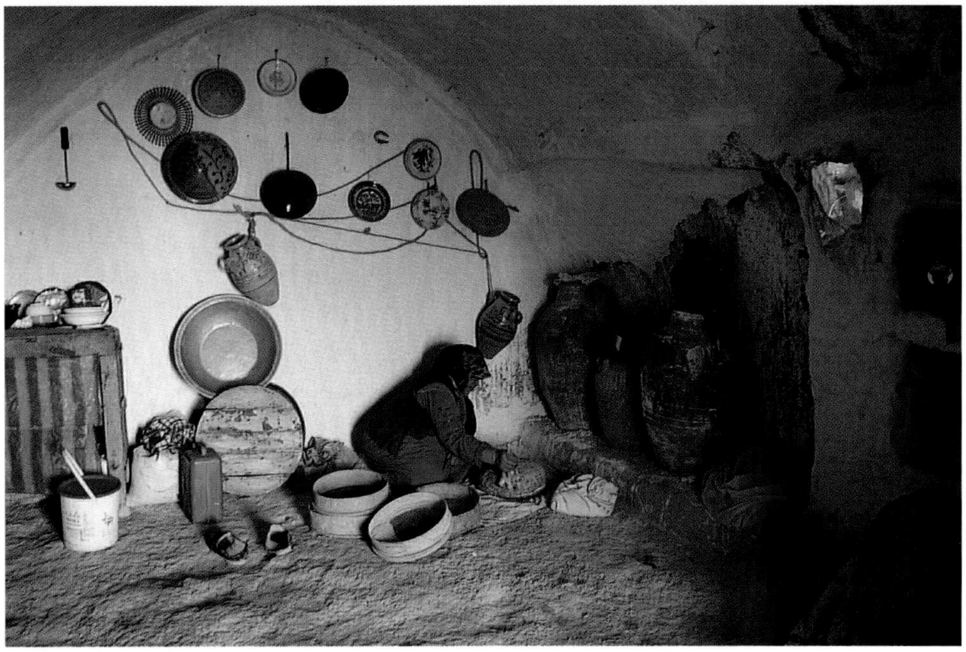

This water even supplies other oases, like that of Matmata, in the mountains of the same name, which appears as one travels in a southwest direction. The land here, if seen from above, is literally riddled with over 700 holes, the entrances to troglodytic homes excavated from the bare earth. Between rare plant tufts and a few shrubs, the setting is truly spectacular. An alien world where 'the living live under the dead', where the living wedge themselves in among the cool folds of the earth's womb, robbing spaces from the shadows with hidden bright white constructions. Below the surface the temperature drops by several degrees. A mild coolness accompanies the visitor along a tunnel until reaching a courtyard, a kind of sizeable well onto which open several living spaces, often having two floors. The only sounds are the voices of women and children, which spend most of their time in front of a loom, creating fabrics that include all the shades of purple and red.

60 right The women of Matmata, of Berber descent, almost always wear the traditional costume. An inseparable instrument is the loom, at which they spend a large part of the day weaving pleasant, multicolored fabrics.

61 The troglodytic houses of Matmata number about 700. They can be accessed through a tunnel that leads to the courtyard, a sort of well around which open the living spaces, often on two levels. The internal temperature is much lower than that outside.

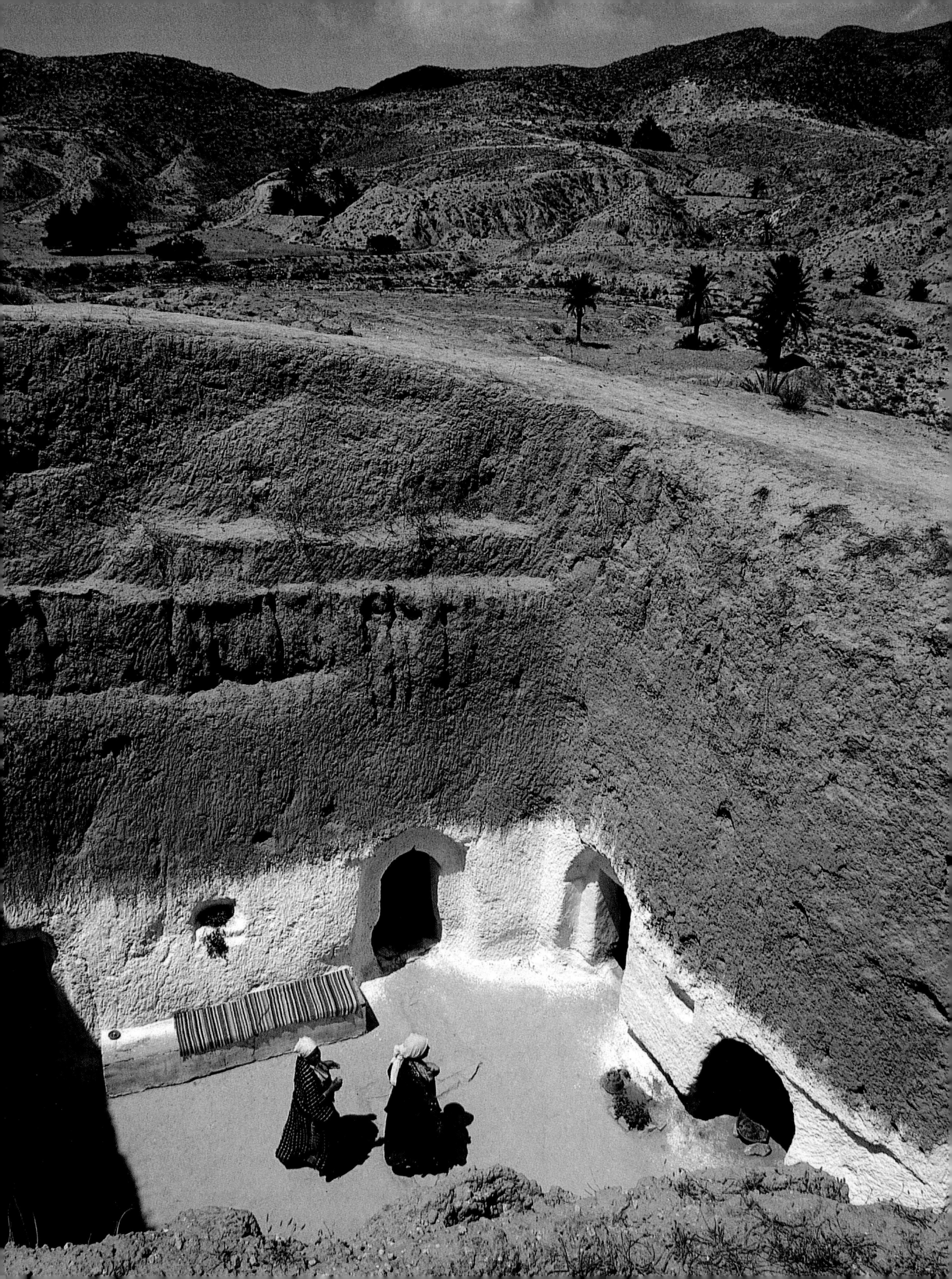

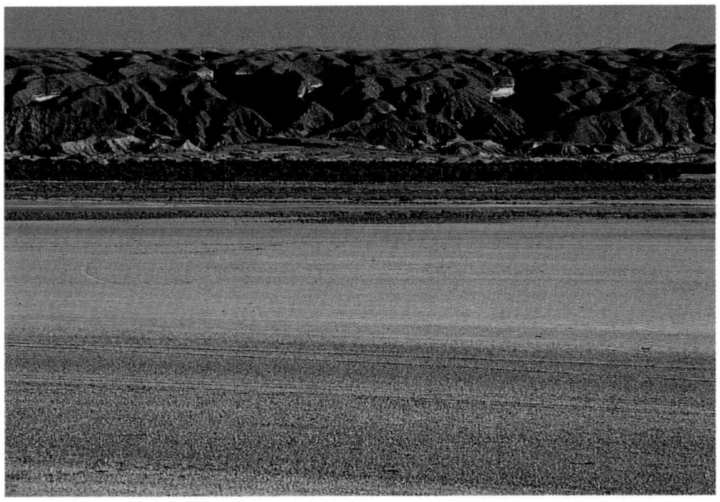

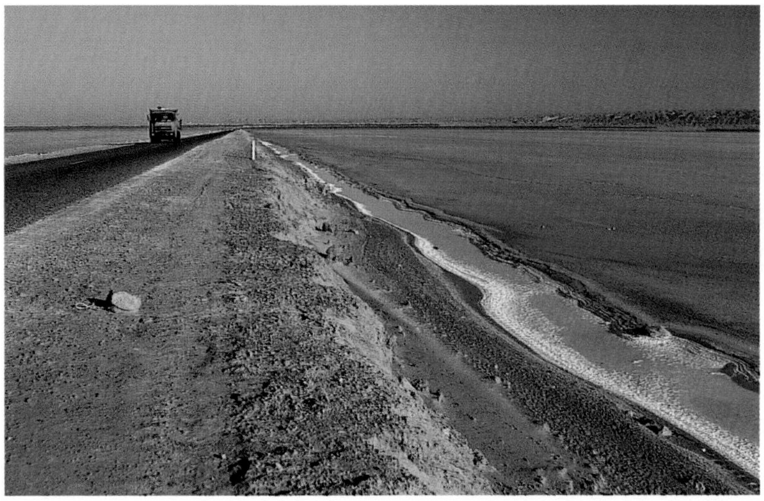

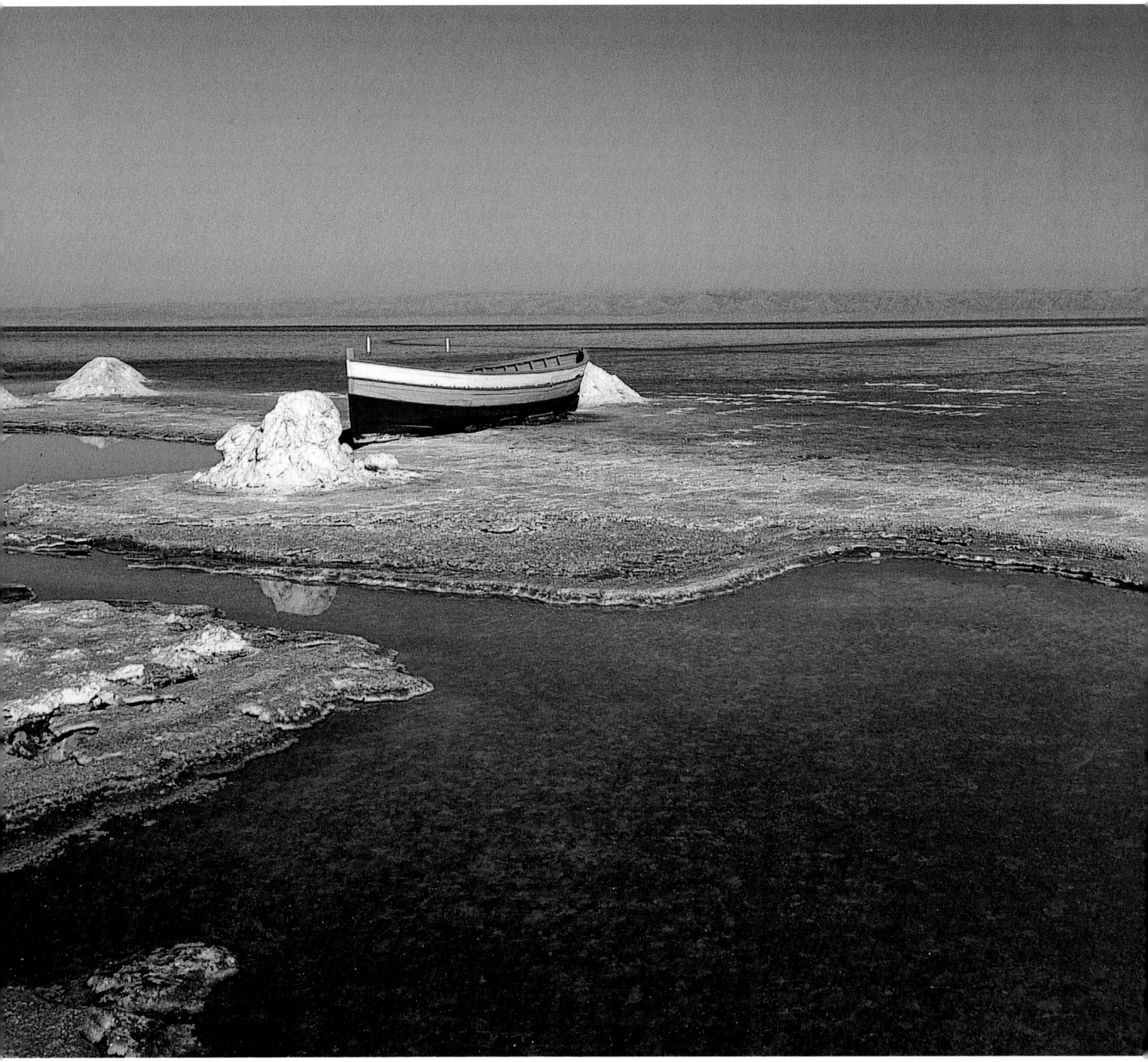

62 top left Chott el-Jerid, in the heart of the country, is the biggest salt lake in Tunisia and the most extensive closed depression in North Africa. Here, the climate is subtropical, with a long summer and an extremely brief winter.

62 top right The road along Chott el-Jerid is used by only a few, rare trucks. All around, the infinite desolation is immersed in a landscape in which the mirage is frequent.

62-63 In Chott el-Jerid, millions of salt crystals that emerge from the surrounding ocean of sand separate and reflect the light in all possible shades. Here, some of the scenes from The English Patient *were filmed.*

Changing direction for a moment and continuing on towards the country's interior, following the path of the dying sun, one will arrive at the region of the *chott*, the great salt lakes. The setting is dazzling. Lost in a genuine ocean of sand, millions of salt crystals, which separate and reflect the light in all its possible shades, crunch under the steps of tourists who adventure to Chott el-Jerid—the largest of the lakes with its 1,776 square miles that make it the most extensive enclosed depression in North Africa. Here, as if by some supreme magic a small stone becomes a pyramid suspended in the air or a tuft of vegetation becomes a tree-filled hill. Mirages appear because of the unequal refraction of the light through certain colored strata of the atmosphere creating a watery illusion on the horizon that acts as an amplifying mirror to distant objects. Around this area, some tracts of golden, crescent-shaped dunes—that have been the ideal settings for the films of the *Star Wars* saga and *The English Patient*—are transformed by the wind into stone sculptures in strange animal forms.

63 top Walking on the crust of salty mud of the Chott el-Jerid, bare of any form of life, is a fascinating experience: the only noticeable sound is the crunch of the salt beneath one's shoes.

63 bottom On the shores of the salt lake, a man gathers 'desert roses', glittering calcareous concretions with a characteristic shape that are rather abundant in the Maghreb in the areas bordering the desert from which they get their name.

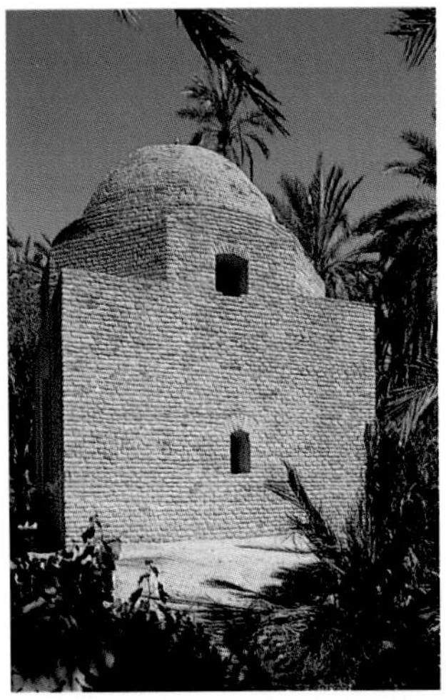

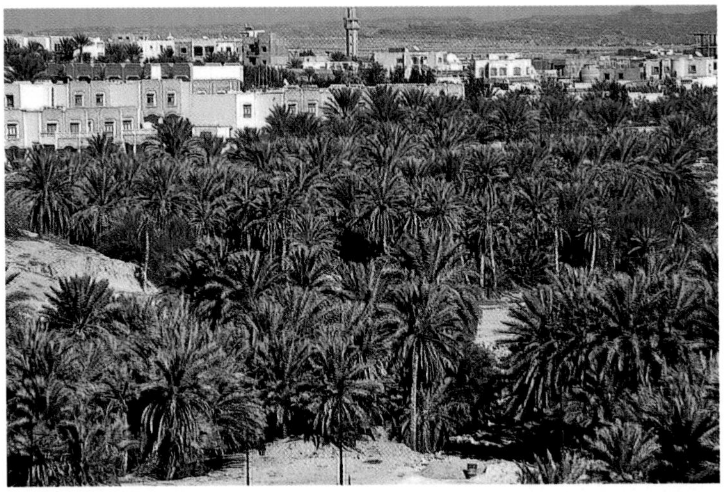

64 top left Squared out of the soft rock of the surrounding areas, plain, and unadorned as required by the tradition of austere simplicity that typifies many minor monuments in Islamic art, the blocks of a marabout *reveal themselves among the leafy branches of Tozeur Oasis.*

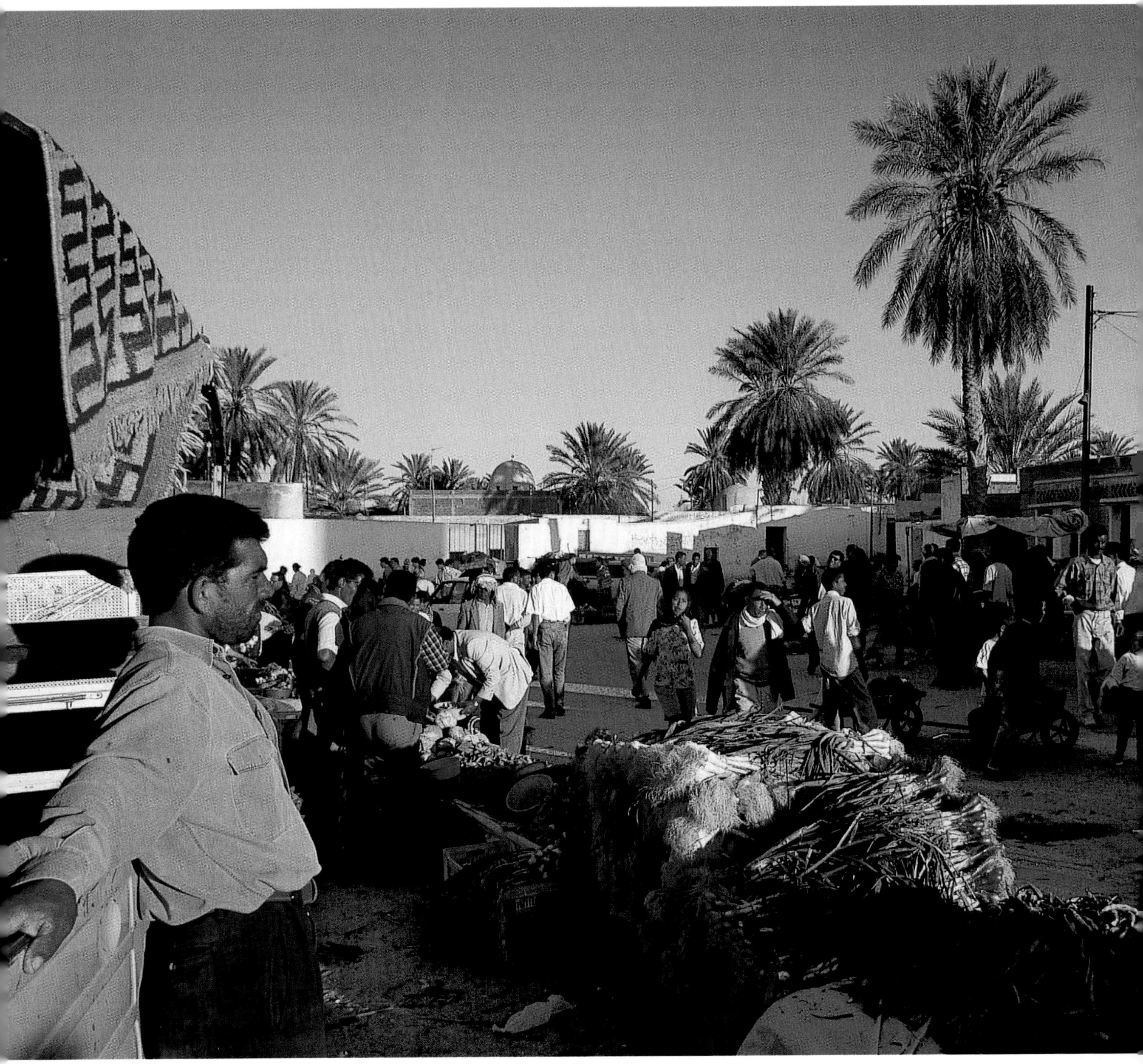

There are other oases. Near the springs life flourishes again, offering unusual places like Tozeur on the north bank of Chott el-Jerid, inhabited by the descendants of the last Byzantines to settle here before the Arab conquest. From here one enters the 'town of the palms' where nearly a half million thin trees produce a variety of marvelous dates. The town is equally marvelous, with its extremely particular architecture of brick houses with facades that depict, when they stick out, motifs inspired by Muslim calligraphy. There is another thing that makes this oasis unique and dreamy: the 'red lizard', a flame-colored train that leads to the discovery of the Selja Wadi ravines, the great bed of an irregularly flowing river where the water, when it is full, gallops like a race horse and rises in the blink of an eye.

64 top right Tozeur is a very famous oasis situated on the northern bank of Chott el-Jerid. The descendants of the last Byzantines to settle in the region before the Arab conquest, in the seventh century, still live here today.

64-65 The market in Tozeur is always very lively. In the 'town of the palms', almost 500,000 plants produce a variety of totally special dates, the famous deglet en nour. Besides fruit, carpets with typical geometric designs are also sold in the local souq.

65 top The desolate ravines of Selja Wadi have been ploughed out of the fascinating bed of an irregularly flowing river. The inhabitants of the place say that, when the riverbed is full, the water flows impetuously like a galloping horse and rises as fast as you can bat an eye.

65 bottom The minaret of a mosque is silhouetted against the cobalt blue sky of Tozeur. In this village, the characteristic red brick buildings can be noticed everywhere, which are often decorated with motifs inspired by the refined Islamic calligraphy.

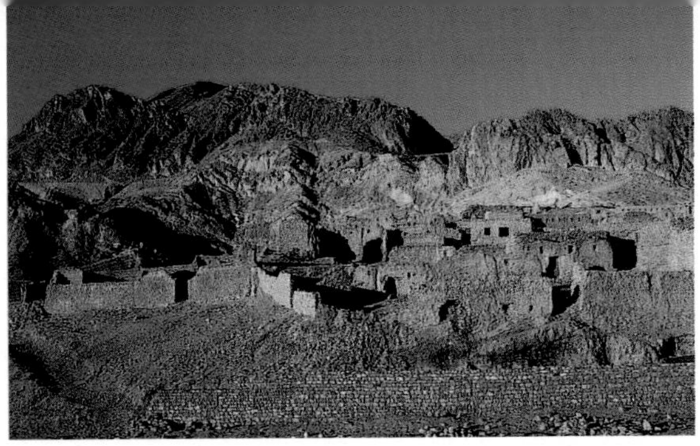

66 top The primitive settlement of Chebika is by now abandoned and in ruins. Built in stone and mud, it is perfectly camouflaged by the bare mountain that overlooks it.

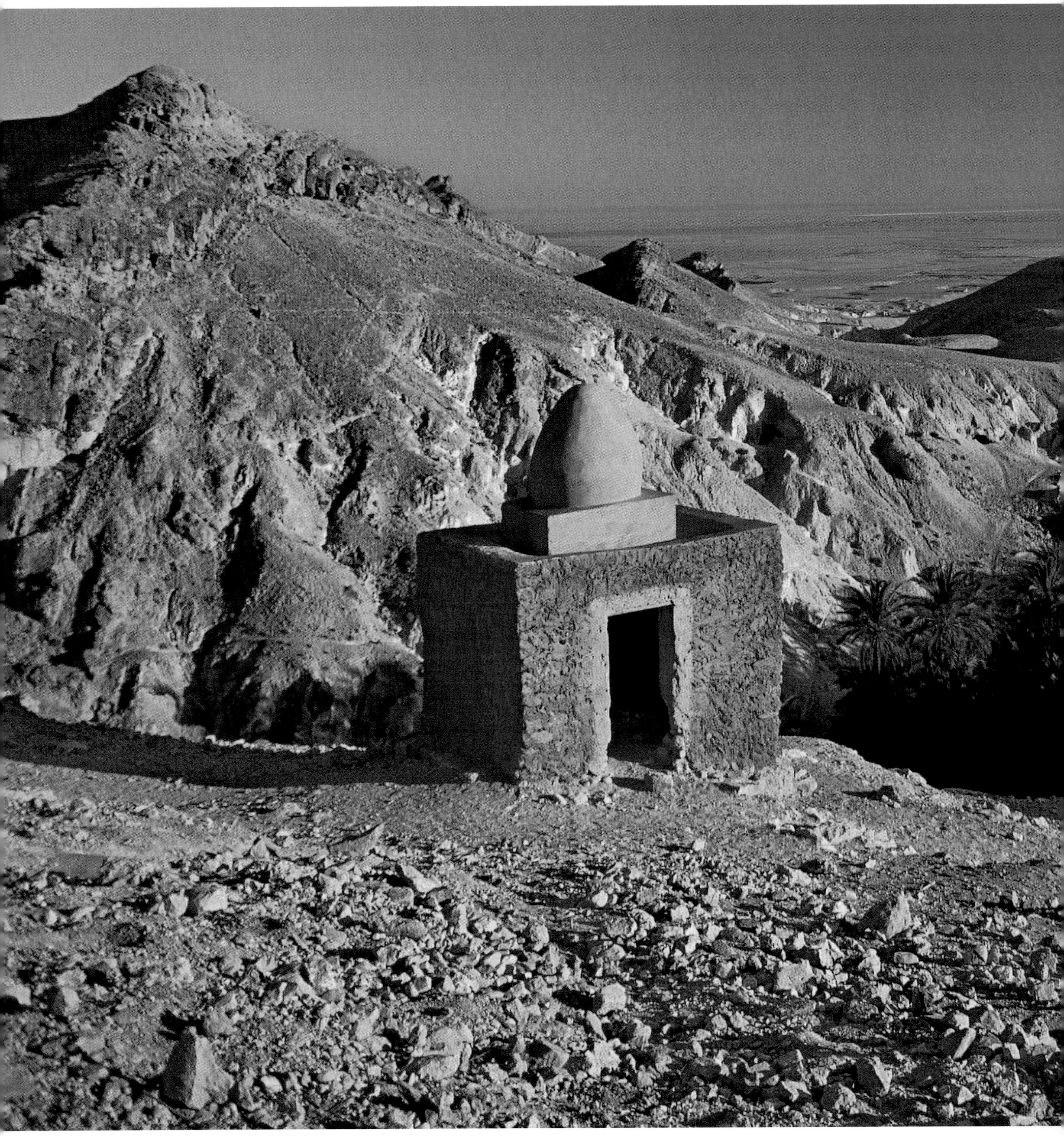

66-67 Chebika, along with Tamerza and Mides, is one of the mountain oases in the central south part of Tunisia. From here, in Roman times, the limes tripolitanus *ran.*

67 top The people of Chebika have by now established themselves along the slopes of the mountain in more comfortable houses . Next to the houses opens the green expanse of date palms.

67 center The oasis of Chebika seems to rise out of nowhere: here the climate is rather harsh, with marked temperature ranges and an average rainfall of six inches per year.

67 bottom The landscape of the Chebika region is decisively arid. A large part of its inhabitants have actually had to emigrate in order to find work in the mines of Redeyef.

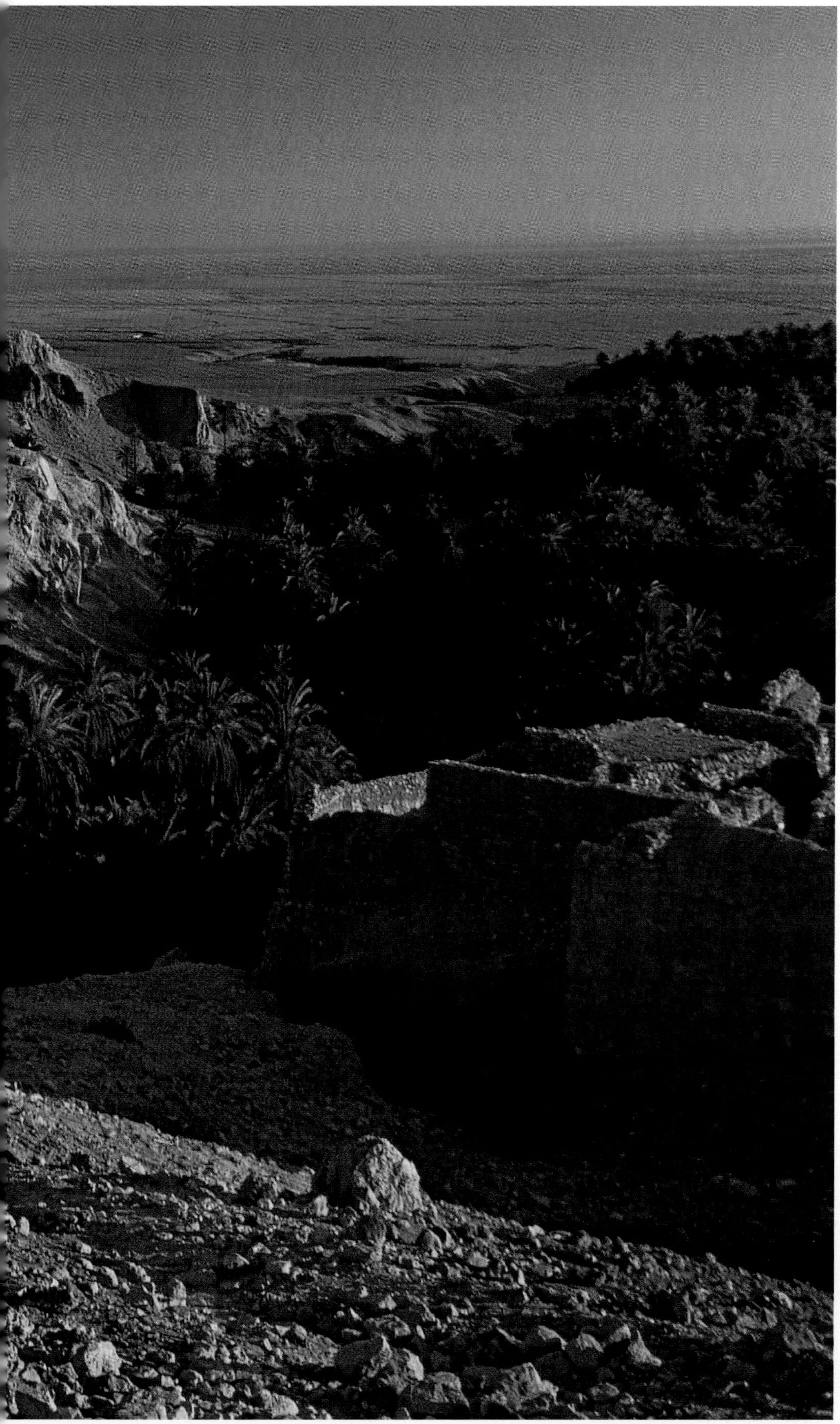

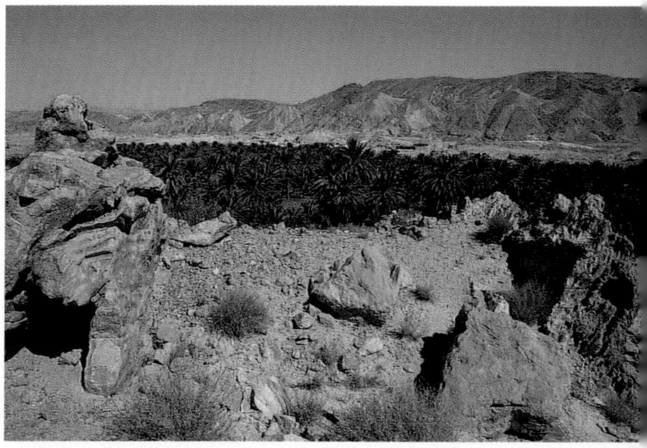

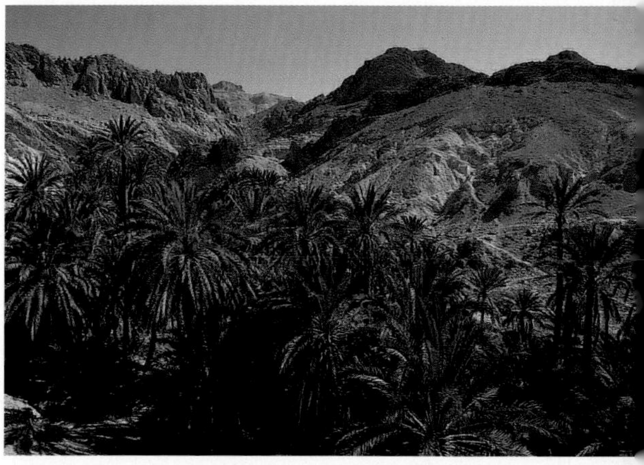

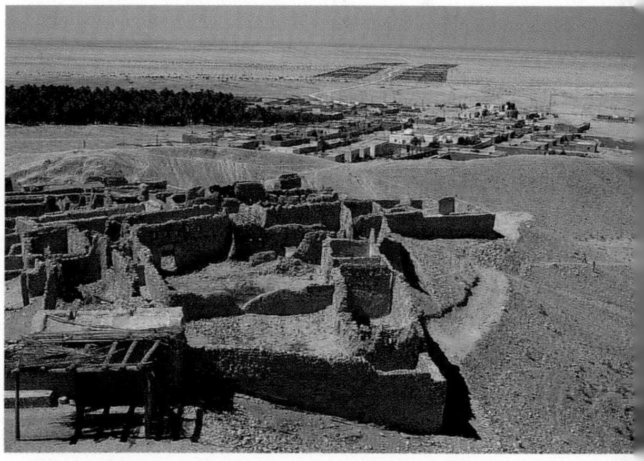

Proceeding clockwise towards the north, Nefta is another oasis challenging the desert. A place of pilgrimage, it is probably the second most important religious center after Kairouan. It has a hundred *marabout* (the tombs of important people, covered with a dome or a conical roof), 24 mosques and is irrigated by an impressive 152 fountains.

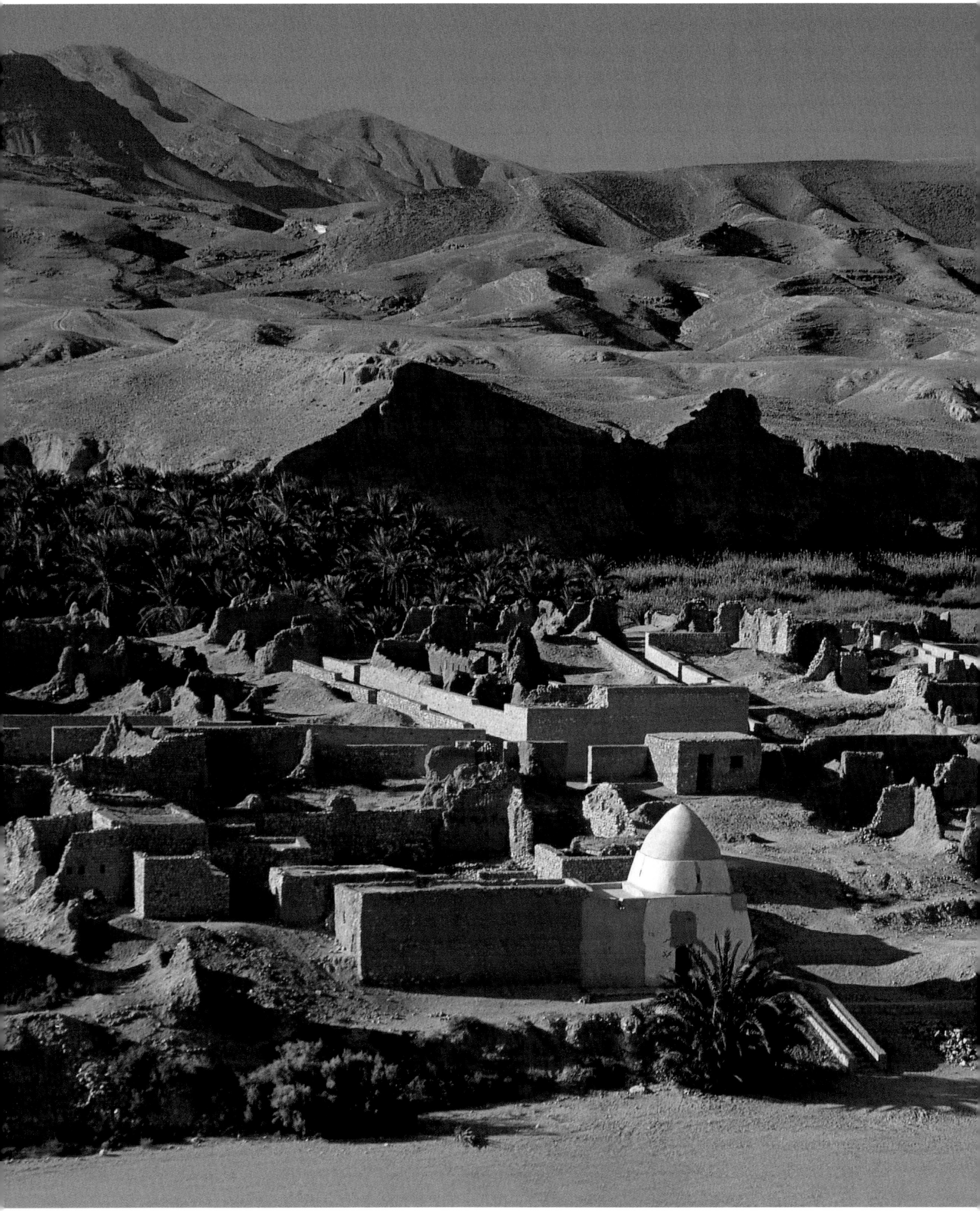

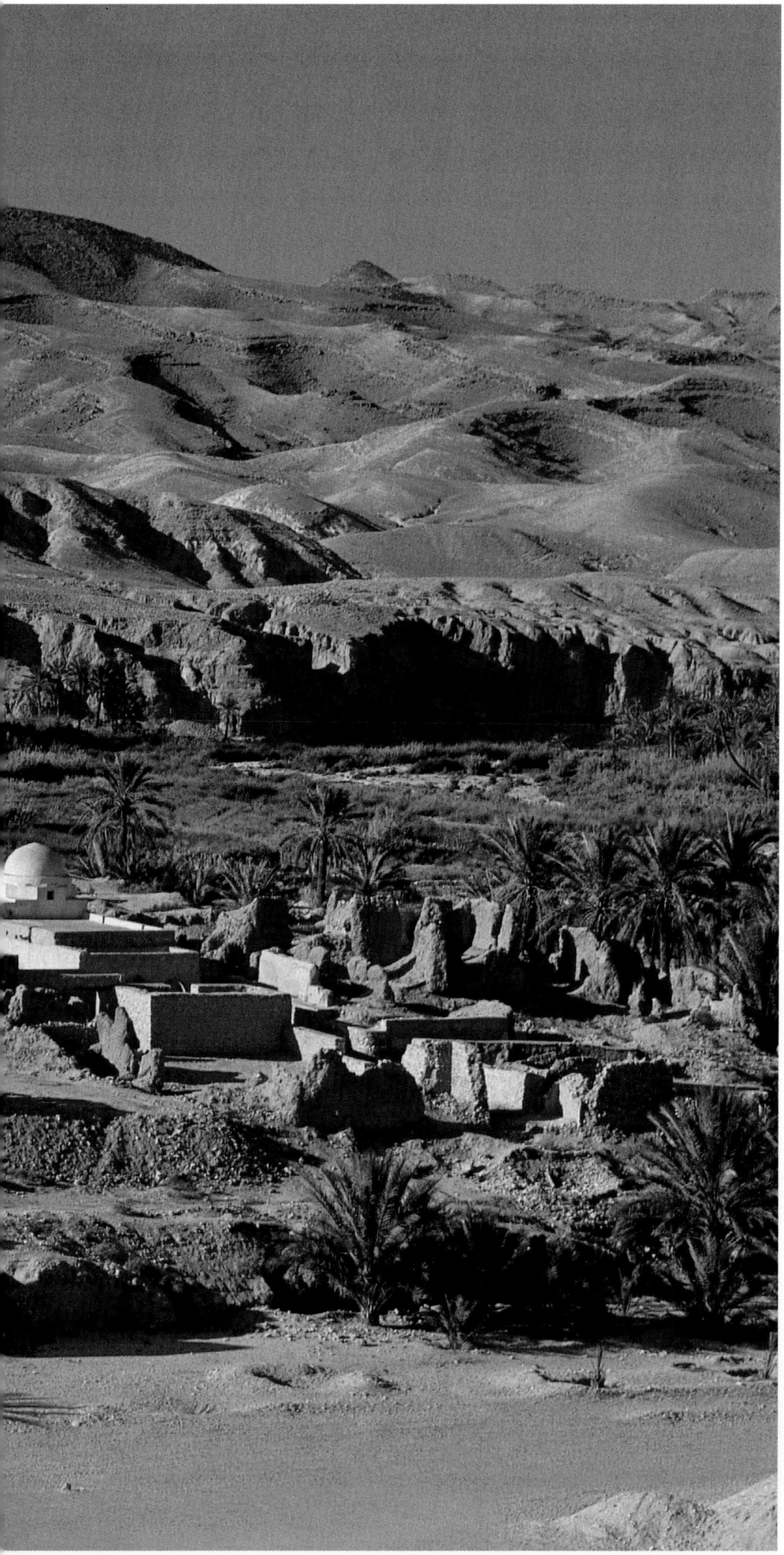

68-69 Between Chebika and Mides, Tamerza stands in an immense amphitheater that opens to the east of Chott el-Jerid.

69 top The troglodyte village of Tamerza, by now deserted, was a Byzantine Episcopal diocese.

69 center A column of tireless camels moves towards the ridges along the Algerian border.

69 bottom Date palms, abundant in the region, are still today one of the main sources of sustenance for the inhabitants of Tamerza.

70-71 Seen from above, the architecture of a ksar *reveals a complex of* ghorfa, *granaries fortified against marauding raids, typical of the central-south of Tunisia.*

Here, the dates are called *deglet en-nour* and they are 'the sweetest in the world', delicate, and transparent. The tour continues with the, by now, all but uninhabited oases Chebika and Tamerza; one is withdrawn halfway up the side of a mountain that, at certain points, gives the unheard of spectacle of a true waterfall, and the other is like a balcony inserted onto an enormous canyon, jutting out over the endless plain that extends until it reaches the salt lake.

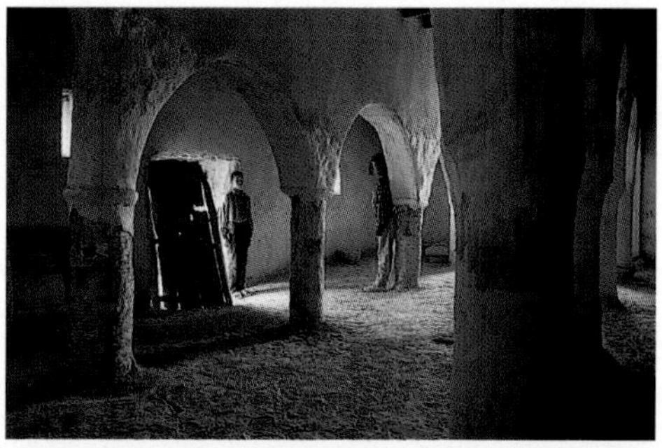

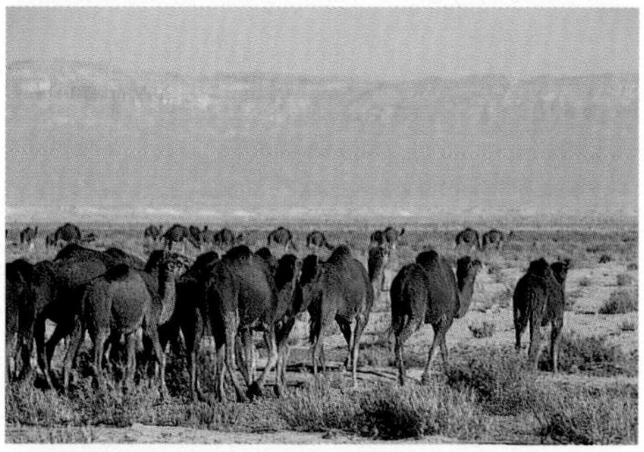

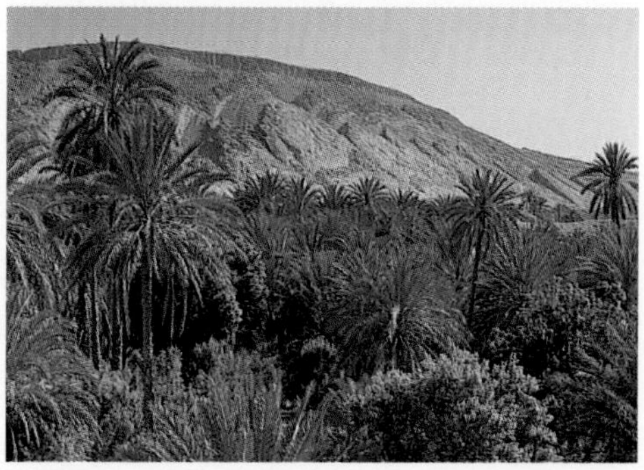

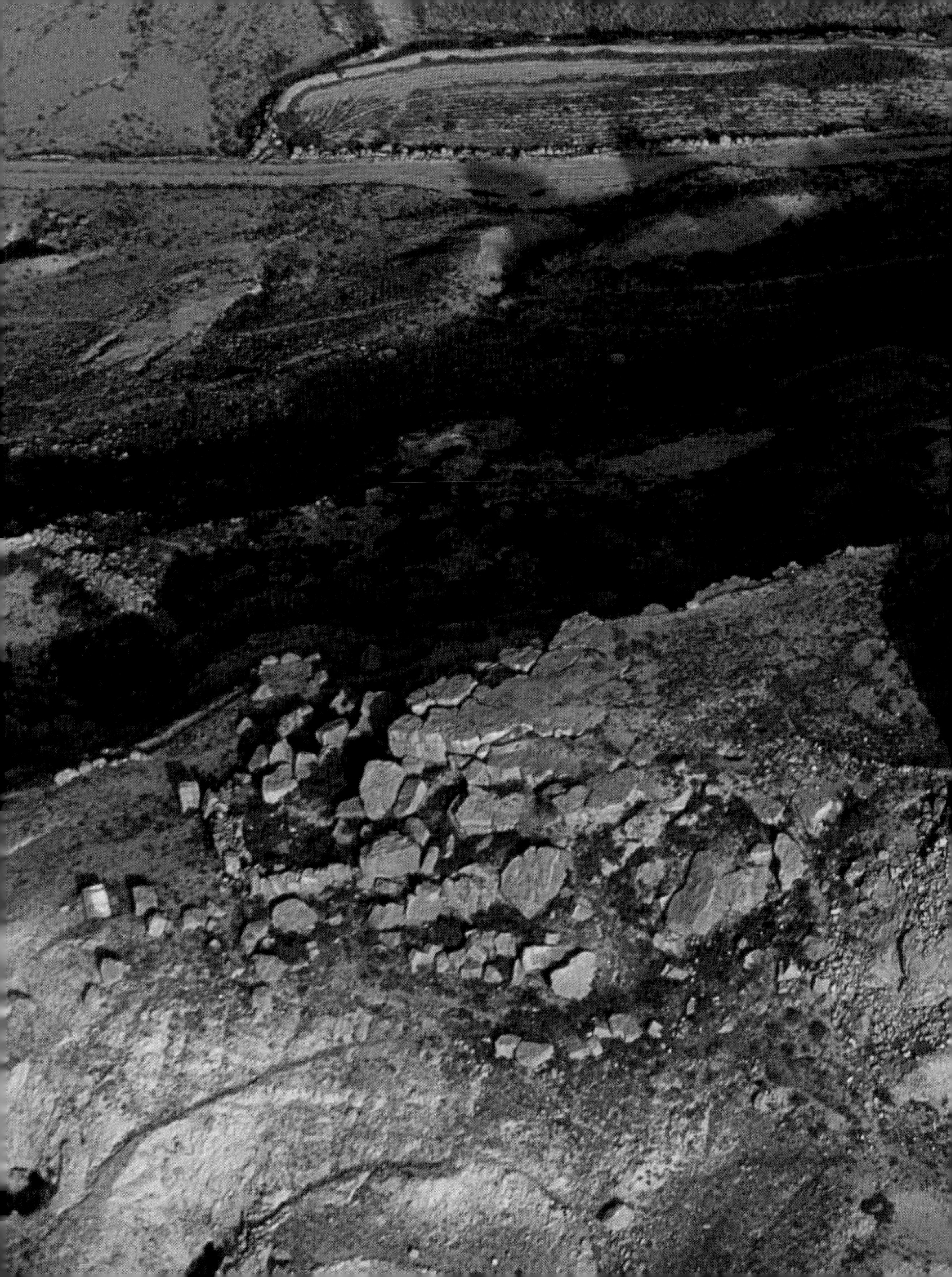

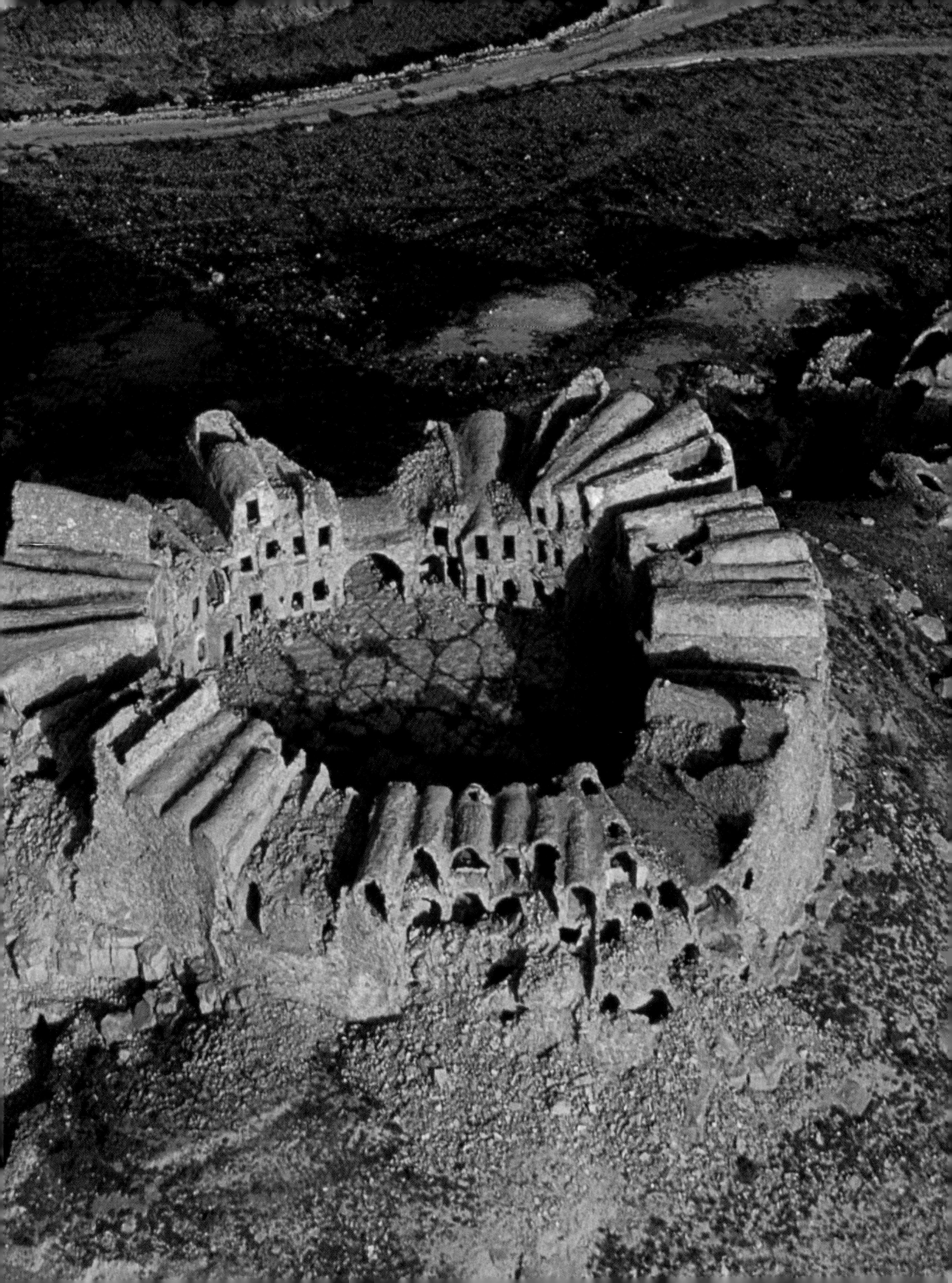

72 top In the oases of Gafsa, a good 100,000 date palms grow, which unfortunately are not very productive. The affluence of the area is owing to the fruit trees that produce apricots, figs and various citrus fruits of remarkable size. The local pistachios are also famous.

72 bottom The pools of Gafsa are 13 feet deep, constructed by the Arabs with recycled materials of Roman origin. The reservoirs collect precious water destined for irrigation, which gushes out of a thermal spring, at 88°F, situated on the bottom.

72-73 Ksar Hadada, south of Gabès, is a combination of fortified granaries where tourists can even stop for a quick stay because a part of the complex has been converted into a hotel. Some scenes from episode one, The Phantom Menace, *of the* Star Wars *saga were filmed here.*

73 top left The kasba *of Gafsa, a city of wide avenues and modern buildings that alternate with cubic, tightly shut huts, typical of the pre-Saharan region, was gutted in 1943 by an explosion in a munitions deposit. Now, the new court building has been established there.*

73 top right Before being abandoned and then newly developed for tourism, the big fortified complex of granaries of Ksar Hadada belonged to a nomad tribe originally from Ghoumerassene.

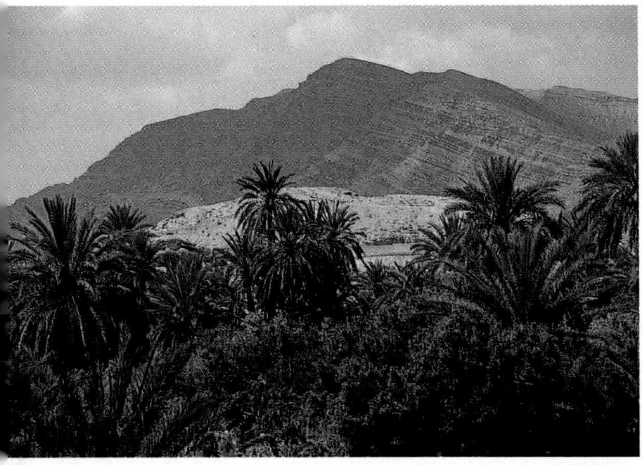

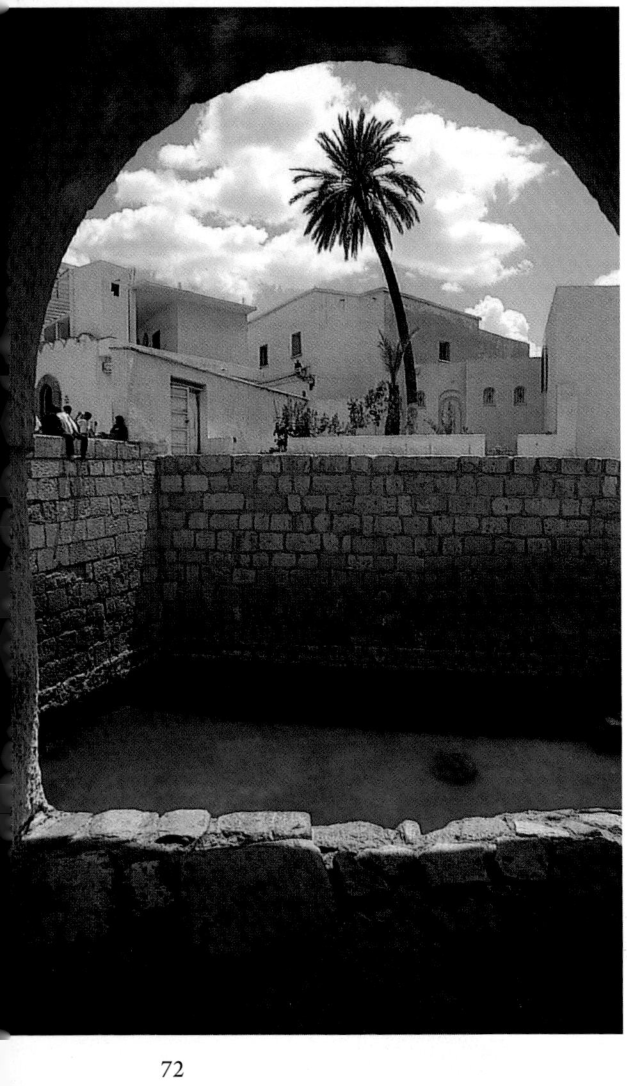

Finally, Gafsa, in reality the most northern oasis of the region, is the true gateway to the desert. Its *kasba* is big and towered and its pools, baths of Arabic origin constructed with Roman materials, are unexpected, where water is collected for irrigation purposes and children attempt daring dives. Yet another brusque change of direction back towards the east and from below Gabès one enters the territory of the *ksour,* the impressive fortified communal granaries of a bright ochre-yellow color like those of Ksar Hadada, where the first episode of *Star Wars* was filmed. One can see towns such as Forum Tatahouïne, with its multicolored market, or Chenini, an earth-colored oasis that crowns a mountain at the center of which, like a cherry on a cake, towers a white mosque. Here there are also troglodytic dwellings and an intense and harsh landscape. Further southwest lays the Nefzaoua, the pre-Saharan zone that was the birthplace of many shepherd tribes. Among the villages, M'Razig of Douz becomes famous once a year thanks to its festival of skilled horsemen, giving whoever arrives down here demonstrations of extraordinary equestrian ability. This is the area where salt deserts are found, those of rock and those of sand, which stretch out to the west towards the Dahar Mountain chain and open onto the Grand Erg Oriental. From here on there is nothing—no vegetation nor permanent settlements. There are only nomads, moving dunes of variable shades (the Erg, sand desert, in the strict sense of the word) and endless spaces: nothing but the wild and indomitable desert.

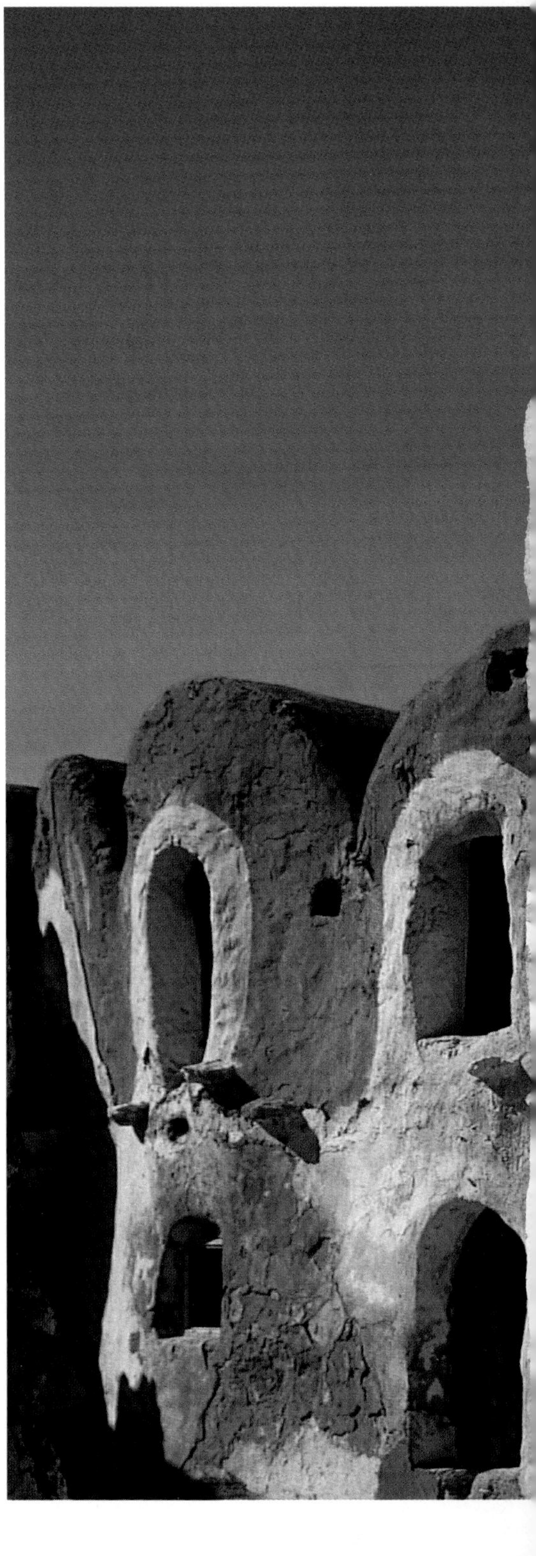

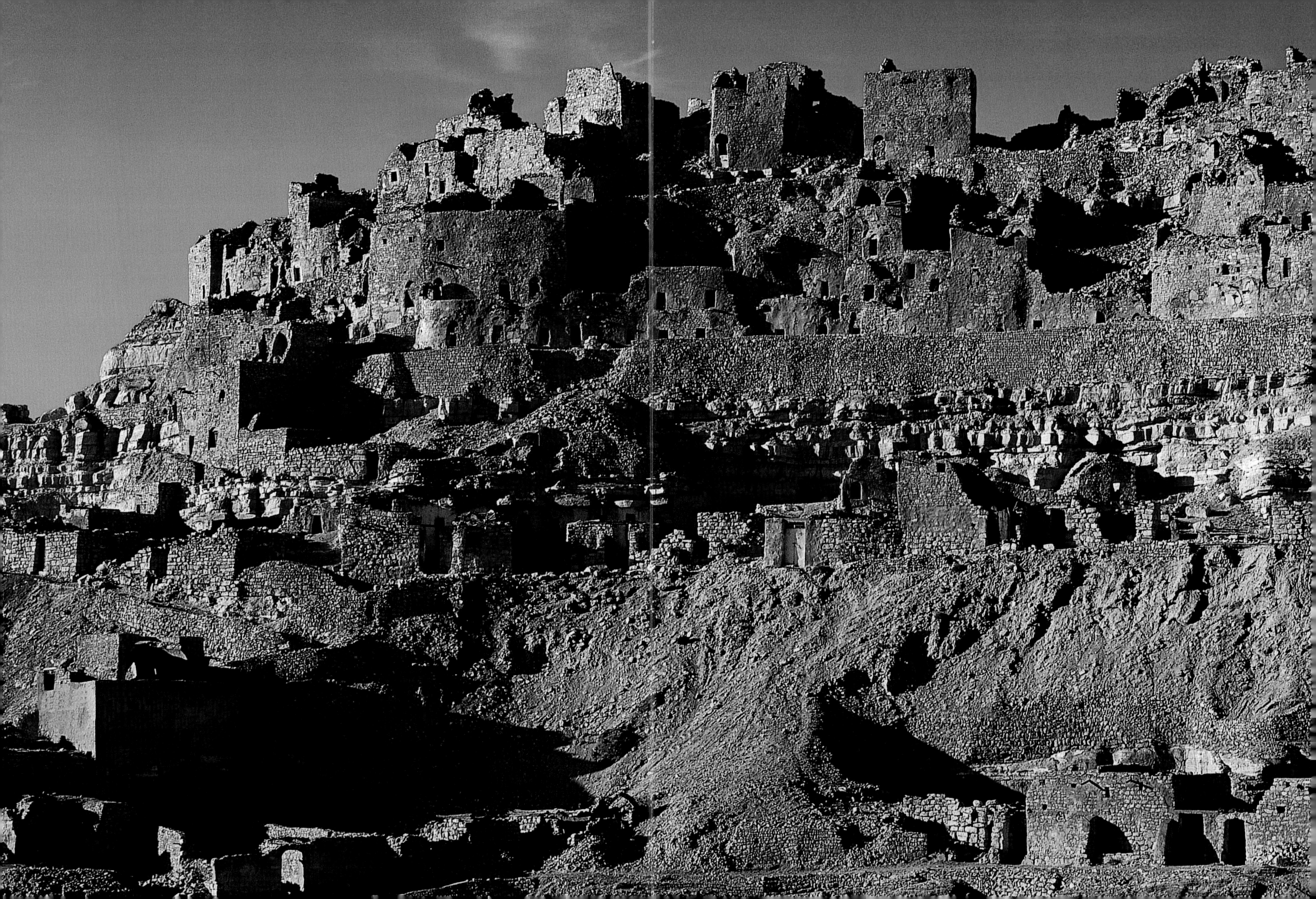

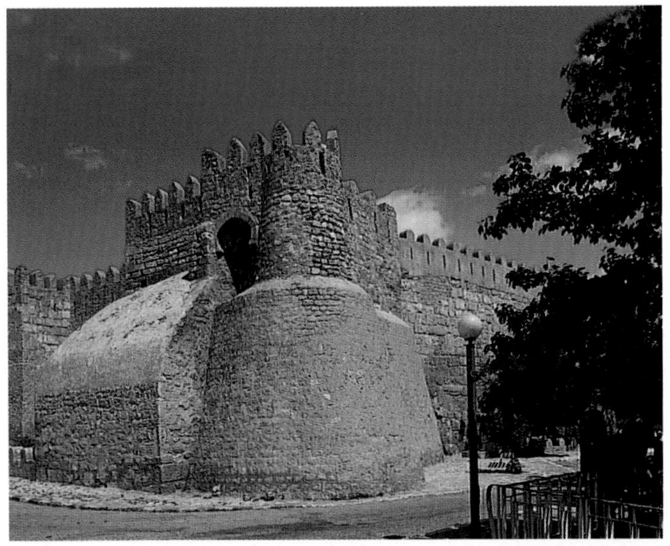

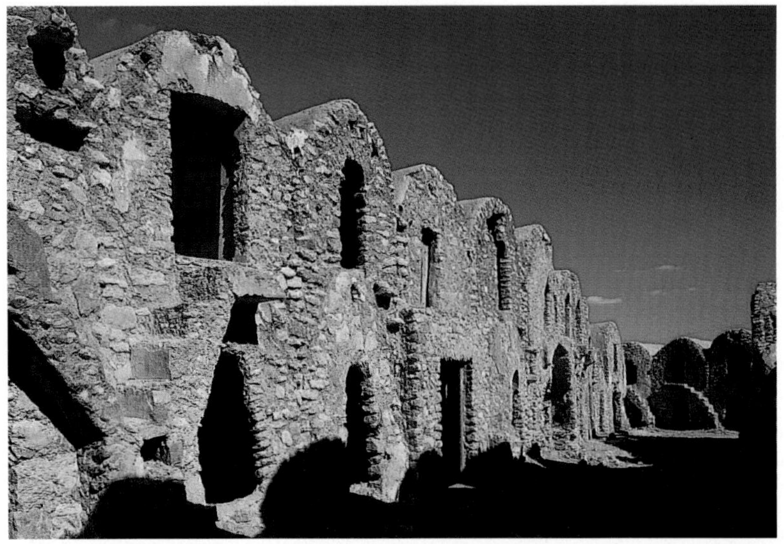

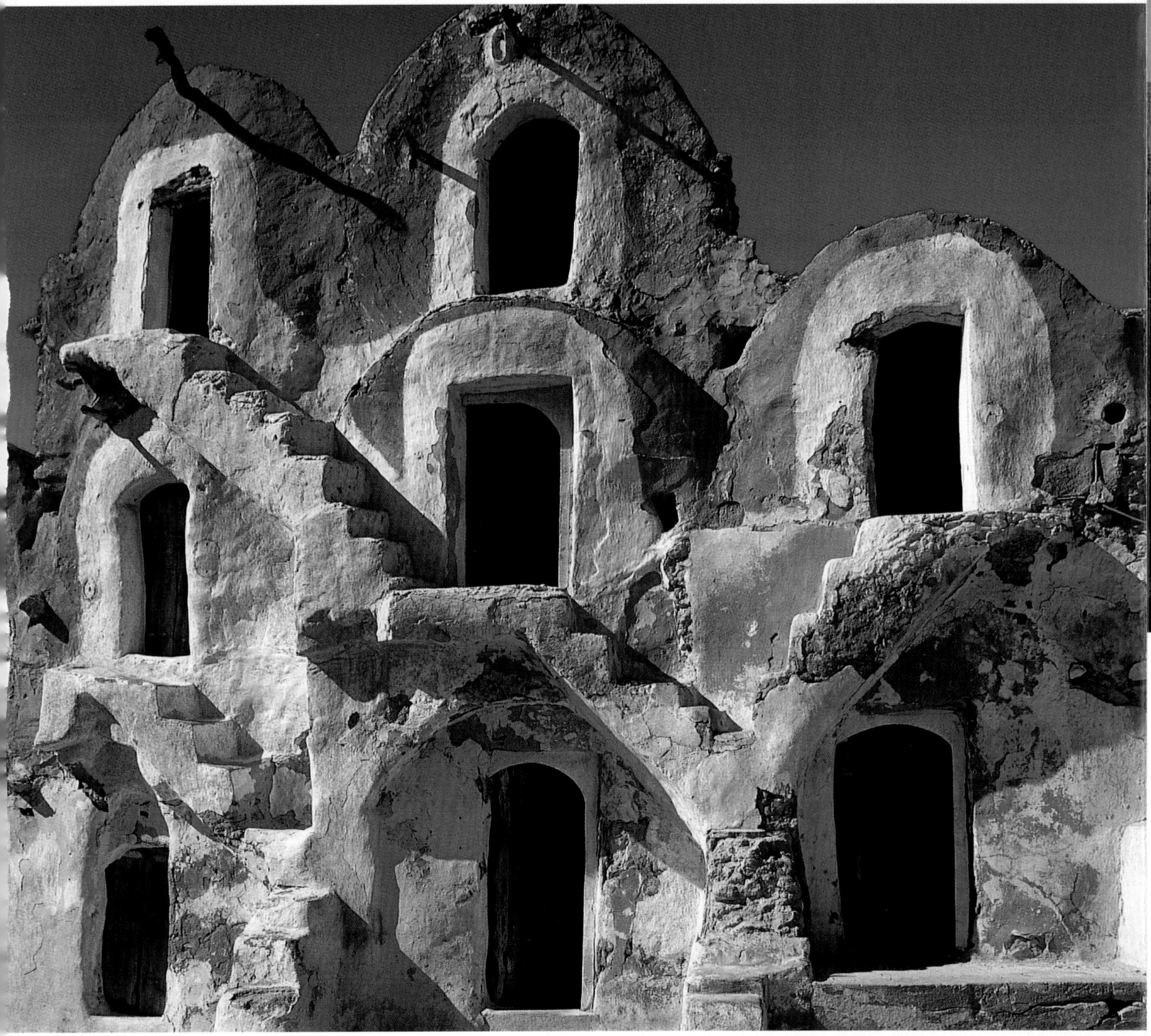

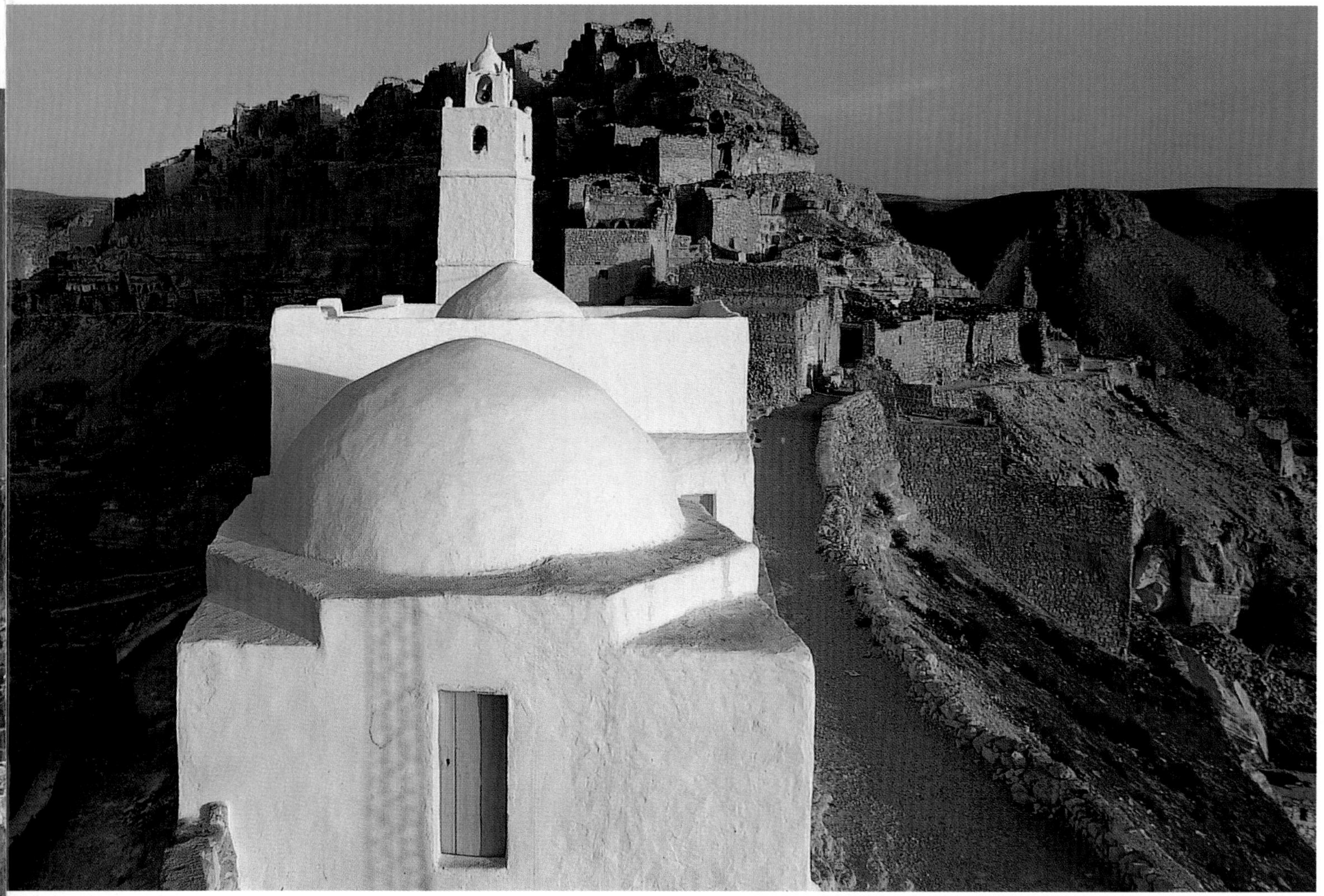

74 In the center of Chenini, a village crowning a high ridge of which it has the same scorched-earth color, a recently restored, bright white mosque stands out, from which a splendid panorama of the whole region can be enjoyed.

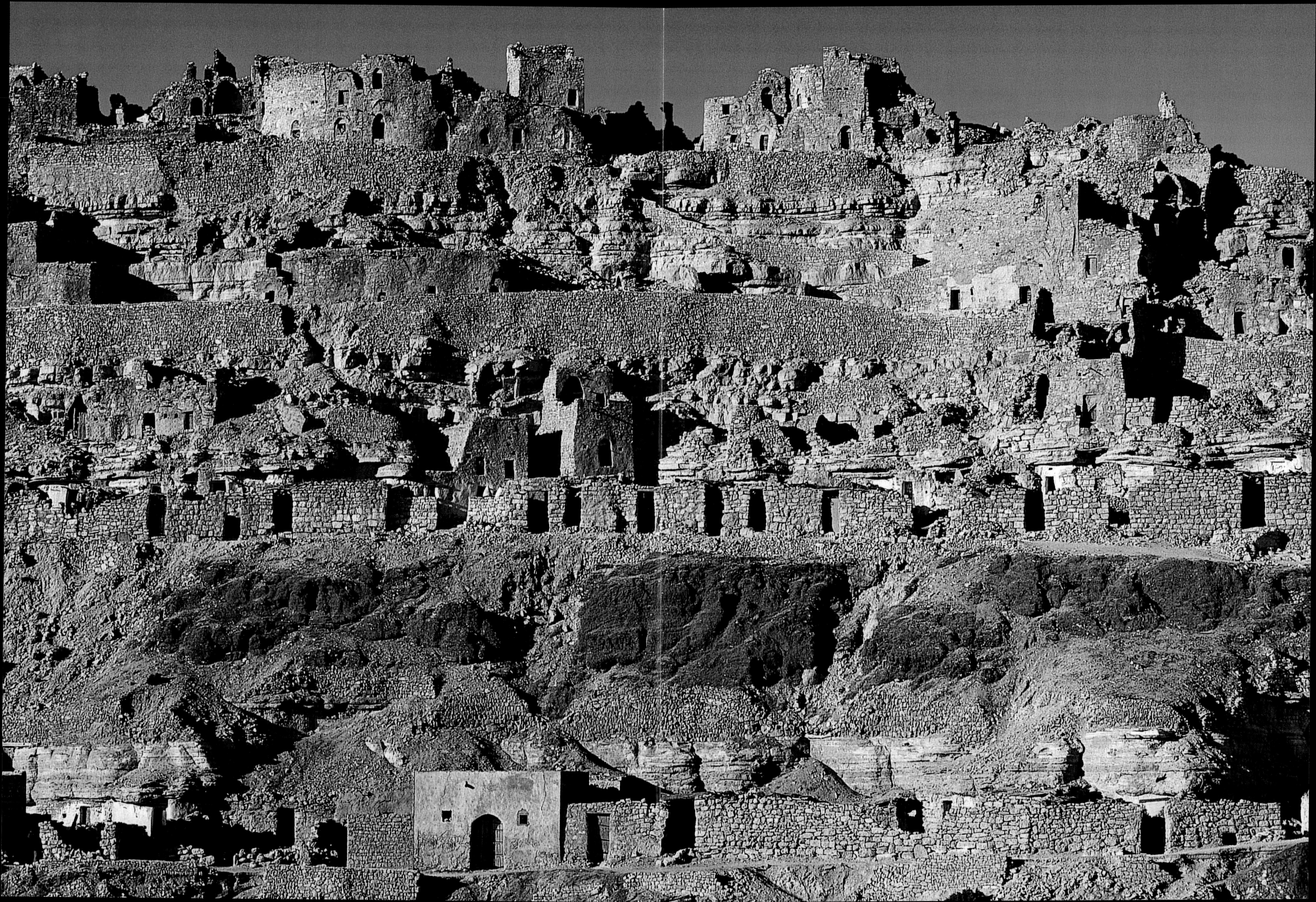

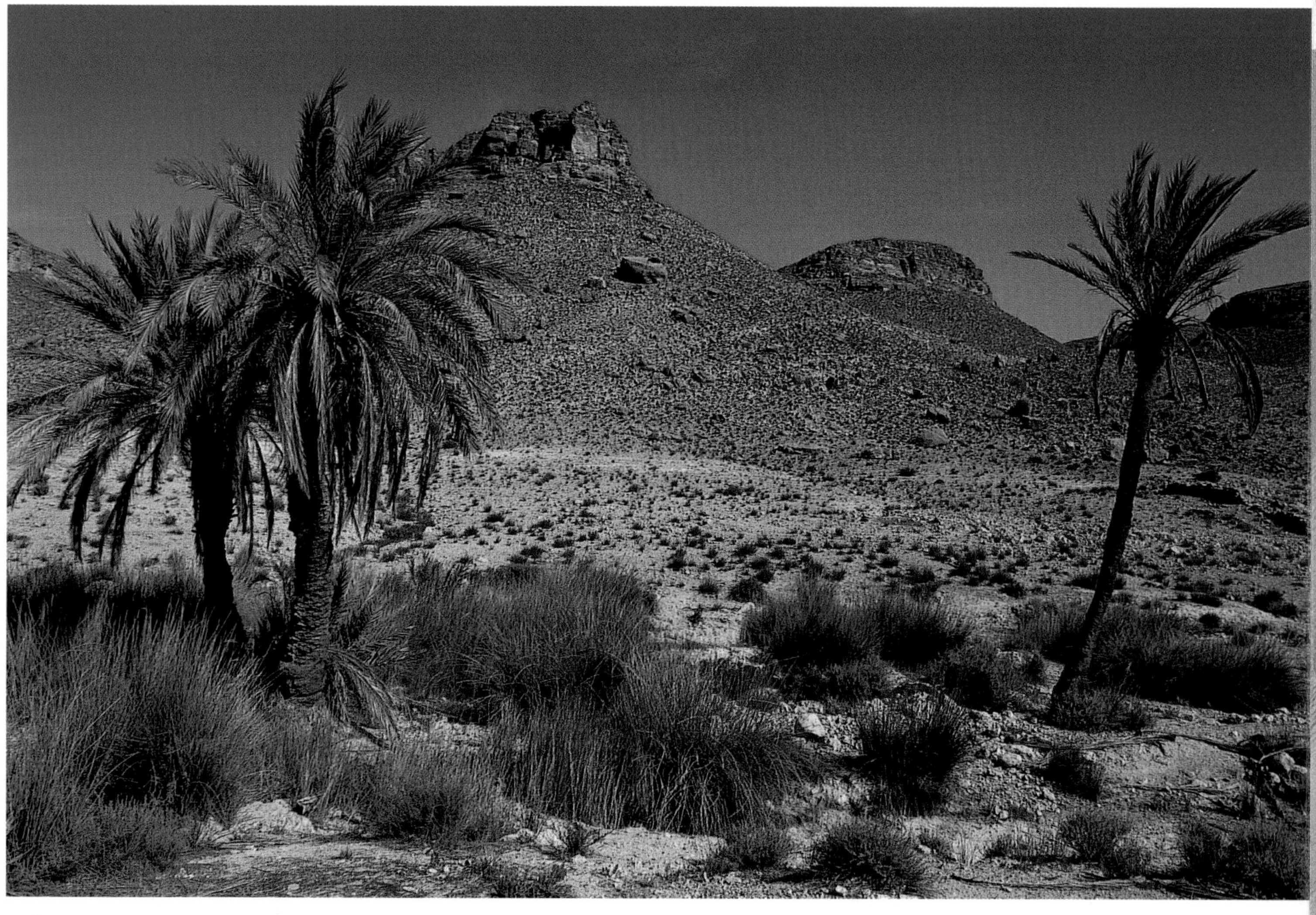

75-78 Chenini appears out of nothing in a spectacular way: given the nature of the land, the buildings, among them an oil mill and an old bakery, can only be noticed when they are seen from relatively close up.

79 The bleak landscape that surrounds Chenini, a very well-preserved Berber stronghold in southern Tunisia, perfectly hides the troglodytic dwellings.

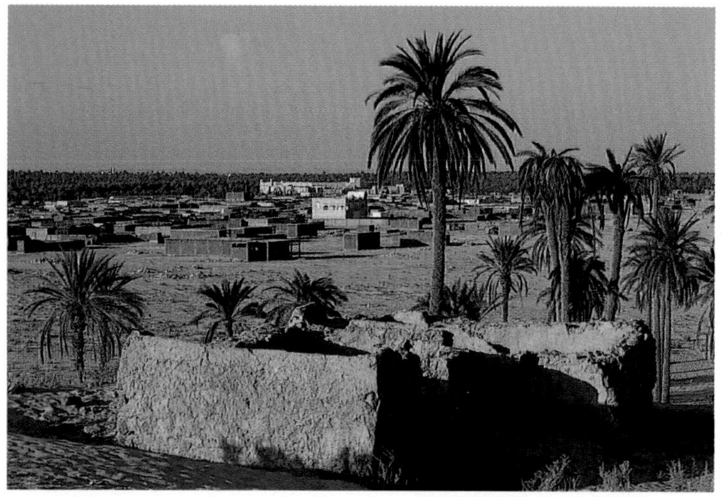

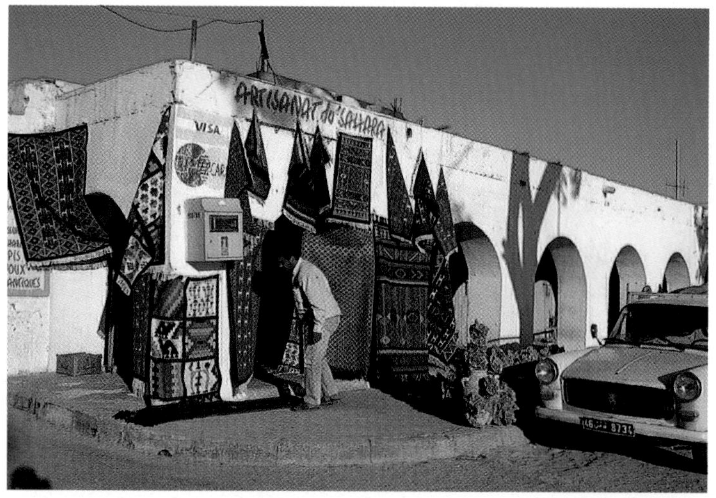

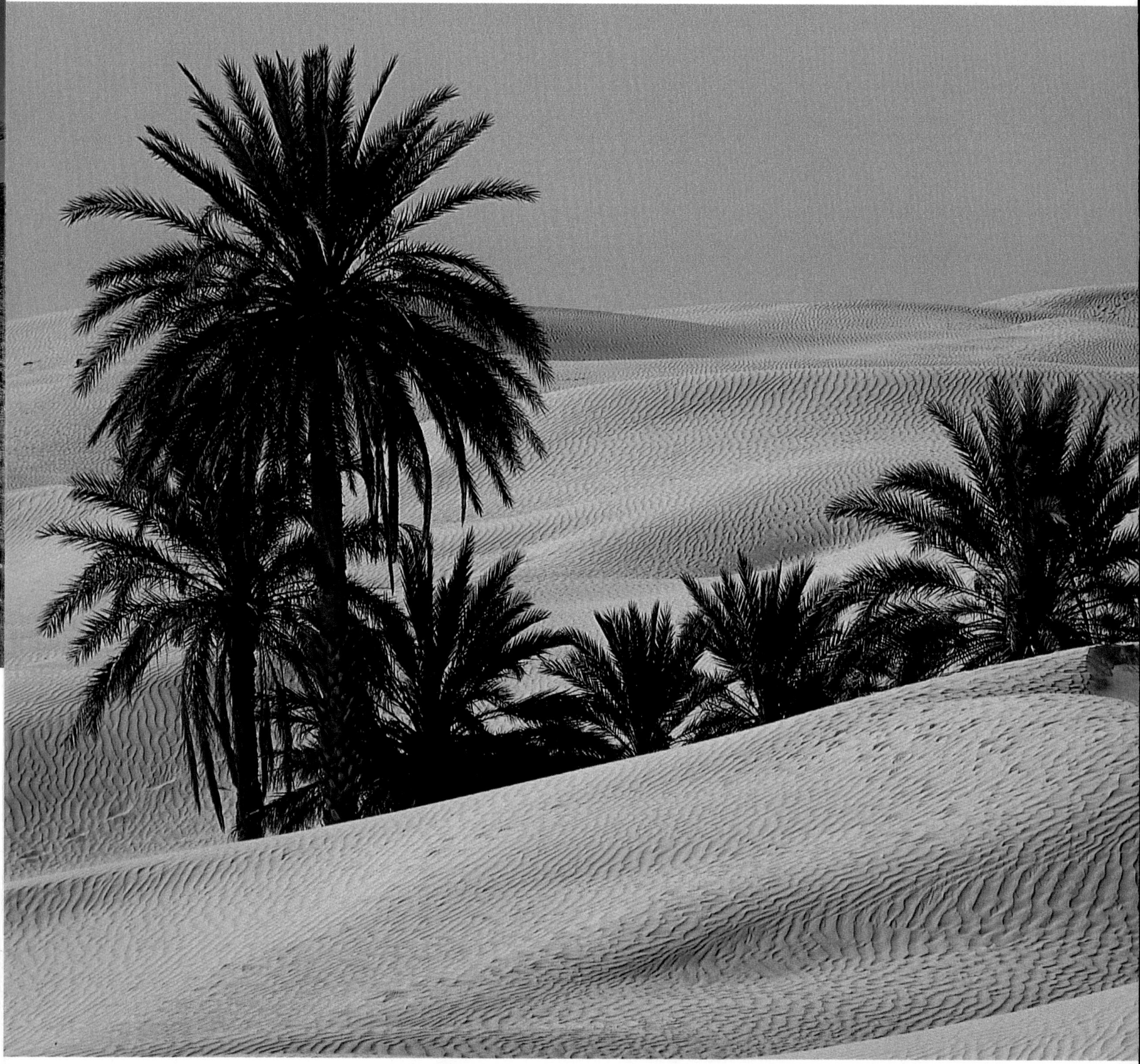

80 top left Around Douz Oasis, new cubic dwellings are materializing, often in the traditional ochre colors.

80 top right The artisan shops in Douz, specialized in jewelry, clothes and camel wool slippers, attract tourists that gather every year in this important center in southern Tunisia to attend the international festival of the Sahara.

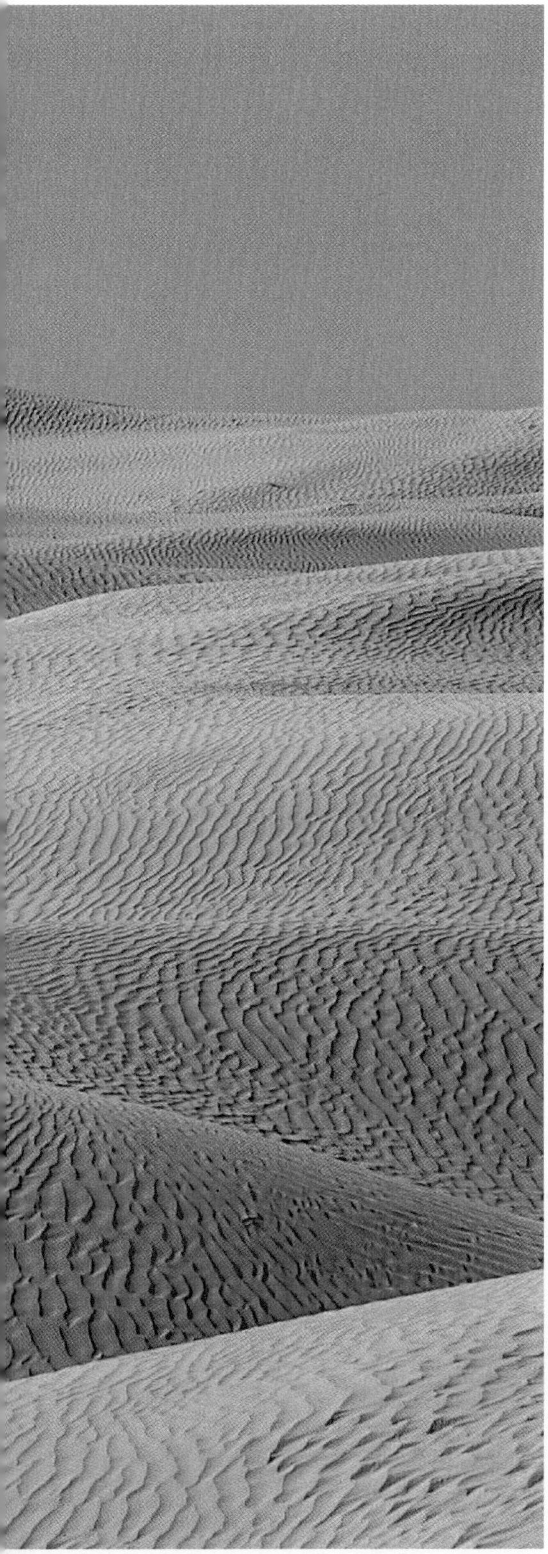

80-81 The sinuous movement of the changeable sand dunes characterizes the region of Douz, extended to the west of the Dahar Mountain chain and opening to the south onto the Grand Erg Oriental.

81 top The cemetery in Douz looks onto an infinite sea of dunes. From here on, nothing disturbs the silence of the desert.

81 center Douz is the best departure point for undertaking fascinating excursions in the desert, on the back of a camel or in a jeep.

81 bottom In the market of Douz, a multitude of people assembles since the region does not offer many other amenities. The city rose around a spring that the inhabitants of the city continue to care for with love, as did the M'Razig nomads six centuries ago.

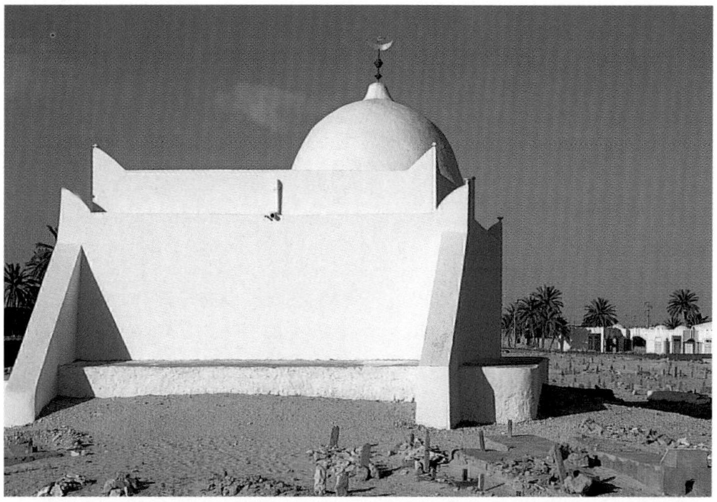

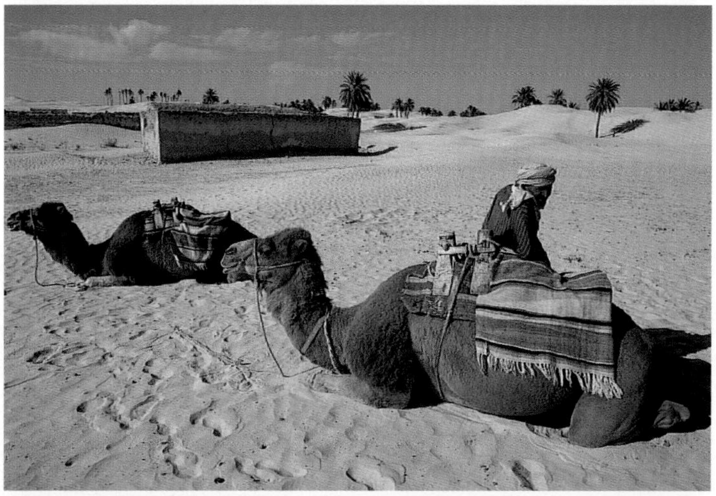

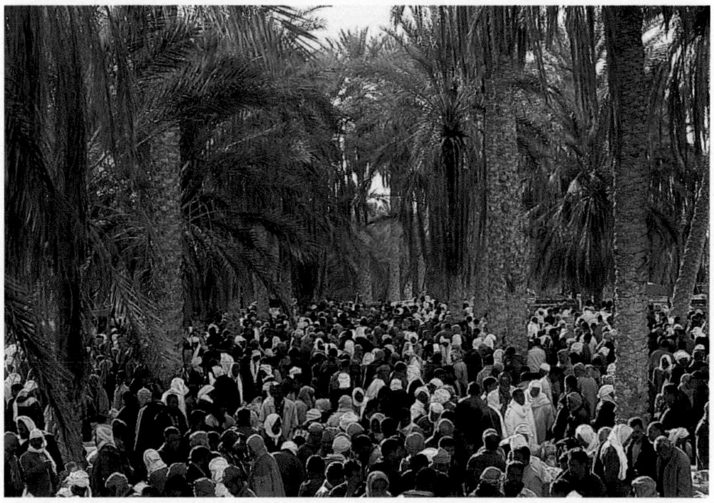

BUILDING BETWEEN THE DESERT AND THE SEA

82-83 Behind the dome of the Great Mosque extends the new part of Tunis. The capital, which looks onto a lagoon within its spacious gulf, occupies the lowlands and the low surrounding hills and is closely tied to the port of La Goulette.

83 top left The modern downtown area of Tunis has expanded along the sides of Avenue Habib Bourguiba that, once past Place de l'Indépendance, turns into Avenue de France and ends opposite the Port of France. This street axis connects the port to the medina.

83 top right The Port of France, the ancient Bab el-Bahr (gate of the sea) at the center of Place de la Victoire, constitutes the entrance through which the visitor enters the labyrinthine alleys of the medina, the old city.

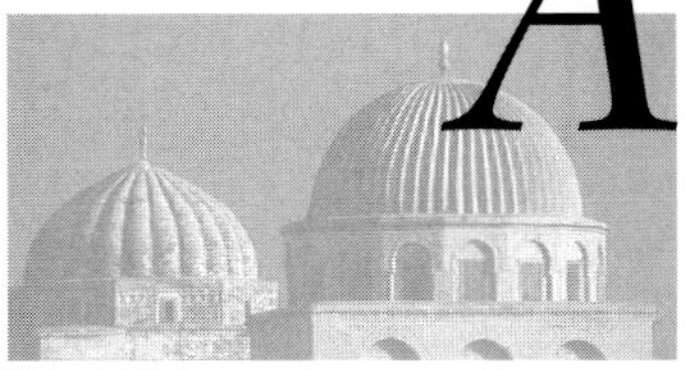

At the beginning, it did not seem so. No one, at the beginning of the fourth century BC—when Phoenician merchants founded it on a hill next to a lagoon—would have bet on the fact that Tunis would become the most important city, the capital of Tunisia. Carthage looked more promising, but then its demise is famous. Tunis, on the other hand, is still there.

International and cosmopolitan, it is a city with both an Arab and European soul. It is not only markets and mosques: there is also a noteworthy colonial neighborhood, which makes it possible to immediately recognize traces of Art Nouveau left by the French Protectorate, for example. A detail here, a balcony sculptured there, a painted front door, the beautiful sights of Tunis must be appreciated as if in a treasure hunt. However, the heart of everything is the *medina,* the old city that, among torturous alleys like the folds in a gown, hides the *souq,* the labyrinthine and clamorous weave of markets where every kind of product is sold, from gold to souvenirs to objects (sometimes even useful) for the home.

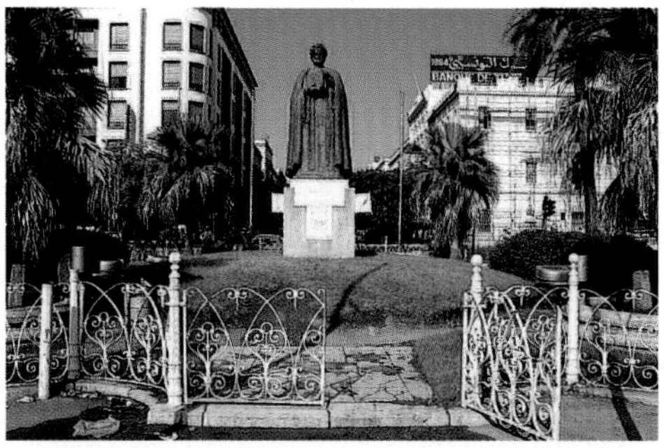

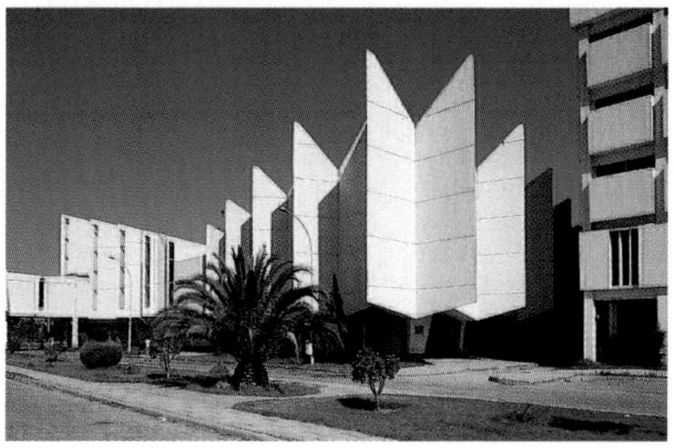

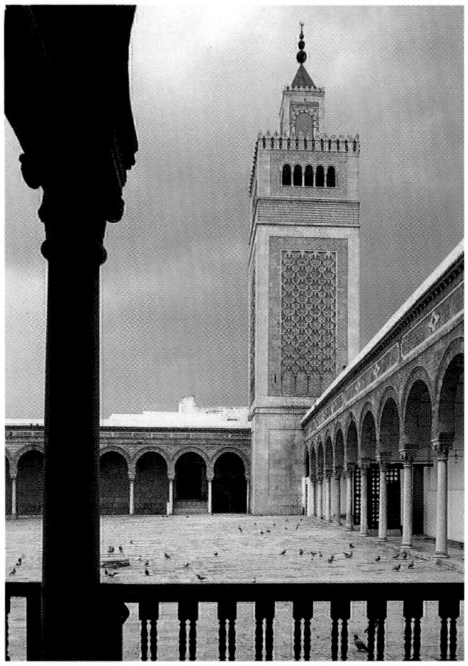

82 left The Great Mosque of Tunis, Jamaa ez-Zitouna, the 'mosque of the olive tree', was built in 732. The immense prayer room contains five naves with ten aisles, from the ceilings of which hang big lamps of Murano glass.

82 top right The monument in Place de l'Indépendance is dedicated to the Bey of Tunis, the sovereign of the city in the past. The title is Turkish and, originally, indicated the commander of the land troops.

82 bottom right The physics department of the University of Tunis, with its avant-garde architecture, testifies to the recent urban development of the city.

The old city is accessible via the French Gate, the old Bab el-Bahr, at the center of the Place de la Victoire (Victory Square). Once past the square, right away there is a pandemonium of languages, a cornucopia of objects, a more or less orderly throng. There is no need to fear getting lost for there is always an exit close at hand, but one certainly feels like a foreigner here.

Then the Great Mosque appears, the largest sanctuary in the capital, founded by an Umayyad governor in 732.

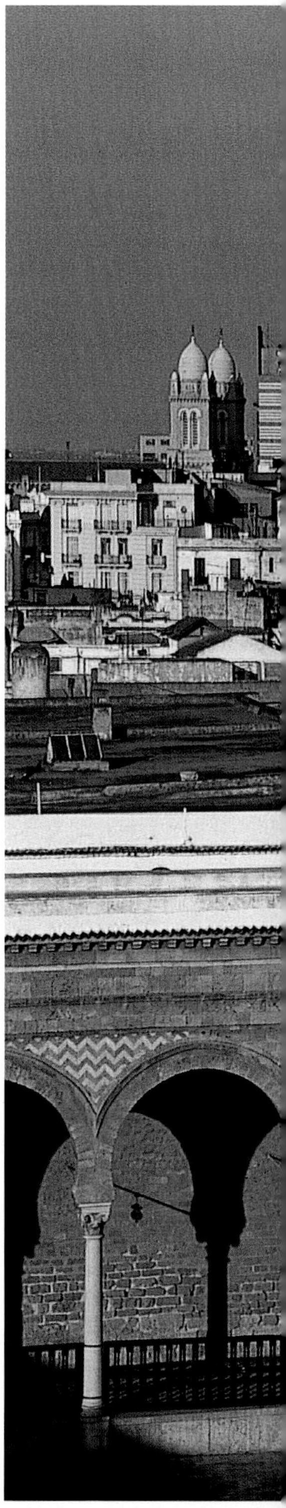

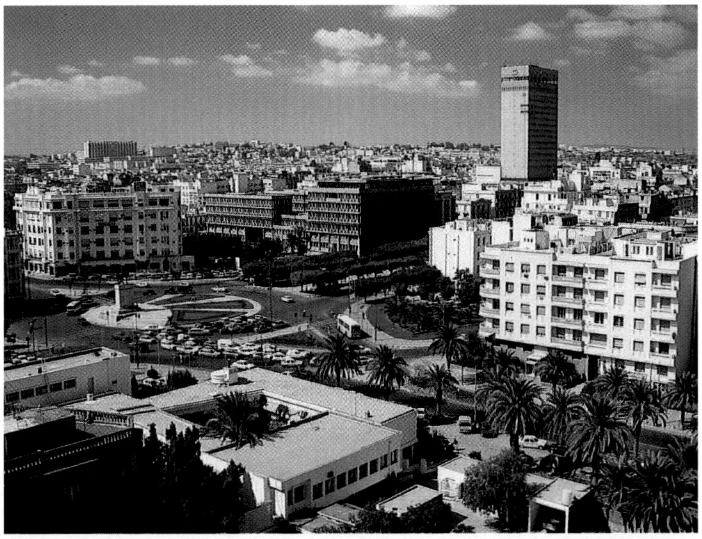

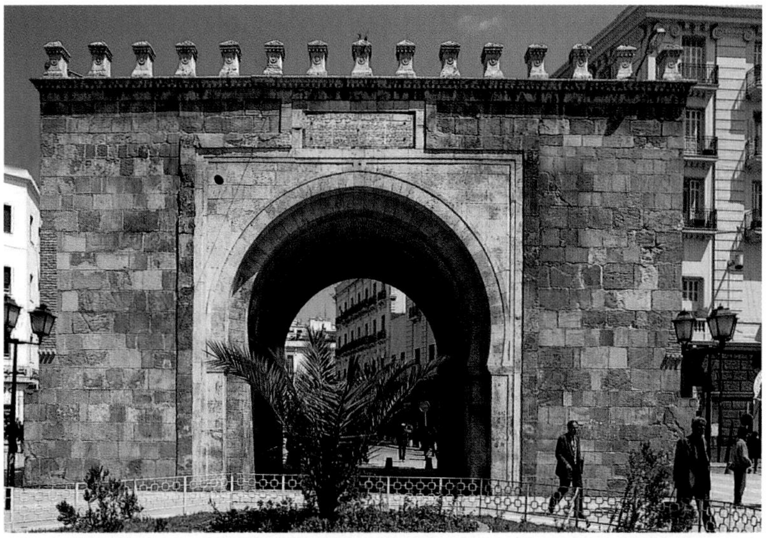

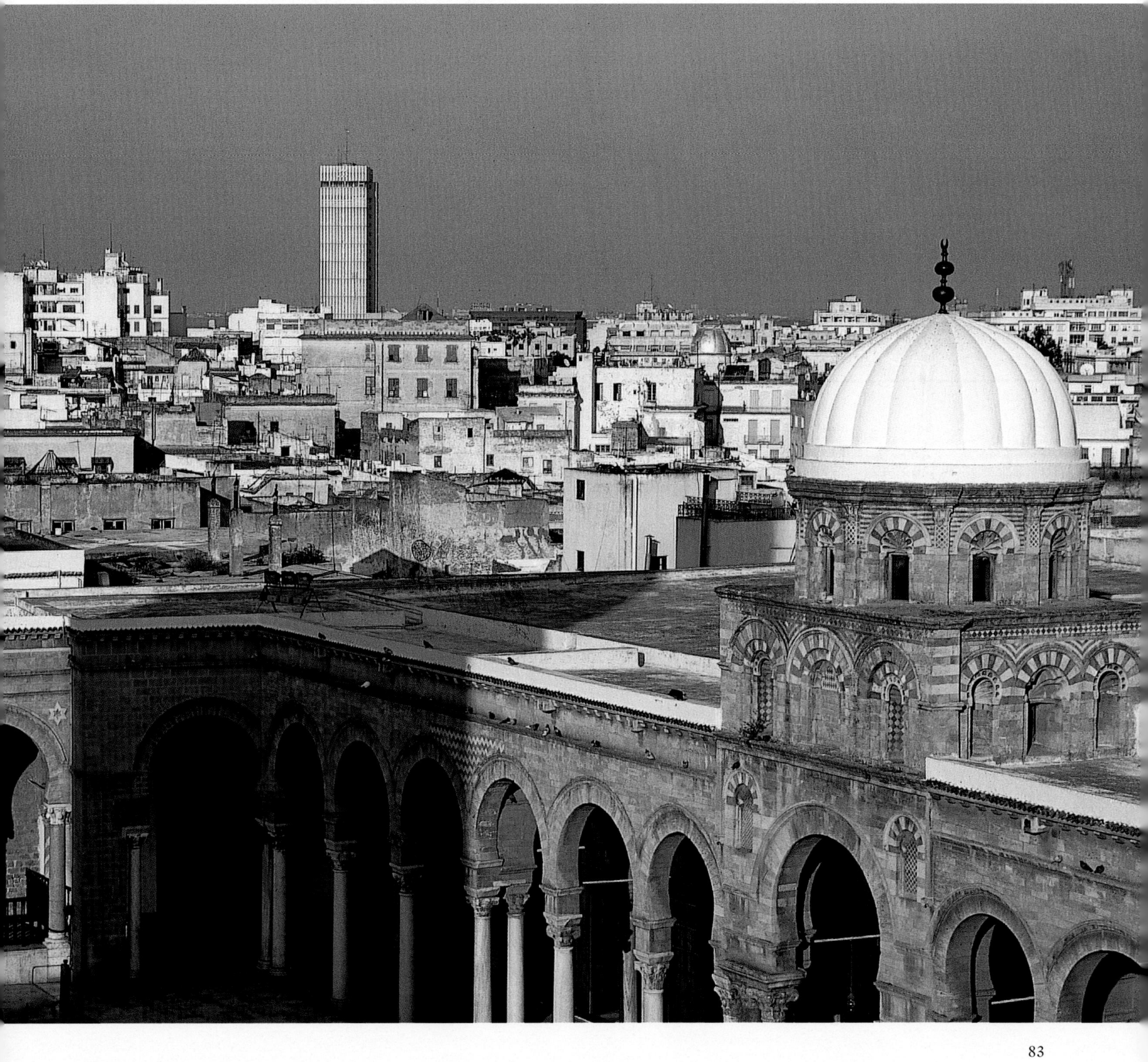

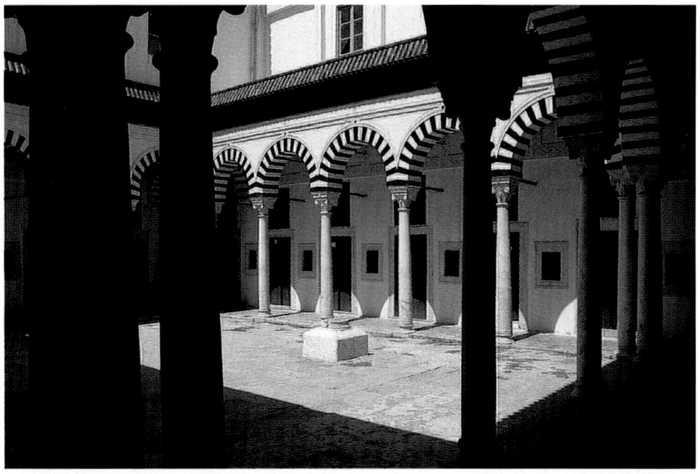

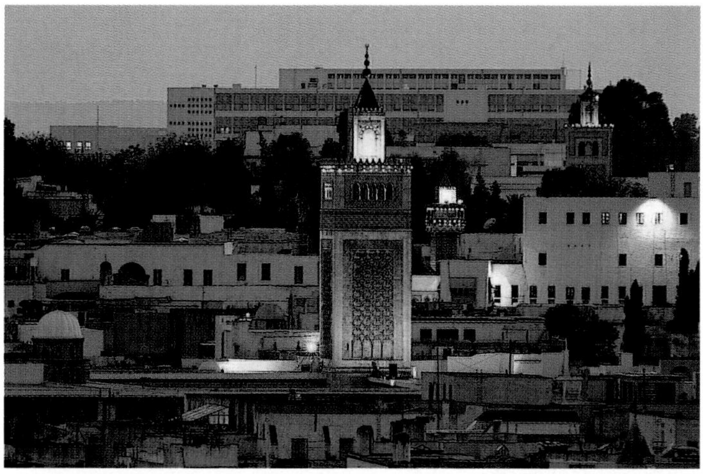

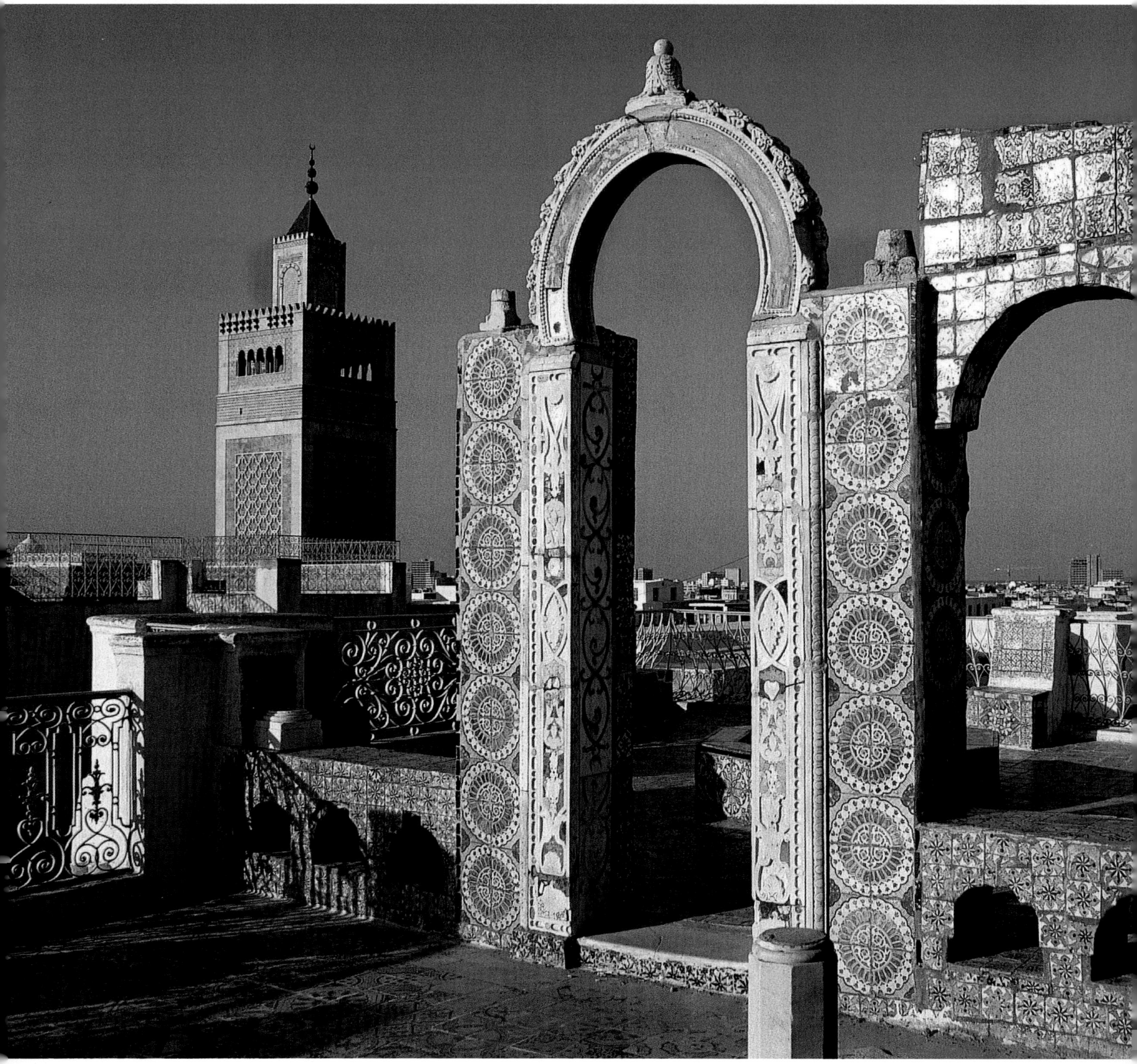

84 top left Often the old house of the medina of Tunis enclose beautiful porticoed courtyards from which the rooms are accessed. All the dwellings of a certain level had a well and a cistern, which assured drinkable water reserves for domestic purposes.

84 top right In this nighttime view of the medina, the minaret of the Great Mosque is still a main player. Generally, Tunisian minarets feature Almohad architecture, in a parallelepiped shape, or Hafsid, hence built on an octagonal layout.

84-85 The Palais d'Orient in Tunis is an ancient building in the wool-dying souq, now converted into a bazaar for selling carpets. From its terrace, among beautiful, colorful majolica tiles dating back to the fifteenth century, the whole medina can be admired, dominated by the minaret of the Great Mosque.

85 left The shops of the jewelry souq display prevalently gold pieces, while stones are not very numerous. This derives from the fact that in Tunisia the weight of jewels (often given in dowries) is of primary importance in determining their worth.

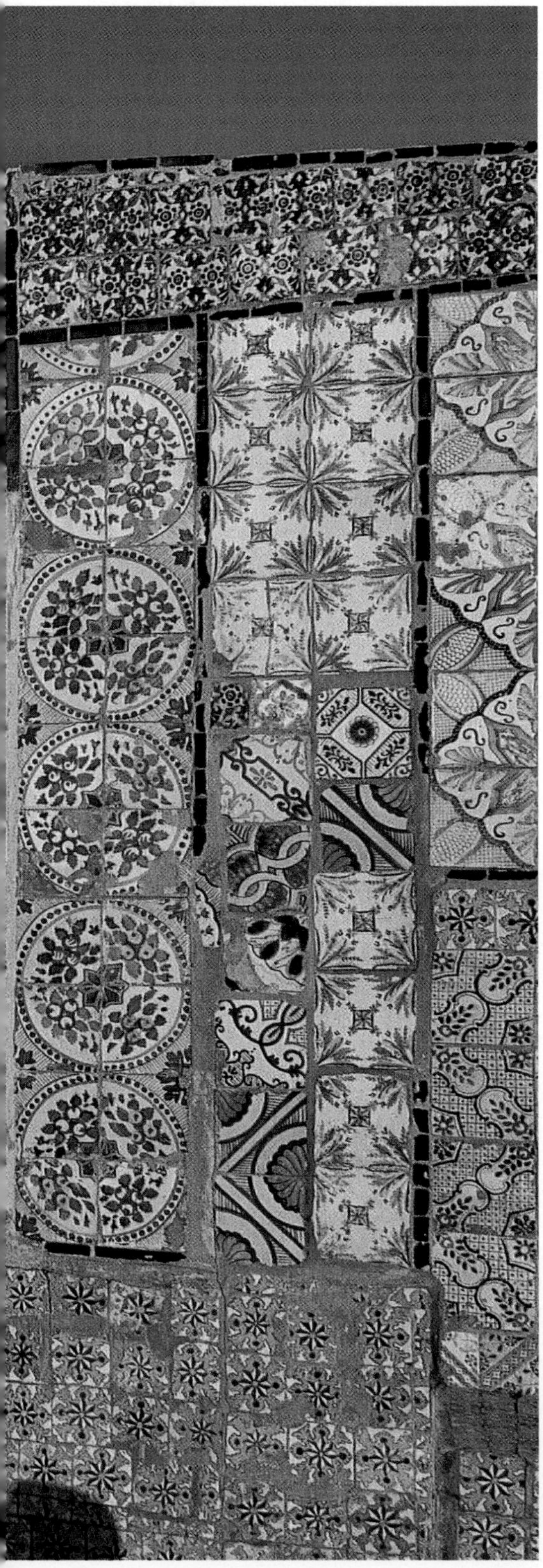

Continuing on, one comes across the el-Attarine Souq, the perfume market, and then the Souq des Etoffes, the cotton market and the el-Kouafi, where they dye above all wool. The Palais d'Orient, a big carpet bazaar, is found here at number 58. From its terrace (one can enter freely), decorated with lovely multicolored majolica tiles from the fifteenth century, one can enjoy a fantastic panorama of the city. The list would go on and on, but the best thing to explore is without doubt the souqs. Tunis is basically a city for living, walking along the very new boulevards, in

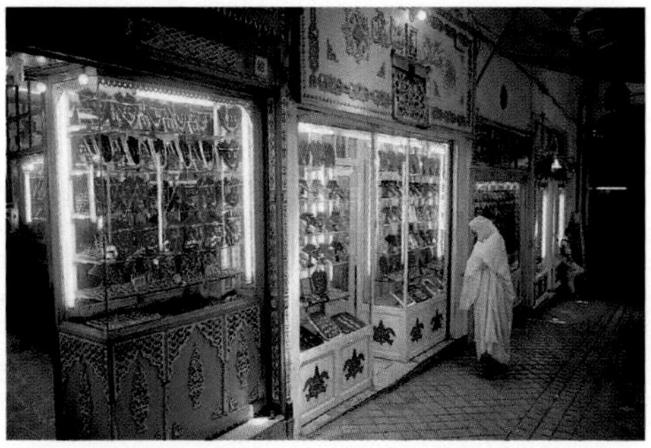

the park or among the ancient mosques, or sitting at the cafés of La Goulette, the civic port and lively, fashionable tourist center.

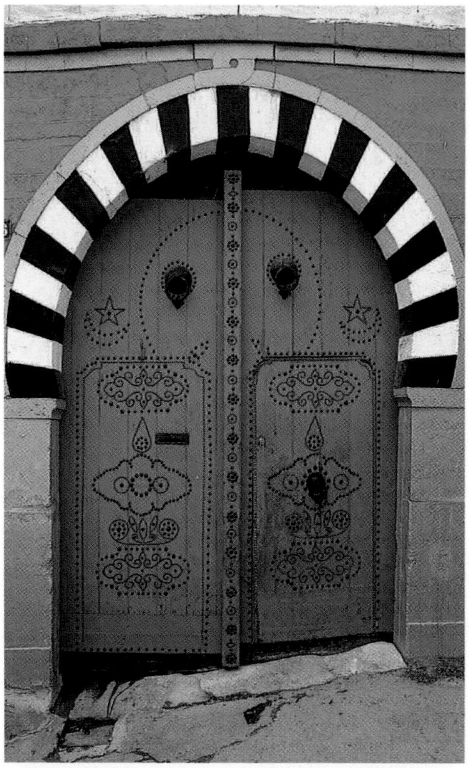

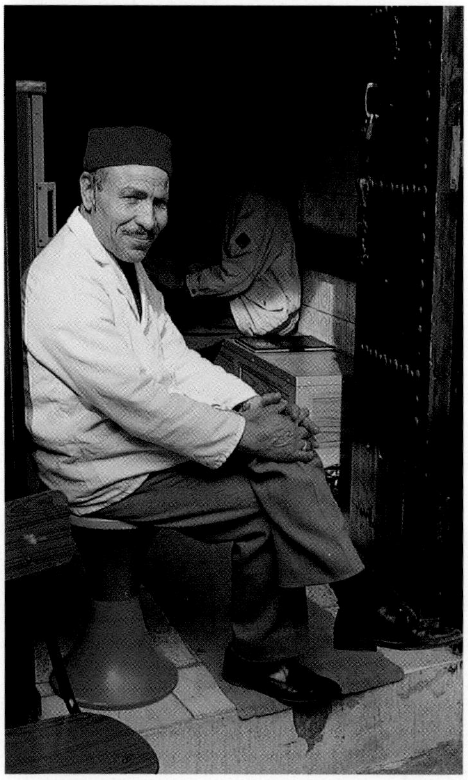

85 top right A typical element in the architecture of the whole country, this gateway in the medina of Tunis features a horseshoe arch, with piers set into a rectangular frame. On the double doors a decoration of nails used in the eighteenth century sticks out.

85 bottom right A barber in the old city waits for clients in the doorway. Taking the Rue des Tamis, one reaches the zone of the souqs, split up according to guilds and arranged around the area in which stands the Great Mosque.

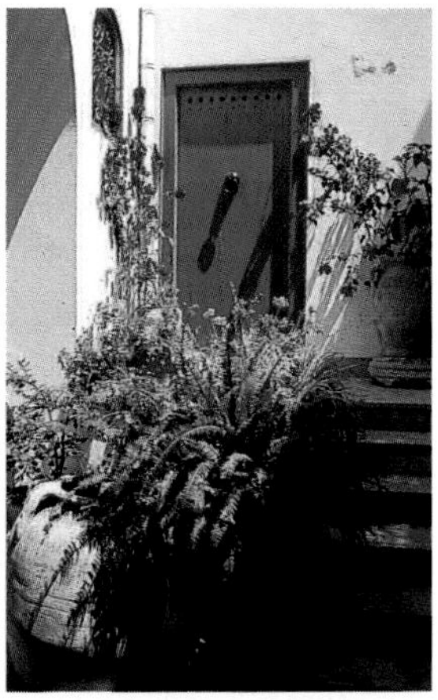
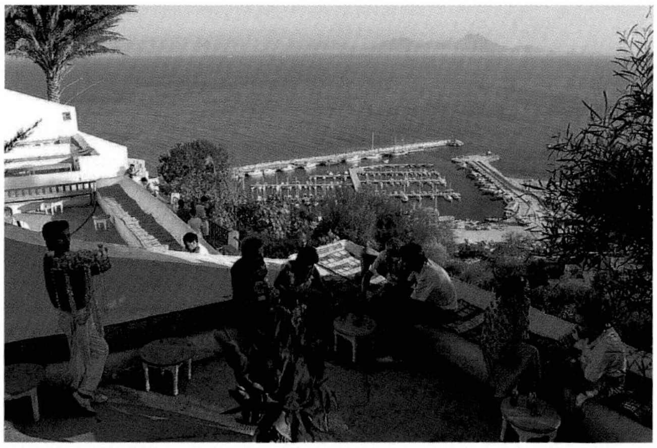
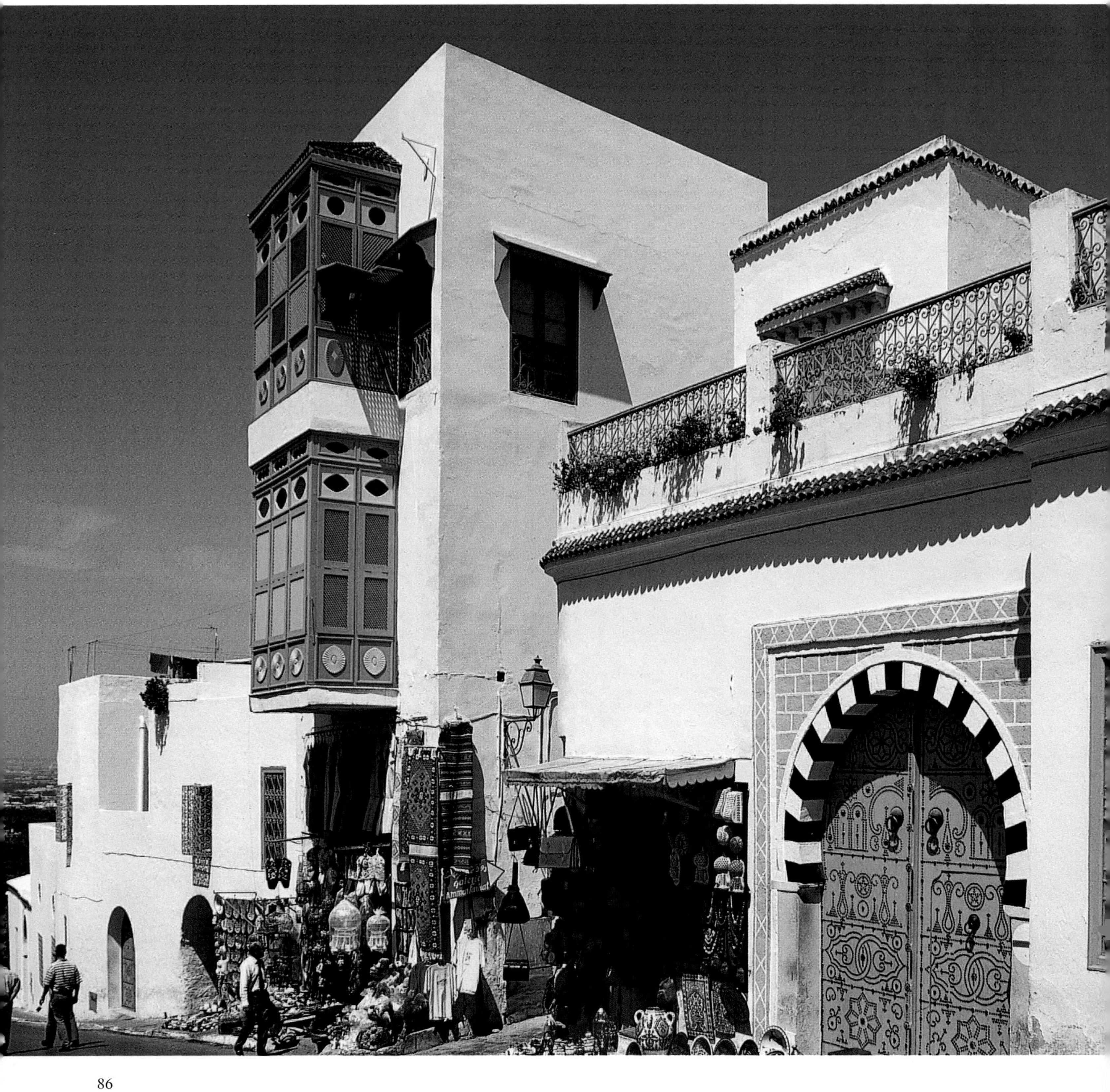

86 top left The doors of houses painted in this particular shade of blue comprise one of the distinctive tracts of Sidi Bou Said, a village that for five centuries represented a preferred destination for disciples of Maghrebian Sufism and that in the twentieth century was dedicated to tourism.

86 top right The tourist port is one of the main attractions of Sidi Bou Said. When swimming in the sea first became popular, over a century ago, special cabins were built here, in which the floors were equipped with openings that allowed women to enter the water discreetly.

86-87 A few miles from the capital, Sidi Bou Said is a quiet and extremely picturesque place. Founded by Abou Said, a good Muslim, it is a typical marabout *village (founded by a religious leader) that has survived the centuries and the advance of mass tourism.*

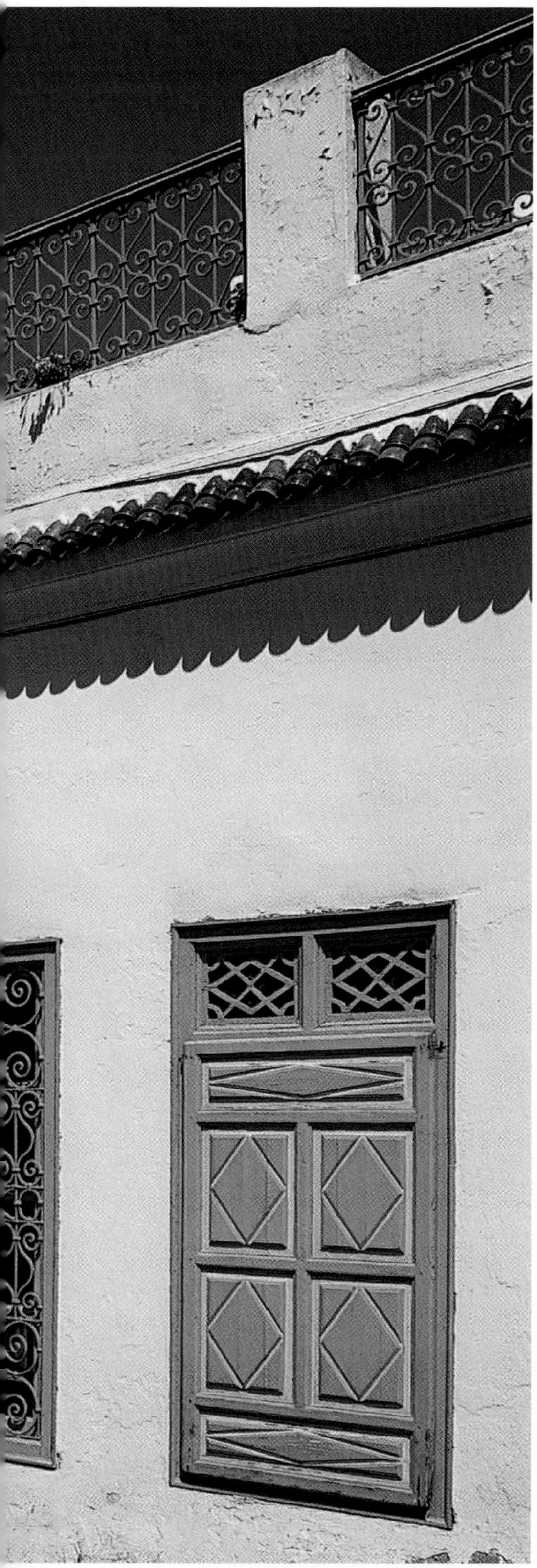

If one wants to take an excursion into the areas surrounding the capital, the ideal place is Sidi-Bou-Said. Delicious is the only adjective to best describe this old village, built in such a way as to survey the sea from the slopes of Mount Manar. At the top of this mountain, where a lighthouse now stands, the Arabs built a fortified monastery, and the little town that grew around it owes its name to the wise man that made it a center for the diffusion of Sufism at the beginning of the thirteenth century. Afterwards, officials, governors and notables turned it into a resort area and in 1915 a government decree approved its reconstruction and restoration. It is now a fashion center frequented by artists, where the beautiful pristine architecture is admired, peppered with the deep blue of the elaborate rounded lattices covering the windows or of the front doors styled with iron studs. Color is the very essence of this place. The daily rite here is sipping a mint tea at the Café des Nattes on the main street: it is unclear which is better, the picturesque atmosphere inside or the view enjoyed from the tables outside.

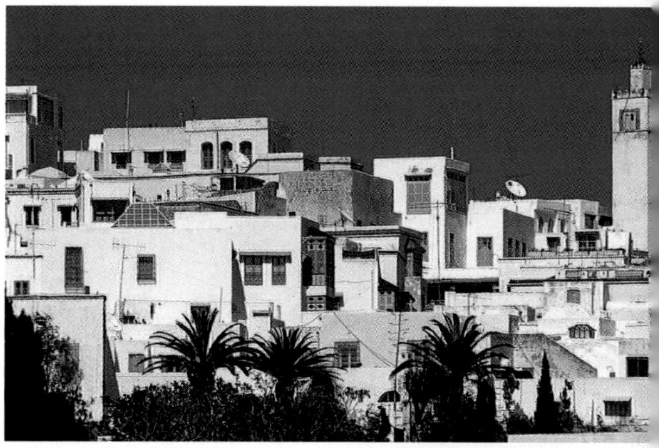

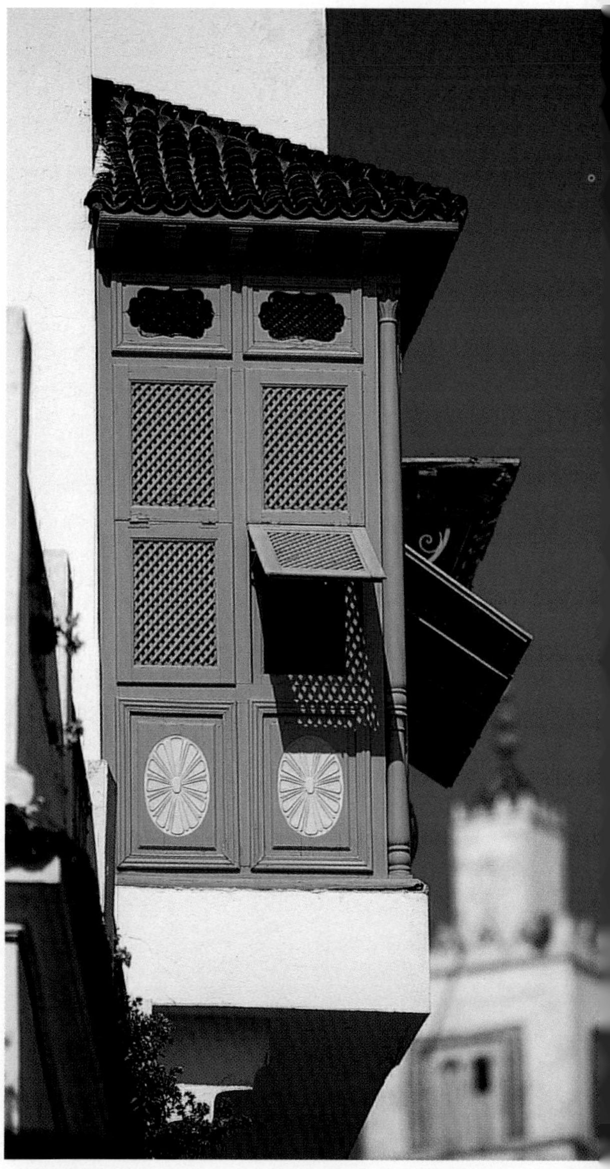

87 top Numbering among the many artists that have stayed in Sidi Bou Said, André Gide and Paul Klee were two of the most enthusiastic. The painter described the evocative village with these words, 'the back of a mountain on which can be seen pop up, with a strict rhythm, the white forms of the houses'.

87 bottom The shutters of the windows, proper architectural elements that make this fascinating place unique, are typical of Sidi Bou Said. The blinding white of the houses and the blue of the grates and front doors, sometimes outlined with a touch of ochre, have always attracted artists from around the world.

88 top In the center of Bizerte, far from the vacationing crowds, the echo of foreign dominations, which have followed one after the other without end since the times of the Greeks from Sicily, is still perceivable in the medina and the fourteenth-century Fort of Spain.

88 center The port of Bizerte has an ancient history, even if the city has not preserved much evidence of its remote past. Established as a Phoenician stopover point, it was conquered by the Syracusians in 310 BC and in the end became the Roman colony of Hippo Diarrhytus.

88 bottom In Bizerte, glimpses full of the characteristic appeal of the Maghreb are not lacking. Long neglected by tourism, in recent years it has undergone a notable boost in this sector: today it is a fashionable city and a well-equipped seaside resort.

88-89 Tabarka, once the Punic city Thabraca, was famous in Roman times for the exportation of lumber from the Kroumirie, wheat and marble. Another important source of income—still profited from today—was red coral, typical of the zone.

89 top left The port of Bizerte often accommodates the pleasure boats of the capital's inhabitants, one of the largest group of visitors to the place.

89 top right The port of Tabarka, settled comfortably in a bay northwest of Tunis, is dominated by a medieval fort, built by Genoese coral merchants.

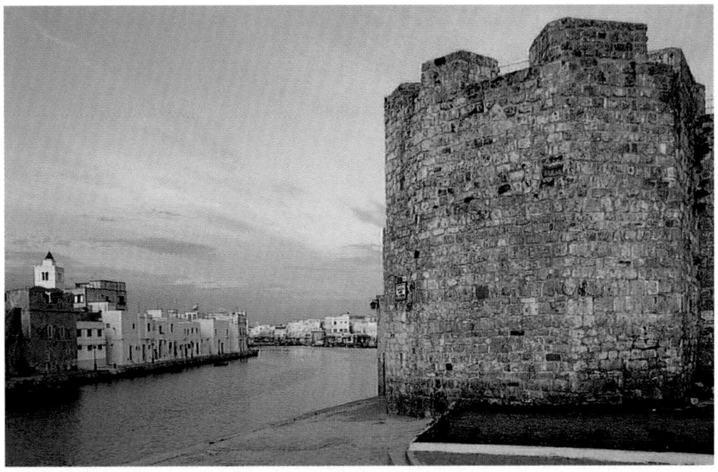

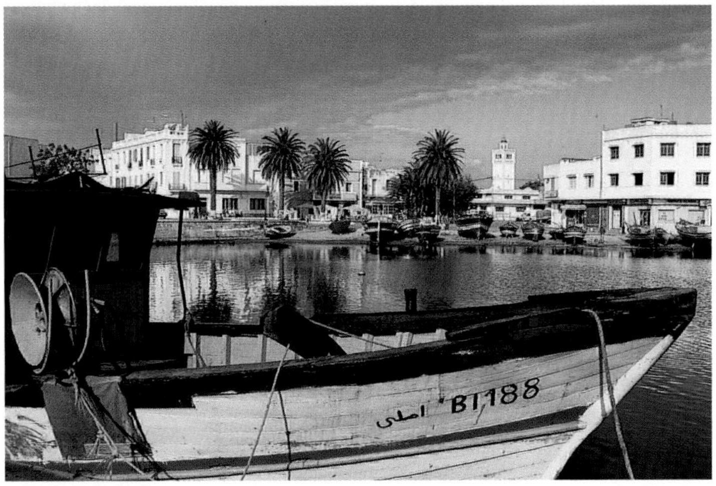

BI 188

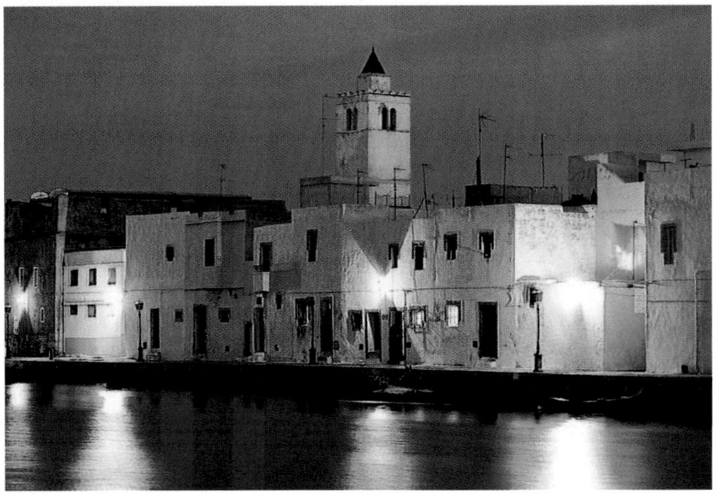

The northern coast is just a quick jump to the west, where Tabarka, settled comfortably at the center of its bay and framed by the spurs of the nearby mountains, and Bizerte, once targeted by the Europeans who saw it as a bridgehead against Berber pirates, stand.

In Roman times, Thabraca, the Punic name for Tabarka, exported wood from the Kroumirie, grain from the plains and marble from the quarries throughout the Mediterranean. From the sea they drew coral, which was an ever-greater source of income for its inhabitants, just like the Genoese, who in the fourteenth century—after obtaining a monopoly over the selling of the 'red gold'—built a fort that dominates the city center. Now the city is an active township, where it is easy to acquire hand-made products of a high quality, above all in wood, as well as jewelry.

Bizerte, on the other hand, is more society-minded, even if it has stayed a quiet coastal city, with the white beaches well equipped for even the most demanding tourists. In the city center, far from the beach umbrellas, the medina, the Spanish Fort, the *kasba* (the citadel) and the old marina still give echoes of foreign dominions, which have followed one other without rest since the times of the Greeks from Sicily. The Carthaginians, Romans, Arabs, who built palaces and gardens, and even Carlos V, who in 1535 occupied the harbor, have also been here. It was later occupied by the French and the Germans and restored to the Tunisians only on 15 October 1963 with their independence.

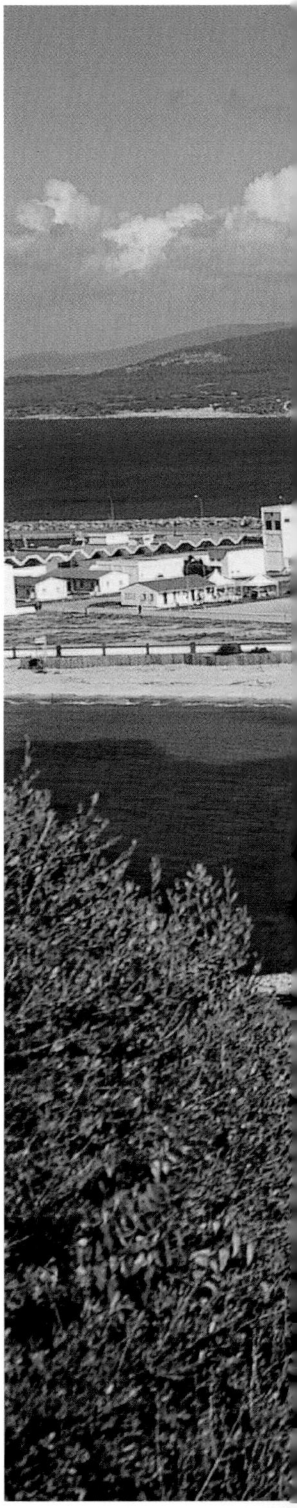

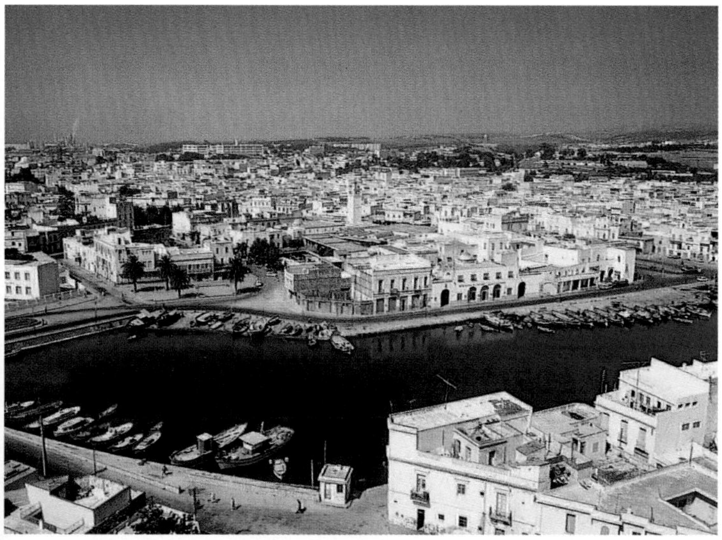

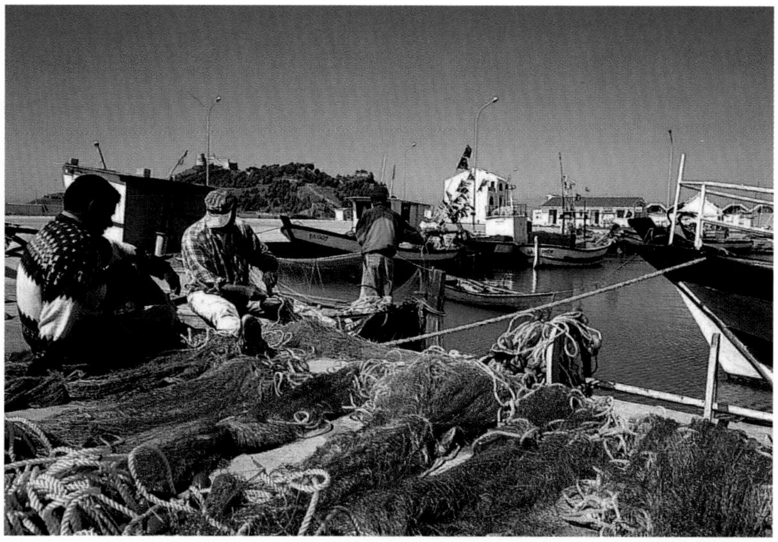

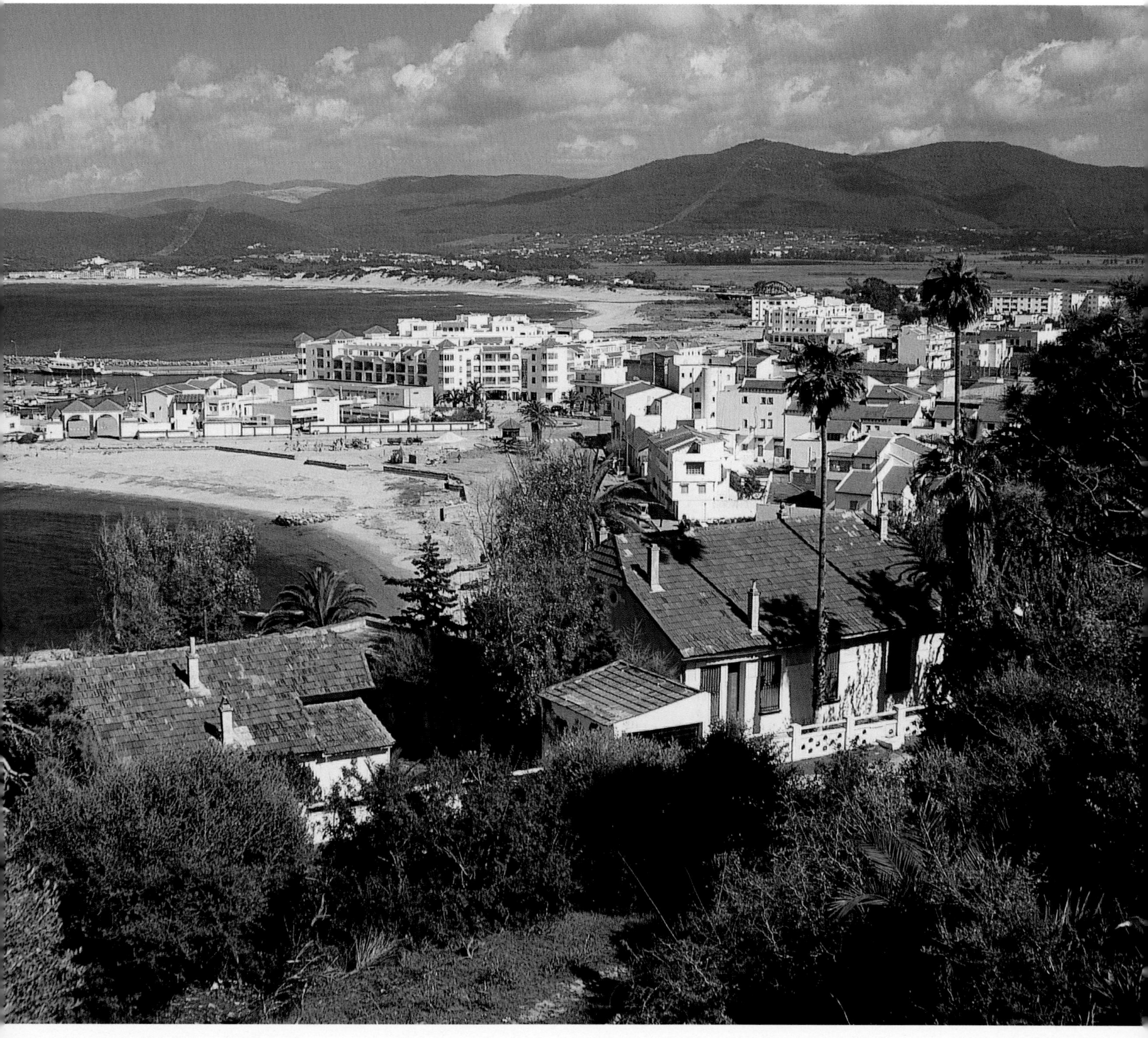

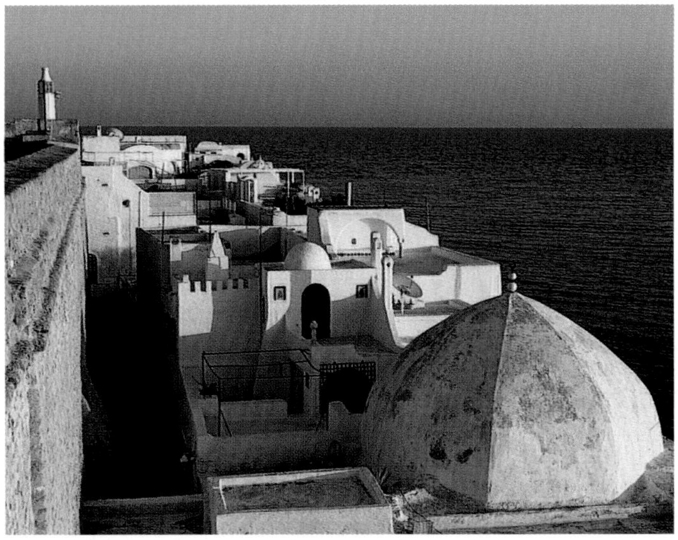

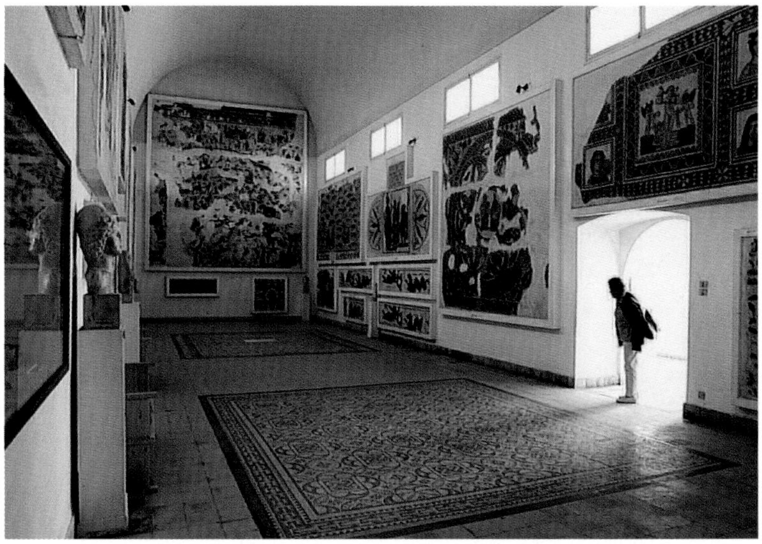

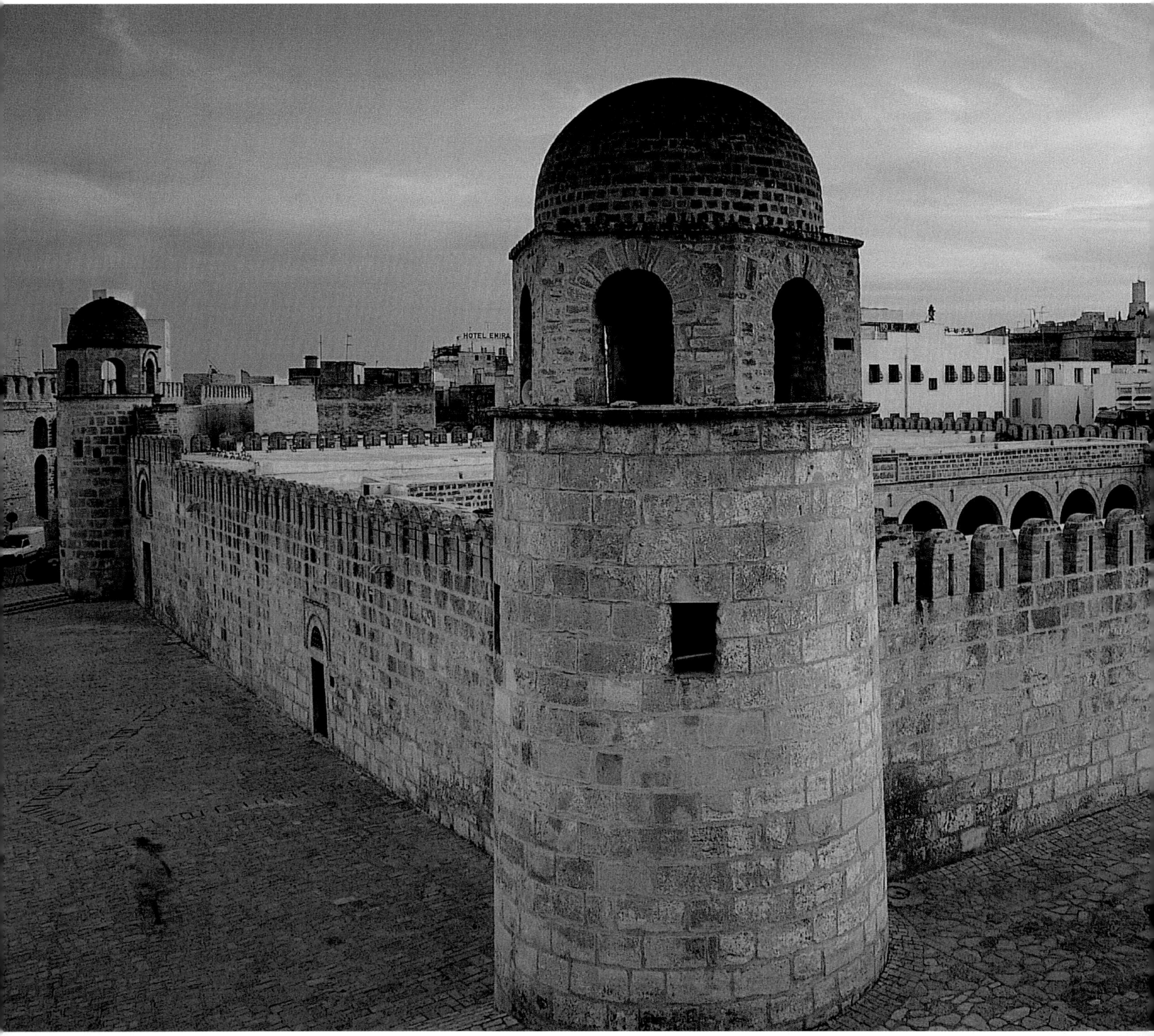
HOTEL EMIRA

90 top left The citadel of Hammamet is surrounded by imposing walls that date back to the fifteenth century. From above them, a beautiful panorama over the sea, the terraces of the surrounding houses and the thousands of bazaars that populate the old part of the city can be enjoyed.

90 top right The Archeological Museum of Sousse is the second most important one in the country after that of the Bardo in Tunis. Located in the kasba, *it boasts a collection of truly remarkable mosaics and exhaustively illustrates the importance of the city in the ancient context.*

90-91 Of quite massive proportions, plain and squared, the Great Mosque of Sousse looks more like a fortress than a sacred building. From the wide porticoed courtyard of the complex, restored in recent years, the prayer room is accessed.

91 top The Great Mosque, built in the ninth century by Emir Abou el-Abbas Mohammed, stands not far from the port of Sousse, visible in the background. This ancient stopover place began to be used by the Phoenicians even before the founding of Carthage.

91 bottom In terms of the attraction of tourism both national and foreign, Hammamet holds a record in Tunisia. With a medina full of shops, a splendid sea and an uninterrupted series of hotels that come one after the other along the coast, it is an ideal place for vacationers.

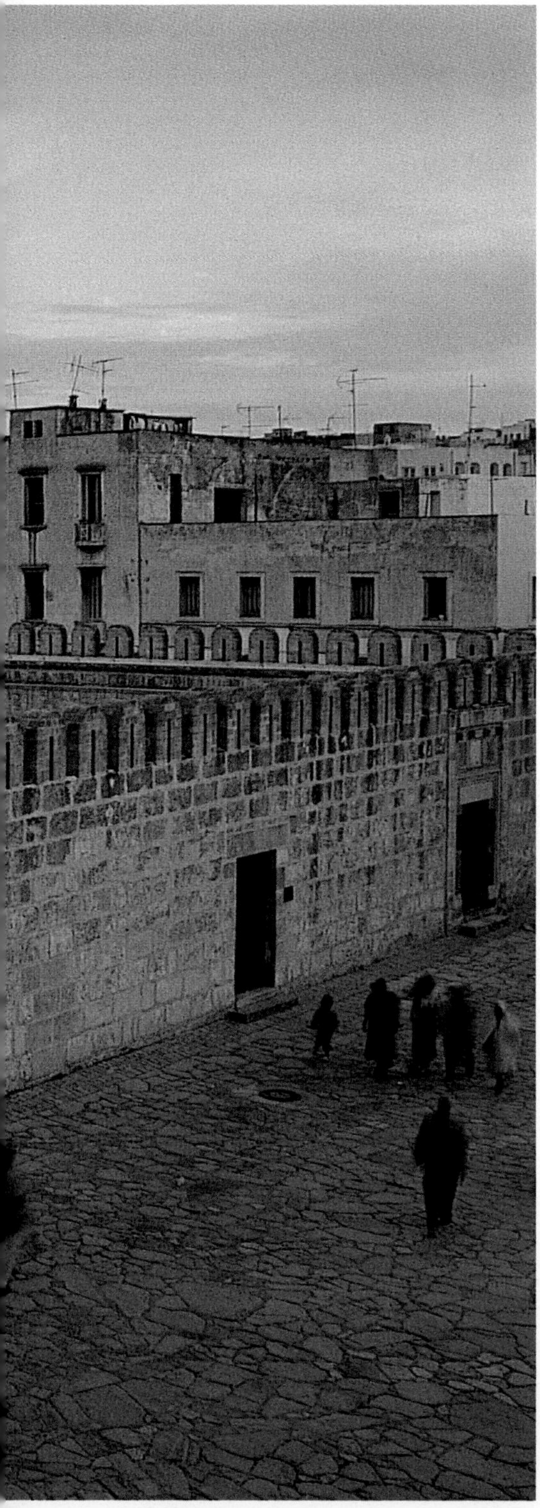

Now, to the east, passing to the other coast, that below Cap Bon, one arrives at Hammamet, the true center of domestic and foreign tourism. Under that cover of hotels, white and as clean as a summer shower, which unrolls endlessly along the coast, Hammamet has also got a soul. It may be hiding in the winding alleys of the citadel, surrounded by fifteenth-century walls, in the courtyards of princely mansions shadowed by flowers and columns or in cafés frequented by celebrities from the whole world, but it is there. A sense of poetry derives directly from the landscape, the mild climate that is so loved by the orange, lemon and tangerine trees, the sand that seems to have been made for the hourglass of time, the heart-rending sunrises, and the terraces jutting out over the sea, where hot pepper and other spices dry in the sun.

The colors here are more concentrated than elsewhere, saturated with a unique light. It all began with the construction of the magnificent villa of the millionaire Romanian aristocrat Georges Sébastian in the 1920s. Thereafter, Klee, Giacometti and Gide arrived, as well as Rommel, who spent that last days of his African stay here, and Churchill, who wrote his memoirs here. A film festival was added to the list, then another and another, until finally, in the 1960s, the consecration of the jet set. Thus, the 'city of the *hammam*', as its name says, famous since antiquity for hospitality and the beauty of its baths both public and private, slowly transformed itself into a tourism mecca with very modern structures and corners that stubbornly resist the assault of civilization.

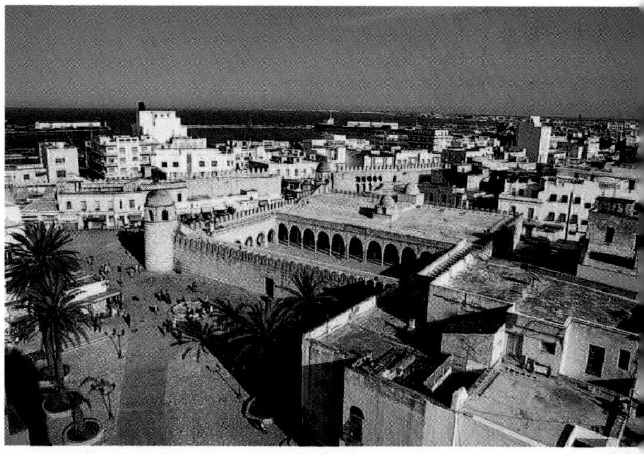

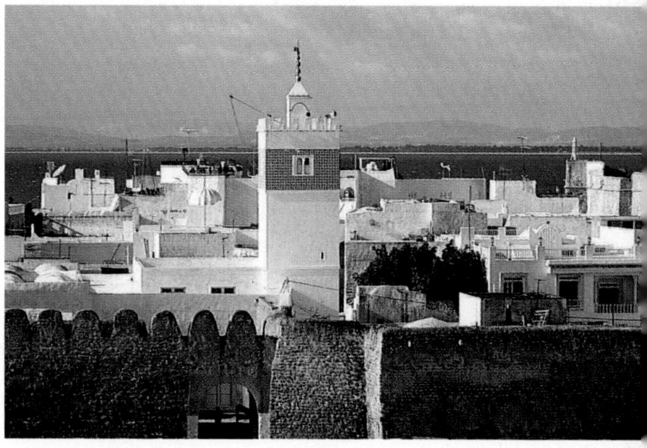

At the end of the Gulf of Hammamet rises Sousse, the Tunisian city most faithful to itself. Since the time of its foundation, in fact, it has grown, but it has remained substantially the same, without betraying its authenticity. Founded by the Phoenicians in the ninth century BC, as always for commercial purposes, it was the third-most important city after Carthage and Utica. Sousse was then Roman, Byzantine and Arab: from here departed Christian drives towards the interior and Muslim landing forces that wanted to conquer Sicily.

92 The Great Mosque of Monastir stands in the area of a majestic ribat, *or fortified convent. Constructed in the ninth century, it was altered and enlarged in the eleventh century by the Ziriti.*

93 left The entrance gate to the mausoleum of the Bourguiba family is emblematic of the volume of precious materials lavished on the completion of the building.

93 top right Behind the famous beaches of Monastir rises the massive ochre-colored structure of the ribat. Buildings of this type were the headquarters of religious warriors that offered protection and hospitality to wayfarers and dedicated themselves to the study and teaching of the Koran.

93 center right Next to the ribat, the Great Mosque of Monastir, contrary to what its name may suggest, has a rather simple and austere appearance.

93 bottom right The Habib Bourguiba Mausoleum in Monastir, built in 1963, is preceded by a spectacular square and boasts a rich decorative apparatus.

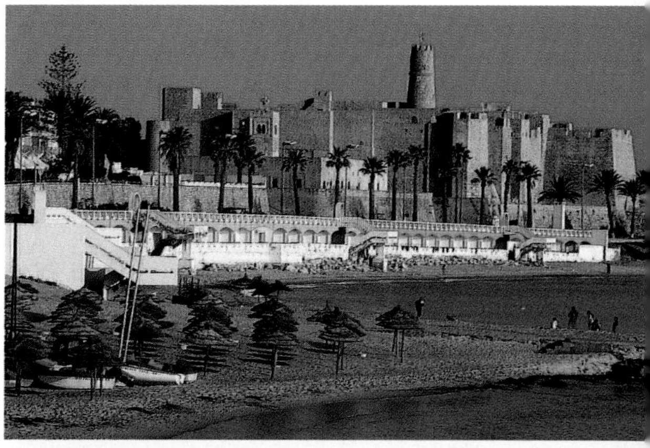

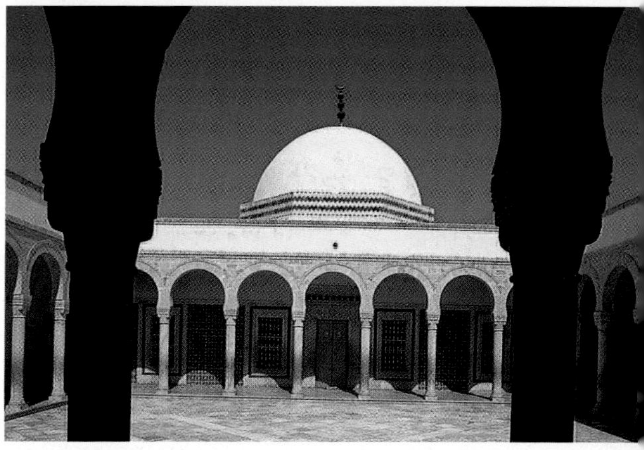

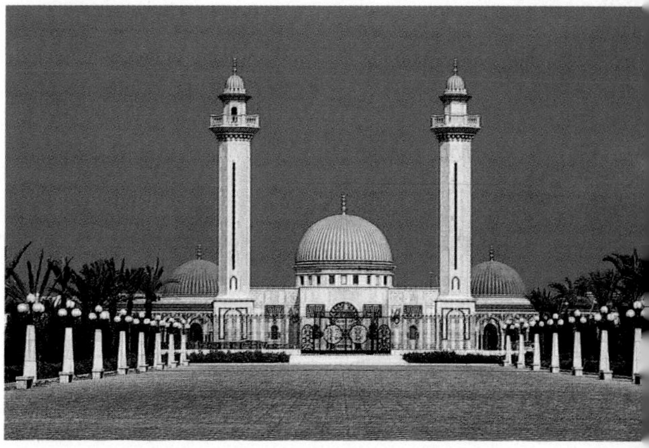

Today it is the capital of the Sahel—the region that includes also Monastir and Mahdia—with its beautiful tourist port, Port el-Kantaoui, which lies very close to the residential areas that, in some cases, allow for the docking of a boat below the houses. To the south, the hotels form a line that follows the coast uninterruptedly for about 50 miles. However, the nucleus of the city is well protected from the layers of modern buildings, which seen from above seem like a river of white milk, in soft, rounded and, above all, low (under 33 feet) forms because at the time of their construction the urban development plan had to follow military-type parameters. Inside this recent part is found the medina, with its surrounding wall dating back to 859. Tall, towered, with merlons that line the patrol pathway, this belt of stone encloses the tower of the *kasba,* the ancient signal tower 98 feet high, and the archeological museum. Accompanied by two luxuriant gardens, the museum exhibits a collection of Roman mosaics second only to that of Bardo. Further on, after the souqs enlivened by goods and loud cries in all the languages of the Mediterranean and beyond, the Ksar er-Ribat, one of the most important testimonies to the presence of Islam in the Maghreb, stands out. The *ribat,* for the Arabs, were monastery-fortresses that housed the cleric warriors that offered protection and hospitality to wayfarers and who also dedicated themselves to the study and teaching of the Koran. This monument is from the eighth century, with a square layout that measures about 130 feet per side, and inside it is located the oldest mosque in Africa, according to sources. In the area and also resembling a fortress, the Great Mosque rises, curiously without a minaret, where the faithful take turns saying their prayers.

As mentioned before, Monastir, the birthplace of Habib Bourguiba, also stands in the Sahel. Its focal point is the city's ribat, the true spiritual and intellectual hub of the region. One of its most special qualities, besides its importance, is its unique status in allowing women to have access to the school both as students and teachers. Not only that: tradition maintains that in Monastir the prophet Mohammed himself pointed out one of the gates of Heaven and that he indicated an infallible method for achieving eternal happiness in the quarters of his ribat. If this is true, given that he was speaking about the next life, certainly the most illustrious intellectuals and the most refined thinkers in the Arab world passed through here, contributing to the transformation of the convent into a proper medieval 'university'. Moreover, this institution maintained connections with the other fortresses: between the eighth and the ninth centuries, the 'road of the ribat'—which ran from Tangiers to Sousse and from there to Monastir and on to Alexandria—was born along the Mediterranean coast of Africa, a path of faith and culture that aimed at the expansion of Islam in opposition to Christianity.

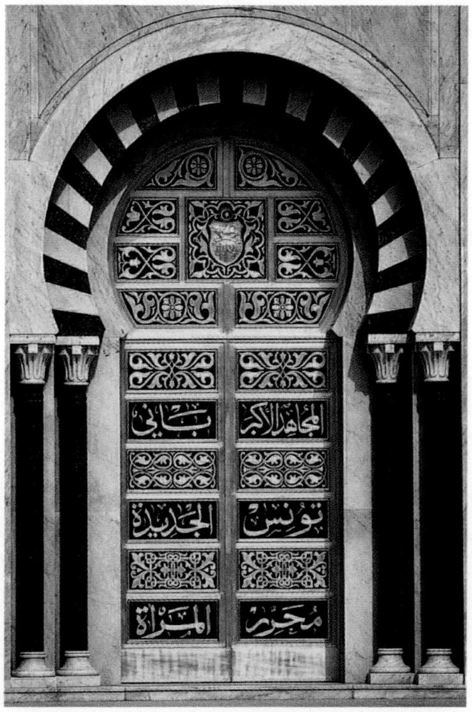

Today the city, which maintained all its prestige until the fourteenth century, has a beautiful mosque and the remains of other ribat, besides the main one. Near the medina, the Bourguiba Mosque was built in 1963, named after the ex-president that contributed decisively to bringing Monastir fully into the modern age.

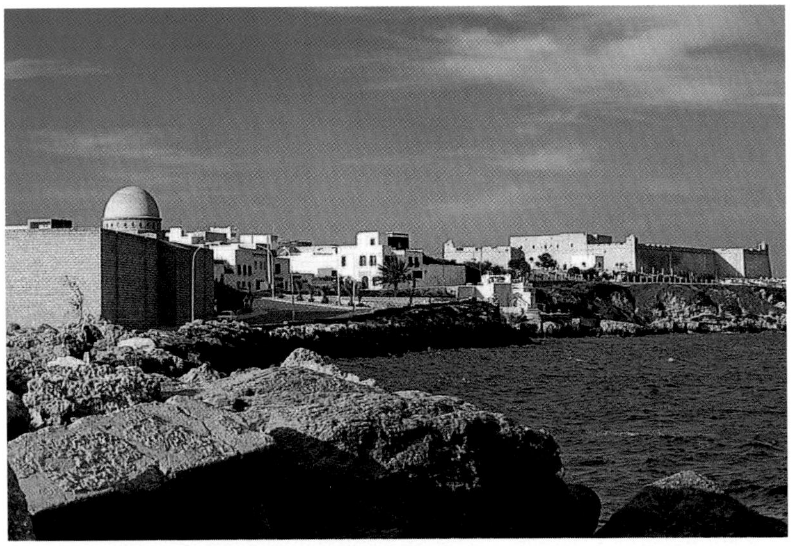

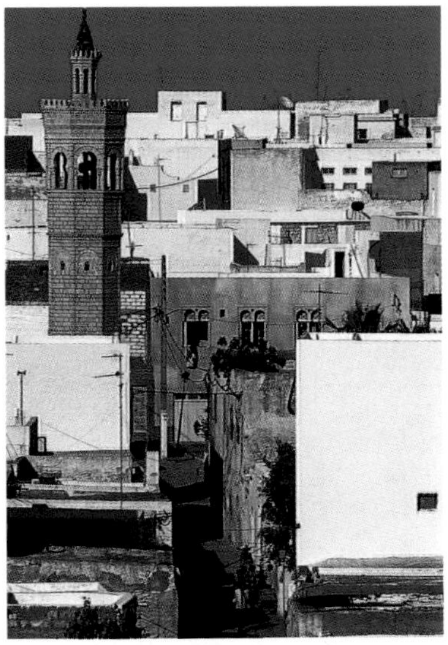

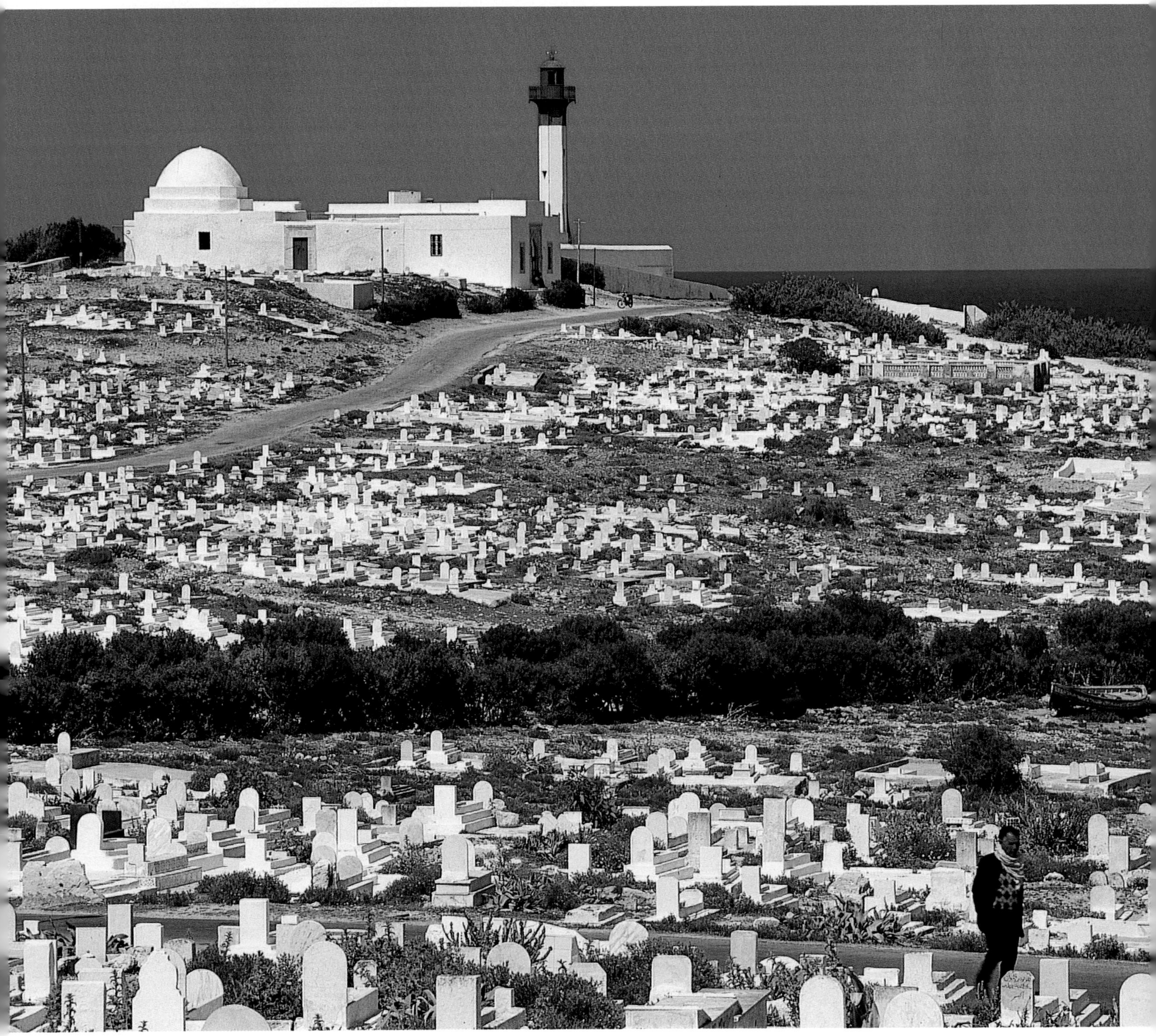

94 top left Mahdia, the 'city of the two crescents', was so-called by the Arabs (to be precise, the Fatimids, who lived there in the tenth century) because it stands on an isthmus, a narrow strip of land that divides almost twin bays, the shape of which recalls the sickle of the waxing moon.

94 top right The clean and attractive houses of Mahdia, overlooked by the elegant and massive structure of an octagonal minaret, are castled on a promontory chosen in the past by the Phoenicians and the Romans for its excellent defensive possibilities. The city owes its name to the Fatimid Obeid Allah, alias Mahdi, 'the savior'.

94-95 All the tombs that cover the Muslim cemetery of Mahdia, looking onto the sea, are oriented in such a way so that the defunct turns his face in the direction of Mecca. The necropolis is no older than the sixteenth century, but the rest of the Shiite burial places from the tenth century are conserved not far away from the lighthouse.

95 left At the end of the nineteenth century, Mahdia became a tourist destination for Sicilians. In return for the hospitality offered them, the guests taught the inhabitants the practice of fishing with lamps.

95 top right The cemetery of Mahdia, bristling with immaculate tombstones along a slope that gently descends towards the sea, is an extremely evocative place, particularly at sundown.

95 center right The Great Mosque of Mahdia, reconstructed around 1960, in large part imitates the ancient Fatimid building, which rose in the tenth century on the initiative of Obeid Allah. In the image, the courtyard surrounded by porticoes on three sides can be appreciated.

95 bottom right Reaching out towards the sea and infinity, Mahdia is sharply silhouetted against the sky when the white houses turn red with the light of the sunset.

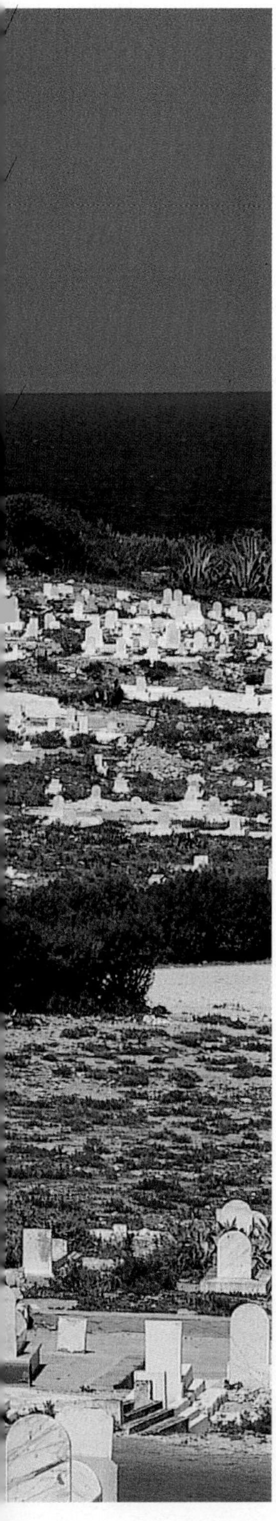

Mahdia is the southernmost of the important cities of the Sahel. The 'city of the two crescent moons': so it was called by the Arabs (the Fatimids, to be precise, who lived there in the tenth century) because of the fact that is was born right on an isthmus, a narrow tongue of land dividing two nearly twin bays with a crescent moon shape.

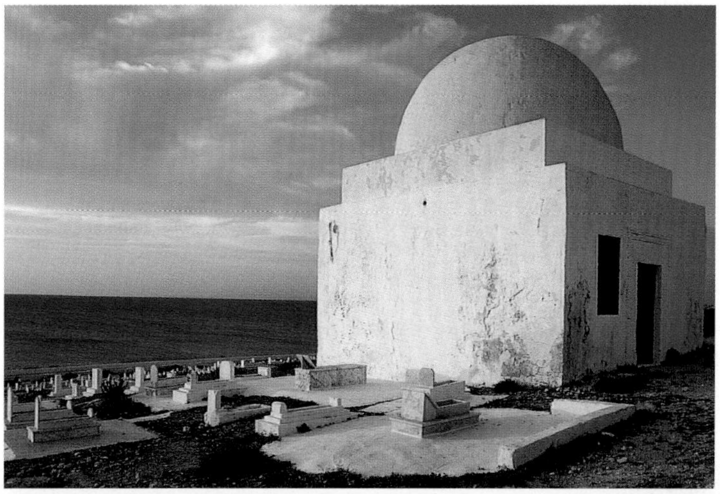

At the end of the seventeenth century the Sicilians started to come here on vacation. They taught the natives to use a fishing light and they built an entire

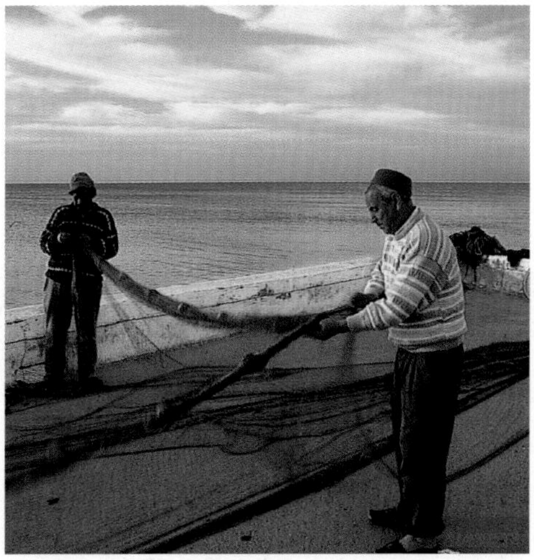

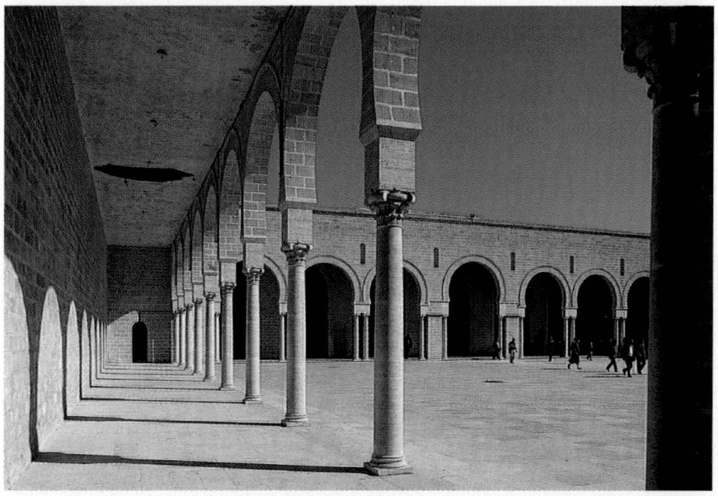

neighborhood situated on the northern bank of the city, opposite the new port.

Neither does Mahdia lack for classic monuments such as a mosque, a fortress and hammam. However, that which is most pleasing about the city is how it penetrates the sky when the white houses turn red in the sunset, opening itself towards the sea and infinity.

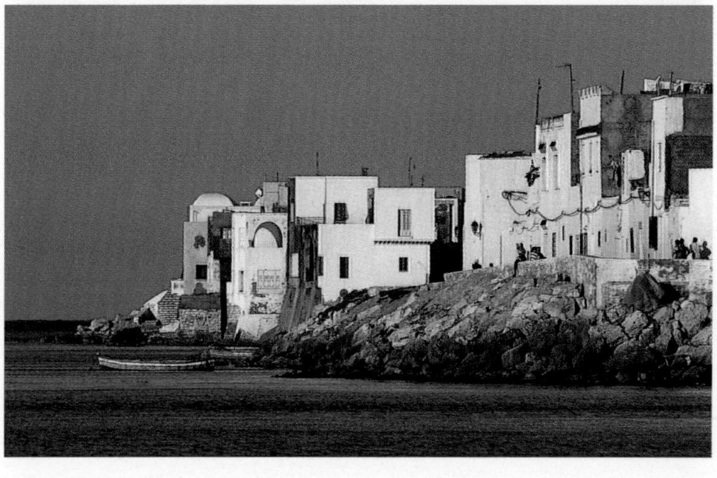

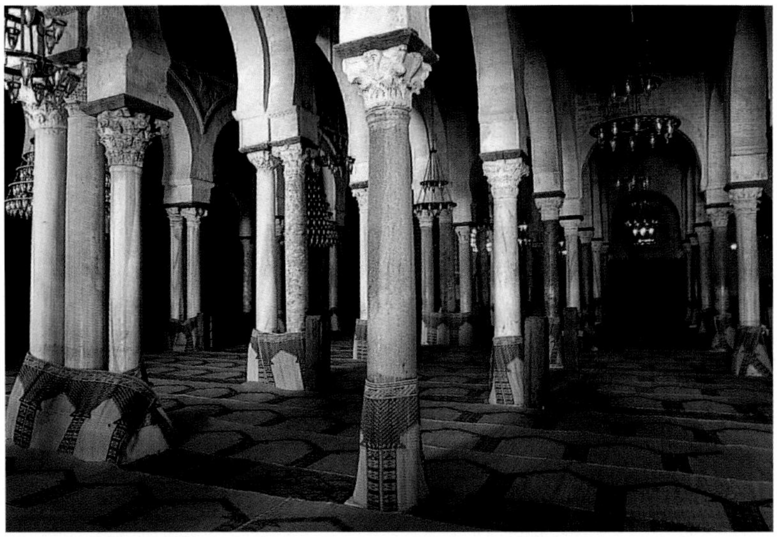

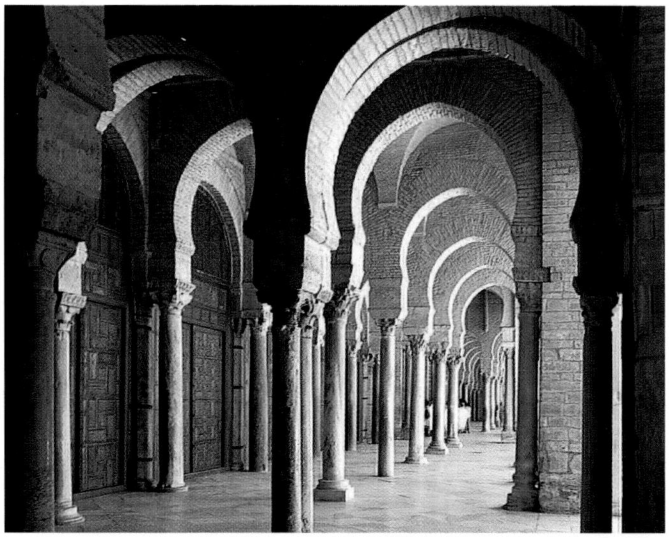

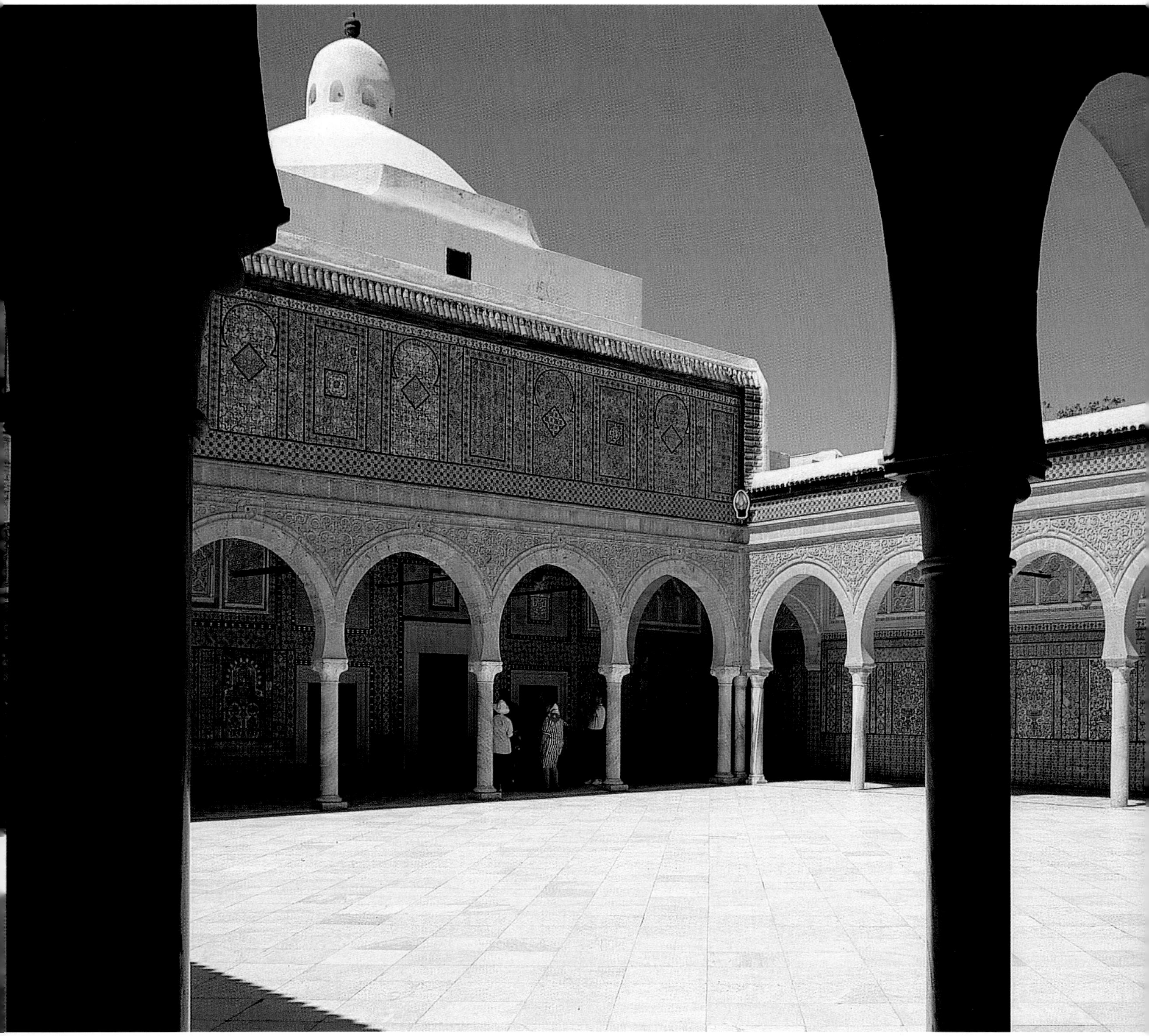

96 top left The Great Mosque of Kairouan in the IX century was renowned academy for the sciences, from geometry to astronomy.

96 top right The Great Mosque of Kairouan was built starting in 670 as wished by the Arab general Uqba ibn Nafa'a and represented the fulcrum of this camp-city, Karawan.

96-97 According to legend, in the Mosque of the Barber (zaouia *of Sidi Sahab, dating back to the fifteenth-seventeenth centuries) in Kairouan, three hairs from the beard of Mohammed are conserved.*

97 top Tall, fortified bastion walls surround the paved courtyard of the Great Mosque of Kairouan, on which rises a pyramid-shaped minaret.

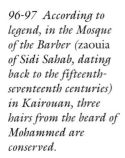

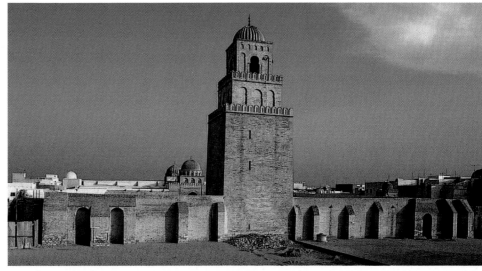

It is extremely important, being the spiritual capital of Tunisia, but inside Kairouan also appears in all its beauty of the savage past. 'On a bare plain like the back of a hand under an obstinately blue sky, the visitor makes out in the distance an Arab city peppered with white domes like ostrich eggs and ringed by ramparts of a dazzling splendor...' From its most secret nucleus, the labyrinth of the tightly shut medina, begin the streets that continue on to form the circle of the walls. On the other side, at the threshold of the desert, the fearsome Muslim warriors departed, scattering themselves to the four winds to conquer lands in the name of Allah. Thus *Karawan* (fortress city), a strategic base founded in 670 by the Arab general Uqba ibn Nafa'a, far from the Byzantine seas was the hub around which turned all of the cultures of North Africa and the Mediterranean. It became an intellectual center without equal of international fame, and in the ninth century, a renowned academy for the sciences, from geometry to astronomy, and translation was established there. With the passage of time, mental illness was studied in Kairouan and some of the most beautiful Tunisian literary works were created here. Architecture flourished, dictating laws everywhere, and religious studies came to be of primary importance in the operating the *medersas,* the Koranic schools, teaching lessons fundamental to Islam.

Today a visit to the city passes through the Aghlabid reservoirs, among the greatest hydraulic works of the Arab world, on seven mighty bastions in the medina.

The tour continues on to the mosques, such as the Mosque of the Barber, where it is said that three hairs from the beard of Mohammed are conserved, or it stays longer in the Great Mosque, with its immense, simply magnificent courtyard, that holds under its vaults the *minbar,* the oldest pulpit in all the Muslim world, composed of 300 engraved teak-wood panels.

97 center The walls of the medina of Kairouan, bordered with rounded merlons, have been preserved in their entirety.

97 bottom Built at the beginning of the fourteenth century, the zaouia *of Sidi Abid el-Ghariani in Kairouan includes a* medersa, *or Koranic school, and the mausoleum of its founder.*

POPCORN

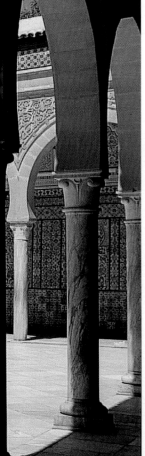

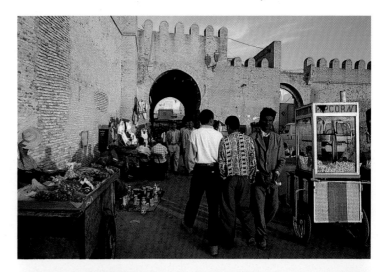

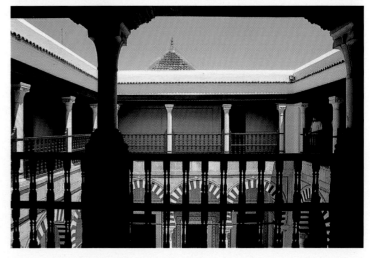

98 bottom The markets of Sfax are located in the area north of the medina, in the opposite part with respect to the entrance gate, in all of the zone contained between the Great Mosque and Bab Jebli. Outside the latter extends a large covered market.

98-99 Hedi Chaker is the main square of Sfax, a city located in the northern part of the Gulf of Gabès. Since become a big commercial hub thanks to the port, it was almost completely rebuilt after the bombings of 1942-43.

99 top left The narrow streets of the medina of Sfax are teeming with visitors intrigued by an infinity of shops and stalls that sell handmade products. This is undoubtedly the most characteristic part of the city.

From the sacred to the profane, or so to say, a *medina* surrounded by merloned walls, mosques and museums is the historic nucleus of Sfax, at the top of the Gulf of Gabès and the second city of the country, which has become a big commercial hub thanks to its port, nearly completely restored after the bombings of the winter of 1942-43.

The pulsing heart of the city center can be dived into through the twelfth-century Bab el-Diwan, the gate that represents the main entrance to the medina. The walls, about a mile long, were built in the ninth century, first out of mud bricks and then out of stone. The renowned regional museum of arts and folk traditions is located inside the Dar Jallouli, a typical aristocratic building in the customary T-shaped layout that dates back to the twelfth century with a majestic interior. The museum holds collections of clothing, fabrics, jewelry, furniture, objects from daily life and a small collection of Arabic calligraphy.

Another building not to miss is the Great Mosque, which stands at the center of the medina, as dictated by tradition, where some of the most important decisions regarding the political life of Sfax were taken. Originally built in the ninth century, it was downsized in the twelfth century in order to create more space for the surrounding residences. The doors of the courtyard are remarkable, sculpted and embellished with medallions featuring floral and geometric motifs that testify to the contact this city had with the Orient.

The souqs also merit a visit. The markets occupy, in the northern zone of the medina, opposite the entranceway, all of the section between the Great Mosque and Bab Jebli, outside of which expands the vast covered market. They are divided into areas of 'expertise', it may be said, and among the most picturesque there is the Souq el-Jamaa, where products made by the nomads are sold, such as matrimonial pillowcases. Outside the walls, on the other hand, the museum of archeology is interesting, outfitted within the town hall in Arab-Muslim style, built at the beginning of the eighteenth century. The massive structure of the Hotel des Oliviers should also be noted, in the same style as the town hall.

99 top right The medina of Sfax, the heart of the city, is enclosed by merloned walls, about a mile or so long. The city walls, completed in two phases starting in the ninth century, first in raw earth and then in stone, are entered through the twelfth century Bab el-Diwan, the main entrance to the old city.

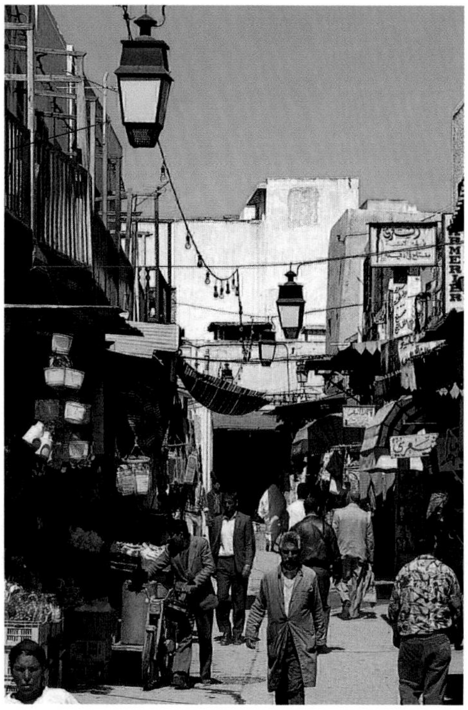

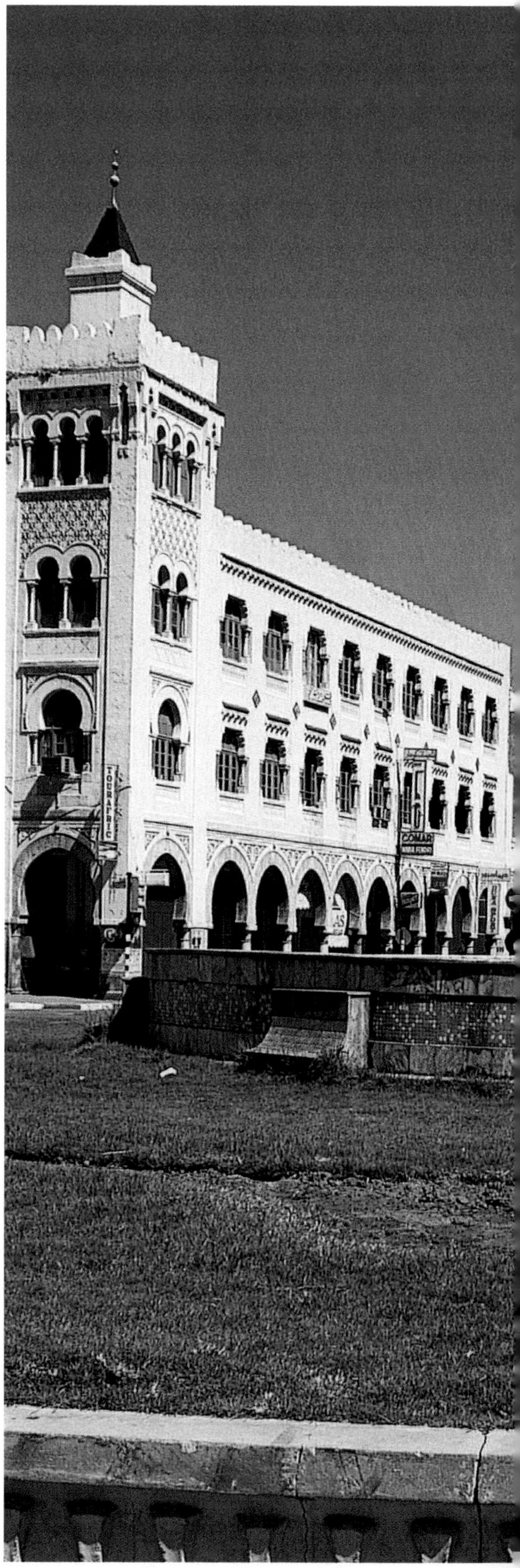

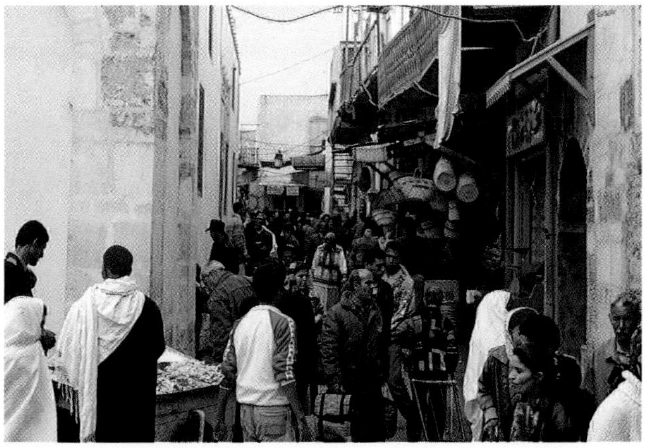

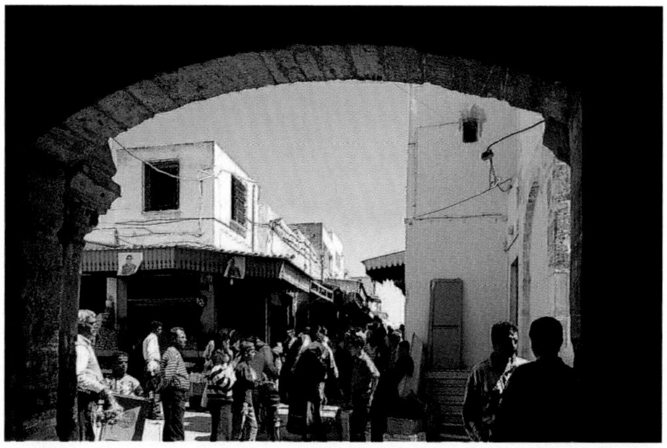

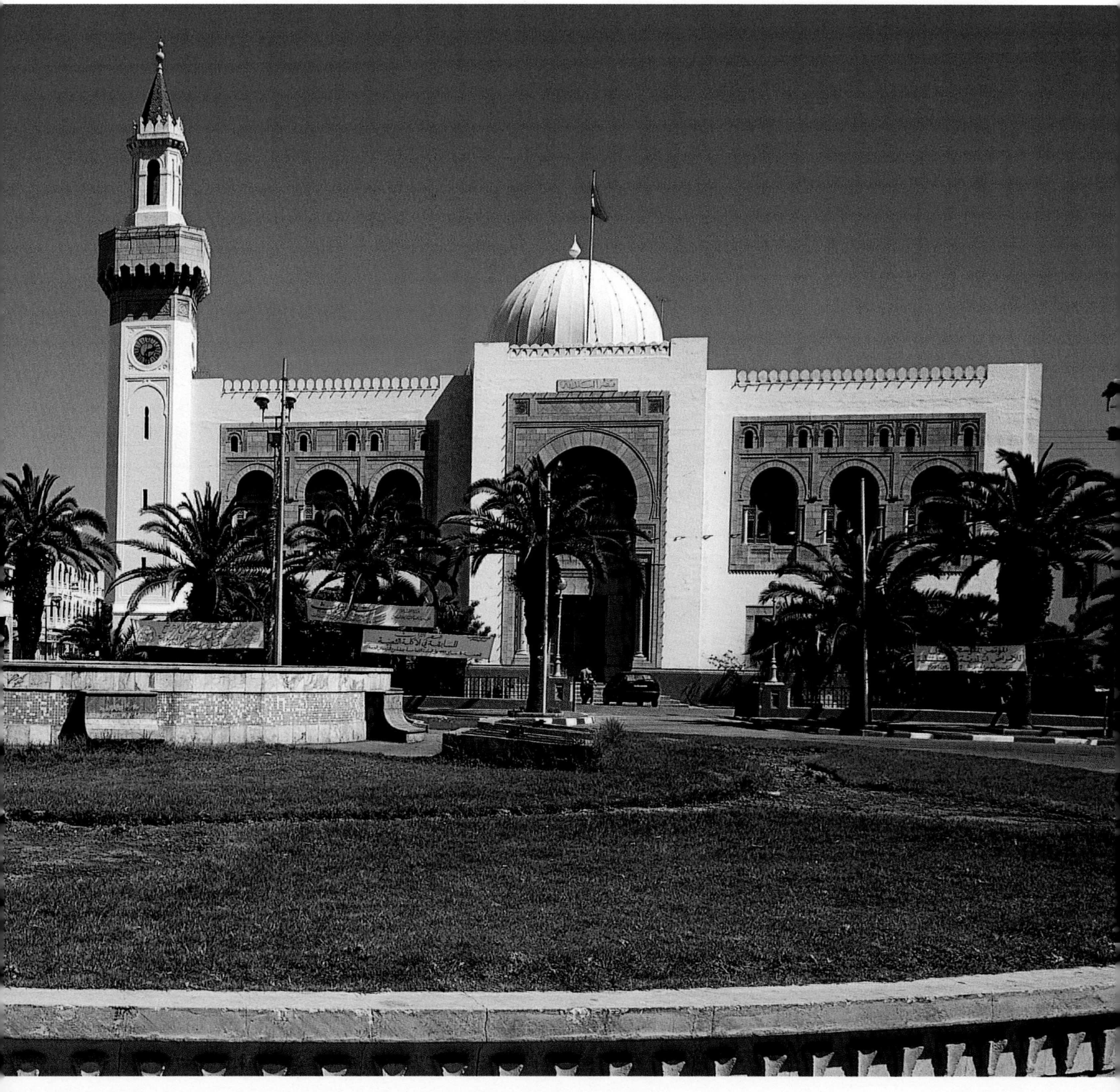

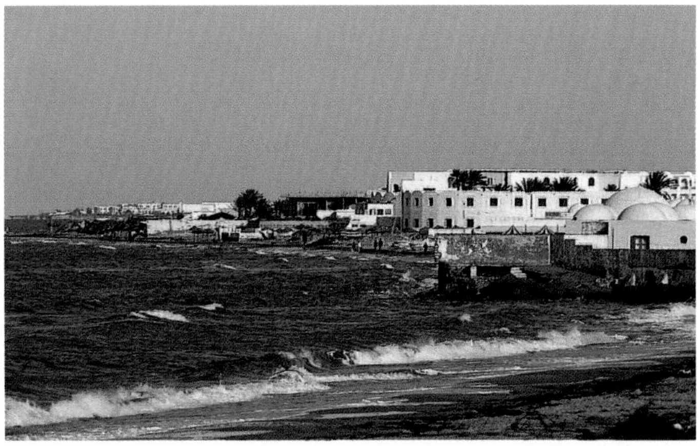

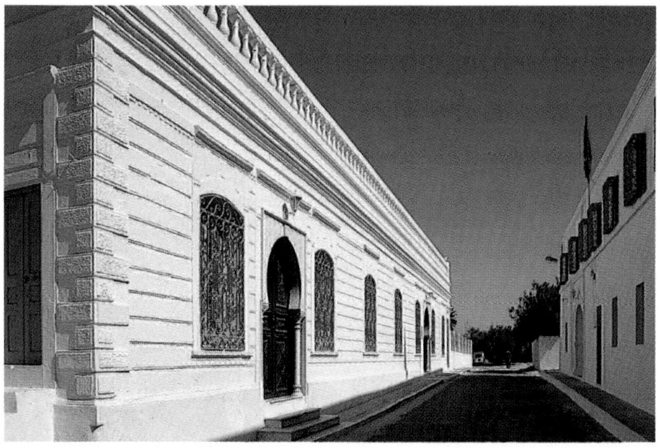

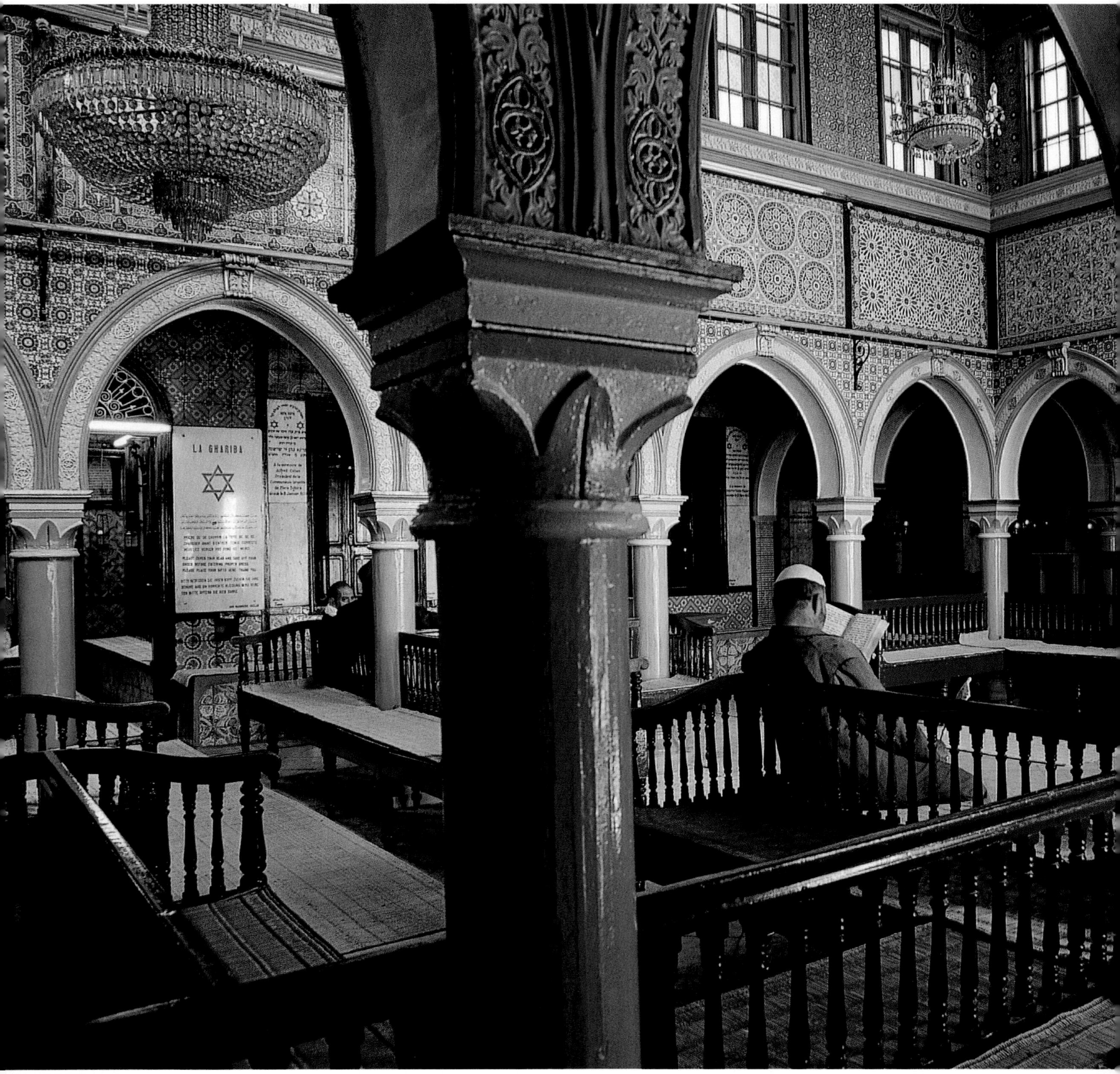
LA GHARIBA

100 top left The eastern coast of Jerba, the home of the Lotus Eaters according to Homer, is perhaps the most beautiful tract of the island's coastline, thanks to the enchanting turquoise sea that laps it and despite the high concentration of very modern hotels.

100 top right On the occasion of Passover, hundreds of Jews from all of North Africa arrive at the synagogue of Jerba. A recent explosion, the cause of which has not yet been determined, partially damaged it.

100-101 The interior of the only synagogue on Jerba Island, the Ghriba, near the village of er-Riadh, is entirely covered with colorful majolica. The building is a highly visited pilgrimage site because it holds one of the most ancient Torahs in the world.

101 The courtyard of the Ghriba, built with two floors of austere porticoes, is frequented by descendants of the first Jewish community on Jerba, which reached the island following the destruction of Solomon's Temple, in Jerusalem, in 586 BC.

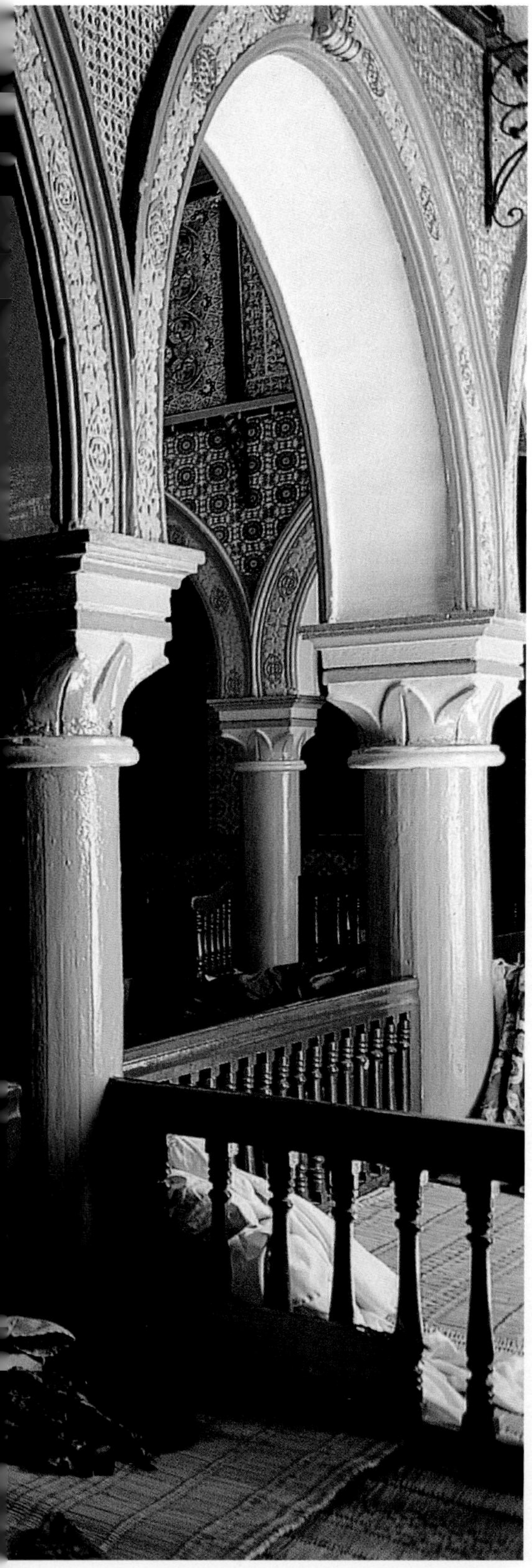

The Kerkenna Islands are situated at the center of the western coast of Tunisia. Historically tied to Sfax, second city of the country, they have beautiful beaches and inviting landscapes: they seem almost a mirage, the air and the earth at the same time. Like a raft anchored on the waves, the rising palms distinguish it in the distance. An hour and a half by ferry is enough to reach this strip of flat land. They do not extend more than about 25 miles in all: the two biggest are, Gharbi, to the west, and Chergui, to the east. They are connected by a Roman dyke, almost 2,000 feet long, surrounded by a handful of uninhabited little islands. They have been known since ancient times, above all for their strategic position, but they started to be permanently populated and to be used as pasture by shepherds from Sfax only in the eighteenth century.

Whoever is lucky enough to take a trip with a *loud*, the typical crafts of the islands, around the Kerkennas can admire the dark green of the palm tree groves that are unfortunately much rarer than in the past. The white, well-grouped houses, the spots of the *marabout* (the tombs of cleric warriors) and their domes sparkling with light. Getting off at the small port of Sidi Youssef on Gharbi for a tour along the only road, which crosses the island. The Kerkennas are one of the last places in Tunisia where they still practice group dances. In August, during the Festival of the Siren, musicians and dancers that seem to have come out of a fresco of Knossos meet here to perpetuate a tradition that is disappearing. Staying with the island theme, the *dulcis in fundo* is represented by Jerba, the island that many academics identify with the mythological land of the Lotus Eaters mentioned in the *Odyssey*. Ulysses lost companions here that, after having eaten some lotus flowers, were bewitched by the beauty of the place and did not want to ever return home again. Without going quite that far, Jerba does offer intriguing sites not yet totally touched by mass tourism, even though it is the second biggest vacation spot in the country. The island, like a big floating oasis consisting of small palm tree groves, gardens and the finest sand, is found in the Gulf of Gabès, and thanks to the temperate climate and the 'sweet air every day of the year', it offers the possibility to bask in the sun along its 74 miles of coast.

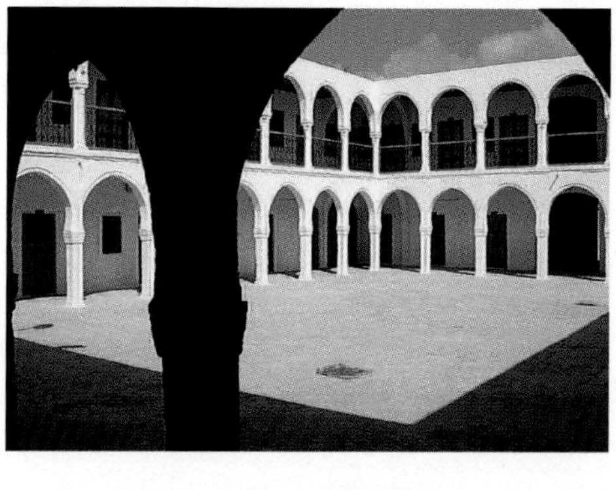

In addition, those who like sport activities can sail, windsurf or join fishermen when they go out on their boats. Or, they can take epic horse rides around the lagoon, exotic walks on the back of a dromedary or even throw themselves into the mayhem of the souq of Houmt-Souk, the regional capital, for an unforgettable shopping experience. Or, finally, they can enjoy the sights of the island, *marabout, mezel* (the little traditional settlements), museums of customs and handiwork and the synagogue, which during Passover becomes a destination for pilgrims from all of North Africa. Inside the synagogue, one of the most ancient torahs in the world is preserved.

THE MOSAIC OF ANTIQUITY

102 bottom left Room VI of the Bardo is known as the 'Bulla Regia' room because finds from this site, which was particularly prosperous between the third and fourth centuries, are gathered here. The photograph shows, from left to right, the statues of Saturn, Apollo, Minerva and Aesculapius.

102 right The Bardo Museum, the pride of the capital, holds the most important archeological collection in the Maghreb. Statuary art is excellently represented, with finds like this head of Jupiter with thick locks of hair.

102-103 In the statuary room of the Bardo Museum, works recovered in the excavation of Carthage are conserved. The exposition is displayed on the patio of the palace, the Hafsid sultans' summer residence between the thirteenth and sixteenth centuries.

Eyes that stare back at visitors from the abyss of time: they are those of the superstars of the Museum of Bardo, just over three miles from the center of Tunis along the Boulevard du 20 Mars 1956. They are the stars for which Tunisia is envied the world over and of which only Tunisia has succeeded in securing and gathering in a building worthy of them. The mosaics seem to be photographs of men and gods, of animals and far-away lands, of a past that, here, takes on the brilliant colors of the present.

The museum was inaugurated on 7 May 1888 with the name of Alaoui, in honor of the last reigning sovereign, Ali Bey. However, it is only a part of the many rooms of the harem, the real Bardo Palace, built by Hafsid sultans as a summer residence. Thereafter, it became the official headquarters of the Ottoman governors who enlarged it. Finally, in 1881, the Bardo stopped being used as a government building but the French resumed the project of a Tunisian governor and had a part of the palace allocated to the collection of national mosaic art. So was born the biggest collection of Roman floor mosaics in the world.

Here, the art is split between the exhibits and the structure itself, creating a single, harmonic environment where the forms are enhanced by the colors and the architecture is adorned with figures that now dominate the walls. In the 'Neptune' Room, for example, domes entirely covered with gold arabesques, frilled with an absolute delicacy, which are surprising

for their lightness can be noted. Wandering in the rooms, famous mosaics appear, like that of *Perseus and Andromeda* (third to fourth centuries AD) that decorated the villa of a wealthy Roman. Here, Perseus, the Greek hero who killed a sea monster, with unexpected dynamism helps the princess Andromeda to leave the reef to which she is chained, while a sea goddess watches the scene.

To explain the complexity and the value of the scene, it is necessary to make a quick digression.

103 top left The Bardo's mosaic collection has no equal in the world, but the rooms of the museum deserve a visit regardless of their archeological contents.

103 top right Overlooked by an elaborate ceiling with multicolored decorations, Room X contains mosaics and statues from Carthage.

102 top left The Arab Museum, dedicated to the applied arts, is located inside the Bardo. The rooms are placed around a patio embellished with majolica, at the center of which stands out a basin in pure white marble.

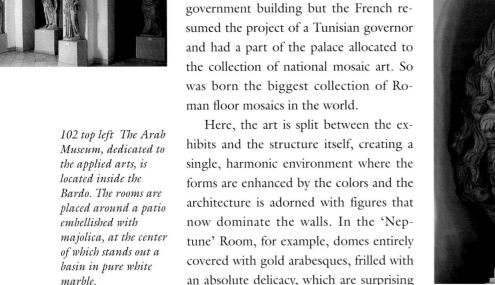

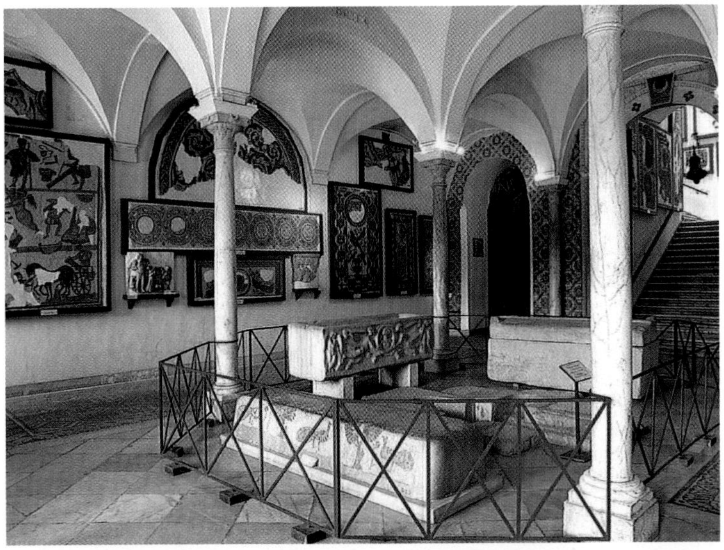

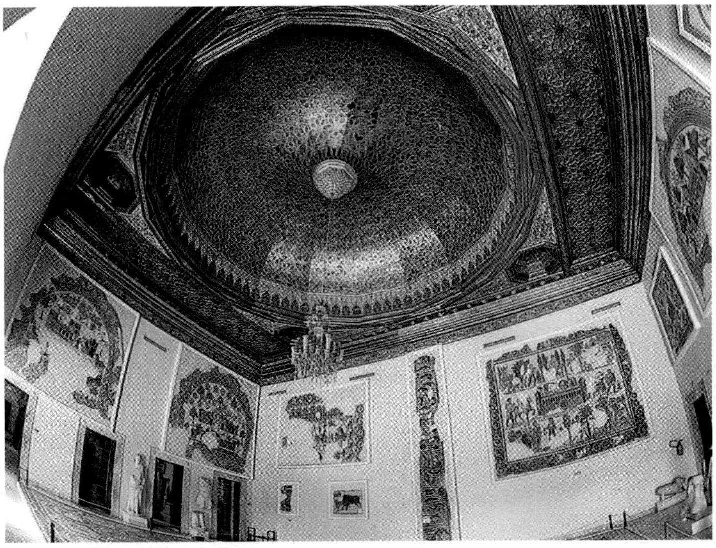

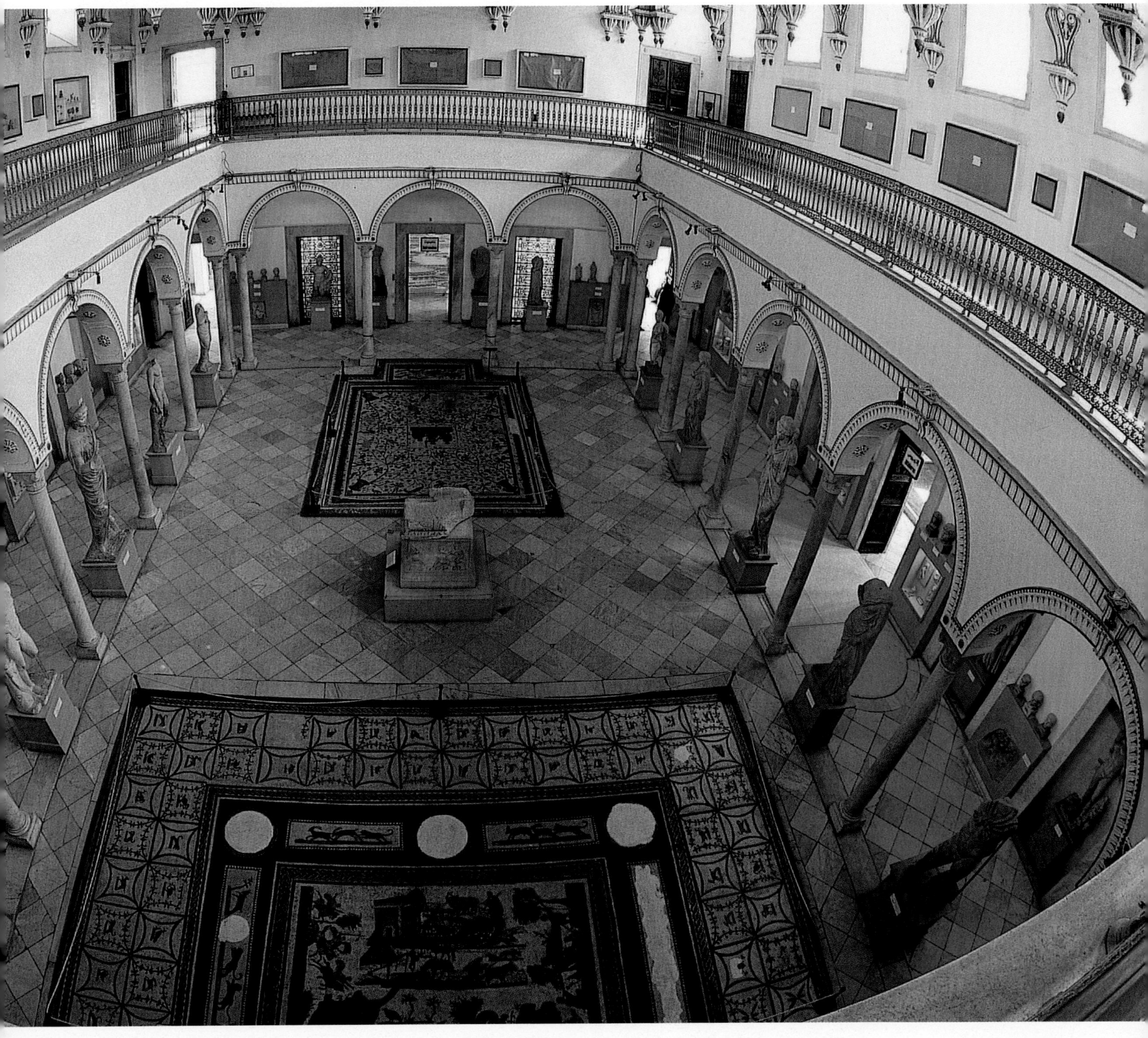

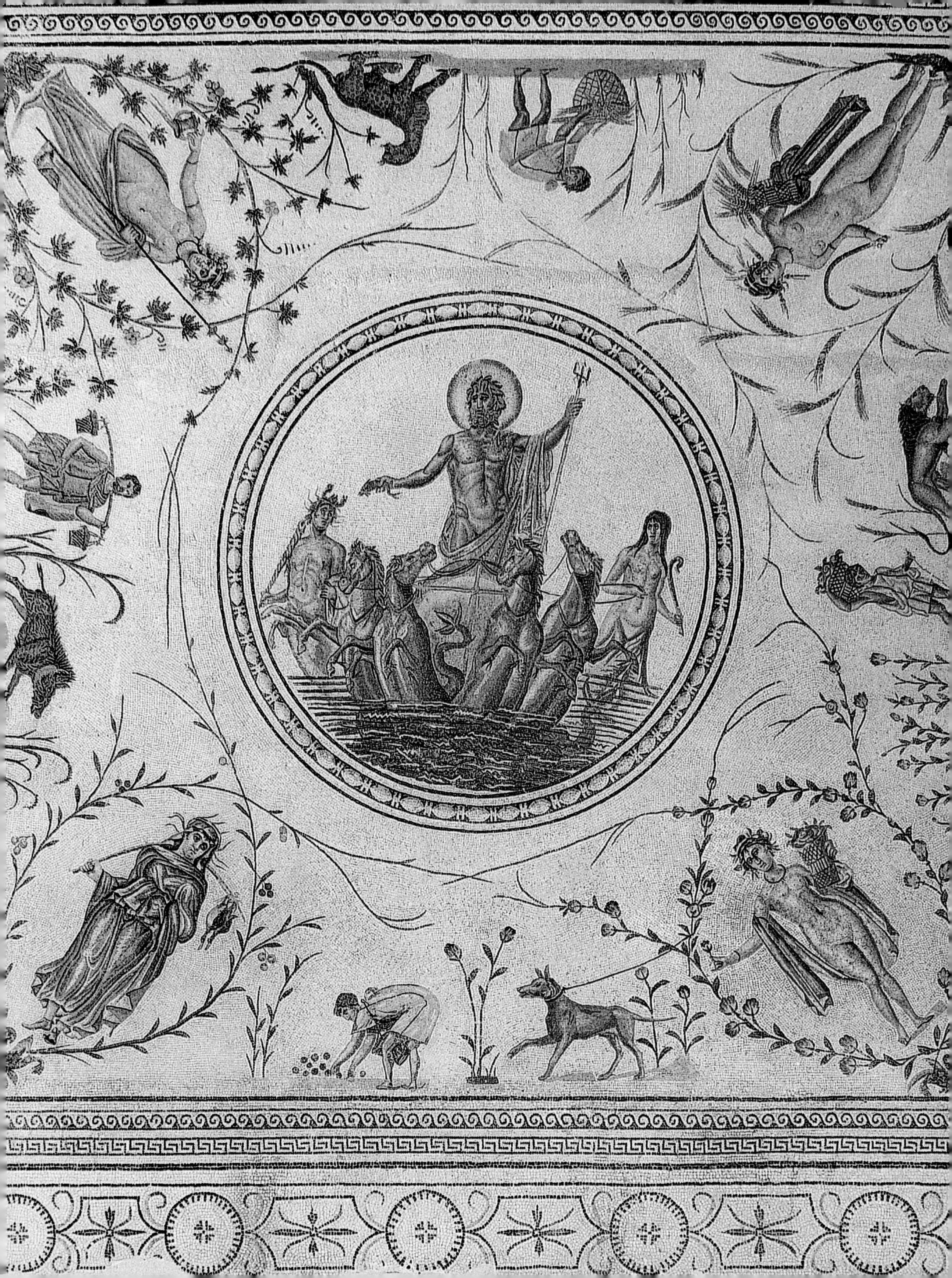

104 In Room XI, known as 'of Dougga', the mosaic of the Triumph of Neptune with the four seasons dominates. Inside the medallion, the god of the sea is portrayed as a divinity of regenerating waters and the passing of time. The feminine figures in the corners are allegories of the seasons. The total effect is of a surprising pictorial delicacy.

105 top The sea and its divinities are one of the main themes in Tunisian mosaic art from the Roman era. Neptune is portrayed here as a personification of the liquid element with a beard of algae that flows as if moved by the waves with monstrous animals that populate the abyss.

105 bottom This splendid multicolored mosaic conserved in the Bardo Museum portrays Perseus who, after having decapitated the Gorgon and shown grasping her head crowned with serpents, liberates Andromeda, exposed to the fury of a sea monster, from the chains that bind her to the rock.

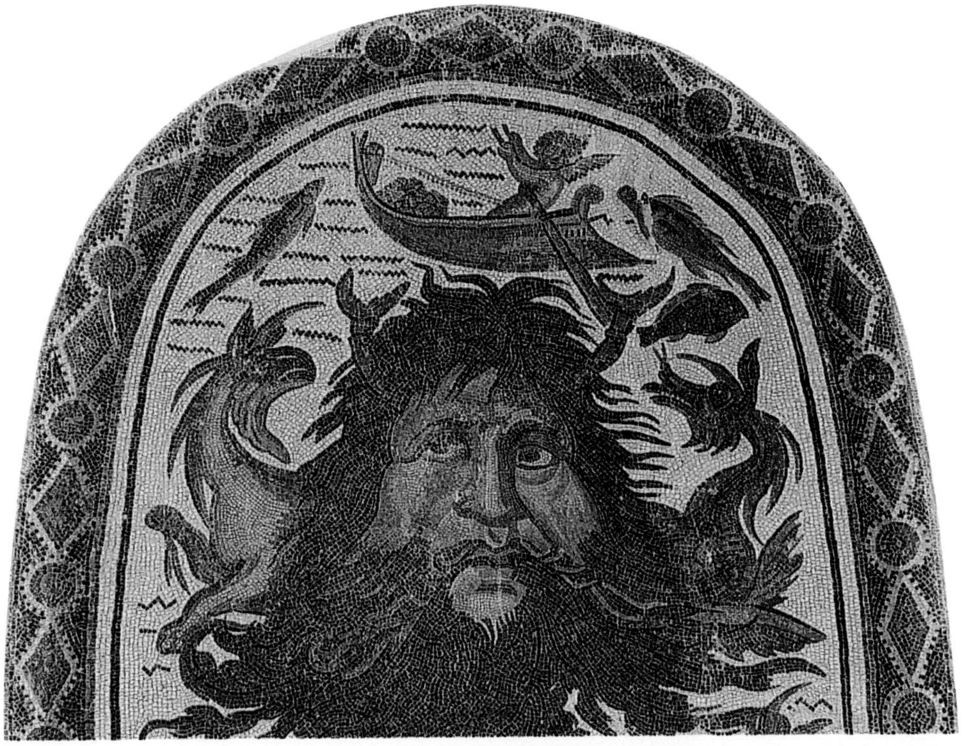

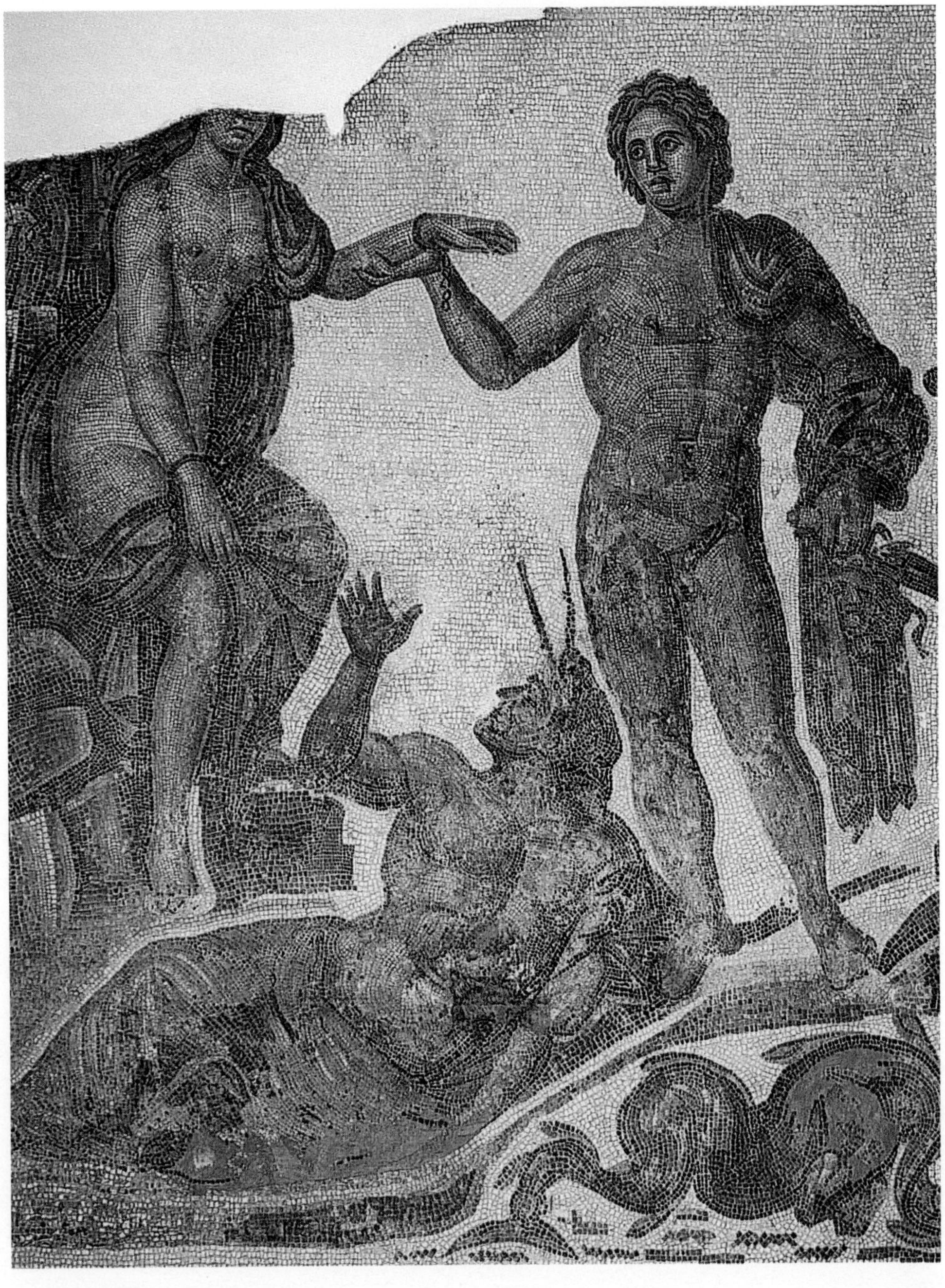

In Tunisia, between the fourth and third centuries BC, during the last days of the Carthaginian rule, *pavimenta punica,* flooring decorated with geometric forms made of river pebbles, stone fragments and uncut terracotta *tesserae,* small square tiles, was developed. Around the middle of the second century, with the Roman conquest, mosaic work underwent a great evolution, probably thanks to Greek, Syracusian and Egyptian workers. The *tesserae* started to become cubes that could be perfectly fit together. This type of workmanship was called *tassellatum:* the tesserae had the dimensions of about a half-inch and served to compose both geometric and figured designs. However, contrary to Roman mosaic art, the African version produced scenes with a more 'flowery' style, inspired largely by oriental models. The mosaics, therefore, sumptuously describe mythological events, hunting or daily life scenes and exotic landscapes, and in all of them a desire to astound with opulence and majesty is noticeable.

The tour of the museum continues up to the second floor to find the 'Sousse' Room, which was the reception room: the present-day name derives from the enormous mosaic (33 by 44 feet) laid on the floor, representing the first *Triumph of Neptune* (second century AD), found at Sousse.

106 top The reduced dimensions of the tesserae *of some mosaics make it possible to achieve high-quality illustrative effects, smoothly blending the colors. The subjects are many: scenes from mythology and daily life, landscapes and still-lifes.*

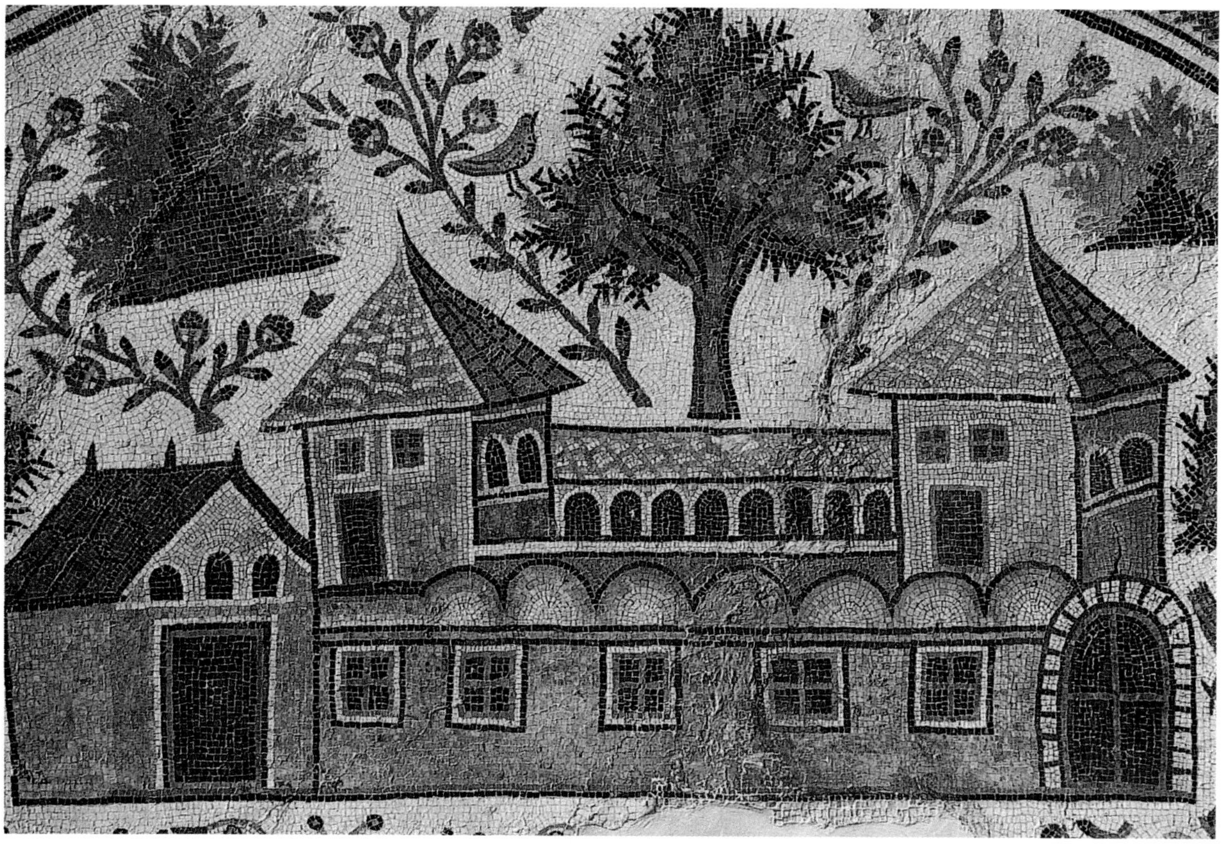

106 left In this mosaic from Utica, conserved in the museum of the capital, Diana is portrayed in an idealized wooded landscape, symbolized by the tree at the center of the scene. The divinity prepares to shoot an arrow at what seems to be an antelope.

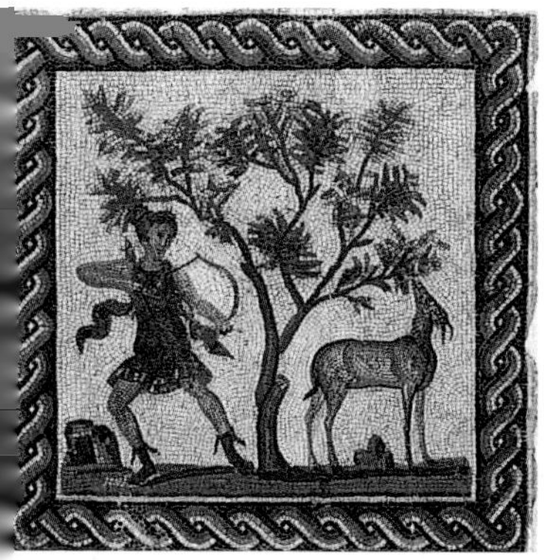

106-107 In the Ulysses mosaic, in the Bardo Museum, the Homeric hero is tied to the main mast so that he can listen to the song of the sirens with impunity, while his companions surrounding him have covered their ears with wax. To the right appear three sirens, portrayed here with half-bird half-woman bodies.

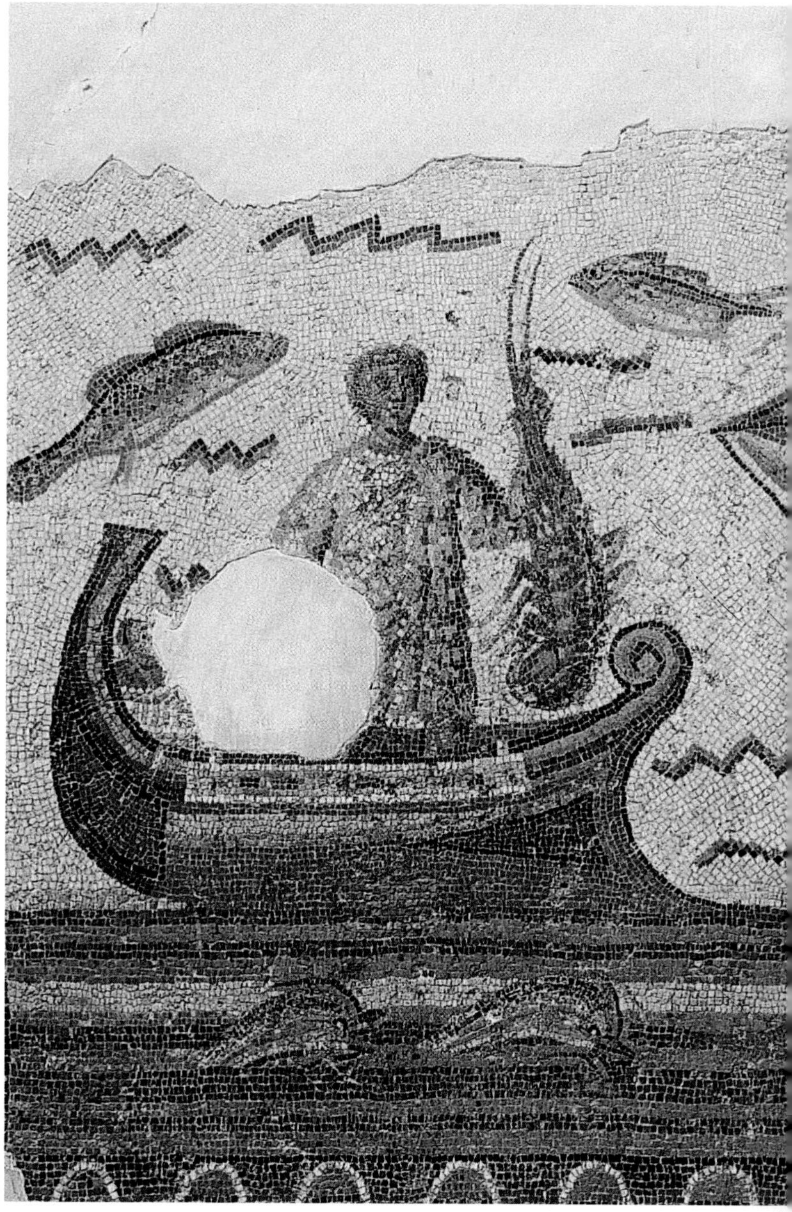

This room, surrounded by a portico under which stand Roman statues from the second and third centuries AD, contains several masterpieces. Among them is found perhaps the most important piece of the museum: the mosaic of *dominus Iulius* (fourth to fifth centuries AD), originally from Carthage. It is an incredible, extremely lively testimony to aristocratic life in Roman Africa during the Early Empire, with figures that seem to move in a perfectly believable scenario. Another very famous mosaic is that of *Virgil and the Two Muses* (third to fourth centuries AD), found at Sousse. On the other hand, the collection of bronze statues that were recovered during the underwater archeology expedition of 1908 (the oldest ever, scientifically) in a wreck off the coast of Mahdia is a curiosity. The load of Hellenistic-period Greek statues, perhaps stolen during the sacking of Athens ordered by the Roman general Silla, is largely intact and worthy of a visit. They merit to be seen as much as the Punic jewelry and the splendid, tragic loneliness of the mosaic of the Minotaur, small and alone, inside a labyrinth traced in black lines. If the opportunity arises to see the museum with few people around, one almost gets the feeling that the works of art are watching them while they walk through the halls pervaded by the deafening silence of images frozen for eternity.

107 top This mosaic from the Bardo depicts a well-known mythological theme: Bacchus and the pirates. The god of wine, kidnapped as a child by some pirates that wanted to sell him as a slave, manages to escape from his persecutors by changing them into dolphins.

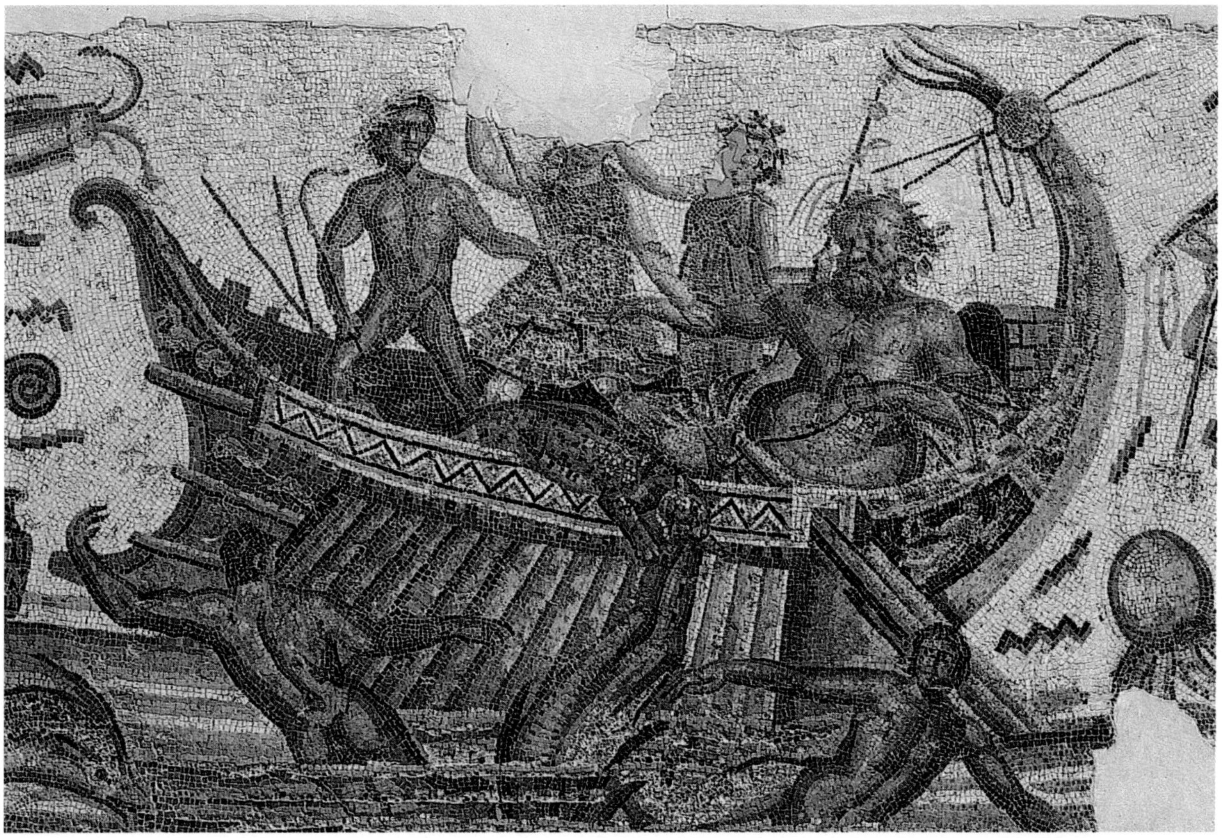

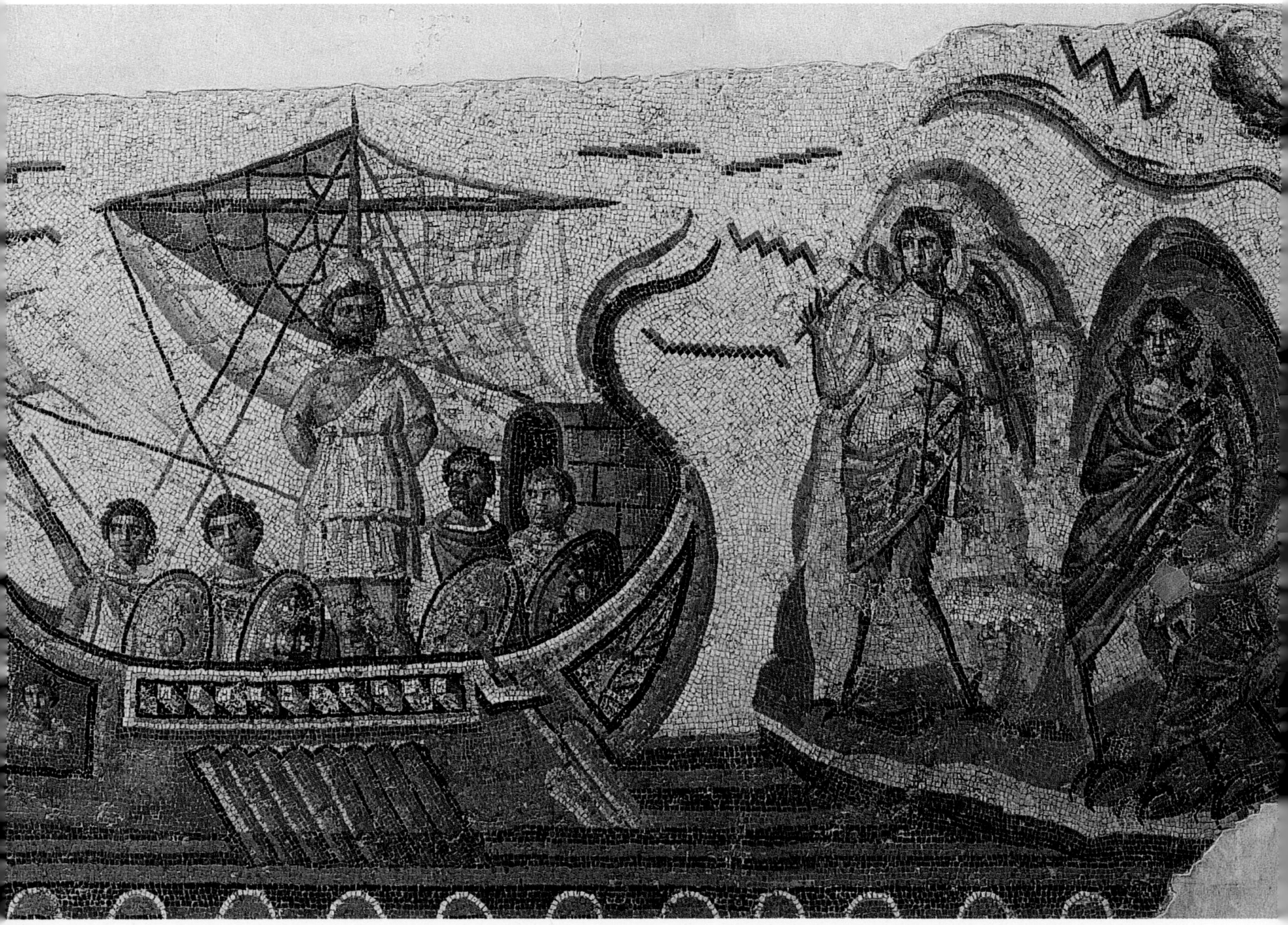

108 top The excavations conducted at the site of Carthage have brought to the light only Roman remains. The Punic city, which would have changed the future of the world had it not been defeated by Scipio Africanus and Scipio the Younger, was completely destroyed by the Romans in 146 BC.

108 bottom This valuable mosaic, whose squares with human and wild subjects alternate with marble intarsia in geometric motifs, was discovered in a Roman-era villa in Carthage. Protected by special laws since 1993, the site is part of the Patrimony of Humanity of UNESCO.

108-109 The Antonine Baths are found in the lower part of Carthage, close to the sea. Begun under Adrian (AD 118-138) and finished by Anthony Pius, it was partially destroyed by the Vandals, according to tradition, and brought again to the light between 1944-56.

It is also necessary to admire the places where these mosaics come from. The first is Carthage, obviously, which was not actually *deleta* totally, as the emperor Cato would have liked. From the magnificent, original city that was about to change the future of the world—if it had not lost the battle of Zama in 201 BC—not much remains, in truth, but the vestiges are interesting.

In the *Aeneid*, it was Dido who founded the city in 814 BC, according to legend, when she disembarked in this Libyan land while escaping from the tyranny of her brother in Phoenician Tyre. At that time, she asked the Libyans for a piece of land where she could settle with her people, but the answer was that she could only have as much as an ox skin would cover. The queen did not lose heart; she cut the skin in strips as thin as hairs and surrounded the present-day hill of Byrsa with them, saying that it would be called *Qart Hadasht*, the 'new city'. Thus was born a commercial emporium, and over the centuries, Carthage became that 'barbaric and magnificent' city that dared to oppose Rome (it was still Dido's fault, because in killing herself when she was abandoned by Aeneas she predicted that 'neither love there shall be between the two peoples nor pact'). It rose again from its ashes thanks to the will of Caesar and had seven centuries of prosperity, but it died definitively in 692 AD when it was taken by the Arabs. The first systematic excavation dates back to 1857, while Gustave Flaubert was writing *Salammbô*—the main character is the daughter of Hamilcar and the sister of Hannibal who dies for love, and whose name is recalled by a neighborhood in the modern Carthage—after which the site was enlarged and investigated by several different research teams.

It is better to begin with a visit to the museum, at the top of the hill, where some truly remarkable relics have been preserved: from the renowned Punic heads bearded with vitreous paste to the Roman mosaics and from the votive stelae to the grotesque masks and big Roman statues, just to name a few examples. Then, the Punic buildings in the area can be admired. Descending towards the lower city, one first glimpses the *tophet* (the sanctuary of Tanit and Baal Hammon, the supreme divine couple), the oldest place of worship in the area. Continuing on, an archeological park is dedicated to the Antonine Baths, the most sensational monument in Carthage, and finally the tour ends with the sites on the outskirts of the city.

109 top left Once Punic Carthage was razed to the ground, the Roman settlement rose on the basis of a program of urban planning, set on a quadrangular layout with street axes intersecting at right angles.

109 top right Byrsa Hill is the site of the first Carthaginian settlement: according to legend, substantiated by the Aeneid, it was Queen Dido who, in 814 BC, fenced in the area of the future Qart Hadasht, the 'new city'.

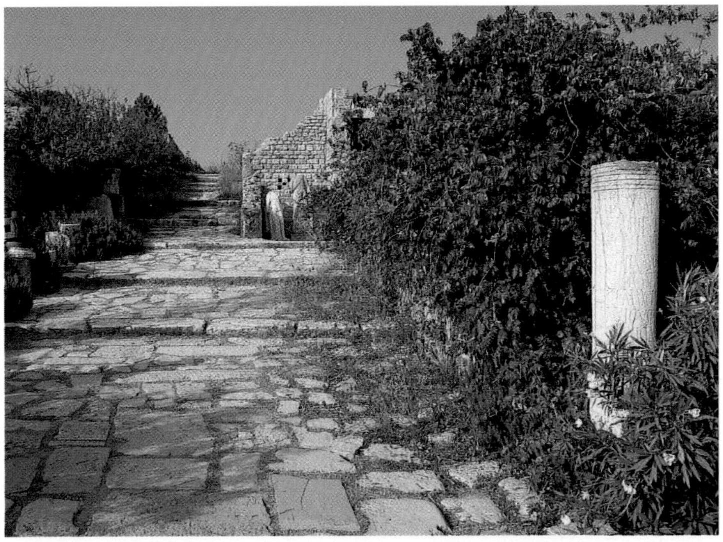
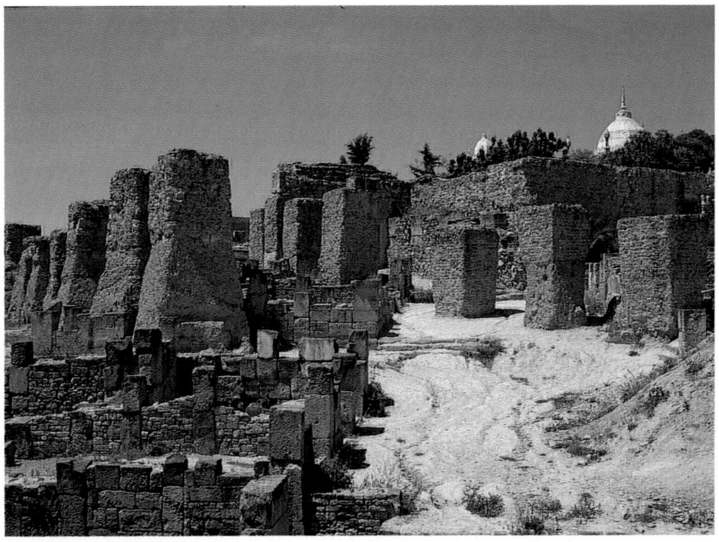
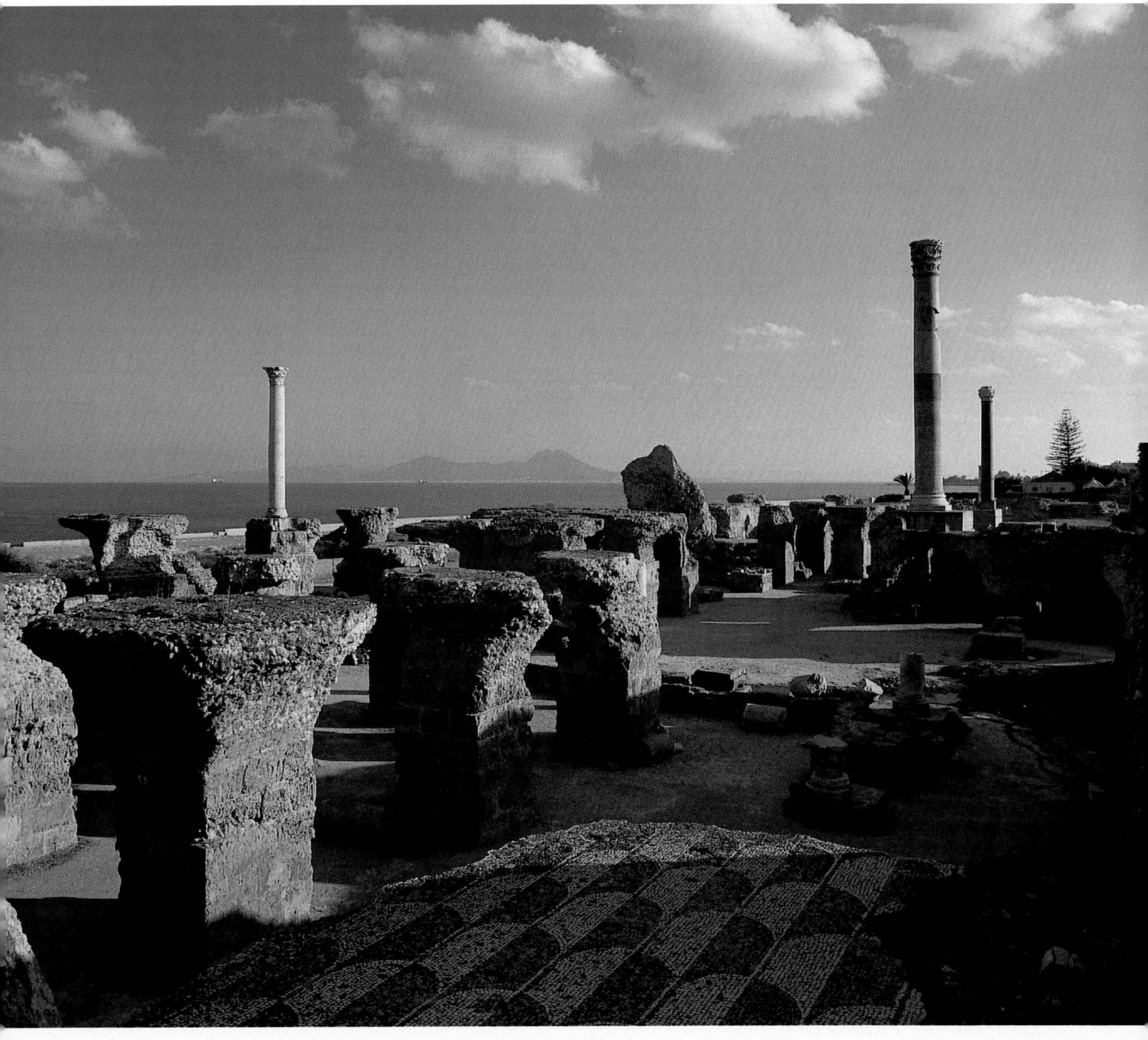

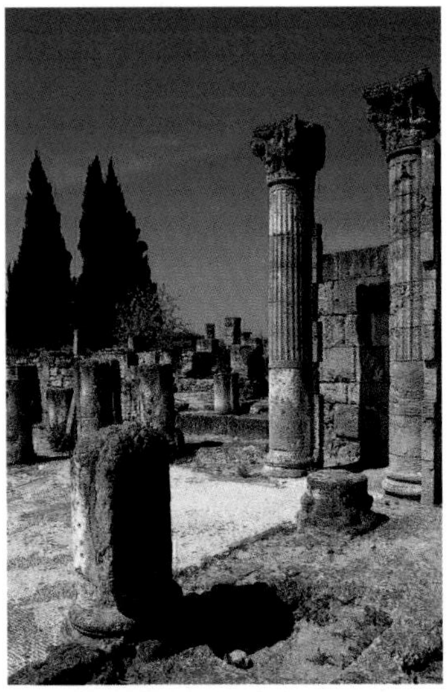

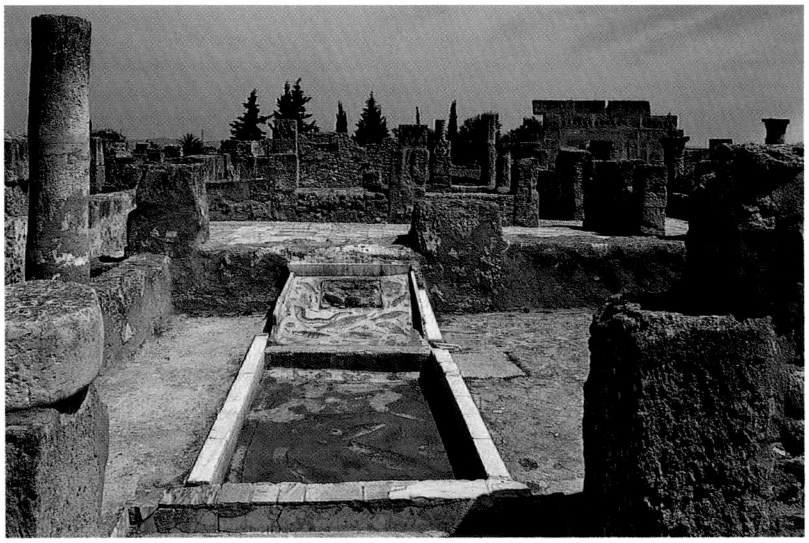

110 top left The House of the Historiated Capitals in Utica gets its name from the two Corinthian capitals, decorated with reliefs on a mythological theme, of the columns in the peristyle, which has two floors.

110 top right The House of the Waterfall conserves one of the exceptional mosaics that can be admired in Utica, decorated with marine motifs.

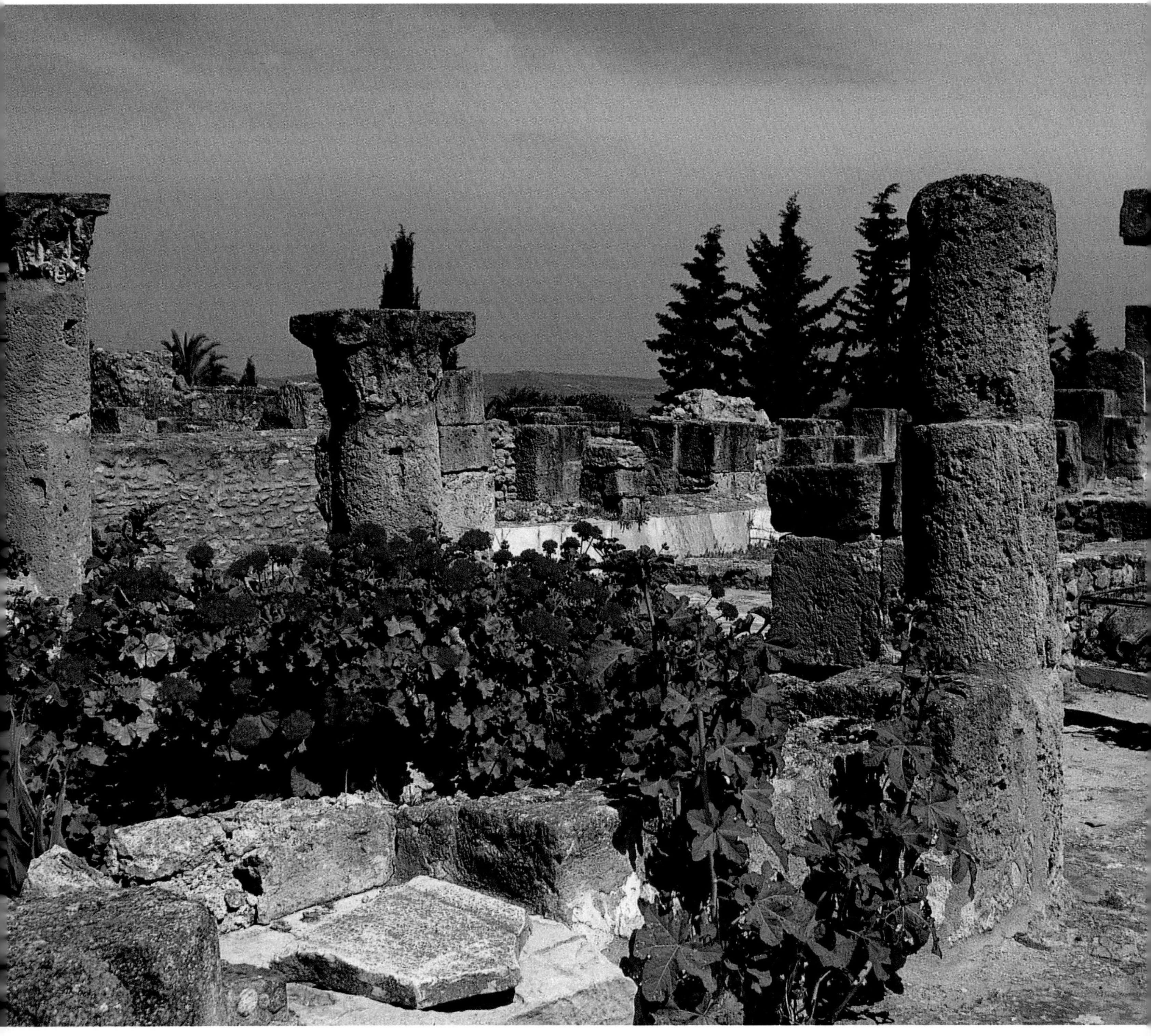

110-111 The House of the Waterfall occupies a large part of the insula *in which the most beautiful dwellings in Utica have been recovered, near the* decumanus maximus.

111 top Utica was the first Phoenician colony, having been founded by refugees from Tyre in 1100 BC, according to the tradition attested to by Pliny the Elder. The city used to be on the sea, but alluvial deposits from the Mejerda have filled the gulf onto which it looked with sand, to the extent that today it is about six miles away from the coast.

111 bottom The mythological themes of the mosaics from Utica are often 'lightened' by characters like this graceful cupid, concentrating on fishing in the water teeming with fish.

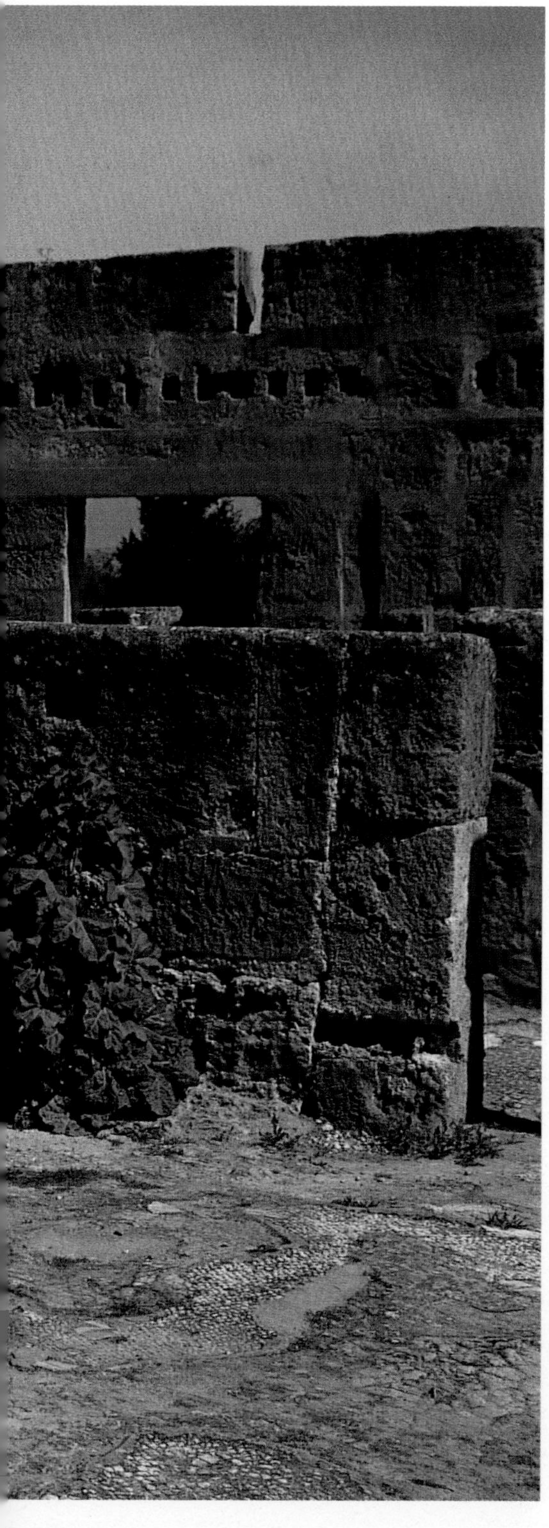

Further north, Utica was the 'biggest city in Libya after Carthage'. Founded three centuries before its 'sister' was by the Phoenician colonists from Tyre, it was an emporium of great importance. Proud, independent and powerful because of its big port, it allied itself with Carthage against the Greeks from Sicily and the Romans, but the Third Punic War went to the enemy, who repaid it with autonomy and favorable conditions for commercial matters.

It was also the capital of the province of Africa, but it later had to cede this honor to Carthage when it rose up again and, consequently, was the theater for battles between the supporters of Caesar and those of Pompey. Cato Uticensis, or Cato of Utica, who was in command of the pro-Pompey faction, killed himself here so as not to fall into the hands of his adversaries.

Utica's highpoint came in the second century AD and its end in the third. Today, the old city is located about seven miles from the coast since the floods of the waterways have left such debris as to distance the famous sea port and almost nothing remains of its past splendor. Among the best-preserved ruins are the House of the Waterfall, with several mosaics, the House of the Historiated Capitals, with stuccoes and Corinthian capitals, and the House of the Hunt. In the Punic tombs in the attached necropolis, many funereal sets of great importance have been found.

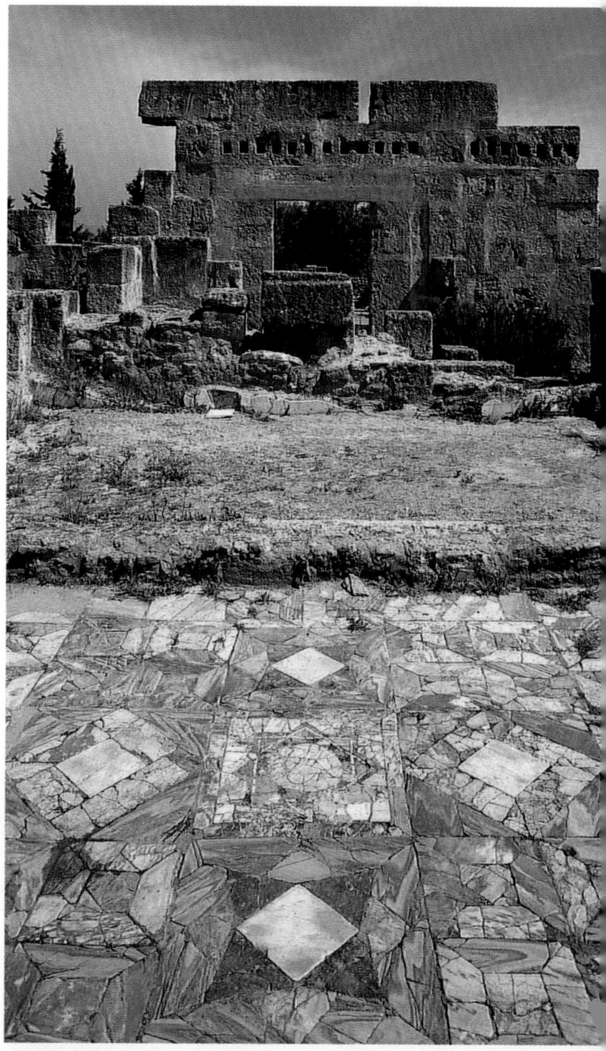

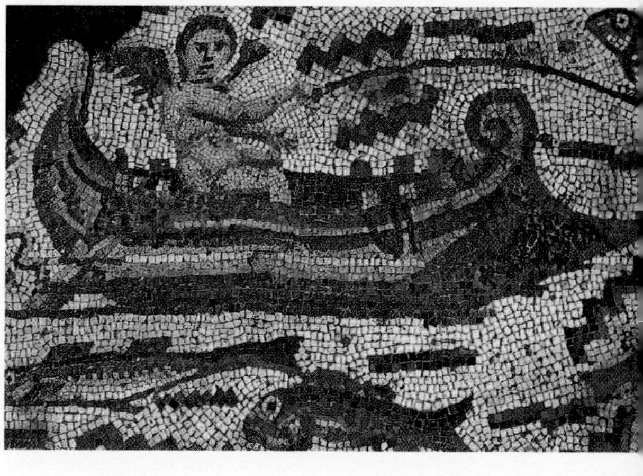

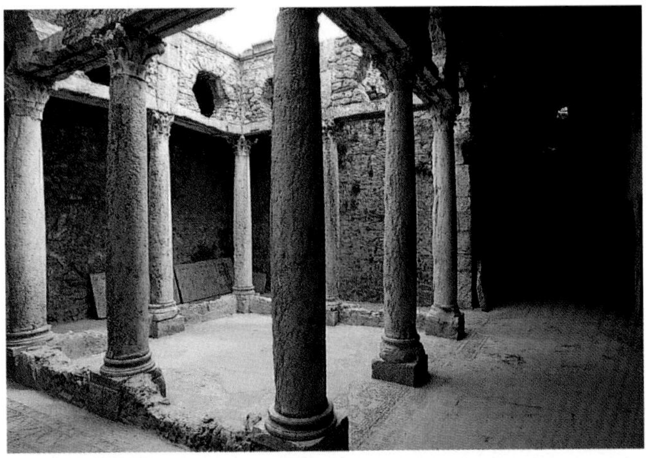

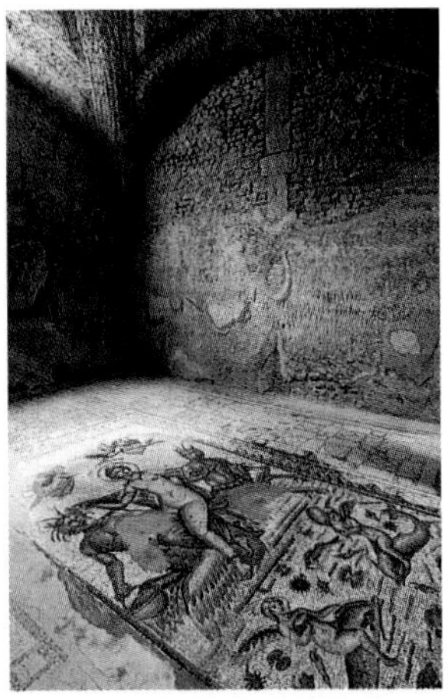

112 top left Among the private dwellings of Bulla Regia, the most well-known is the House of the Hunt, whose name derives from a valuable mosaic with a hunting scene conserved in the Bardo Museum. Onto the arcaded courtyard open several rooms of the abode.

112 top right The House of Venus Marina, known erroneously as 'of Amphitrite', has taken its name from a magnificent floor mosaic that is still found on site. The work depicts the goddess of love on the back of unusual centaurs, with cupids in a marine context at her sides.

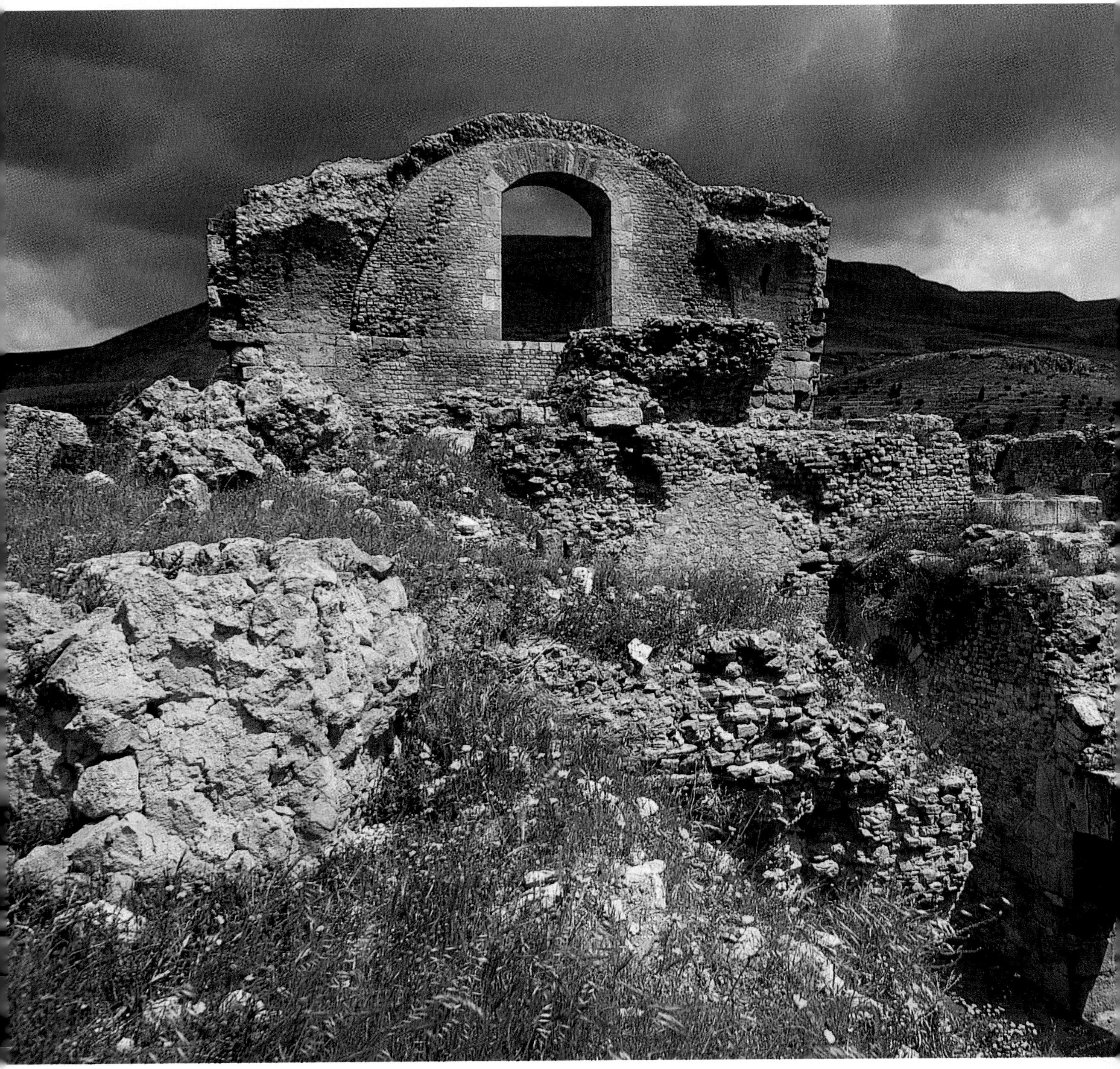

112-113 Bulla Regia, established at the foot of the southern slopes of Jebel Rebia, was the residence of Numidian kings in the second century BC, before it entered into the Roman sphere of influence. It is located in the Kroumirie, the forest region in the north of the country, from which the Romans procured the animals exhibited in circuses.

113 top The panorama of Bull Regia must not deceive. The city hides 16 feet deep its beautiful features; the multicolored mosaics that decorate the living spaces of the private residences, the most luxurious of which were semi-interred, in order to offer shelter during the hot summer months.

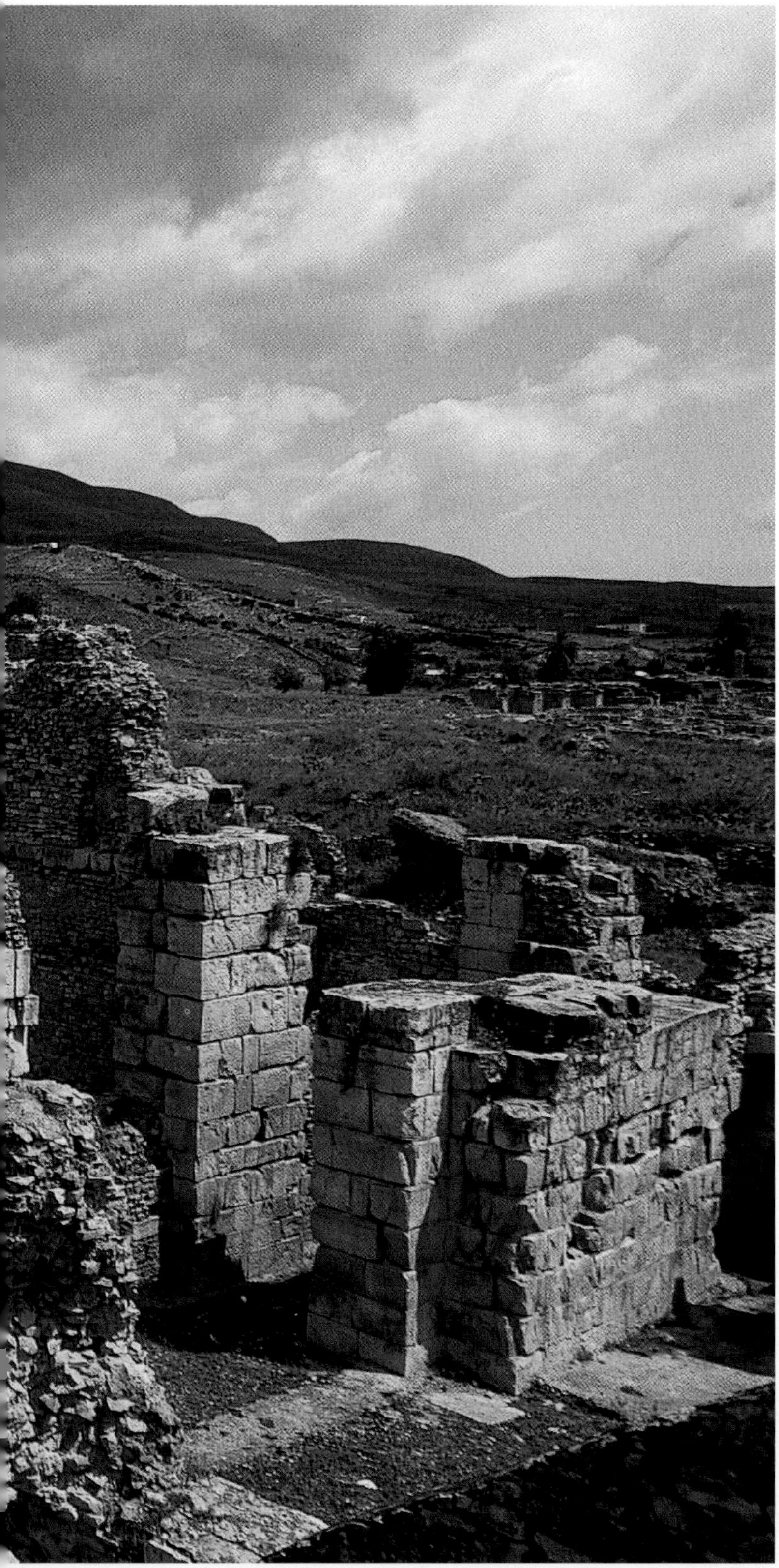

The ruins of Bulla Regia, situated further south and inland, are also very interesting. First a residence of nomad kings (second century AD) and then an imperial Roman city, the city prospered until the medieval era. Besides a beautiful theater and the baths, it boasts a rarity: Roman houses semi-interred up to 16 feet deep, with gorgeous mosaics left in place, built by ingenious architects to escape the heat. Among the most spectacular the House of the Hunt, the House of Fishing, and the House of the Venus Marina. A few miles to the west, the small town of Chemtou, with its marble quarries, baths, a theater that has highly significant subterranean galleries and the very new archeological museum.

113 bottom The theater of Bulla Regia was used until the end of the fourth century AD. Built between the second and third centuries AD and very well conserved, it was richly adorned by statues now on display in the Bardo Museum.

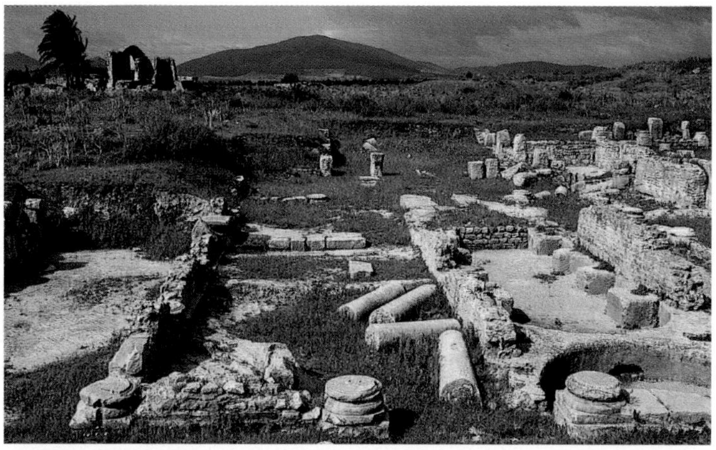

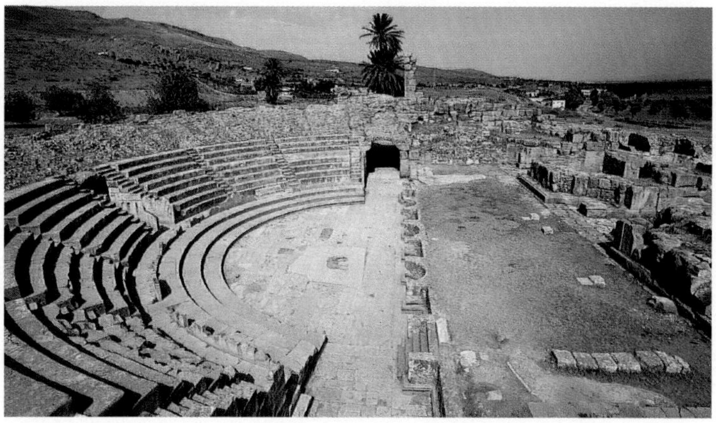

114 top The Capitol of Dougga is one of the most famous monuments in the country. Dedicated to the Capitoline triad, it dates back to the second century AD. Modified during the Byzantine era, it maintained a part of the portico, some statues and the monumental steps.

114 bottom The norm in buildings of this type, a rich statuary apparatus adorned the stage of the theater of Dougga. An inscription recalls that a citizen remembered for having been elected to a top sacerdotal position donated the monument.

114-115 Dougga, the ancient Thucca (fortress), is considered among the most important Roman cities of Africa. Located a few miles west of Tunis, the well-preserved ruins stand in a very evocative natural environment.

115 top left The House of the Clover is the most vast in Dougga. Constructed within AD 250 and then renovated, its name derives from the trefoil disposition of the three apses that embellish one of the rooms. The Roman residential area covered about 62 acres.

115 top right The theater of Dougga was erected between 168 and 169 AD. Modest in size, it is very well preserved and features a cavea 49 feet tall, which rests on the living rock. It was able to hold up to 3,500 spectators in 19 sections of tiers.

Only a couple miles further south, Dougga is probably the most vast and well-preserved Roman city of Africa. It is unforgettable. The treacherous king of Numidia Massinissa conquered Dougga between 160 and 155 BC. He settled there and his heirs were perceptive enough to take the side of the Romans against Carthage. After the destruction of Carthage, Dougga was not occupied but was annexed in 46 BC by Caesar to the new province of Africa and it prospered quickly. It grew again in 205 AD when it was named a *municipium* by Septimus Severus and then a colony in 261. In testimony to this prosperity, stupendous public buildings have survived that between the second and fourth centuries AD rivaled those of other provinces for their architectural luxury and magnificence.

Built on a hill, the Roman settlement

spreads over about 62 acres and it is totally shaped to the slope with a labyrinth of winding alleys and houses with double entrances, characteristic even today of typical Mediterranean villages. The heart of the city is entered by passing through the Square of the Rose of the Winds, which takes its name from the engraving in the pavement of three concentric circles with the names of the 12 winds (third century AD). Next, there is the spectacular Capitolium from around 166 AD, dedicated to the Capitoline triad, Jupiter, Juno and Minerva. It held up to 3,500 spectators, divided into 19 sections of tiers, and had an impressive stage with tall shafts of Corinthian columns that made it visible even from afar. Then, the arch of Alexander Severus appears, from which the Libyan-Punic mausoleum, lonely and majestic on a stretch of level ground, is seen, an extremely rare, intact example of a royal Numidian tomb from the second century BC. Everything was built with a vast profusion of means, but the affluence of the rich is seen in the baths as well, like those of the Cyclops, so-called for the mosaic featuring Vulcan's forge conserved at the Bardo. It was the Byzantine era that dropped a veil of silence over the city, which was never, however, completely abandoned. In 1889, methodical excavations began and are still ongoing.

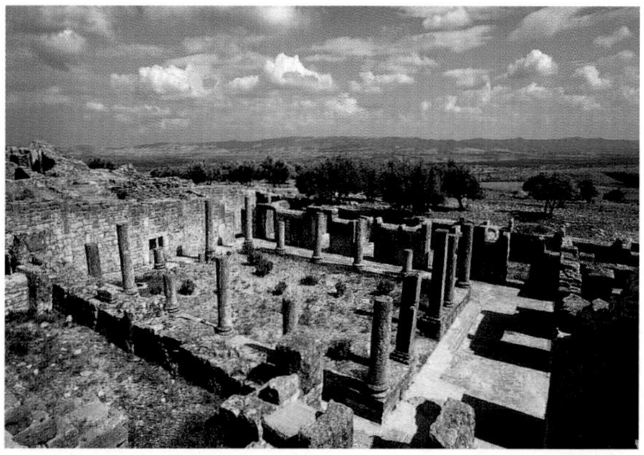

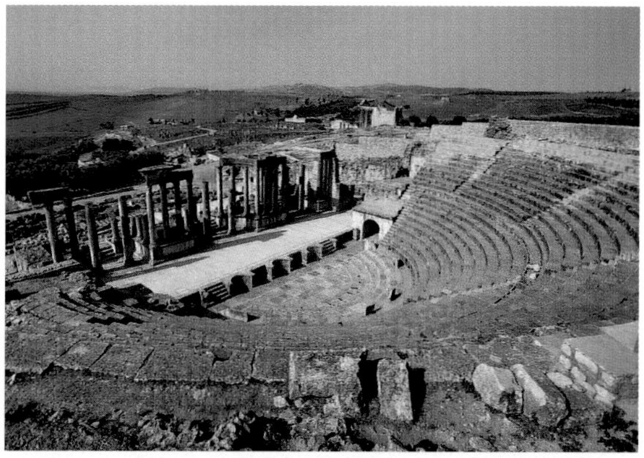

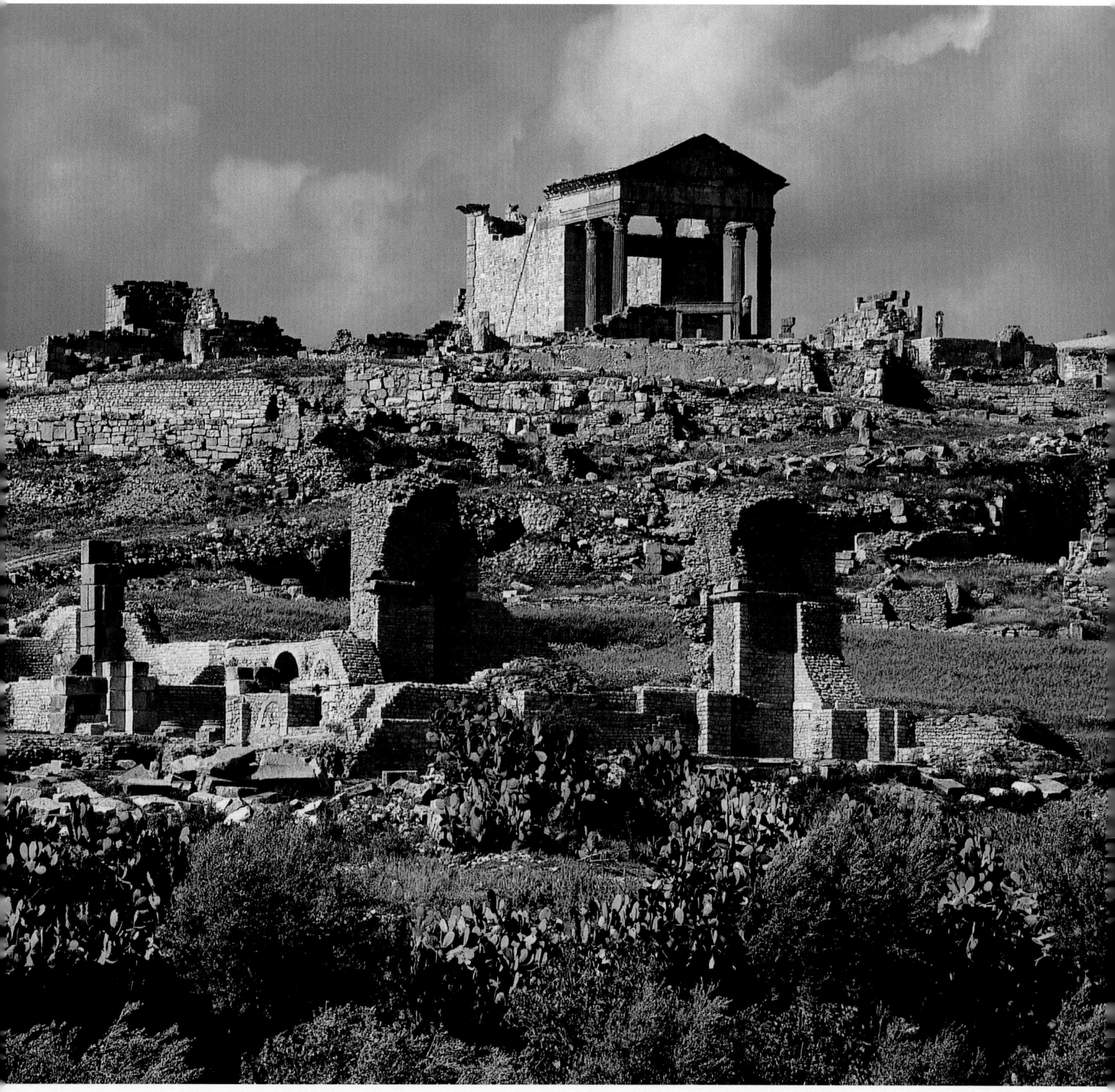

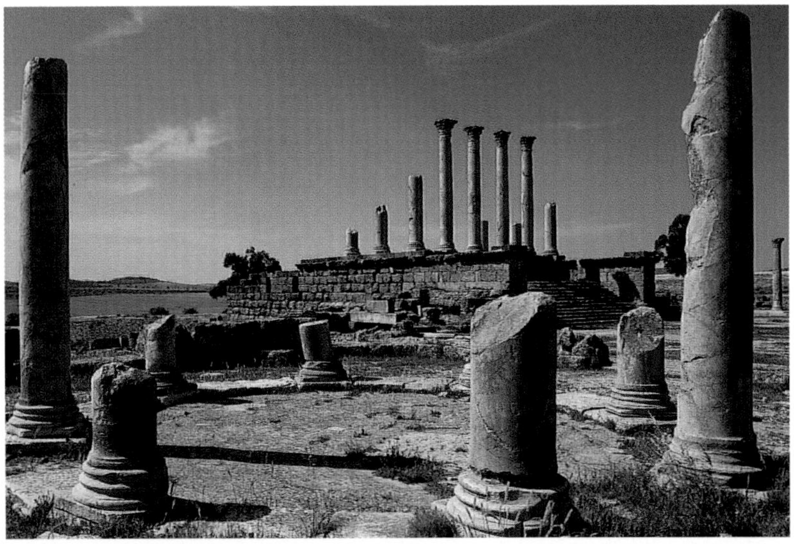

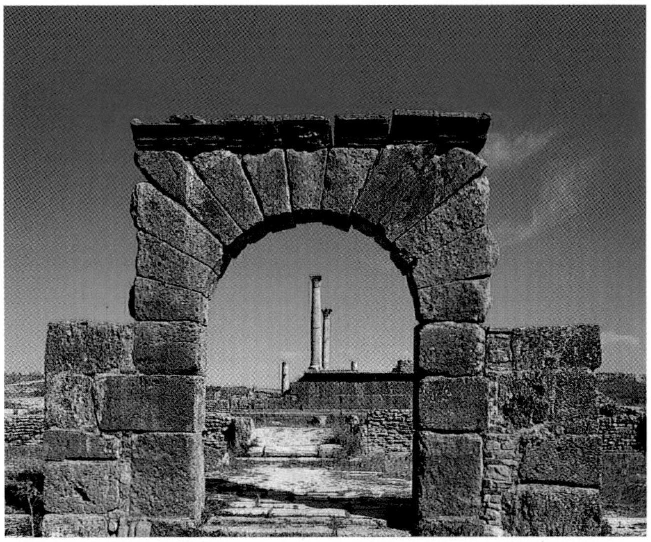

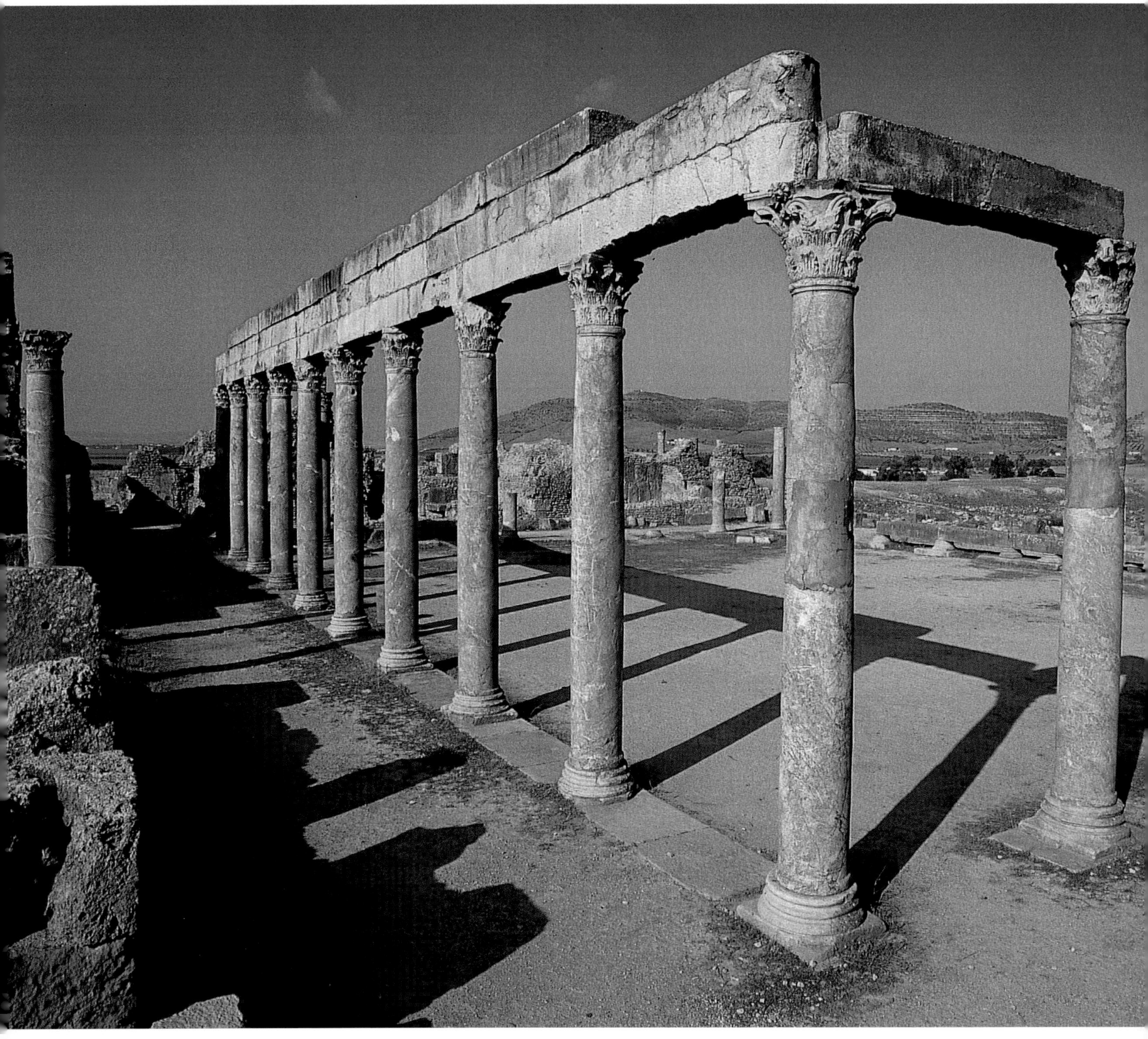

116 top left According to some historians, the origin of Thuburbo Majus goes back to Augustus, who would have gathered an original nucleus of colonists here. For others, it became Roman only during the time of Adrian, a moment in which a great period of urban development was recorded, as testified to by the notable extension of the excavation area.

116 top right Structured with big blocks and rather linear forms, this arch gave access to one of the two bathing establishments identified in Thuburbo Majus, called, on the basis of certain inscriptions recovered at the site, thermae hiemales *and* aestivales, *in other words the winter and summer sections of the building.*

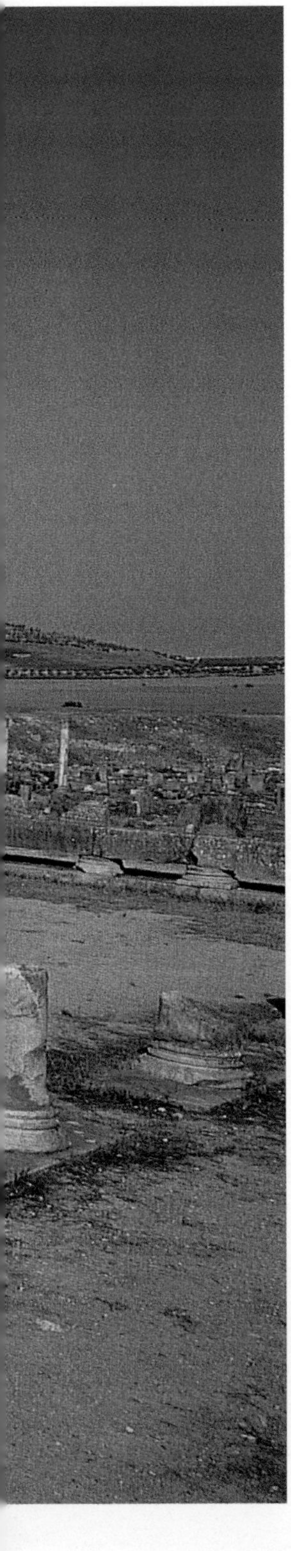

116-117 The ruins of Thuburbo Majus are located about 37 miles south of Tunis. In the foreground of the image, the remains of the portico of the Palaestra of the Petronii can be observed, which took its name from Petronius Felix and his children, who donated it to the city, as an inscription tells, in AD 225.

Thuburbo Majus, on the other hand, is at the same latitude but further to the east, closer to the coast. It is a Punic city, 37 miles from Tunis, that became Roman during the time of the emperor Adrian, and that underwent great urban development (up to 12,000 people lived there) as testified to by the remarkable range of the excavations. For a non-exhaustive but sufficient visit, about an hour and a half will do. The Capitolium, one of the most important in all of Africa dating back to 168 AD, the Palaestra of the Petronii from 225 AD, where the inhabitants came to exercise before going to the baths, and the summer baths from 361 AD, in their definitive shape with very refined decoration, are not to be missed. However, the houses are the main attraction of the site. They get their name from the multicolored mosaics recovered here, now conserved at the Museum of Bardo, which allow for the reconstruction of the lives of the ancient residents in all their political and social aspects.

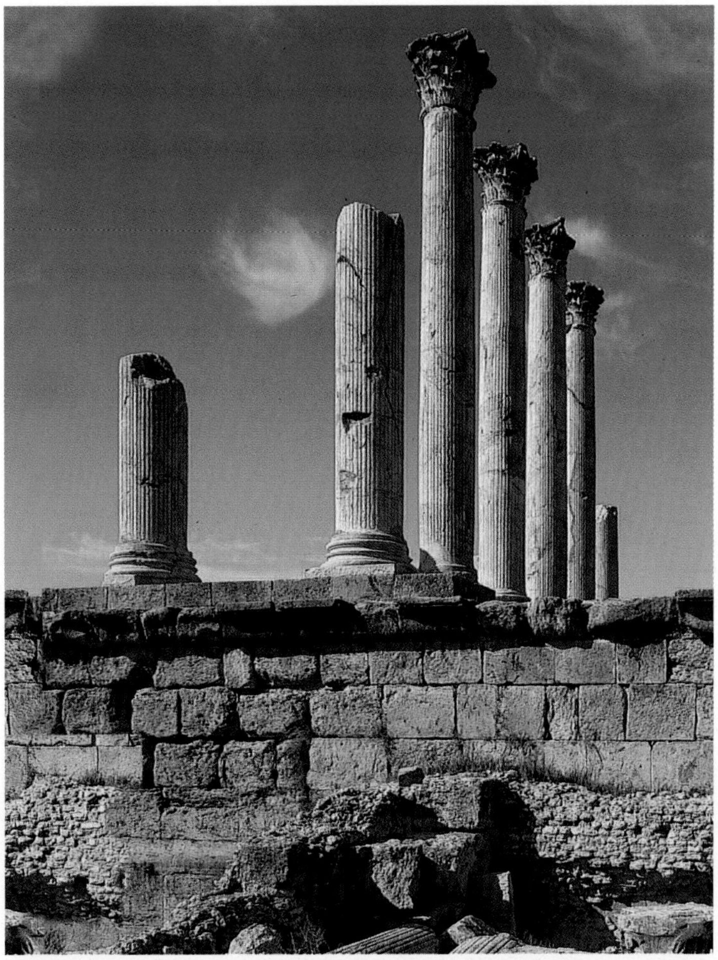

117 top Of the Capitol of Thuburbo Majus, built in AD 168, only the podium and the Corinthian columns are visible today. After its destruction, it housed an oil mill, in which a beautiful monumental head of Jupiter now conserved in the Bardo Museum was found.

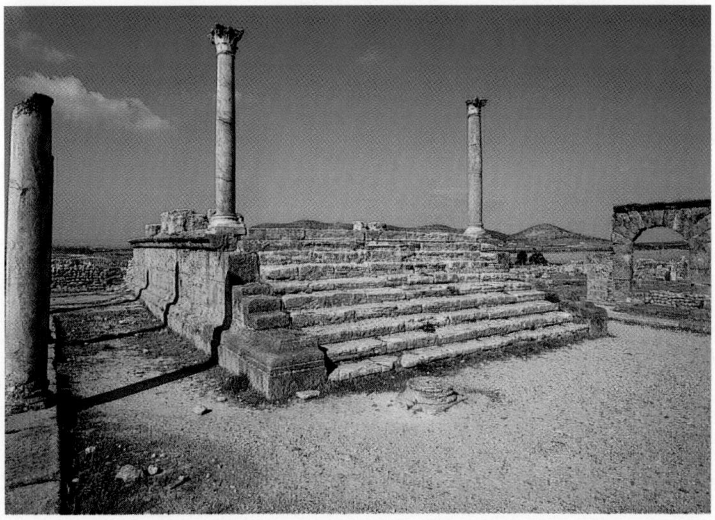

117 bottom The temple of Baalat, in Thuburbo Majus, is a small sanctuary resting on a tall podium. Erected most likely under the Antonines, it owes it name to a fragment of a clay statue found here, which portrays a feminine divinity sitting on a throne.

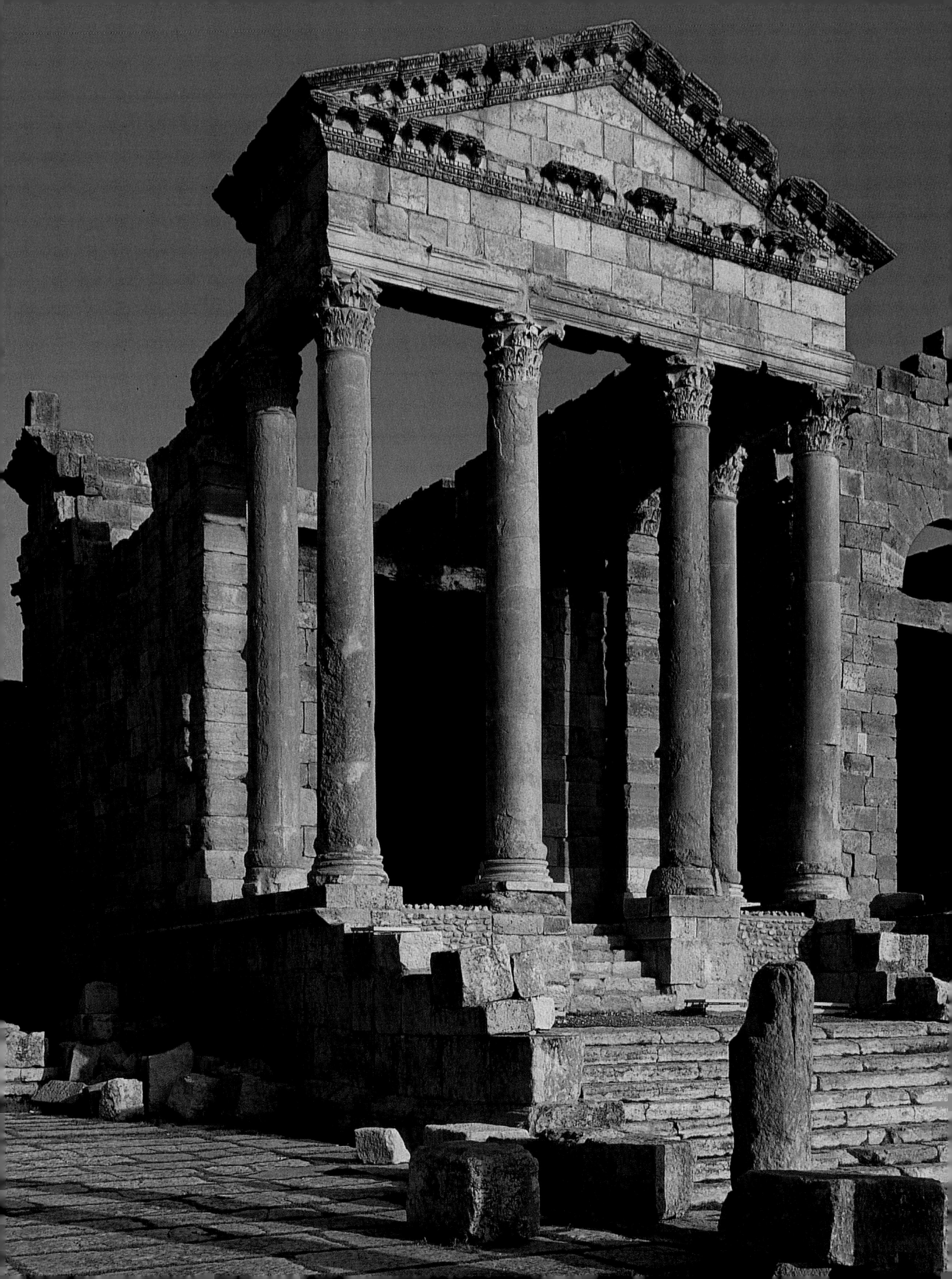

118 The Capitol of Sbeitla, the ancient Sufetula, a Roman city founded in the first century AD, was composed of three temple buildings. In the image, the left one is visible, which shows itself to be in an excellent state of preservation.

119 top The arch of Diocletian, in Sbeitla, marks the southern border of the Numidian kingdom. With only one barrel vault between two niches framed by columns on the front of each side, the monument demonstrates a common typology in Roman Africa.

119 center top Within the 1,401-foot perimeter of the ellipse, the amphitheater of el-Jem, dating back to the beginning of the third century AD, could contain up to 27,000 spectators.

119 center bottom The monumental forum of Maktar is dominated by the massive structure of the triumphal arch dedicated in 116 AD to Emperor Trajan. The construction was later incorporated into the fortifications of the Byzantine era.

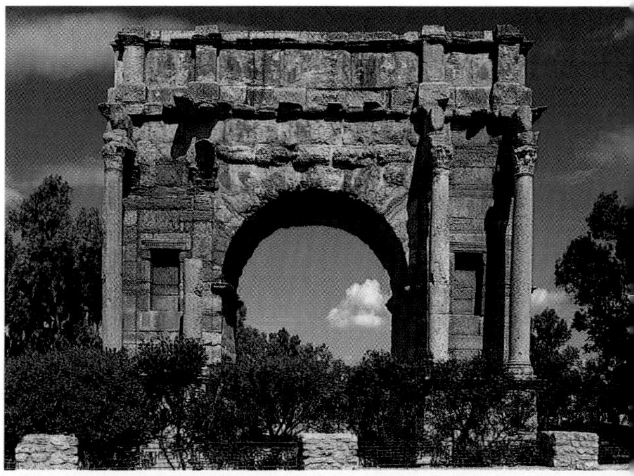

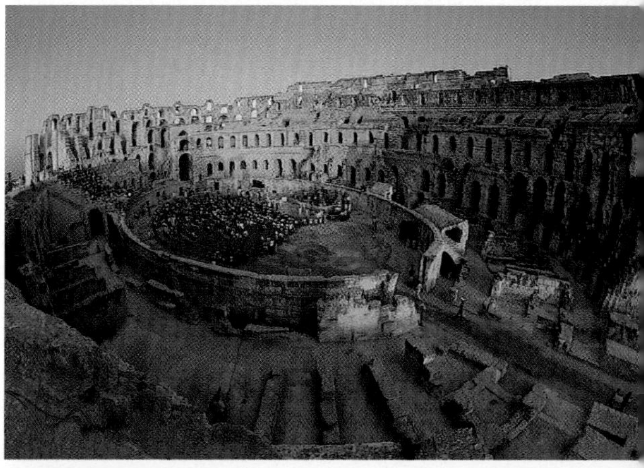

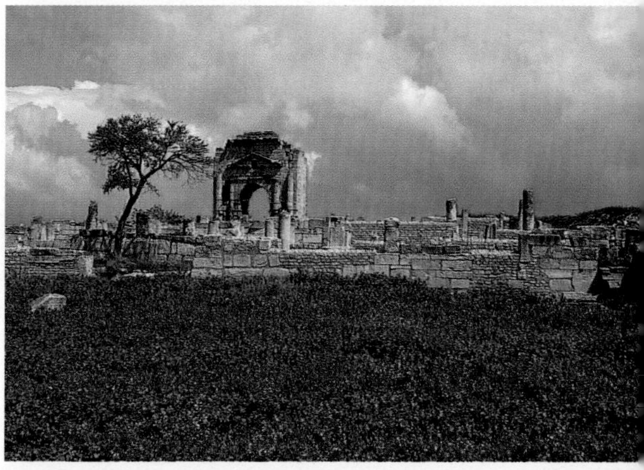

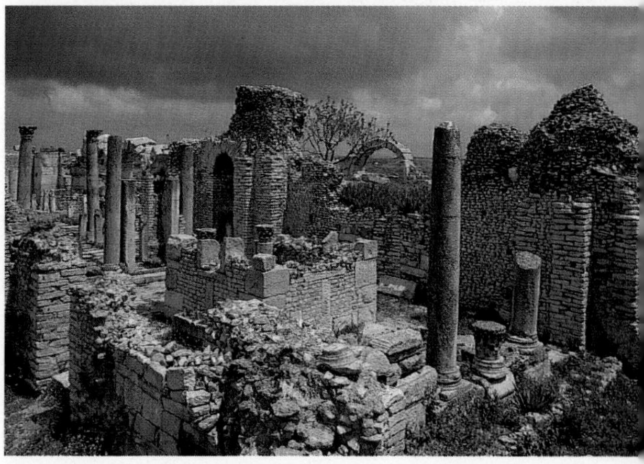

Maktar, further to the south, reveals itself to visitors at a quota of around 3,380 feet. With its imposing ruins in the middle of Numidian territory, it was the place where Scipio Africanus lay in wait for Hannibal before the battle of Zama. The Mactaris of the Romans was in fact an important place both from a strategic and commercial point of view, since it overlooks one of the passageways through the Great Ridge. The result was, therefore, a place of union between various cultures and the Punic influence is felt above all in the religion, with the important cult of Baal practiced in the sanctuary at the bottom of a gorge. Its period of maximum splendor was in the second century AD, as testified to by the forum from those years, perfectly paved, onto which is grafted the triumphal arch in honor of Trajan. The baths are in an excellent state of preservation, as is the arch of Bab al-Ain, at the entrance to the new city. However, the most particular monument is the Schola Juvenes, where what could be called a paramilitary school, which employed young men in a militia that operated like a police force, had its headquarters.

Sbeitla marks the southern border of the Numidian kingdom. The ancient Sufetula was in the territory of the steppes of the nomads, and it emerged from the abyss of time only in later times, when the rich patrician Gregory, governor of Carthage, decided to move there. In 647 AD, with the defeat of the Byzantine army, Greco-Roman Africa died and the Arab one was born. Today, in a 124-acre archeological area, it can be seen how the Roman city was divided into *insulae* (quadrangular blocks of residential buildings), with the inevitable baths, the capitol and the triumphal arch, but that which is most striking here is the Christian presence. The churches are numerous and are among the most beautiful in the northern part of the Black Continent.

El-Jem, finally, is closer to the coast. It can be recognized from far away by an apparition that borders on being a mirage: an out-and-out Colosseum, 'a stone oval, a seal with which Imperial Rome marked a steppe good only for sheep and dromedaries'. With a good 1,401 feet of elliptical perimeter, it was the third biggest amphitheater after that of Rome and Capua, capable of accommodating 27,000 spectators: a magnificent construction that has risen up in the solitude of this region of the country since the beginning of the third century AD. For the Romans, it was not only a place for games but also a sort of enormous water collector, which was ingeniously channeled by a series of technical devices. This allowed the cultivation of olive trees in the middle of this hard and inhospitable land.

119 bottom Maktar, situated in the interior of the country, to the north of Kairouan, saw its period of maximum splendor during the second century AD, as testified to by the forum, perfectly paved, on which rises the triumphal arch dedicated to Trajan.

THE ART OF REJOICING

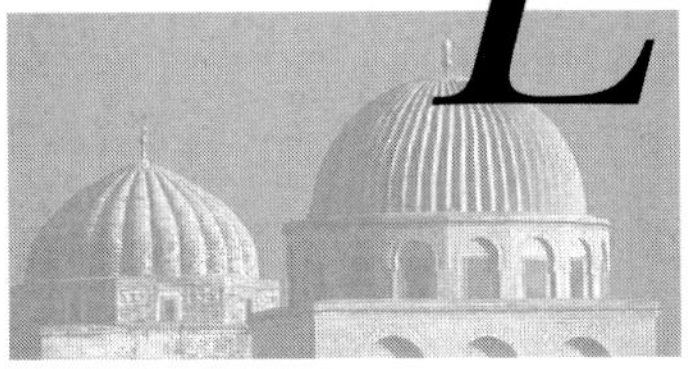

Looking at the calendar of holidays, one would say that the Tunisians are really a happy people. Starting with the celebration of the New Year and proceeding in chronological order there is the ceremony at the end of Ramadan and then the big holiday that commemorates the sacrifice of Abraham. Then, there are circumcisions, weddings with a gathering of relatives, musical and dance festivals, parades and equestrian acrobatics. The holiday is still a strong source of attraction for the inhabitants of this country, who sometimes have only this opportunity, in all the year, to exchange news and household goods, to look for a husband or wife or to buy a horse or trade a herd of goats. As far as traditional clothing is concerned, western styles have seriously made a dent in the conservative heritage of attire. Today in the big cities, women dress as they please, even with only their heads covered, but in small towns and in the southern part of the country they often are seen wearing typical clothing.

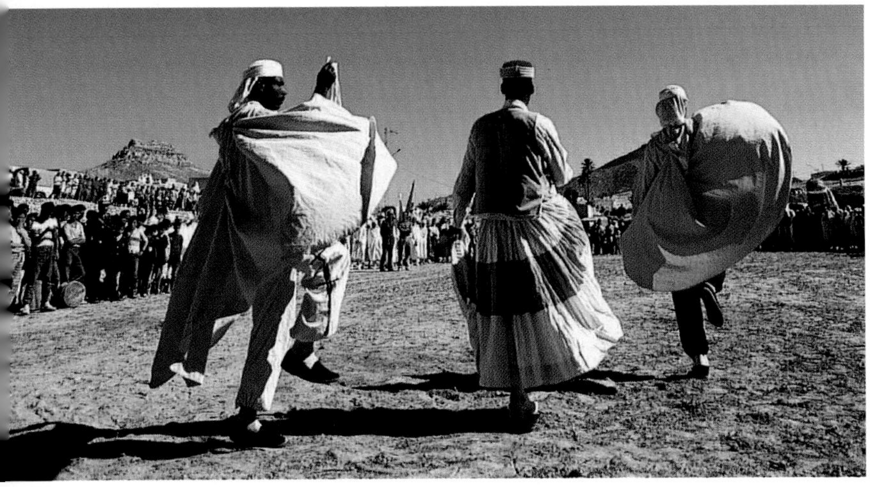

120 In Douz, during the festival that is held in December, men and women perform in various collective dances, among them those 'of possession', during which the dancers may fall into a trance.

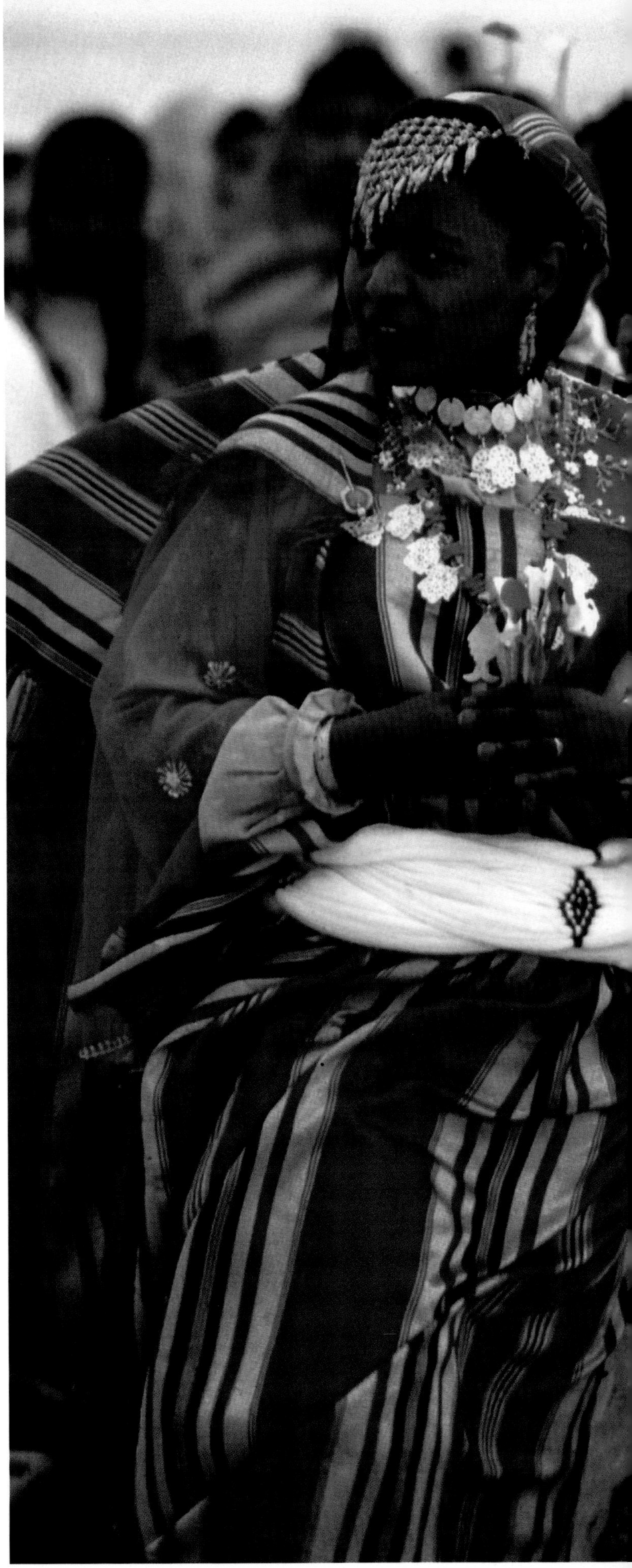

120-121 A group of Berber women dressed up in traditional costumes take part in the international festival of the Sahara, which is held in Douz, a town in Nefzaoua, the pre-Saharan region.

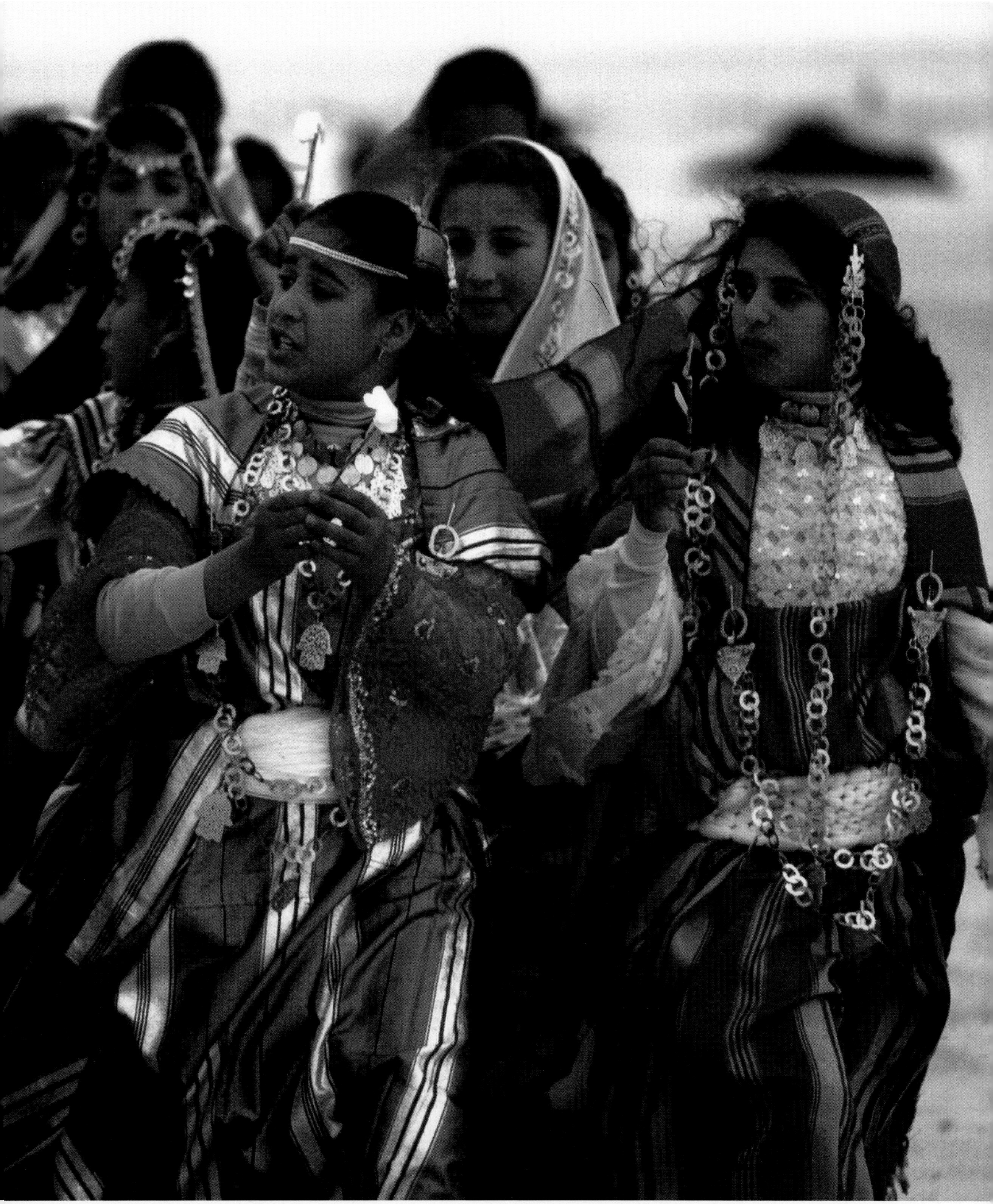

122 top The M'Razig of Douz, a village that comes out of its tranquil ways once a year thanks to the winter festival that is held there, have been horsemen for generations and offer spectators demonstrations of their extraordinary equestrian abilities.

122 bottom A group of musicians performs during a party in the mining town of Metlaoui. Dressed in the traditional bournous, *the performers have added a personal touch to the outfit with green scarves.*

122-123 Camel-drivers prepare to compete in the race that is held on the occasion of the international festival of the Sahara, in Douz: the other attractions at this festive event are the nomad folklore shows and hunting with greyhounds.

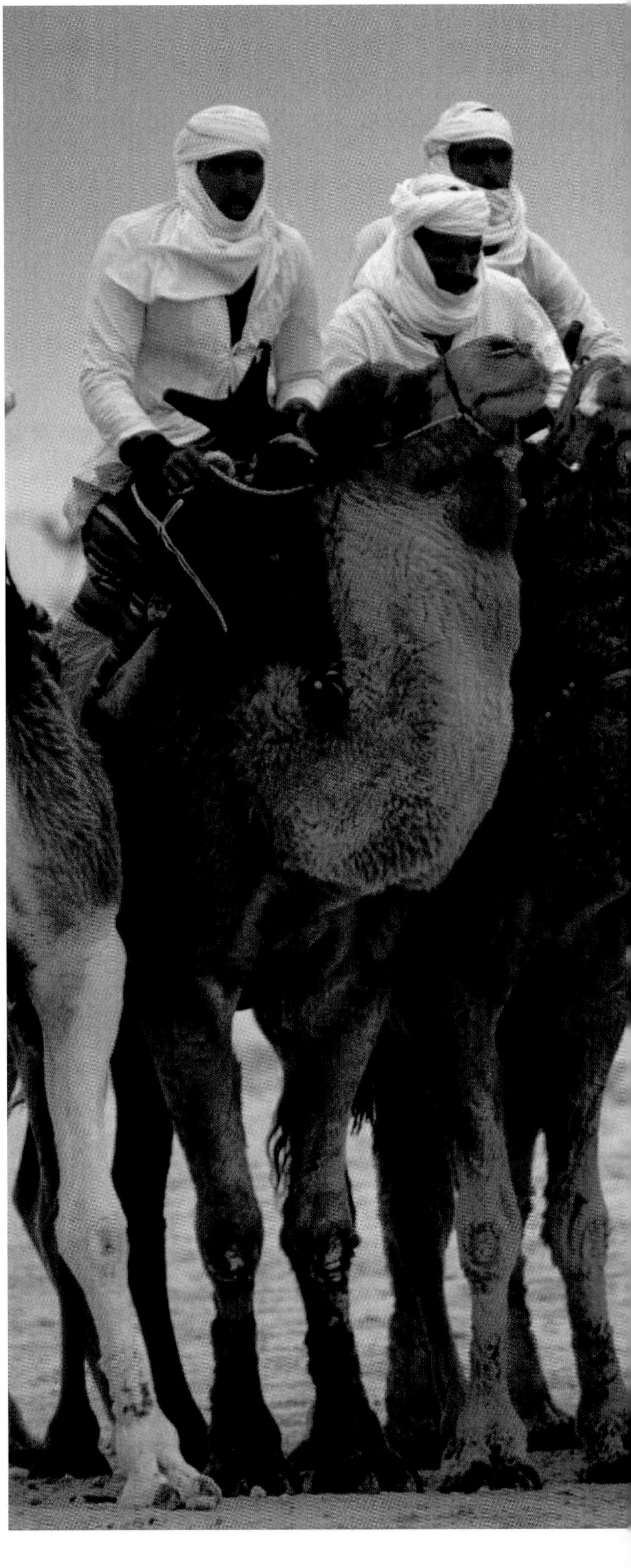

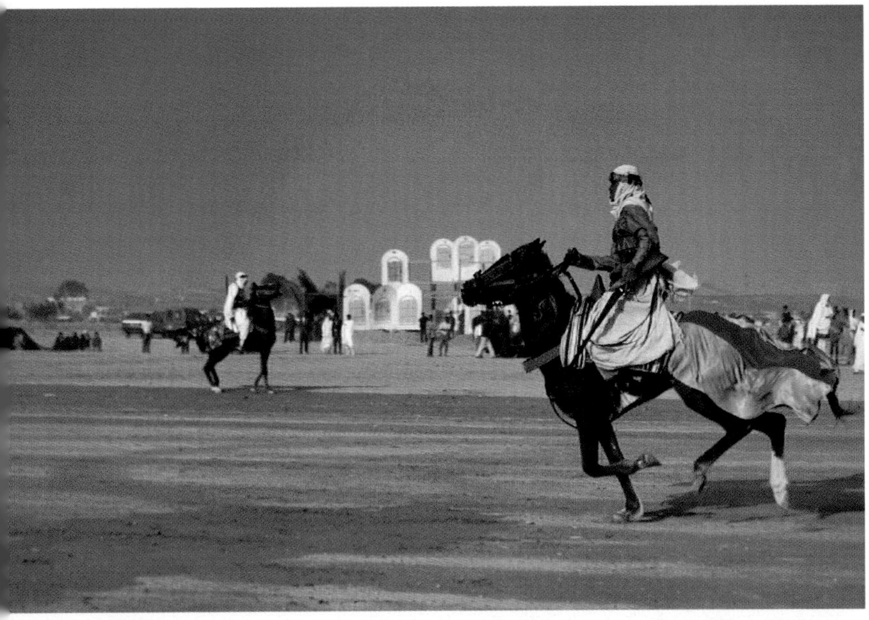

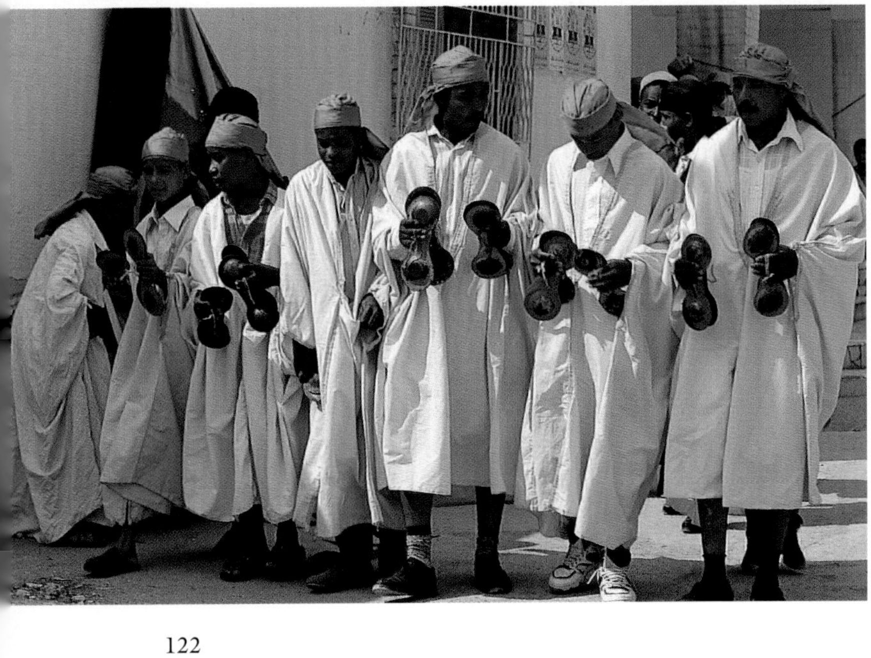

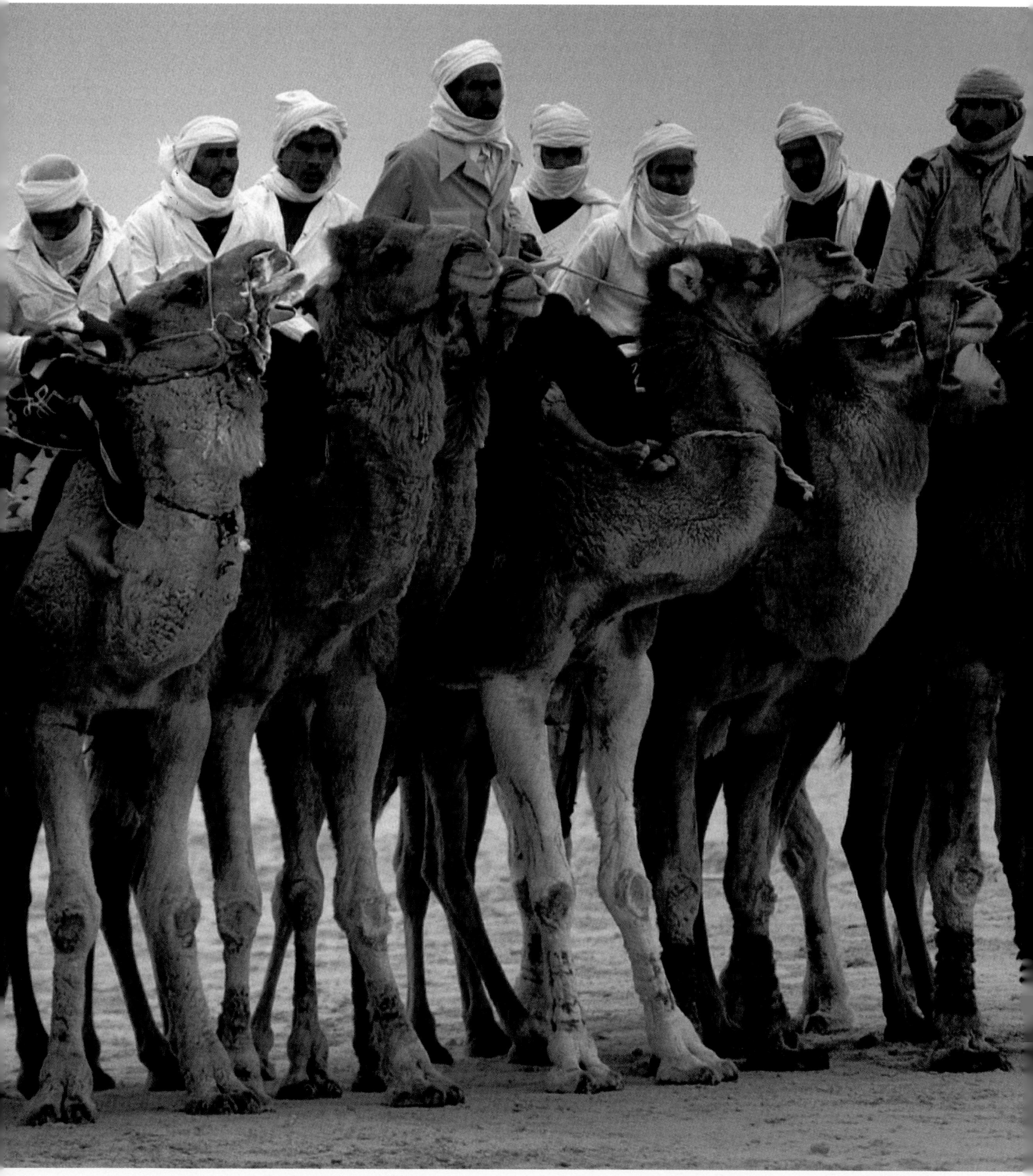

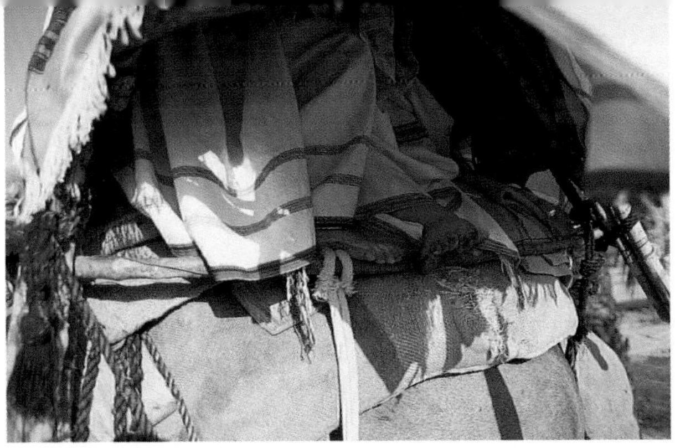

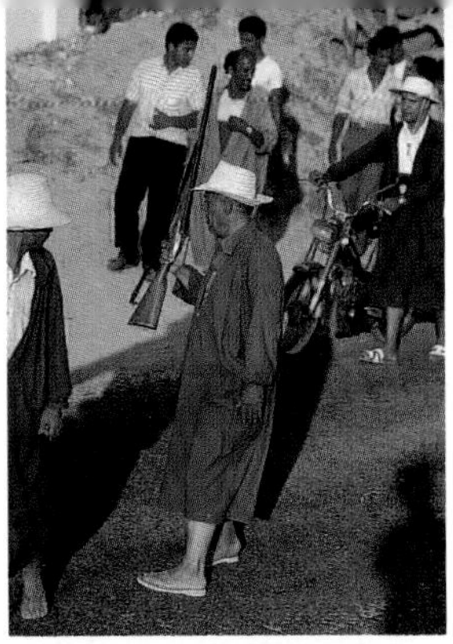

124 top left The bride's feet, which stick out from her clothes, are painted with henna, as tradition requires. Even her hands are decorated with symbolic designs traced in the same natural dye.

124 top right Shooting into the air is a typical custom at Arab weddings. During these parties, all the relatives compete to show, in various ways, their generosity towards the wedding couple.

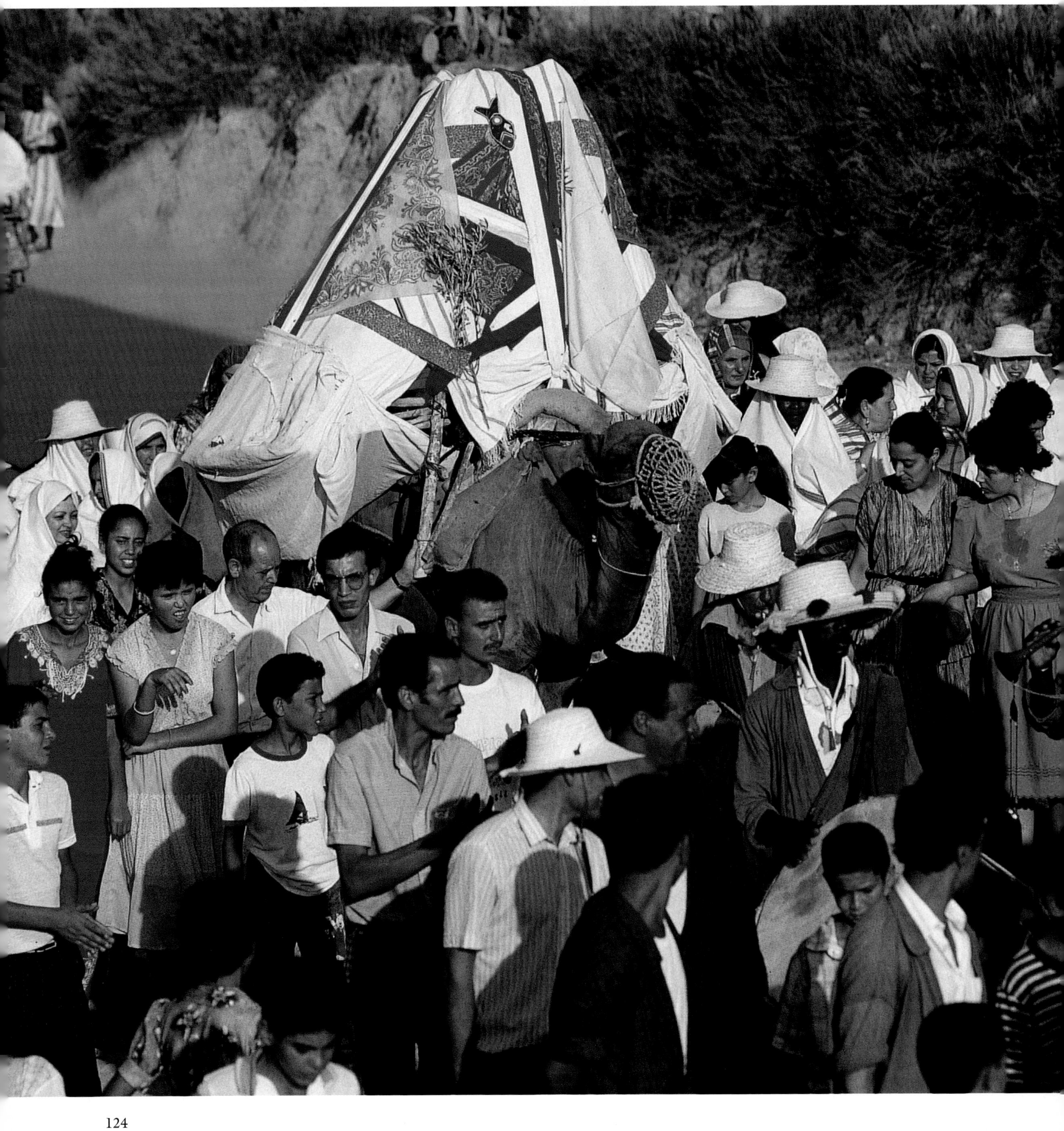

124-125 *A wedding in Jerba requires the presence of a large bridal procession that gives a thunderous accompaniment to the event. Weddings are normally celebrated in summer.*

In reality, manner of dress denotes, as everywhere, the rank and social position of the person who wears it, but this is more noticeable on holiday occasions.

In this case, fashion returns to traditional norms, and women, under long veils, hide elaborate dresses, sewn or only draped, as in antiquity. For city women, the most common outfit is a simple tunic, cut and sewn, which, however, never lack embroidery and, as an accessory, a solid-color scarf and decorated shawls. Women in the country, on the other hand, wear the malya, a dress draped and fastened with silver pins, almost always woven at home by their own hands. Men that reside in the city wear a garment that originated in the sixteenth century called the *jebba*, an article of clothing open at the chest, sleeveless and that falls to mid-calf. Elsewhere, puffy trousers or a simple, very wide tunic can be worn. Also for men, the traditional head covering is the *fez*, a red wool cap, which was still considered just a support for a turban in the eighteenth century. Only later did it become a head covering in its own right. That which counts, however, is 'the good suit', rich with embroidery, in lively colors, with above all a lot of gold, which for everyone, men and women, is a symbol of power and wealth.

During the holidays, dressed to the nines, the people play instruments and dance. Music and dancing are fundamental components of Arab culture. Dances range from belly dancing, which is danced alone, to the group dances of the south to those called 'possession' or ecstatic dancing, during which dancers can fall into a trance. However, the important thing is to move and express oneself to the rhythm of the music, whether traditional or not. One of the classical compositions is the *malúf*, in 13 sittings of instrumental and vocal performances.

125 top A bride, entirely covered in veils, is about to be brought before her future husband. In the past, in the weeks preceding a wedding, the women were fed with sweets and particularly nutritious foods until they acquired those abundant and healthy shapes that would have honored the groom.

125 bottom The jahfa is the kidnapping of the bride, who is put in a canopy and placed on the back of a camel decorated with silk hangings in lively colors.

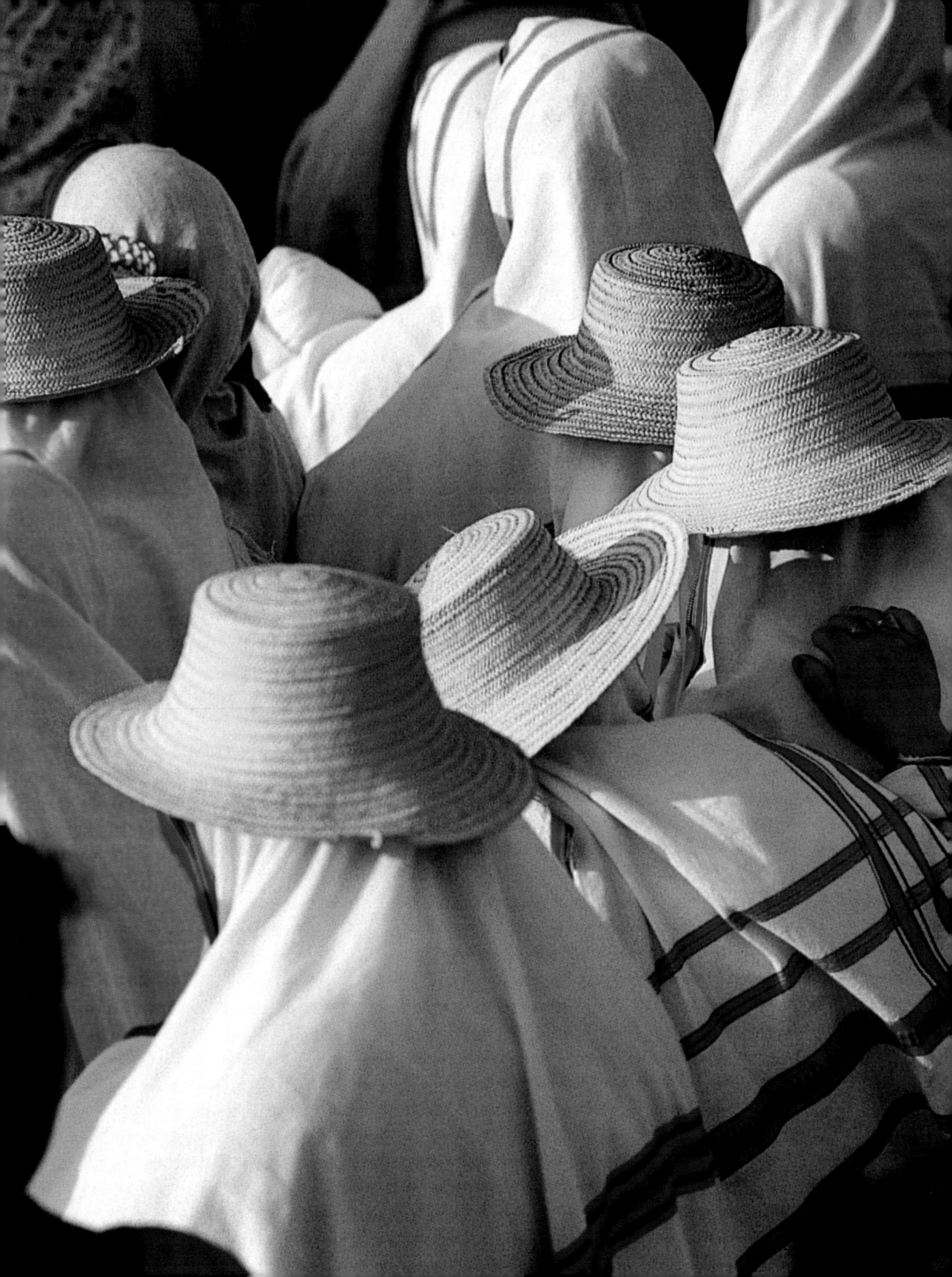

126 Women that go to the market on a holiday dress with particular care: besides the fouta, *a white veil held in place by a thin ribbon tied around the neck, they also wear a characteristic hat of woven palm fronds.*

127 left The use of the veil, once obligatory, has never disappeared from the rural areas of Tunisia. For the women of Jerba, for example, it is totally normal to wear the fouta, *which, on the other hand, traditionally covers only the hair and not the face.*

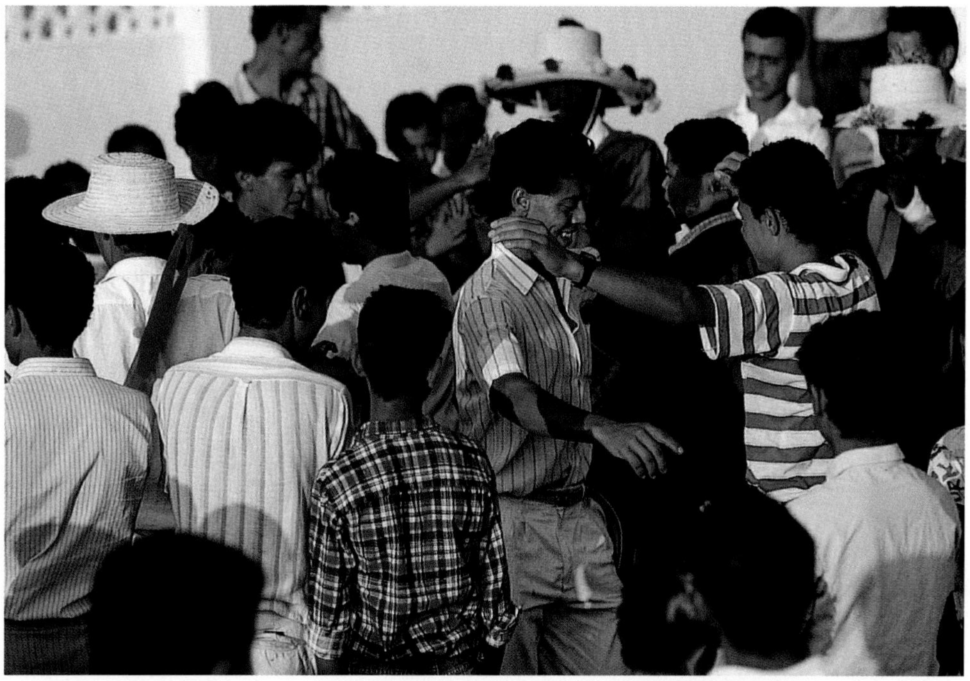

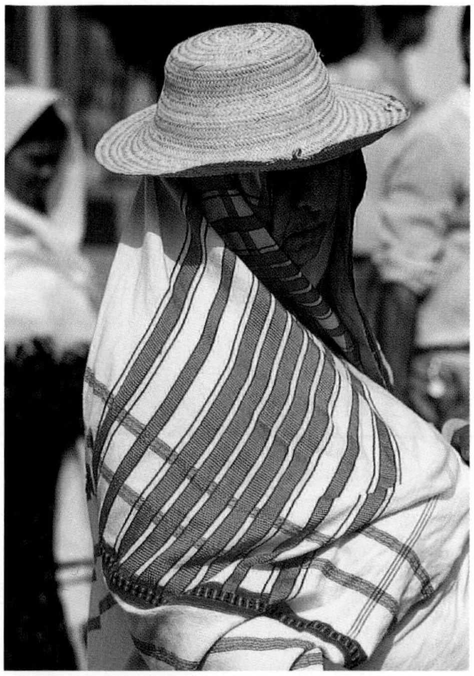

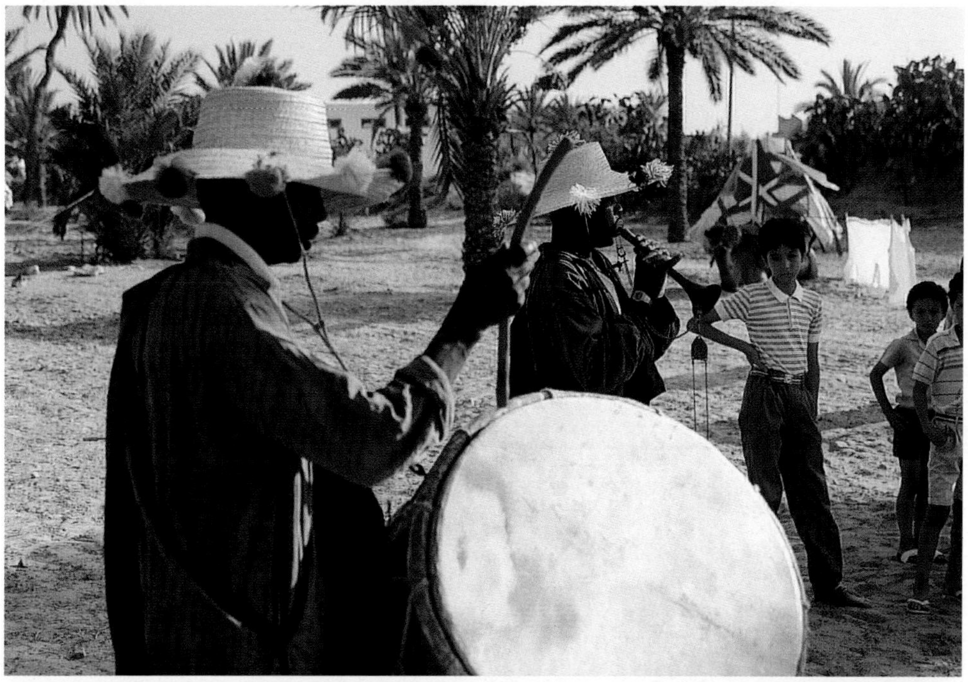

127 top right During wedding celebrations, in Jerba as elsewhere, dancing breaks out suddenly. Music and dancing are the true life and soul of the party.

127 center right To celebrate marriages, the traditional tabbala *musician-dancers are sometimes hired, who descend from the ancient African slaves.*

127 bottom right The female guests at a wedding in Jerba get ready to yell the high-pitched youyou. *This cry, which constitutes a feminine privilege, is done by combining a yell with a vibration of the tongue.*

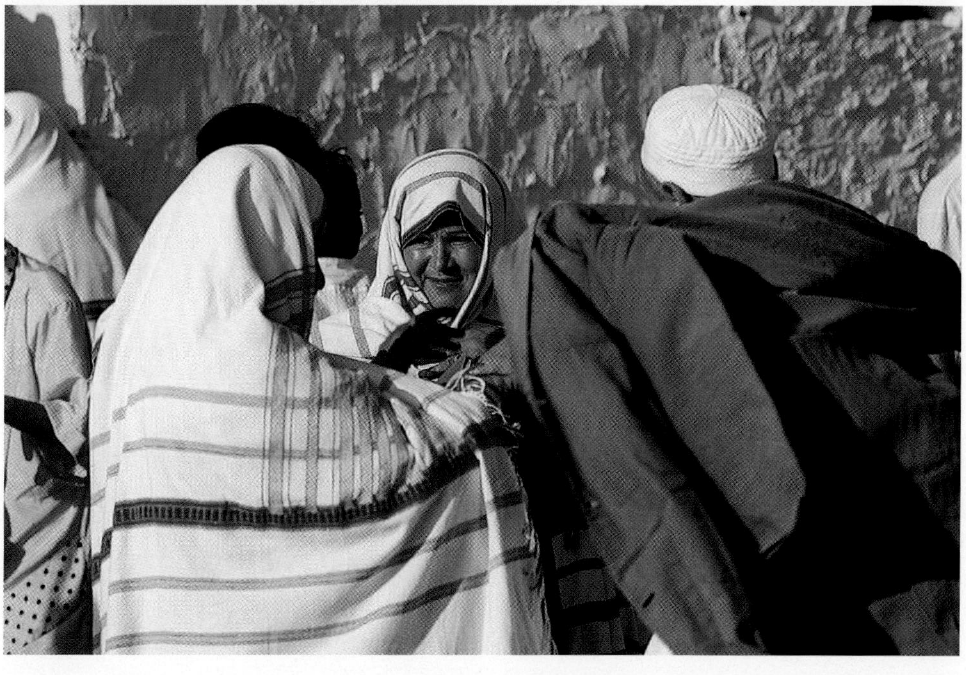

128-129 *A woman
with the* fouta (right)
*is accompanied by
another that is
wearing the* houli
jerbi, *the typical dress
of Jerba Island, made
in a fabric with yellow,
red and purple squares
and embroidered with
golden and silver
thread.*

There is nothing better than a party for showing off one's jewelry. A type of charm against evil, a way to make oneself more beautiful, an economic safeguard in case of abandonment by fiancés or husbands—these are the main purposes for Tunisian valuables. In gold or silver, handmade in filigree, in fretwork or wrought-metal, they draw on oriental, Turkish and European motifs typical of a people that live between the Mediterranean and Europe. There are four main styles: that of the city of Tunis, which is inspired directly by the jewelry of Turkey or the Old Continent; that of the east coast, of Syrian and Egyptian origin; that of the Western world, as transformed in Algeria; and that of the south, from the area of Medenine.

Today the jewelry that is given in dowries to future brides has been substituted with, in many cases, a sum of money, and jewellry is no longer worn on the head, at the wrists, around the neck and on the ankles, all at the same time as in the past. However, its apotropaic function, as a charm against evil forces, has remained. Necklaces often contain elements indicating the number five, a symbolic and protective figure, or any of its multiples. There is also the fish and the horn, a symbol of fertility and a powerful good-luck charm, as well as the hand of Fatima, daughter of Mohammed, whose five fingers represent the pillars of Islam and is very powerful against the evil eye. In the medinas of Tunis for gold and of Jerba for silver there is jewelry to suit all tastes. Sometimes, authentic antique pieces can be found but this does not happen often.

*128 top A woman of
Jerba flaunts a
enameled pendant.
The art of enameling
spread through North
Africa after the non-
Christians were
thrown out of Spain.*

*128 bottom Once
only married women
could wear jewelry,
which was given them
by their husband
when they got
married.*

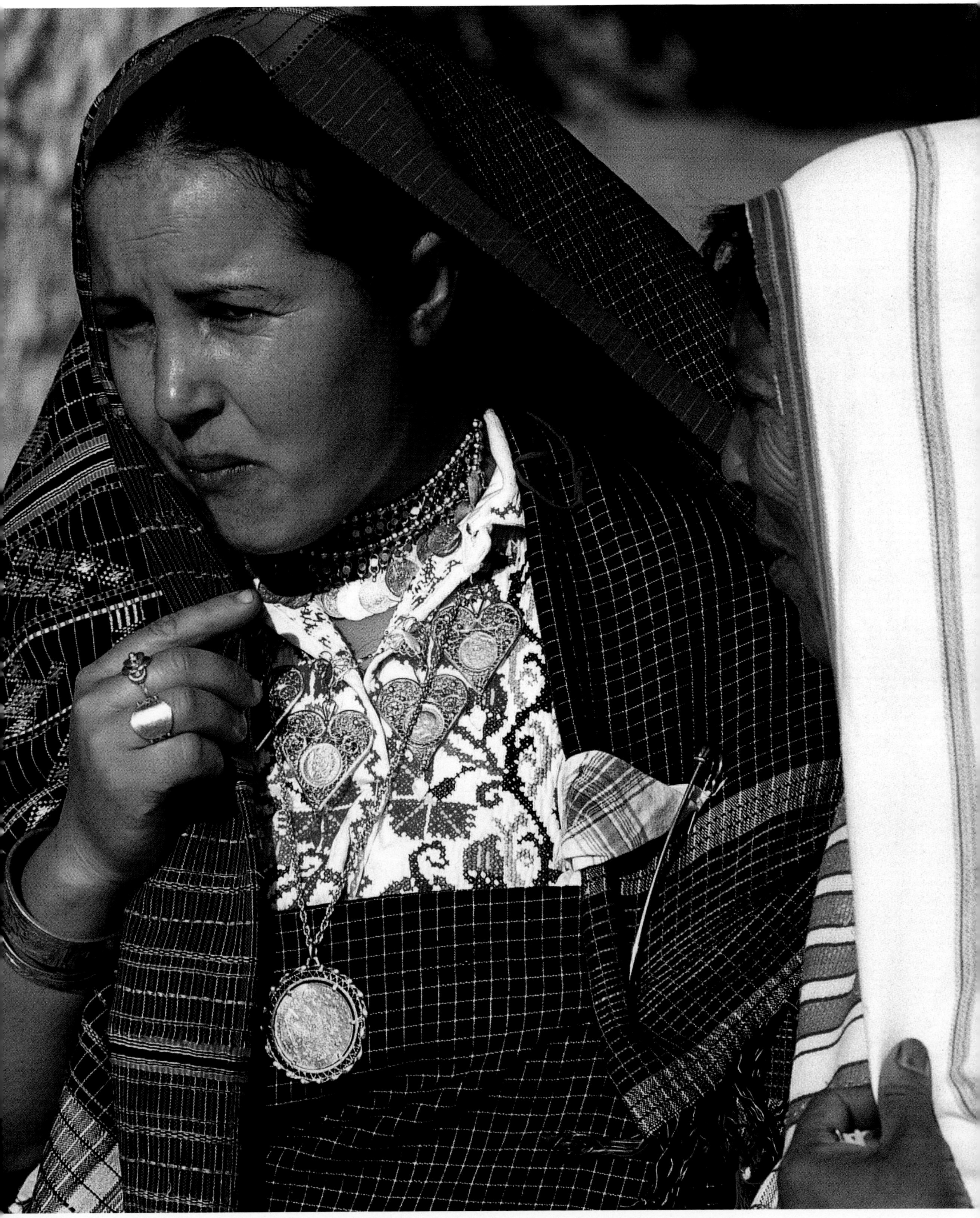

130 top The weaving of carpets on Jerba is an exclusively female occupation, since men can only participate in that of clothes and blankets.

130 bottom A carpet merchant on Jerba waits for customers. The price of a piece is calculated on the basis of the quality of the wool, the designs and the density of the knots, which varies between 40,000 and 160,000 per square yard.

131 Identifiable according to color, design, and weave type, Tunisian carpets are divided into four kinds: the zerbia, *the* alloucha, *the* mergoum *and the* kilim, *like those seen in the illustration.*

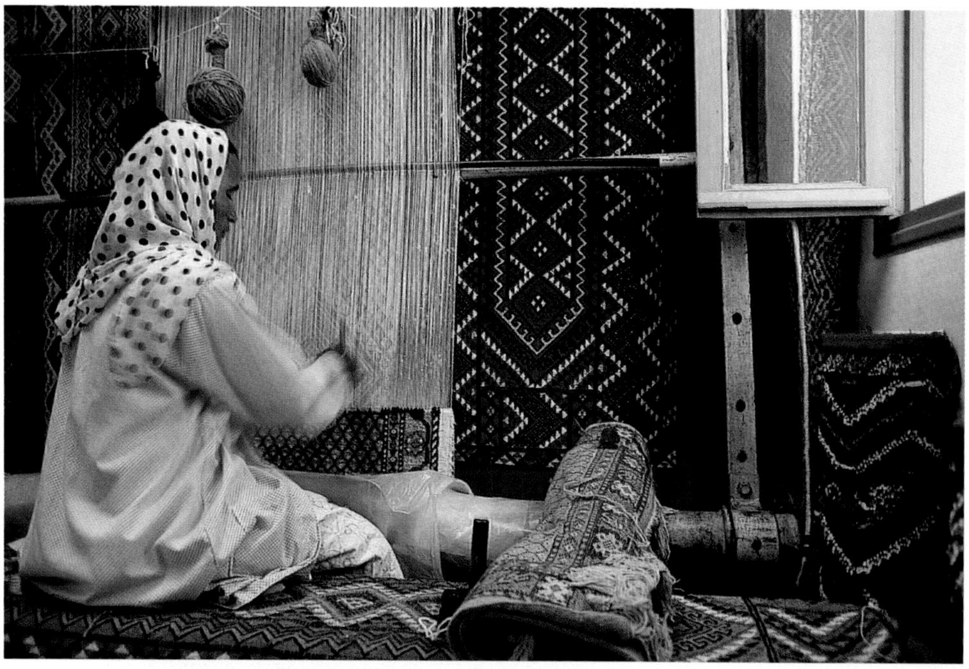

On important occasions, dancers twirl to the sound of music or people chat sitting on carpets. An inevitable piece of the culture and the Tunisian dwelling, be it a house or a tent, the carpet is almost a form of art.

The most common are the *kilim* and the *mergoum,* both with geometric motifs and lively colors. Women usually weave the carpets and men sell these bits of happiness in wool, silk or cotton.

Among the most precious carpets, however, are the *zerbia,* or the knotted ones, a handiwork typical only of Kairouan, with designs that the artisans learn when they are children, featuring ancient tribal symbols.

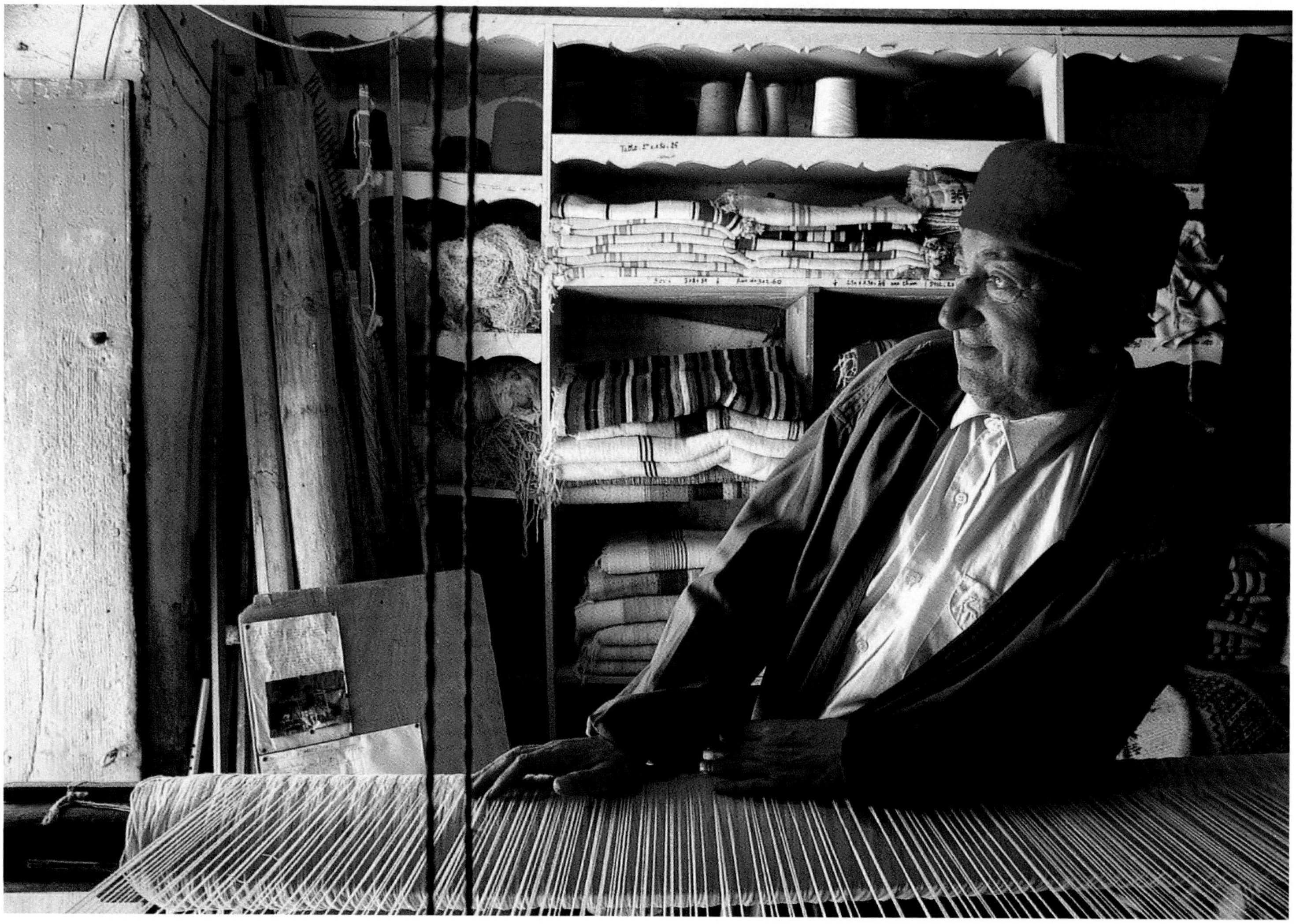

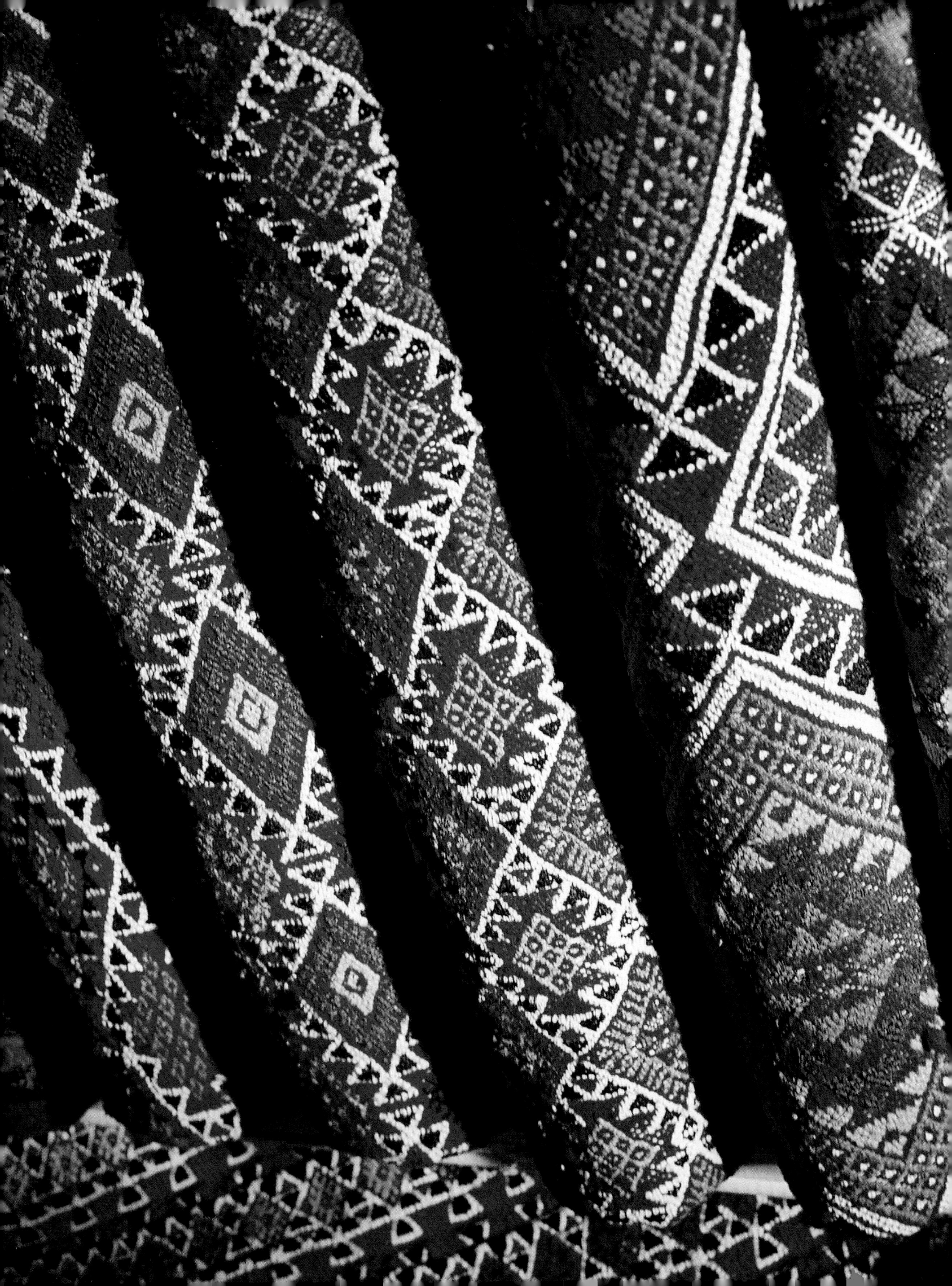

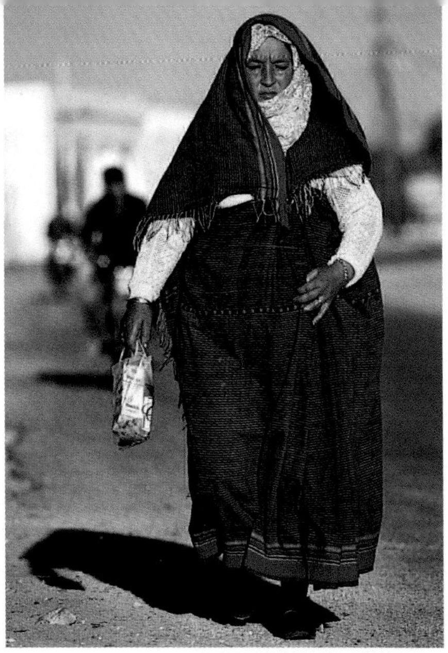

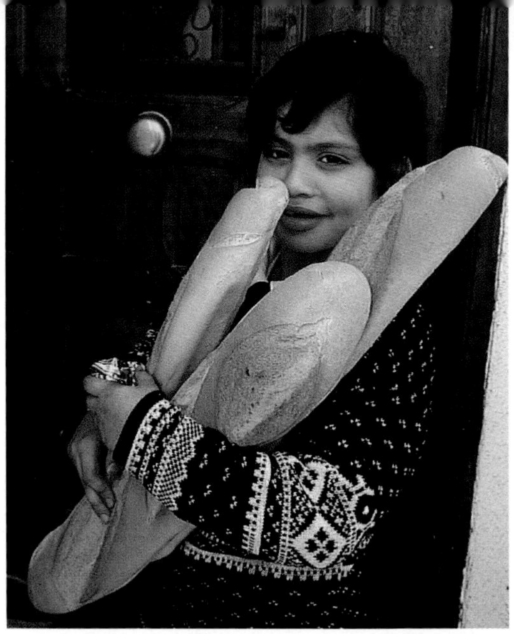

132 top left Women that wear the typical costume in Tunisia are quite common, above all in the south of the country and on the islands.

132 top right The French left a notable mark on Tunisian cuisine: the baguette is, as a matter of fact, even more common that the khubz, *the Arab bread made with white flour.*

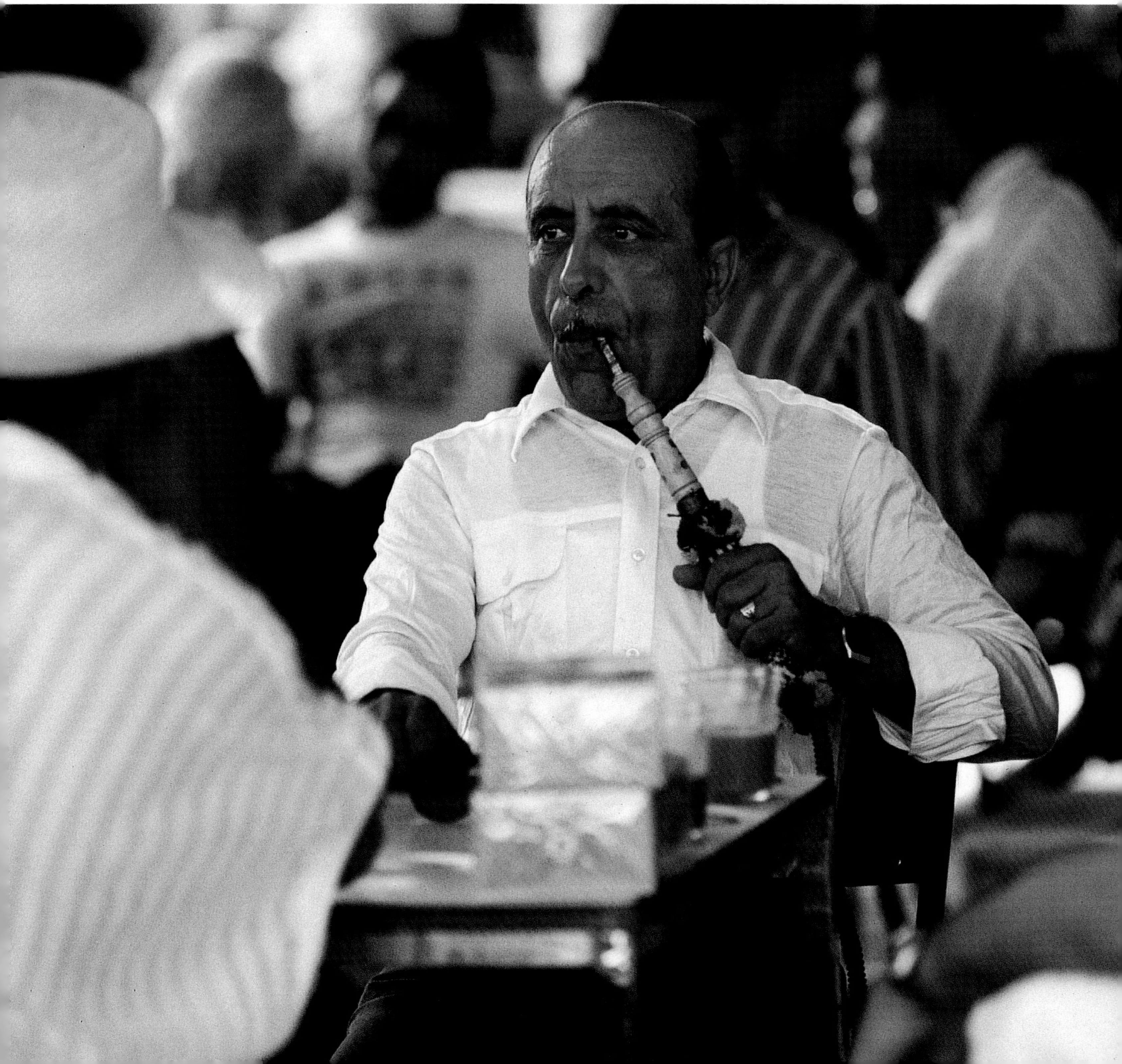

132-133 In the cafés of Midoun, on Jerba, men meet after work to smoke the narghila *and chat with friends.*

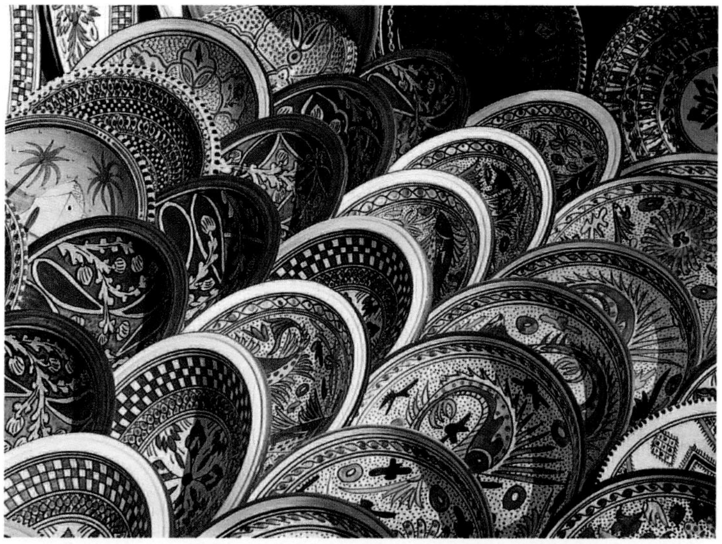

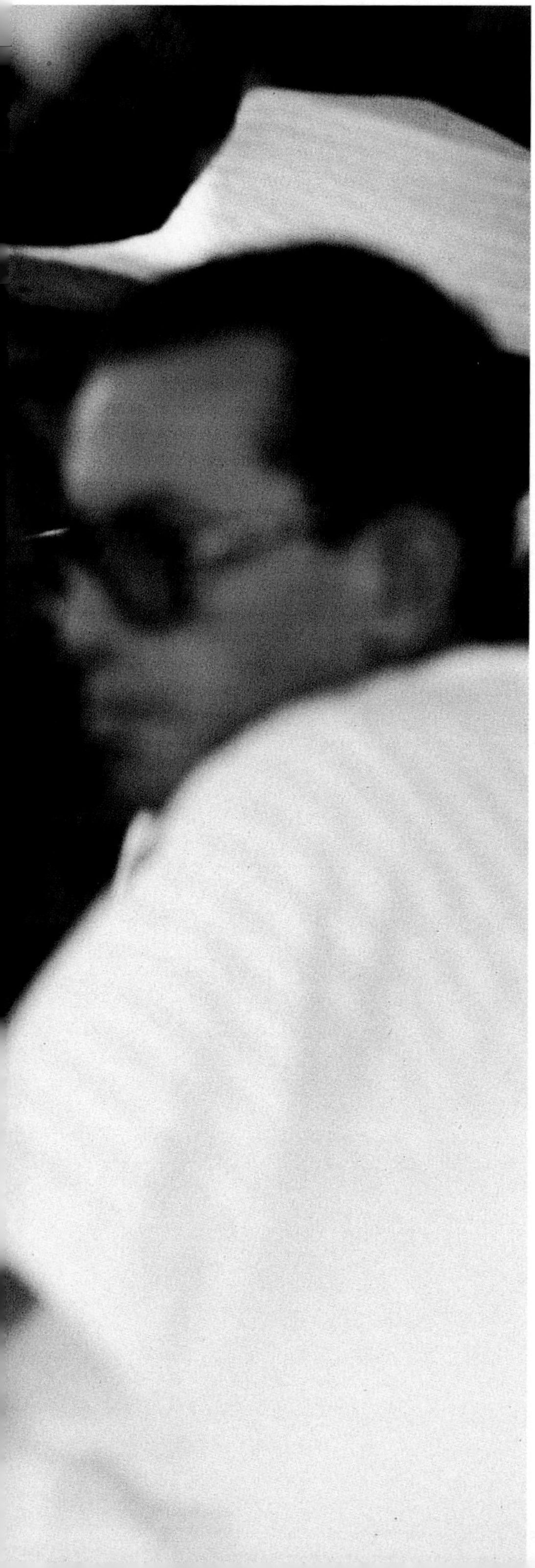

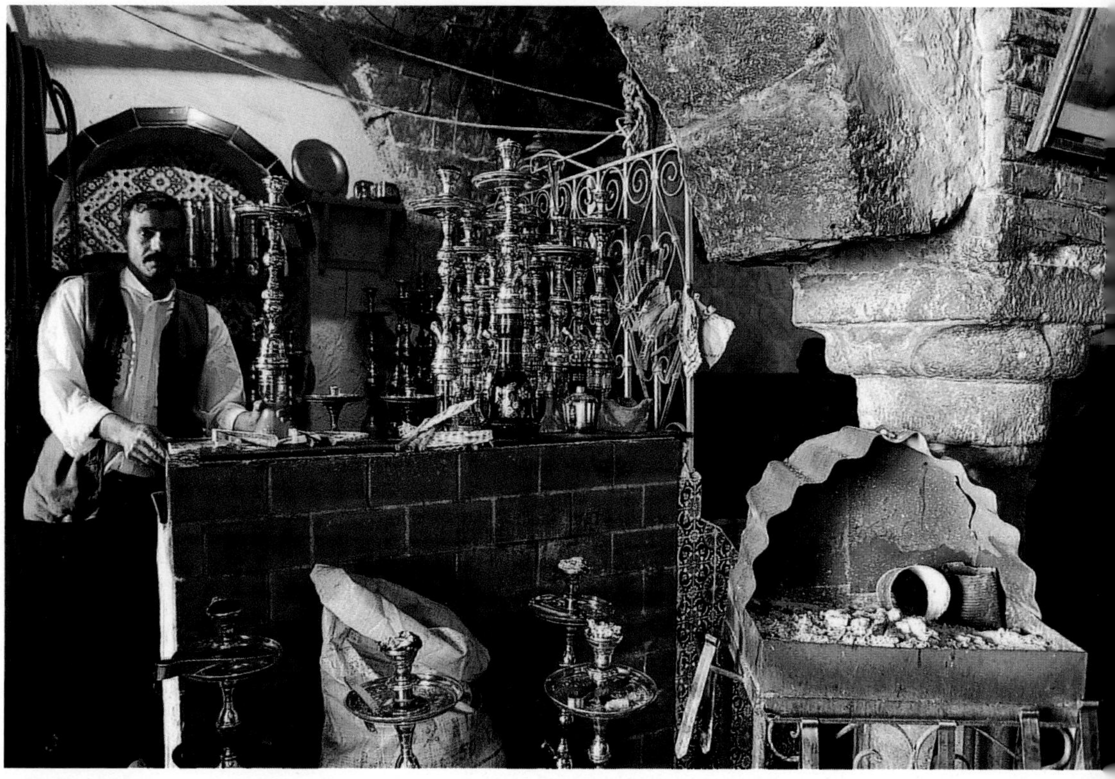

The people eat using typical ceramics, in gaudy colors that range from green to yellow to blue, shiny and sparkling under the midday sun, decorated with fish, floral motifs and olives.

The French, finally, left an indelible mark on the Tunisian cuisine: the baguette is actually more common than the *khubz,* Arab bread made with white flour. This influence is also noticeable in the *chakcouka,* a mix of vegetables cooked in a pan that is similar to ratatouille. However, apart from the 70 varieties of dates, the cuisine is domineered by strong flavors: the spicy and hot mutton, the sugary desserts made with honey and the mint tea, thirst-quenching, refreshing and unforgettable.

There is also the classic couscous, a base of semolina flavored with a stew of choice, made with chicken, lamb or mutton, not to mention the *tajine,* a type of pâté baked with legumes, meat, chicken, tuna and cheese.

133 top Settled comfortably on the sides of the streets to glisten in the sun, the ceramics of Houmt-Souk, on Jerba, create appealing colorful corners. Among the characteristic motifs that decorate them, the fish stands out as the design typical of the island.

133 bottom The narghila *corner, in a popular café in Bizerte, has just been displayed for the arrival of customers. This very particular pipe is filled with a light tobacco, often fruit flavored, much enjoyed also by women.*

INDEX

PHOTO CREDITS

Marcello Bertinetti/Archivio White Star: pages 9 top left, 10 top left, 16-17, 58 top right, 58-59, 59 bottom, 82 top right, 82 bottom right, 83 top left, 84 top left, 84-85, 85 top left, 86 top right, 89 top left, 93 bottom left, 93 center right, 93 bottom right, 97 top, 101, 106 bottom left, 109 top, 119 center top, 124 top left, 124 top right, 124-125, 125 top, 125 bottom, 126, 127 top left, 127 top right, 127 center right, 127 bottom right, 128 top left, 128 bottom left, 128-129, 132 top left.
Antonio Attini/Archivio White Star: pages 11 bottom right, 108 top, 108-109, 112 top left, 112 top right, 113 bottom, 114 bottom left, 115 top left, 115 top right, 116-117, 117 bottom, 118.
Alfio Garozzo/Archivio White Star: pages 1, 9 top right, 8/9, 10 top right, 10-11, 11 top left, 15 bottom left, 15 top right, 46 top left, 46 bottom left, 46 top right, 46 bottom right, 47, 47 right, 48 top left, 48 bottom left, 49 top left, 49 top right, 48-49, 50 top left, 50 center left, 50 bottom left, 51 inalto, 50-51, 54 top left, 54 top right, 54-55, 55 top , 55 bottom, 56 top, 56 center, 56 bottom, 57 top left, 57 top right, 56-57, 58 top left, 59 top, 60 top left, 60 top right, 61, 62 top left, 62 top right, 63 top, 63 bottom, 64 top left, 64-65, 65 bottom, 67 top, 67 center, 67 bottom, 68-69, 72 top, 72 bottom, 73 top left, 74, 79, 80 top left, 80 top right, 80-81, 81 top, 81 center, 82 left, 83 top right, 82-83, 84 top right, 85 top right, 85 bottom right, 86 top left, 86-87, 87 top, 87 bottom, 88 top, 88 center, 88 bottom, 89 top right, 88-89, 90 top right, 90-91, 91 bottom, 92, 93 top right, 94 top left, 94 top right, 94-95, 95 bottom left, 95 top right, 95 center right, 95 bottom right, 96 top left, 96 top right, 96-97, 97 center, 97 bottom, 98 bottom right, 98-99, 99 top right, 100 top left, 100 top right, 100-101, 102 top, 102 bottom left, 102 bottom right, 103 top left, 103 top right, 102-103, 104, 105 top, 105 bottom, 106 top, 106-107, 107 top, 108 bottom, 109 bottom, 110 top, 110 bottom, 110-111, 111 top, 111 bottom, 112-113, 113 top, 114 top right, 114-115, 116 top left, 116 top right, 117 top, 119 top, 119 center bottom, 119 bottom, 122 bottom, 130 top, 130 bottom, 131, 132 top right, 132-133, 133 top , 133 bottom, 136.
Giulio Veggi/Archivio White Star: pages 3-6, 12, 13 top left, 13 bottom left, 13 top right, 13 bottom right, 15 top left, 15 bottom right, 60 bottom left, 62-63, 64 top right, 65 top, 66 top, 66-67, 69 top, 69 center, 69 bottom, 72-73, 73 top right, 75-78, 81 bottom.
Angelo Colombo/Archivio White Star: map pages 14-15.
Maria Ancenay/Marka: page 90 top left.
AP Presse: pages 43 bottom, 45 bottom.
Yann Arthus-Bertrand/Corbis/Grazia Neri: pages 52-53, 70-71.
Bettmann/Corbis/Grazia Neri: page 45 top.
Biblioteque National France: page 33 top.
Biblioteque National Tunisia: pages 36 bottom, 37 bottom left.
Gerard Blot/RMN: page 33 bottom.
Giovanni Dagli Orti: pages 27 bottom, 28-29, 34 bottom, 34-35, 35, 37 right, 39 center.
Araldo De Luca: page 24 top left.
Double's: pages 2-7, 34 top.
Mary Evans Picture Library: pages 24 bottom right, 24-25, 25 bottom.
Werner Forman Archivi/Index: pages 31 center, 31 bottom.
Fototeca Storica Nazionale: page 38 top.
Hulton Deutsch Collection/Corbis/Grazia Neri: pages 38 bottom, 40 top left, 41 top, 40-41, 42-43, 43 top.
Index: page 36 top.
Lapi/Roger Viollet/Contrasto: page 42.
Erich Lessing/Contrasto: page 23 bottom.
Frances Linzee Gordon/LPI: page 122 top.
Lipnitski/Roger Viollet/Contrasto: pages 44/45.
Mestiri family - http://www-edu.gel.usherb.ca/mestiri/ Mchenik.html: pages 40 top right, 40 bottom left.
Photos 12: pages 27 top right, 32, 33 center, 39 bottom.
E. Poupinet/Marka: page 91 top.
Marc Riboud/Magnus Photos: page 44.
Hans Georg Roth/Corbis/Grazia Neri: pages 18-19.
Scala Group: page 120 bottom.
S.A. Corbis/Grazia Neri: pages 30, 31 top.
The Bridgeman: pages 26, 27 top left, 28 bottom.
The British Museum: pages 20 top, 20 bottom, 23 top left, 23 top right, 29.
G. Tomsich/Marka: page 99 top left.
Roger Viollet/Contrasto: pages 39 top, 43 center.
Patrick Ward/Corbis/Grazia Neri: pages 120-121, 122-123.
Roger Wood/Corbis/Grazia Neri: pages 21, 22.

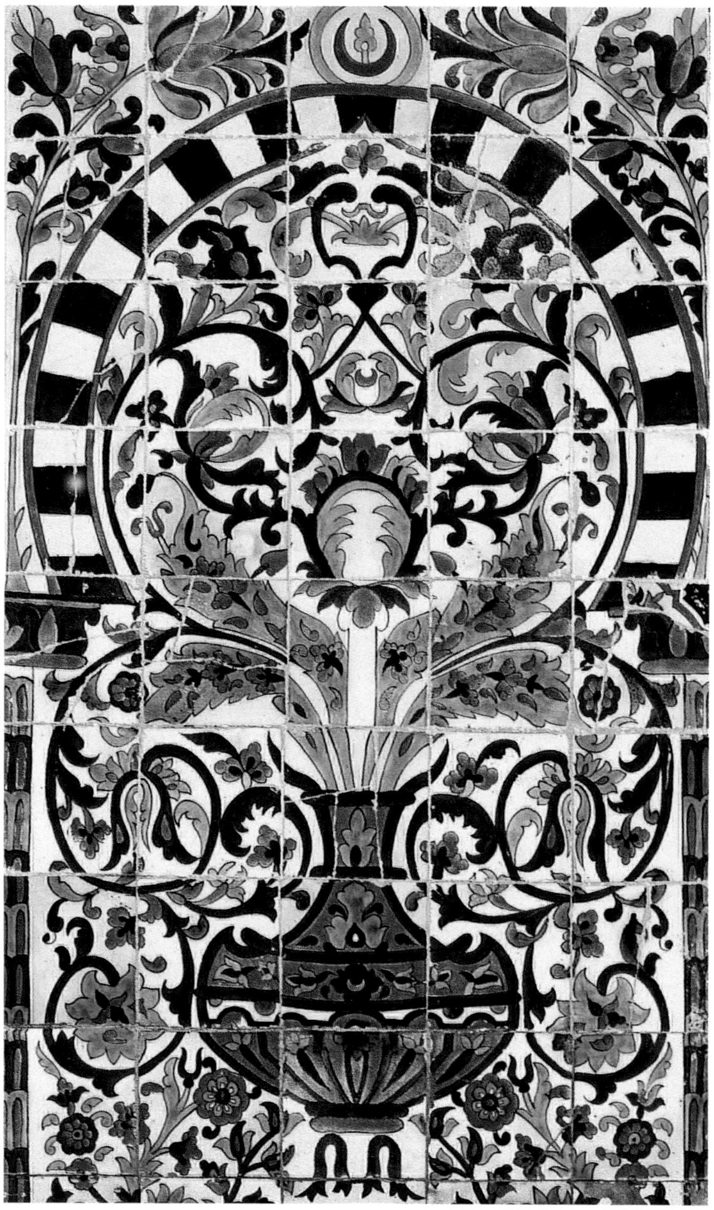

136 The multicolored majolica tiles are an absolute main character in Islamic religious decoration, as are floral themes, given the prohibition to portray human figures in sacred places. The detail shown is part of the splendid decoration of the zaouia, or the seat of a religious brotherhood, of Sidi Sahab, in Kairouan, the sacred building better known as the Mosque of the Barber.